BENJAMIN
BRITTEN

A LIFE FOR MUSIC

BENJAMIN
BRITTEN
A LIFE FOR MUSIC

NEIL POWELL

A John Macrae Book
Henry Holt and Company
New York

Henry Holt and Company, LLC
Publishers since 1866
175 Fifth Avenue
New York, New York 10010
www.henryholt.com

Henry Holt ® and ®are registered trademarks of
Henry Holt and Company, LLC.

Library of Congress Cataloging-in-Publication Data
Powell, Neil, 1948–
  Benjamin Britten : a life for music / by Neil Powell.—First U.S. edition.
    pages cm
  Includes bibliographical references and index.
  ISBN 978-0-8050-9774-0
  1. Britten, Benjamin, 1913–1976. 2. Composers—England—Biography. I. Title.
  ML410.B853P68 2013
  780.92—dc23
  [B]   2012051536

Henry Holt books are available for special promotions and premiums.
For details contact: Director, Special Markets.

Originally published in the U.K. in 2013 by Hutchinson

First U.S. Edition 2013

Printed in the United States of America

1 3 5 7 9 10 8 6 4 2

In memory of Adam Johnson
1965–1993

You great composer, I little composer.

Dmitri Shostakovich

I want to say, here and now, that Britten has been for me
the most purely musical person I have ever met and
I have ever known.

Sir Michael Tippett

CONTENTS

ILLUSTRATIONS

PREFACE

In writing this book, I've proceeded from assumptions which may not be universally shared but which I hope will be vindicated in the following pages. The first is that Benjamin Britten was the greatest of English composers—rivalled only by Henry Purcell and Edward Elgar—and one of the most extraordinarily gifted musicians ever to have been born in this country: these are slightly different things, of which the latter is perhaps the more clearly incontrovertible, and they certainly don't suggest that he was infallible. The second is that he was specifically a man of the East Anglian coast, which is inclined to foster (as those of us who have lived by it know) a particular cast of mind, in whose life and work we should expect to discover kinships with Suffolk artists and poets such as Constable and Crabbe. The third is that his fondness for adolescent boys and his devotion to his partner, Peter Pears, represent distinct and complementary aspects of his sexual nature; his conduct in both cases was exemplary and is therefore the occasion for neither prurience nor evasiveness. And the fourth is that in two phases of his career—the periods of his involvement with the 'Auden Generation' in the 1930s and of his formative work with the Aldeburgh Festival from 1948 onwards—he contributed to cultural life in ways which go beyond those to be expected of any composer and performer, however great.

This is not a book by a musician, by which I mean that although I can struggle with a score I don't read it fluently nor do I hear it accurately in my head; if I take the score to the piano, a further lengthy struggle ensues, from which I usually retire in defeat. For people such as myself, notated music examples in biographies are a form of reproachful torment, so I haven't included any. I write about music as I hear and understand it, in very much the same way as I've written about poems and novels in books about authors: the reader who is used to literary biographies will, I hope, feel perfectly at home here. And because I approach Britten's work from this direction, I've been particularly interested in the relationship between his music and its literary sources, in some of his song settings and in operas such as *Peter Grimes*, *Billy Budd*, *The Turn of the Screw* and *Death in Venice*. For the musicologist, there are other studies of Britten by people whose scholarly and technical expertise astonishes me and to whom (as the Bibliography and Notes will testify) I remain greatly indebted.

Both the Britten Estate and the Britten–Pears Foundation kindly gave their approval to this project at the outset, although they obviously bear no responsibility for the finished book. My agent, Natasha Fairweather, has been an unfailing source of encouragement and support, while Sarah Rigby, my editor at Hutchinson, read and annotated my draft text with exemplary care: I've acted on far more of her suggestions than is habitual for an obstinate author and it's been a pleasure to work with her. I'm also deeply grateful to the following people, whom I've listed in alphabetically democratic style, for their help and advice at various stages of my work on Britten: John Amis, Amanda Arnold, Alan Britten, Nick Clark, Paul Driver, Roger Eno, Maurice Feldman, Caroline Gascoigne, Jonathan Gathorne-Hardy, John

Greening, Jocasta Hamilton, Rex Harley, Ray Herring, David and Mary Osborn, Philip Reed, Jonathan Reekie, Peter Scupham, Margaret Steward, David Stoll, Malcolm Walker, Martin Wright. Extracts from the letters and diaries of Benjamin Britten and from the travel diaries of Peter Pears are © The Trustees of the Britten–Pears Foundation and are not to be further reproduced without prior permission.

The best of all companions to the music of Britten, whether in the concert hall or on record, was my friend Adam Johnson. I have constantly wished that I could try out ideas and phrases on him while writing this book, which he would certainly have improved. It is dedicated, with love, to his memory.

N. P.
Orford, 2012

CHAPTER 1

BRITTEN MINOR

1913–30

1

The Suffolk coastal resort of Lowestoft, where Benjamin Britten was born in 1913, was described in the mid-nineteenth century as 'a handsome and improving *market town*, *bathing-place*, and *sea port*' which, 'when viewed from the sea, has the most picturesque and beautiful appearance of any town on the eastern coast'.[1] This was just before the arrival of the railway in 1847 and the massive development of South Lowestoft, between Lake Lothing and the previously separate villages of Kirkley and Pakefield, by Sir Morton Peto of Somerleyton Hall. Thirty years later, Anthony Trollope would choose Lowestoft as the setting for a pivotal chapter in his novel *The Way We Live Now*, transporting three characters – Paul Montague, Winifred Hurtle and Roger Carbury – to the town: Paul rashly meets Mrs Hurtle there and bumps into Roger, who has been his rival for the hand of another woman. At that time, South Lowestoft's principal building was the Royal Hotel of 1849: though unnamed by Trollope, it is evidently the scene of Paul Montague and Winifred Hurtle's meeting. In one filmed version of *The Way We Live Now*, part of the episode takes place on a hotel balcony, from which the former lovers watch the sun set over the sea; but this is something they couldn't have done in Lowestoft, since it is the most easterly point on the English coastline, although on a clear morning you might see the sun rise. What is just as likely to greet you, if you look out from the Victorian houses of Kirkley Cliff Road, across the slender green space of the bowls club towards the beach and sea, is an easterly onshore breeze and sleet in the wind.

During the early years of the last century, one of these houses, 21 Kirkley Cliff Road, was occupied by a dentist, Robert Victor Britten, his wife Edith Rhoda (née Hockey) and their family. A semi-detached villa with its entrance lobby to the left-hand side, it was to contain a dental practice for most of the twentieth century and is now a small hotel called Britten House; opposite, next to the bowling green, there's a car park adorned with aluminium seats and cycle racks, flying-saucer lamp posts and a few municipal saplings in little gravelled squares. Robert Britten, whose father ended up running a dairy business in Maidenhead, where he died in 1881, had originally hoped to be a farmer, but this ambition was thwarted by his lack of the necessary capital. Instead, he trained at Charing Cross Hospital before working as an assistant dentist in Ipswich and, in 1905, setting up his own practice at 46 Marine Parade, Lowestoft; three years later, his growing family and increasing prosperity prompted him to move the mile further south to Kirkley Cliff Road. There, every day at eleven o'clock, he would habitually leave his ground-floor surgery for a fortifying mid-morning whisky, ascending to the first-floor sitting room which he called 'Heaven'; downstairs, he seems to have implied, was the other place. There's a hint in this habit of that continuous rumbling dissatisfaction, not unlike toothache, with which Graham Greene so memorably burdened his dentist, Mr Tench, in *The Power and the Glory*. Yet, probably because he didn't relish his profession, Robert Britten's patients found him sympathetic and friendly; he was able to share and respond to their feelings to a greater extent than a more enthusiastic practitioner of his craft might have done.

Robert had met his future wife while studying dentistry at Charing Cross, but there was already a connection between their two families: Edith and her sisters had attended the same school as Robert's sisters – Miss Hinton's School for Girls, Maidenhead – where Florence Britten and Sarah Hockey were exact contemporaries. Edith's father, William Henry Hockey, was a Queen's Messenger at the Home Office: the family's staff flat had a misleadingly grand address in Whitehall, and it was from there in September 1901 that the eldest daughter married Robert Britten at St John's, Smith Square. Edith was a strikingly attractive and talented young woman who might have expected something better than marriage at the age of twenty-eight to a dentist four years her junior, had it not been for her socially compromised background: her father was illegitimate and her mother sufficiently unstable to have spent much of her life in homes. But Robert was young, handsome and something of a challenge, for drink and recklessness had already ruined both of his brothers. Determined to save her husband and children from a similar fate, Edith's prescription was moderation and music, and it seems to have worked.

By 1913, Robert was thirty-six and Edith forty years old: they had three children – Barbara (born in Ipswich on 11 June 1902), Robert or Bobby (born in Lowestoft on 28 January 1907) and Elizabeth, known as Beth (born in Lowestoft on 10 June 1909) – and they thought their family complete. So their fourth child was what parents are sometimes apt to describe, with a knowing and self-congratulatory smile, as a 'mistake'. He was born at 21 Kirkley Cliff Road on 22 November, which is the feast day of St Cecilia, the patron saint of music. As if that were not omen enough, he was given the first name not only of his father's younger brother but, as Edith at least would have been very well aware, of England's most eminent living composer, Edward Elgar, who in the preceding five years had produced a flurry of major works including the two completed symphonies (1908, 1911), the violin concerto (1910) and *The Music Makers* (1912). But the Brittens' youngest son would always be called by his middle name – Benjamin or 'Beni', 'Benjy' and finally 'Ben' – and, as we shall see, he would grow up to have mixed feelings about Elgar.

His father had no interest in music: he was, said Britten, 'almost anti-musical, I'm afraid'.[2] The musical ability and ambition was all on his mother's side: of the seven Hockey children, at least three pursued musical careers, most notably Edith's brother Willie, who was organist at St Mary-le-Tower in Ipswich, conductor of the Ipswich Choral Society and a professional singing teacher. He gave his nephew, for his ninth birthday, a copy of Stainer and Barrett's *A Dictionary of Musical Terms* (1889), which in ordinary circumstances might have seemed an over-ambitious or over-optimistic present. By this time, Benjamin would sometimes stay with his Uncle Willie and Auntie Jane at their home in Berners Street, Ipswich, from where his earliest surviving letter home was written on 25 April 1923: in this, he is more excited by a visit to the railway station and the sight of a new L&NER engine, 'green with a gold rim round its chimmeny', than by anything specifically musical. Nevertheless, Marian Walker, a family friend, remembered that when she asked Britten 'Where did your music come from?' he replied: 'I had rather a reprobate old uncle, but he was intensely musical, and I think it was he who originally told me that he preferred to *read* a score rather than hear anything played.'[3]

So where *did* his music come from? Uncle Willie, supplying the crucial distinction between the practitioner's pleasure in the score and the listener's in the performance, is clearly part of the answer. But little Benjamin showed conspicuous ability, or so his doting mother supposed, from the moment his infant hand touched the piano in the upstairs drawing room: 'Dear pay pano,' he would demand at the age of two, liking to think 'Dear' was his name because that's what people called him.[4] Edith was particularly keen that he should be a musical genius, since her two daughters were as unmusical as their father while Bobby, her elder son, preferred to play ragtime; she convinced herself that her younger son would one day be ranked as the 'fourth B', alongside Bach, Beethoven and Brahms – although, as things turned out, a more relevant trinity of Bs would be Bridge, Berg and Berkeley. There is a peculiar photograph, taken when he was about seven years old, of the small boy seated at the piano, upon which half a dozen open scores have been ingeniously displayed: whether they are parts to be played simultaneously or pieces to be performed in rapid succession isn't clear; but the photograph is evidently intended as a joke, since another taken at about the same time shows him tackling a single piece in the ordinary way while, seated on the sofa, his mother listens politely and an unmusical sister reads a book. The point of the first photograph, of course, is that this is a child of prodigious virtuosity; yet virtuosity isn't the same as creativity. 'Where did his musical skills come from?' isn't the same question as 'Where did his music come from?' The latter may prove the more difficult and interesting of the two.

Benjamin received his first semi-formal musical instruction from his mother at the age of five or six; two years later, he began piano lessons with Miss Ethel Astle ARCM, the younger of two sisters who ran the nearby pre-preparatory school called Southolme, at 52 Kirkley Cliff Road. Although he would later praise Miss Astle's 'impeccable' teaching, adding that those with whom he subsequently studied at the Royal College of Music 'commented on the really first-rate ground-work that I had received',[5] there is no reason to suppose that she was anything much more than a perfectly decent and unexceptional provincial piano teacher. She used the 'Seppings Music Method', a rather cumbersome contraption consisting of blocks and cards to be fitted on to wooden staves: like many another 'progressive' educational invention of the era, it looks to the uninstructed eye to be more trouble than the conventional grind, although her pupil would remember his 'early musical days' with Miss Astle as 'always interesting and entertaining'.[6] She was also a regular participant at Mrs Britten's fearsome musical soirées where, according to a fellow performer, there was 'one piece that she always played, and played quite well . . . and it absolutely horrified me, the whole performance'.[7] These soirées, though partly designed to show off the musical talents of her younger son, were equally an expression of Edith's social ambition: the status of dentistry as a profession was ambiguous, so that the Brittens belonged neither to the gentry nor to the tradespeople, and musical parties were one way of joining, or even creating, a cultured social circle. Visitors to the Britten household noticed how, on other occasions, Bobby would have been instructed to play something light and welcoming as the guests arrived; while if Benjamin were playing the square piano in the attic on a warm day with the windows open, a crowd would gather on the pavement beneath to listen. Edith's apparently fantastic expectations of Benjamin's musical ability were thus complicated by something altogether more local and pragmatic: music as a means of social advancement. Robert Britten was less bothered than his wife about his status; as for the illustrious prospect of his younger son's musical career, he thought the whole idea was absurd. His cautious scepticism, it should be added in his defence, sprang less from his hostility to music than from his own experience of disappointed ambitions. Nevertheless, the combination of an obsessively pushy mother and a sternly unconvinced father might have been enough to put a less committed child than Benjamin off music for life.

Among Edith Britten's circle of musical acquaintances was Audrey Alston, a clergyman's wife who lived at Framingham Earl, just south of Norwich. Her son John was almost the same age as Benjamin; the two boys would play duets together, each mother privately certain that her own son would be the greater musician. Audrey herself was the viola player in the Norwich String Quartet and in 1923, when he was ten years old, she took Benjamin on as a viola pupil. She was evidently a fine musician and a gifted teacher, but her influence was to be even more momentous in other ways. Firstly, and most simply, she got Ben away from Kirkley Cliff Road, Lowestoft, which contained his entire life: family, home, piano teacher, pre-prep school and prep school. Secondly, she encouraged him to attend concerts in Norwich: since his father refused to have either a gramophone or a radio in the house, his childhood experience of live perform-ance had been restricted to what was possible in the sitting room or at church (he said that his early knowledge of orchestral music came from 'ploughing through the great symphonies' in piano duet arrangements with family or friends). Thirdly, she was a friend of the composer Frank Bridge, who stayed with the Alstons when he conducted *The Sea* at the Norwich Triennial Festival in October 1924 and again three years later when he returned to conduct the premiere of the festival's commission, *Enter Spring*. On this occasion, Audrey Alston introduced her prom-ising pupil, still a thirteen-year-old in his last year at prep school, to the composer: it was a meeting which was to have the most profoundly influential and far-reaching consequences for Benjamin Britten's musical future.

Thus, the answer to the simpler question – 'Where did his musical skills come from?' – is actually quite straightforward: from his genes; from his mother and his uncle; from a piano teacher in Suffolk and a viola teacher in Norfolk; from home and church. In all this, his experience was not so different from that of thousands of other children: when he claimed, in 1968, to have 'come from a very ordinary middle-class family',[8] he was almost telling the truth. Attempting to answer the more difficult question – 'Where did his music come from?' – will suggest, among other things, why that 'almost' is there.

We need, first of all, to return to Kirkley Cliff: to the fact that it is, precisely, a cliff, although a fairly modest one. The sound of the North Sea – or the German Ocean, as it was still called in 1913 – rattling over the pebbled beach and beating against it was Ben's constant childhood companion from the day he was born; he once told Donald Mitchell that 'the sound of rushing water'[9] was his earliest memory, although to his sister Beth he said, more prosaically, that the sound he remembered was the gas hissing as he was born. As a boy, he would spend hours on the beach below the family home, often playing a solitary version of tennis against the concrete wall at the foot of the cliff; he was a strong swimmer, too, unintimidated by rough seas or tricky cross-currents. Even when he was a student in London he longed to return to the sea; and, from the moment he bought the Old Mill at Snape in 1937 until his death in 1976, his own permanent home would always be within a mile or two of it. He always needed, he said in 1960, 'that particular kind of atmosphere that the house on the edge of the sea provides'.[10] But if the North Sea can be companionable, it can also be destructive. The Brittens' aptly named Nanny Walker always took the children on interesting afternoon walks and, when asked where they were going, liked to reply, 'There and back to see how far it is':[11] a favourite destination was nearby Pakefield, so they could discover whether any more houses had lately fallen over the cliff. Today, the lanes there still peter out uncertainly where other vanished lanes should be, while the parish church stands within a few feet of the coastal path, rather than in a village centre. And the sea has a further effect on the lives of those who grow up or live adjacent to it: the ordinarily accessible world is reduced by half. The inland dweller has four points of the compass and all the directions in between to choose from; the inhabitant of Lowestoft cannot, except by swimming or taking a boat, go anywhere in the 180 degrees between north and south via east. Suffolk coastal places share a sense of being at the end of the road: this *genius loci* contains feelings of limitation and restraint which can also be intensely creative.

Secondly, there is the matter of young Benjamin's relationship with his family. His sister Beth said that their mother spoilt her younger son terribly: there was some excuse, for he had been dangerously ill with pneumonia at the age of three months and may only have survived because Edith, who was breastfeeding him, 'expressed the milk, and fed him with a fountain-pen filler, [when] he was too weak to suck'.[12] It was fortunate for Ben, Beth thought, that he hadn't been an only child, for in that case Edith's devotion might have been calamitously suffocating; but in crucial respects he *was* an only child. His brother, with whom he didn't especially get on, was six years older: too distant, in the telescoped time scheme of childhood, to be useful as a near-contemporary companion and for much of the time away from home as a boarder at Oakham School. His sisters were largely excluded from his private world of music, although Beth would make an exception for the military bands who played on the South Pier, especially the Grenadier Guards, 'for both Ben and I had a crush on the conductor and would dare each other to speak to him'.[13] However, the whole family would participate in plays and pantomimes: at the age of six, Benjamin appeared at the local Sparrow's Nest Theatre in a production of Charles Kingsley's *The Water Babies*, playing the part of Tom, 'dressed in skin-coloured tights with tiny fins sewn to his shoulders and heels'.[14] He also wrote plays of his own, often about what he called 'The Royal Falily' (an early and curiously prescient enthusiasm), as well as poems with excruciating Cole Porteresque rhymes: 'Poor wee pussie cat! / Oh! a matter of fact, / you're much nicer / than all the mice er!!!'[15] But these were in every sense diversions from the main focus of his creative talent. That Robert Britten could appear to be sternly unsympathetic – 'hard' on his younger son is a word that recurs in contemporary recollections of him – seems simply to have strengthened Benjamin's musical resolve, as well as helping to shape a ruthlessly competitive side of his character which was strikingly unlike any stereotype of the sensitive, introverted composer.

Mr Britten made a decent living from dentistry; but with a house to run, including servants and nannies, and four children to educate at fee-paying schools, his resources were often stretched; he was, said his younger daughter, 'not a mean man, but expenses weighed heavily on him'.[16] The composer's 'ordinary middle-class' background certainly included the ordinary middle-class game of keeping up appearances. One such appearance, as we've already seen, was the impression created for visitors and passers-by that the household was continually engaged in civilised music-making. Another was the Brittens' Sunday-morning departure for church in the family car: once there, however, Robert would drop off his wife and children before driving away to call on patients, invariably ending up at a farmhouse pub in the appropriately named village of Sotterley; after Sunday lunch, he would wallow in his weekly hot bath (he took cold baths on weekdays) before setting off to enjoy an evening with his chums at the Royal Yacht Club in Lowestoft. It's a useful reminder that Robert was a more complex character than he may have at first appeared: although he was a conventionally authoritarian father, who expected his children to stand when he entered a room, there was also a hint of rebellious independence about him. In this combination of opposites, he suddenly seems much more like his younger son than we might otherwise have guessed.

Benjamin's childhood geographical environment and the tensions within his family both fostered the sense of apartness which is a prerequisite of creativity. So – a little more surprisingly, since it offered nothing in the way of musical education – did his prep school, South Lodge.

2

Britten supplied his own account of his schooldays at South Lodge in the sleeve note he contributed to the 1955 Decca recording – by the New Symphony Orchestra of London, conducted by Eugene Goossens – of his *Simple Symphony*:

Once upon a time there was a prep-school boy. He was called Britten mi., his initials were E.B., his age was nine, and his locker was number seventeen. He was quite an ordinary little boy; he took his snake-belt to bed with him; he loved cricket, only quite liked football (although he kicked a pretty 'corner'); he adored mathematics, got on all right with history, was scared by Latin Unseen; he behaved fairly well, only ragged the recognised amount, so that his contacts with the cane or the slipper were happily rare (although one nocturnal expedition to stalk ghosts left its marks behind); he worked his way up the school slowly and steadily, until at the age of thirteen he reached that pinnacle of importance and grandeur never to be quite equalled in later days: the head of the Sixth, head-prefect, and Victor Ludorum. But . . . there was one curious thing about this boy: he wrote music. His friends bore with it, his enemies kicked a bit but not for long (he was quite tough), the staff couldn't object if his work and games didn't suffer. He wrote lots of it, reams and reams of it. I don't really know when he had time to do it. In those days, long ago, prep-school boys didn't have much free time; the day started with early work at 7.30, and ended (if you were lucky not to do extra prep.) with prayers at 8.0 – and the hours in between were fully organised. Still there were odd moments in bed, there were half holidays and Sundays too, and somehow these reams and reams got written. And they are still lying in an old cupboard to this day – string quartets (six of them); twelve piano sonatas; dozens of songs; sonatas for violin, sonatas for viola and 'cello too; suites, waltzes, rondos, fantasies, variations; a tone-poem *Chaos and Cosmos*; a tremendous symphony, for gigantic orchestra including eight horns and oboe d'amore (started on January 17 and finished February 28); an oratorio called *Samuel*; all the opus numbers from 1 to 100 were filled (and catalogued) by the time Britten mi. was fourteen.

Of course they aren't very good, these works; inspiration didn't always run very high, and the workmanship wasn't always academically sound, and although our composer looked up oboe d'amore in the orchestra books, he hadn't much of an idea of what it sounded like; besides, for the sake of neatness, every piece had to end precisely at the bottom of the right-hand page, which doesn't always lead to a satisfactory conclusion. No, I'm afraid they aren't very great; but when Benjamin Britten, a proud young composer of twenty (who'd already had a work broadcast), came along and looked in this cupboard, he found some of them not too uninteresting; and so, rescoring them for strings, changing bits here and there, and making them more fit for general consumption, he turned them into a SIMPLE SYMPHONY, and here it is.[17]

Subjecting a sleeve note to close reading might seem odd, but this is an extraordinary document. We need to bear in mind the date, 1955, for two reasons: firstly, because the archness of tone, though unquestionably present, would have seemed far less obtrusive at the time; secondly, because the recent spate of high-profile homosexual arrests and prosecutions – Britten himself was interviewed by the police in December 1953 – made this a dangerous moment for self-revelation. But self-revelation there certainly is, if we care to look for it. To start with, there is the insistence, exactly consistent with his assertion that he came 'from a very ordinary middle-class family' but contradicted by almost everything else in the piece, that 'Britten minor' – his brother Bobby would have been styled 'Britten major' – was 'quite an ordinary little boy'. In the opening lines, 'quite' appears no fewer than four times, and on each occasion its qualifying effect is crucial: here, it means that he wasn't at all ordinary. In 'only quite liked football', it firmly implies that there was something wrong with football, rather than with Britten minor, whose ability to rise above this mundane game is at once confirmed by his kicking 'a pretty "corner"' as a casually parenthetical skill. The 'pinnacle of importance and grandeur never to be quite equalled', destablised by its ironic 'quite', topples towards insignificance; while the mock-modesty of 'he was quite tough' manages to suggest that he may have been very tough indeed.

The dated prep-school slang was both an enduring habit – throughout his life, Britten used the *School Boy's Pocket Diary*, delightedly entering his personal details in the conventional juvenile fashion – and a code. In fondly recalling his locker number, he discloses his continuing affection or even need for school-like order; while his reference to the snake-belt which he took to bed with him suggests something still more personal, a talismanic, almost fetishistic attachment to objects associated with his schooldays. No one coming across the note in 1955 would have been in the least bothered by the 'contacts' with cane and slipper, which were still commonplace implements of prep-school discipline, but an attentive reader might have been struck by the mixture of coyness and relish of 'left its marks behind' in the subsequent parenthesis: the merest hint of a preoccupation which was to recur in his work. And as for that 'pinnacle of importance and grandeur', it is comical partly because we will more readily associate such terms as 'the Sixth' with an eighteen-year-old on his way to university than with a thirteen-year-old at prep school and partly because, even as prep schools go, South Lodge was a small one with fewer than fifty pupils: a school photograph of 1923 shows thirty-seven.[18] The hours of study may have been long, but there is no evidence to suggest that the academic standards were at all exceptional. Yet it was precisely this – in the dialectical fashion which is so often the way with creativity – that led the young Britten to compose music: paradoxically, had he been given more time and encouragement to do so at school, he would almost certainly have written much less. South Lodge provided him with the sense of pressure and discipline which would always be a feature of his working habits as a composer. 'I often thank my stars,' he said in a 1960 BBC interview with his friend the Earl of Harewood, 'that I went to a rather strict school where one was made to work and I can, without much difficulty, sit down at 8.30 or 9 o'clock in the morning and work straight through the morning until lunchtime.'[19]

South Lodge was a tall and exceptionally ugly early-Victorian house on the opposite side of Kirkley Cliff Road, adjacent to the beach and the sea; the school had been founded in 1862. Soon after Britten went there as a day boy in September 1922, its proprietor, 'an ancient clergyman named Phillips',[20] sold it to his mathematics master, Thomas Jackson Elliott Sewell MA MC, known to parents as 'The Captain' and to pupils as 'The Beak'.

Sewell was not just a close neighbour of the Brittens; he had taught Ben's elder brother Bobby and courted his twenty-year-old sister Barbara, before dropping her in favour of a young woman whose dowry enabled him to buy the school. Since this completely disrupted Barbara's life – she left home, trained as a health visitor in London and formed a relationship with an older woman, whom even the Britten parents must have recognised as a lesbian – it seems a little strange that Sewell remained sufficiently in favour with the family for Ben to have been sent to his school; but the compensatory advantages included proximity to home and to his music teacher, Ethel Astle, as well as relative cheapness compared with boarding at some more distant establishment. Yet it seems that he may have boarded briefly at South Lodge – perhaps while his parents were away from home for some reason – since, in the Harewood interview quoted above, he said that he 'used to disconcert the other children by writing music in the dormitory and all that kind of thing'.[21]

His days there were less cloudless than he later chose to recall. Although records of South Lodge are sparse – the school, which was twice destroyed by fire,[22] moved premises several times, ending up at Old Buckenham Hall in Norfolk – it's clear that 'Britten mi.' spent much of his time towards the bottom of his form. Like his father, he notably failed to subscribe to some aspects of the place's conservative orthodoxy: a master, perhaps Sewell himself, once barked at him, 'Stand up the boy whose father voted Liberal!'[23] In his final term, he wrote an essay on the subject of 'Animals' which caused deep offence and received a mark of nought because it protested against bloodsports and cruelty instead of taking the approved pro-hunting, pro-shooting line: he thus anticipated the adult self who in 1931 would set to music W. H. Davies's anti-hunting poem 'Sport' and in 1936 compose *Our Hunting Fathers* in collaboration with Auden. The Britten scholar Mervyn Cooke says that, as a result of the

'Animals' essay, Britten 'left his prep school in disgrace',[24] but this is an overstatement: both his mathematical ability and his outstanding success in the Associated Board's music exams had made him too conspicuous a favourite of Sewell's to be undone by a single essay. Even though there was 'no music at all' at South Lodge, according to Britten (apart, he added, from 'the end of each term, on the last evening' when 'we sang some songs'),[25] Sewell was shrewd enough to realise that this remarkable young musician, whom he envisaged as a future concert pianist rather than as a composer, might bring honour and prestige to the school. Britten was also a successful sportsman, vice captain of his school's cricket team and junior county tennis champion, yet even on the cricket pitch he wouldn't be allowed to forget his musical destiny. 'For this reason,' his schoolfriend Alan Lyon, who was the team captain, remembered, 'he always had to field in the deep and when a high ball was hit to him the Headmaster, Captain Sewell, fearing for his fingers, would shout from the boundary, "You're not to catch it, Britten! You're not to catch it!"'[26]

Although Sewell was an able teacher of mathematics and of classics, this is not why he was chiefly remembered by his pupils. One recalled that he was 'very fond of beating boys – which one didn't understand in those days . . . at that age. But obviously there must have been a little bit of a fixation.'[27] 'You got beaten on the slightest pretext, with a hell of a palaver,' said Britten's South Lodge friend John Pounder. 'For really extra special beatings the whole school was assembled, and the criminal was brought out before them, and then was led away to a dormitory above the school room. We always said that Sewell liked beating boys, but we were much too frightened to complain.'[28] Sewell, according to another contemporary, removed boys' trousers and underpants before beating them 'to enable me to see what I am doing'.[29] Interviewed by the *Guardian* in 1971,

Britten said: 'I can remember the first time – I think it was the very first day that I was in a school – that I heard a boy being beaten, and I can remember my absolute astonishment that people didn't immediately rush to help him. And to find that it was sort of condoned and accepted was something that shocked me very much.'[30] That is a different tone from his 1955 recollection of South Lodge, and a different kind of partial truth: what he didn't – and couldn't – say on either occasion was that Sewell's fondness for beating 'left its marks behind' in a more complicated psychological way. It would be naive to accept at face value the suggestion that Britten was simply dismayed by violent corruption of the young, which is why it became a recurring theme in his work; there's too much obsession and excitement for that to be the whole truth. But what we might more usefully do is to accept calmly that his sexual character contained a sadomasochistic element which he transformed into a source of creative energy while, no less admirably, treating the sequence of boys to whom he became devoted with exemplary gentleness and generosity.

It makes even less sense than usual to speak, in Britten's case, of his being young or old 'for his age'. He acquired 'from the very first day I was in a school' – and by this he obviously means South Lodge rather than the tiny and innocent Southolme – an awareness of the power and excitement of violence, but that doesn't imply that he could yet connect it with anything sexual. He was out of phase with himself: in some respects, precociously well informed; in others, startlingly innocent. And this was partly a consequence of the confined geographical orbit in which he lived: many boys, at nine or ten years old, do some significant growing up while talking dirty in a gaggle on the bus or train home from school, but Britten's home was just along the road; even the traditional rituals of cigarettes, obscenities and sexual exploration 'behind the bike sheds' would have been denied to a serious boy who didn't need a bike to get there and who, when the long school day was over, mainly wanted to go home and compose. Moreover, he remained in this highly protective environment for an unusually long time, not going on to board at Gresham's School, Holt, until he was nearly fifteen.

Nevertheless, some transforming experience seems to have occurred towards the end of his final year at South Lodge, 1927–8. It was, in any case, a momentous time for him, the year in which he achieved all those unrepeatable schoolboy honours as well as the year in which he met the composer Frank Bridge: he possessed the outward confidence of a talented boy who knew exactly where he wanted his talent to take him. There could hardly have been a more auspicious moment for some sort of sexual awakening to take place. Much later he told the director and librettist Eric Crozier that he had been 'raped by a master at his school': he didn't say which school, and the absence of a qualifying adjective such as 'prep' or 'private' suggests that he was referring to his public school, Gresham's, rather than South Lodge. But assuming (for the time being) that he *was* talking about South Lodge, he didn't say 'headmaster': so he would have meant not Sewell but one of the assistant masters, who in prep schools were often young men filling in a year before or after university. It may well have been a provocative remark designed to disconcert a professional colleague with whom he had a fairly edgy relationship, although the biographer Humphrey Carpenter pointed his suspicious finger at an 'opportunity' suggested by Britten's diary entry for 13 June 1928: 'Set off to play Match against Taverham, but I only get 1/2 way and I go back to School in Capt. Sewell's car as I am not well. Lie down at school and come home after and go to bed.'[31] But after three days' illness, he returned to his diary – and to an entry unmentioned by Carpenter – on 17 June: 'Am much better, go to the Colemans' to tea, I got up at 12 o'clock . . . Rewrite some songs, written on Friday and Saturday namely Dans les bois, and begin to rewrite Nuits de Juin.'[32] Was this, for young Benjamin Britten, the moment in childhood when a door opens and lets the future in?[33]

Probably it was. But I suspect that the way in which the door opened for him was far less sensational, though no less profound, than Carpenter suggested. For this was the year in which his friendships with two of his South Lodge contemporaries – John Pounder and, especially, Francis Barton – became intensified by the emotional force of adolescence and further sharpened by the sense that, with his imminent departure from the school, they might be about to end (although, as we shall see, they both continued well into adulthood). Francis, the son of a Sussex clergyman, was a lively, bright boy who looked and was, but didn't act, two years younger than Ben. There's a charming photograph, taken that summer term, of the pair smiling from an open railway-carriage window at Lowestoft station: perhaps they're setting off for one of those away cricket fixtures, wearing their badged South Lodge caps, Ben in a smart jacket and prefectorial tie, Francis in his striped blazer. Francis, leaning over Ben's outstretched arm, grins with impish dimpled pleasure; yet Ben's smile has something more subtle and complex, even proprietorial, about it. Surely, he was in love: though this wasn't a word he could have used to Francis, in the privacy of his dreams or his creative consciousness he can't have had much doubt about it. Those three days of illness, so near the end of the summer term, may well have been the catalyst which transformed his emotional turmoil into astonishingly mature musical utterance: he began work on the *Quatre Chansons Françaises*, his first truly adult compositions. The future had definitely been let in.

3

Britten's extravagant-looking claim, in his 1955 note, that by the time he was fourteen 'all the opus numbers from 1 to 100 were filled (and catalogued)' is actually a massive understatement. According to the definitive catalogue of his juvenilia prepared by the Britten–Pears Foundation in 2009,[34] he had composed no fewer than 534 works by the end of 1927, which was shortly after his fourteenth birthday; the peak year was 1925 (128 works), closely followed by 1926 (108). Not all of these would have been granted the honour of an opus number, of course, but the sheer quantity of effort, energy and invention is staggering. The earliest surviving piece – a song entitled 'Do you no my Daddy has gone to London today' – dates from 1919, when Britten was five or six years old. The following year, he composed another song, 'The rabbits stand around and hold the lights', which clearly illustrates his fascination with the 'dots and dashes' and the musical sounds they might represent, although he had yet to grasp the exact connection between them: 'I am afraid it was the pattern on the paper which I was interested in and when I asked my mother to play it, her look of horror upset me considerably.'[35] The words don't match the vocal line; the vocal line doesn't match the accompaniment; neither key signature nor time signature relates to what follows, which is, as Mrs Britten discovered, unplayable. But what remains oddly impressive is the seven-year-old's determination to put down on his own paper so much of what he has observed in other music; and there is something quite subtle about his dynamic markings, which take us from *ff* piano introduction through *pp* central passage (where, aptly, 'Fairys are singing . . .') to *f* conclusion. In that, coincidentally or not, there's a hint of the life to come.

Those rabbits are from the years before he had begun his lessons with Ethel Astle; a piece such as the 'Fantasie Improptu' of 1922–3 belongs to a different world. The notation is clear, neat and playable: no doubt, this is the result not only of Ethel Astle's tuition and the Seppings Music Method but of Uncle Willie's birthday present, *A Dictionary of Musical Terms*. The opening bars are adapted from Wagner's *Siegfried Idyll*, of which a piano reduction was among Mrs Britten's favourite pieces; that the young composer should therefore have used it in a work of his own for piano seems understandable enough. What is much more remarkable is his attempt, a few months later, to write for a range of instruments he had never heard, let alone spelt, in the 'Walzt', signed 'E. B. Britten, Op. 3, No. 3' and scored for 'Solo Violin, Flauti, Hoboem, Clarinett in C, Fagotti, 2 Trombe in C, 2 Corni in C, Timpani, Violon, Viola, Celli, Kontra-Bassi'; the solo violin line was one he would recycle, most notably in the 'Sentimental Saraband' from the *Simple Symphony*. In the summer of 1924, he completed a volume of *12 Songs for Mezzo-Soprano* to be performed by his mother, presumably with himself as the accompanist, two of which – 'Beware!' and 'O that I'd ne're been married' – he was to revise for publication in the late 1960s: as with the *Simple Symphony*, one notices both his judiciousness in the retrieval of juvenilia and his baroque spirit of creative thrift. He wrote reams of piano music during 1925–6, much of it grouped into series, of which the most ambitious was *Twenty-Four Themes*: a waltz for every major and minor key, combining the example of Bach's 48 Preludes and Fugues and the influence of Chopin's 24 Etudes. In June 1926 he composed and scored an 'Ouverture' which his proud father submitted as an entry for the BBC's Autumnal Musical Festival Prize Competition: it was, explained Mr Britten in his covering letter, 'written by a lad of 12 years, in nine days: written in his very few spare moments snatched from the hourly routine of his "Prep" school (in the very early mornings, for instance)'.[36] Perhaps he was overdoing it a bit, as he was when he claimed that his son had 'only an elementary knowledge of harmony' and 'no instruction of any kind in orchestration or counterpoint'.

Two months later, while staying miserably with a family friend in Kent (he had suffered from 'bad diherea', his room was 'pested with *wapses*' and he wanted 'Daddy to come soon'), Benjamin wrote home to describe the Queen's Hall concert he had attended with his sister Barbara and her friend Helen Hurst: 'It was all modern music, and I have taken a great like to modern *Orchestral* music.' There was Schelling's now forgotten 'Suite Fantastique for piano and orchestra', which was 'only a show of technique(?)', 'a Delius piece called "Life's Dance", this was lovely; and Holsts planets which were lovely';[37] he went on to transcribe correctly the 'gorgeous' 5/4 rhythm of 'Mars'. Britten's own 'Suite Fantastique for large orchestra and pianoforte obbligato' dates from the same year and was written for his parents' silver wedding anniversary, although quite what they were intended to do with it is unclear. Soon after this, Benjamin embarked on the tone poem *Chaos and Cosmos*, 'although I fear I was not sure what the words really meant'.[38] But 1927 was principally the year of the string quartet, of which he composed twenty-nine. The 'Quartette in G', begun in the spring for Audrey Alston and the Norwich String Quartet, was extensively drafted and redrafted – there are over thirty manuscript sources in the BPF archive – and he further revised it at the beginning of 1928, so that he could take it to his first lesson with Frank Bridge on 12 January.

Bridge and Britten had first met, introduced by Audrey Alston, at the Norwich Festival premiere of Bridge's *Enter Spring* in October 1927. 'We got on splendidly,' Britten recalled, 'and I spent the next morning with him going over some of my music.'[39] Bridge was so impressed that he made a radical suggestion: Benjamin should move to London and lodge with his friend Harold Samuel, from whom he would receive daily piano lessons, while Bridge would teach him composition. This was all too much for his conservative father – who was uneasy about Bridge, according to Beth Britten, because 'He had long hair, was very excitable and talked a lot'[40] – and his possessive mother. In fact, both parents quite sensibly recognised the outside chance that their son's musical talent might even now dry up: he still needed to continue with his ordinary education, just in case. They decided that he should remain at home until the following summer and then go on to public school as planned; nevertheless, he would make regular trips to London for lessons with Samuel and Bridge. It sounds a messy sort of compromise, but – since it involved considerable expense, inconvenience and negotiation with schools for days off during term time – it was actually a huge gesture of confidence.

Bridge, born in 1879 and thus of Britten's parents' generation, was to become the musical father young Benjamin had hitherto lacked. His reputation, which now at last seems secure, was in the 1920s somewhat precarious: the shock of the First World War and its associated upheavals in European culture had transformed an extremely competent, well-mannered Edwardian composer into a challenging modernist. It was as if, for a reader of poetry, Henry Newbolt had suddenly turned into T. S. Eliot, and much of Bridge's previous audience were alienated by the change. Writing only a few years after the composer's death in 1941, the musicologist Jack Westrup would say that Bridge was by then primarily known to amateur singers 'as the composer of one or two effective songs';[41] and the discography in the same volume suggests that, although by 1946 some dozen of his most celebrated pupil's works had been recorded, there was not a single gramophone record available of music by Frank Bridge.[42] His reputation was further muddied by the tendency of listeners to search in his orchestral master-piece *The Sea* (1910) at first for the scene-painting of Debussy's

La Mer (1904) and later for premonitions of the interludes in *Peter Grimes* (1945), while many mid-twentieth-century music lovers must have first encountered his name (perhaps asking themselves 'Who?') in the title of Britten's *Variations on a Theme of Frank Bridge* (1937).

But Bridge's strength was as a composer of chamber music and, had he remained true to the spirit of such relatively unchallenging earlier works as the *Phantasy Piano Quartet* of 1910, not only his musical career but Britten's might have taken a very different course. Instead, by the time Britten began studying with him, he had already published his Third String Quartet (1926) which, in the words of the composer Anthony Payne, 'proclaimed that an English composer could achieve a rapprochement with Berg and Bartók without surrendering his independence of vision'.[43] It was followed in 1929 by the marvellous Second Piano Trio: this, says Payne, 'inhabits an unprecedented world, one of the masterpieces of twentieth-century English, indeed European chamber music'. Britten himself described it as 'one of the finest pieces of extended musical thinking of our time'.[44] Although it was 'unprecedented' in English (if not in European) music, the language of the piece is unthreateningly bitonal rather than atonal, its character often beguilingly melodic. In the first movement, the forward lyrical momentum is checked by the piano's clusters of open fifths; then, after a searching central section and a tense allegro passage, the movement resolves into fragile tranquillity. Next comes a busy scherzo with a neurotic pizzicato motif, spreading out into a central melodic idea which has moments of zany, almost folksy charm. In the slow third movement, a memorably haunting melody is offset by another repetitive motif, ticking away like a clock or a time bomb; while the final hurtling allegro leads to a restatement of the first movement's second theme and, eventually, to a sort of provisional calm. These were among the components of the creative sound-world inside Bridge's head when he began teaching Benjamin Britten, and it would show.

It's probably fair to say that Bridge wasn't a natural teacher. He made no concessions to his young pupil's age or stamina, subjecting him to 'mammoth' lessons of 'immensely serious and professional study': 'I remember one that started at half past ten, and at tea-time Mrs Bridge came in and said, "Really, you must give the boy a break." Often I used to end these marathons in tears; not that he was beastly to me, but the concentrated strain was too much for me.'[45] It wasn't just the epic duration of these lessons that wore Britten out: 'Not only did he keep my nose to the grindstone, but he criticised my work relentlessly.'[46] 'I used to get sent to the other side of the room; Bridge would play what I'd written and demand if it was what I'd really meant.' For this, the pupil remained permanently grateful:

> I badly needed his kind of strictness; it was just the right treatment for me. His loathing of all sloppiness and amateurishness set me standards that I've never forgotten. He taught me to think and feel through the instruments I was writing for: he was most naturally an instrumental composer, and as a superb viola player he taught me instrumentally.[47]

That is the sort of thing an adult might retrospectively say to justify a worthwhile experience he didn't much enjoy at that time, but Britten's diaries tell a different story. 'Had an absolutely wonderful lesson,' he wrote after his first one, on 12 January 1928, setting the tone for future entries on the same subject. (That evening, though, *Peter Pan* was also 'wonderful', a word he tended to overuse.) On 26–28 April he was in London for three successive days and three lessons with Bridge, which he recorded in his diary: '26 Thursday: Lesson from Mr Bridge 11.0–12.45. Very nice and helpful . . . 27 Friday: Lesson from

9.45–12.0. Mr Bridge gives me score of his "An Irish Melody" . . .
28 Saturday: Lesson from 9.45–12.15.'⁴⁸ He said nothing else
about the Saturday lesson, hastening on to the 'wonderful'
Beethoven concert at the Albert Hall that afternoon. He
copied out the main details from the programme and pasted
this into the diary: the *Egmont* overture, the second piano
concerto and the Choral Fantasia; the soloists were duly noted
and the New Symphony Orchestra was conducted by 'DR.
MALCOLM SARGENT', to whom he would seldom sound quite
so respectful. The previous afternoon, following a Prufrockian
'Dinner at Ruths . . . gramophone after, and ices', he had gone
off to 'Buy Ravel's "Introduction & Allegro" for Harp etc. at
Augeners'.

'I was beginning to get more adventurous,' he later recalled.
'Before then, what I'd been writing had been sort of early 19th
century in style; and then I heard Holst's "Planets" and Ravel's
string quartet and was excited by them.'⁴⁹ Ravel's String Quartet
in F major dates from 1903; the Introduction and Allegro for
harp, flute, clarinet and string quartet, composed three years
later, may have made an even deeper impression on the young
composer, for whom the exploration of just such restricted yet
colourful instrumental groupings would develop into a lifelong
preoccupation. At this crucial point, in the last few months of
his long years at South Lodge, he was already assimilating an
eclectic range of musical influences: the standard repertoire
favoured by his mother, typified by that Beethoven concert;
the teaching of Bridge, English-rooted but excitedly informed
by composers of the Second Viennese School; and his own
largely independent discovery of modern French music, such
as that of Debussy and Ravel. The logical compositional
outcome might lie somewhere between the 'early 19th century'
style which had previously dominated his work and the
modernist bitonality of Bridge, a late romanticism with

chromatic tinges; and that is indeed the musical language of his *Quatre Chansons Françaises*.

Britten began work on these songs some six weeks after those three eventful London days in April, during those mysterious other three days in June when he was visited in rapid succession by illness and inspiration. Everything about the *Quatre Chansons Françaises* is extraordinary, starting with the fact that a prep-school boy could so confidently embark on setting such intense French texts as two poems apiece by Victor Hugo and Paul Verlaine; he jettisoned his setting of a fifth poem, 'Dans les bois' by Gérard de Nerval. He found the poems in *The Oxford Book of French Verse*, so he may not have known anything yet about *symbolisme* in general and the Verlaine–Rimbaud milieu in particular: he would come, fully informed, to Rimbaud when setting his prose poems in *Les Illuminations* (1939), yet even here there's a sense of the fourteen-year-old Britten using French as a means of distancing and encoding, to provide seriousness and obliqueness. It was, after all, still the language conventionally spoken in front of servants, so that they wouldn't understand. In opening with a deliriously evocative setting of Hugo's 'Nuits de juin', he aptly registers the time of year and his own feverish state and perhaps also intends an allusion to Berlioz and his *Les Nuits d'été*. Then comes Verlaine's 'Sagesse', with its plaintive oboe-led underlining of the conclusion, 'Dis, qu'as-tu fait, toi que voilà / De ta jeunesse?' The third song is by common consent the most remarkable. The poem, Hugo's 'L'Enfance', is about a five-year-old child who continues to sing and play while his mother is dying, and dies, of consumption: the flute's instantly memorable nursery-rhyme motif becomes compromised and melancholic as the song proceeds, and the juxtapositions of lightness and darkness have an almost cinematic vividness, prefiguring Britten's film scores of the 1930s. At about this time, and certainly after he went away to school in the autumn, he began to experience terrifying nightmares, which must have been connected with the Hugo poem, about his own mother's death. The final 'Chanson d'automne', like the other Verlaine poem, is treated by Britten emphatically as a farewell to innocence: 'Je me souviens / Des jours anciens / Et je pleure . . .' The orchestral writing throughout *Quatre Chansons Françaises* is astonishing for a boy who had yet to study orchestration and had very seldom had the opportunity to *hear* an orchestra: he seems, with Bridge's encouragement, to have absorbed elements of Berlioz, Debussy, Ravel, Wagner and Berg. By the time he completed the work, in August 1928, his prep-school days were over.

4

'I like this place quite, but I feel horribly strange and small,' wrote Britten to his 'darling Mummy and Pop' on 21 September 1928, after spending his first night in Farfield, his boarding house at Gresham's School, Holt. He was sharing a study with three other boys who were 'quite nice', although Marshall, who was captain of the study, had 'a rotten old gramophone, on which he plays miserable jazz all the time!'[50] That note – a bit prissy and joyless for a boy two months short of his fifteenth birthday – is one we shall hear again: it would both restrict his range of pleasures and concentrate his talent, a quid pro quo of which he gradually became helplessly aware. He had met some of the staff, including 'a funny little chaplain', and he was eager to report, with the pride befitting a former head prefect and victor ludorum, that he was in 3b, 'not at all a bad form . . . above Purdy [from South Lodge] . . . and Dashwood from Aldeburgh'. He had not yet met the Director of Music, Walter Greatorex.

Two days later, he had. Greatorex famously greeted him with

the words, 'So you are the little boy who likes Stravinsky.' When Britten had finished playing some late Beethoven, he asked, 'And who taught you that?' before going on to tell him that he had 'a very flimsy technick (?) . . . that it was hopeless for a boy of my age to play late Beethoven and that my love of Beethoven will soon die'. When they came to the Chopin Polonaise in C sharp minor, Greatorex first disputed Britten's dynamic inter-pretation of bars 5–8 – 'I played them *f*, he said they ought to be *pp* practically' – and then, which was worse, showed how he thought it should be done, 'playing with no two notes together, and a gripping touch, and terrible tone. I don't think much of his ~~technick~~ (oh I don't know) technich (?)!' Greatorex 'as good as said it would be no good whatsoever for me to go into the musical profession' – although 'as good as said' may mean he said something rather more equivocal – after which Britten dramatically concluded: 'Music in this school is now finished for me!' But that didn't prevent him from admitting, a few lines on in the same letter, that 'This school is not half as bad as I expected', nor from saying how much he had enjoyed the previous evening's choir practice ('great fun, I sing alto you know') and that day's 'very nice service in the Chapel'. This service, with its plainsong and unfamiliar hymns, was different from the resolutely 'low', evangelical style to which he was accustomed, and it was somewhat spoilt by the inevitable organist: 'Mr Greatorex, who played the organ, does not play well.'[51]

Poor Walter Greatorex: almost everyone sides with the bumptious new boy against him. Yet a pampered and sheltered fourteen-year-old – homesick, 'longing for November', a small fish in a big pond for the first time in his life – is not necessarily a reliable witness. He chose to take Greatorex's remark about Stravinsky, whose work he had in fact not yet come across, as a sarcastic slight; whereas a more mature boy, or one accustomed to the quizzical ways of public-school masters, might have detected a note of wry admiration or even camaraderie. For his part, Greatorex must have felt that it would do no harm to take this precocious young pupil of Frank Bridge down a peg or two, and he wasn't entirely wrong: after all, the main purpose of Britten being at Gresham's was for him to acquire some general education and School Certificate passes, just in case his musical ambitions came to nothing. Greatorex would have been well aware that an overconfident prodigy would be just as likely to disrupt the school's musical life as to enhance it; he may also have recognised that a somewhat humbled Britten would stand a better chance of fitting in socially. It was by no means the first time that he had encountered creative genius among his pupils. The writer Michael Davidson, whose brother-in-law Christopher Southward taught the violin in Greatorex's department, remembered him saying: 'There's a boy you'd like to meet – writes very good verse I think. His name's Auden.'[52] Davidson was then a 26-year-old journalist in Norwich, the poet W. H. Auden a sixteen-year-old pupil at Gresham's. There followed, wrote Davidson, 'a poetical relationship which for two years or so absorbed me'; so it was a bold and perceptive introduction, whether or not Greatorex knew or cared that both Auden and Davidson were, like him, homosexual. At that time Greatorex was 'a principal worshipper' at the Southwards' home, The Beeches, which was something of a sanctuary for writers and musicians. He was clearly no philistine; equally clearly, his conservative musical instincts and his old-fashioned keyboard technique would have been intolerable to a forward-looking pupil of Bridge. Although Greatorex, born in 1877, was actually only two years older than Bridge, he seemed to belong to a different generation and a different musical world.

Auden, who was at Gresham's less than a decade earlier, had a very different estimate of Greatorex as man and musician. It was to him, Auden said, that he owed 'my first friendship with a grown up person . . . he was what the ideal schoolmaster should be, ready to be a friend and not a beak, to give the adolescent all the comfort and stimulus of a personal relation, without at the same time making any demands for himself in return'.[53] Musically, 'he was in the first rank. I do not think it was partiality that made me feel, later when I heard Schweitzer play Bach, that he played no better.' Robert Medley, another member of the 1930s Auden circle who was at Gresham's during the early 1920s, wrote that he and his contemporaries 'never penetrated the mystery of how it was that Greatorex, whom we regarded as one of the great musicians in the land, came to be stranded in Holt'.[54] Stephen Spender, also at Gresham's, remembered the boys debating whether he was 'the eighth or the ninth greatest musician in England'.[55] In their day, Greatorex was known as 'The Ox', in Britten's as 'Gog', which suggests that his impressive figure with its domed head and stern late-Beethovenian scowl had solidified into something still more imposingly mythological.

Gresham's had been chosen by the Brittens because the school 'didn't actively hate music, as so many other public schools did';[56] it offered music scholarships, was within a reasonable distance of home and had a reputation of being generally fairly civilised. Although an old foundation, dating from 1555, it had only recently attained public school status and it prided itself on having broken with a number of nineteenth-century traditions. Most boys slept in individual cubicles rather than dormitories; they were not compelled to join the cadet force, though if they wouldn't join they had to explain why not; and they had to subscribe to an 'honour system', which meant that they would report their own and others' transgressions to their housemasters. Auden, while acknowledging the decency of the idea, said that it turned the school into a fascist state and made innocent boys neurotic (though elsewhere he would argue that childhood neurosis was a usefully creative thing). In a diary entry of 1929, Britten agreed: 'I think the "Honour System" is a positive failure in Farfield . . . Atrocious bullying on all sides, vulgarity & swearing. It is no good trying the Honour System on boys who have no honour. Boys, small & rather weak are turned into sour & bitter boys, and ruined for life.'[57] He may well have been right, although the note of primness is striking, especially in a private diary: he seems overanxious to insist, even to himself, that he is wholly unlike his boorish contemporaries, as if trying to fend off any suspicion that he might be less than impeccably virtuous. Britten thought he disliked Gresham's, but what he actually disliked was being in close proximity to a large number of insensitive, uncreative people: he always would. When, for instance, he discovered that 'If you are original, well you are considered a lunatic, & consequently become unpopular',[58] he was making a discovery which applied well beyond the confines of his or any other school. During his two years at Gresham's, he was frequently ill, despite which – as his letters home show – his spirits usually seemed to rise in the peaceful isolation of the sickroom.

The high point of Britten's first term at Gresham's was to be his escape from it, when in early November he travelled to London for lessons with Harold Samuel and Frank Bridge. His diary entries for 9 and 10 November record his 'Wonderful Lesson' with Samuel, the 'absolutely wonderful' concert at the Queen's Hall that evening (the Hallé under Sir Hamilton Harty playing symphonies by Schubert, Beethoven and Brahms) and his 'very nice' lesson with Bridge the following morning. But they are interesting in another way too. The entry for 9 November opens: 'Set off for London at 8.40 in morning by train, very slow. Mrs Fletcher takes me to Sheringham in car. Meet Mummy at Ipswich. Get to Liverp[ool] St[reet] at 1.20.' And the entry for 10 November closes: 'Barbara takes me to

King's Cross, Ruth takes Mummy to Liverp. St. I get to Holt feeling absolutely miserable, cold and hungry at 7.19.'[59] He had spent well over eight hours of the two days on trains, a circumstance which would become familiar during the years he shuttled between Holt, Norwich, Lowestoft, London and the Bridges' country home in Sussex, though his father would drive him to and from school in the family car which Britten grandiloquently renamed the 'Rolls-Crossley'. What he observed or experienced in the long solitary segments of these train journeys is unrecorded, but they made a lasting impression on him. When, much later, he came to set eight poems by Hardy in *Winter Words*, perhaps the most deeply personal of all his song cycles, Britten chose not only 'At the Railway Station, Upway', which includes the boy with the violin (although in his own case it was a viola), but also 'Midnight on the Great Western', where the final stanza describes his young self's predicament with quite astonishing accuracy:

> Knows your soul a sphere, O journeying boy,
>   Our rude realms far above,
> Whence with spacious vision you mark and mete
> This region of sin that you find you in,
>   But are not of?[60]

He would always feel warily ambivalent about the 'region of sin' which he was either 'in' but not 'of' or, just as uncomfortably, 'of' but not 'in'.

His other escape from Gresham's was back into the world of his home and his prep school. Basil Reeve, a close friend and contemporary from Lowestoft and himself a gifted musician, remembered how completely Mrs Britten continued to dominate her younger son: even when Britten was in his mid-teens, 'I could only see him with her permission.'[61] The fact that the

Reverend Cyril Reeve, Basil's father, was vicar of St John's, Mrs Britten's preferred church, was one obvious recommendation; while Basil's musicianship meant that he could be roped in to perform at her private concerts. So there were clear reasons why 'Ben's mother decided I was a good person for Ben to know', as Reeve told Donald Mitchell. 'That's really how it happened. So she arranged his life. His mother really made him a great musician. That's absolutely clear to me.'[62] Although she seems to have arranged a strict timetable even for Basil's visits, it was possible within this for the two boys to evade her direct supervision by walking into the town to Morlings music shop, where they might buy scores, listen to records, or even set about playing piano duets; it was on these walks that Benjamin told his friend about his mother's determination that he should become 'the fourth B' and his own developing ambition to be a rather different kind of composer. He hadn't yet begun to question the supremacy of those other three Bs, whom he continued to arrange in a fluctuating private hierarchy: 'Brahms has gone up one place,' he noted in November 1928; 'Beethoven is still first and I think always will be, Bach or Brahms comes next, I don't know which!'[63] In ways she may not have understood, Mrs Britten was right in her belief that Basil was 'a good person for Ben to know', both for the easy-going equality of their friendship and for the unpressurised pleasure of their music-making beyond her home.

She also approved of her son's friendship with that other clergyman's son, Francis Barton, after whom he urgently enquired in his letters home to her from Gresham's. Francis was still at South Lodge: on leaving the school, Britten had been 'frightfully sorry to say good-bye to . . . Francis Barton especially. He has been a ripping boy.'[64] It isn't always easy to read the nuance of outdated schoolboy slang, but 'ripping' implies both excellence and excitement (as in the phrase 'ripping yarns') and is an emphatic compliment; in Britten's school-inspired *Alla*

Quartetto Serisoso: 'Go play, boy, play' (1933), the movement dedicated to Francis is 'Ragging', a word from much the same
segment of the verbal palette. The Bartons were, in the words
of Francis's sister Joy, 'a noisy, happy go lucky Rectory family'
from Sussex, so Francis would have been a boarder at South
Lodge. The two boys could continue to meet in Lowestoft when
their respective schools' holidays or half-terms didn't exactly
coincide, as was evidently the case in May 1929: 'FRANCIS
comes to tea,' wrote Britten in his diary. 'I fetch him to go for
a walk (at 3.0) along the Beach. He has to go (worst luck!) about
5.45. So we don't really see much of him. He looks so young
(he is 13), about 11, but when he talks he might be 15!!! All the
same he is a marvellous kid.'[65] There, though faintly, is
the template for Britten's future relationships with the boys he
befriended: they would have to look young but be intelligent
and devoted; in return, they would receive the wisdom and
affection of a brilliant older friend. In Francis's case the relationship prospered: he came to stay with the Brittens that summer
– 'It's been topping having him, & I miss him dreadfully' – and
Benjamin made several visits to the Bartons, on one occasion
taking Francis and Joy to meet the Bridges at their country
home. Nor did their disparate paths in adulthood – Francis
ended up as a major-general – sever their friendship: 'He is a
great contrast to most of my friends,' Britten later wrote, 'being
in the Marines, a Tory, & conventional, but he is so charming
& ingenuous, that he is decidedly bearable!'[66] In the period of
such left-leaning, unconventional projects as *Night Mail* and *Our
Hunting Fathers*, that 'great contrast' would have been something
of an understatement, but he was growing ironic: in 1937, he
described Francis, wistfully or wishfully, as 'my paramour at
South Lodge'.[67]

Many people think so readily of the adult Britten in terms
of his friendships with younger boys that it almost comes as

a surprise to discover that, back at Gresham's, he developed a close friendship with an older boy, Oliver Berthoud, a sixth-former who left at the end of Britten's third term. 'The only reason why I don't want the end of term is because Berthoud is leaving . . . He has been marvellous to me, in spite of being a house-pre . . .'[68] Carpenter says that Britten had become the 'object' of Berthoud's 'attentions', and this in itself wouldn't have been at all improbable: the curly-haired blond child had by now grown into a darker, leaner, good-looking teenager with an engagingly wry and knowing smile. But Carpenter's implication is, as so often, crude and simplistic: Berthoud was a talented pianist and his role was essentially collaborative and protective in the face of an institutional philistinism which both boys disliked. He eventually became headmaster of Trinity School, Croydon, from where he wrote to Britten on 16 March 1971 a letter which vividly captures the quality of their friendship as well as their occasionally anarchic musical life at Gresham's:

> I recall quite clearly, for instance, the occasion when you and I and Christopher Eyres were playing the Mozart E flat trio in three different keys simultaneously, and Mr Greatorex marched in looking more than ever like the 'late' Beethoven. However, when he found that it was not three rugger hearties wrecking the place but three of his right-hand boys in the music department, he retired baffled. I also remember your sight-reading at the piano the first few pages of the miniature score of the Schubert C major quintet, which neither of us had heard but of which I was about to acquire the records. Your being able to do this struck me as positively miraculous.[69]

Walter Greatorex emerges in a kindlier light here too; and even Britten's unquenchable contempt for his performing skills can't disguise the fact that they developed a fairly amicable working relationship in which Greatorex gave him the run of his music room and allowed him to listen to his records (which is where he did, as it turned out, for the first time hear and like Stravinsky).

By the middle of his second year, Britten's irritation with Greatorex was tempered by amused tolerance: 'Gog seems to have meant what he said last term about performing one of my bally works this term,' he told his parents on 19 January 1930. 'He asked me for one yesterday; and so I thrust the nicer modern one into his hands – but he nearly choked & so I had to show him the silly small one, and he even calls that one *modern*!!!'[70] The 'bally work' – which was performed at Gresham's on 1 March by Britten (viola), Joyce Chapman (violin: she was a member of the music staff and Britten's viola teacher at the school) and the inevitable Walter Greatorex (piano) – was reviewed with guarded enthusiasm in the school magazine: '[Britten] contributed a Pianoforte Trio in one movement called "Bagatelle", in which he played the viola part. Written in a modern idiom, the Trio shows that Britten has already advanced a considerable distance in the technique of composition. He should go far and we take this opportunity of wishing him every success in the future.' In his diary, Britten wrote: 'It goes very badly! My thing is quite well appreciated but not understood.'[71] The audience's incomprehension was perhaps not so surprising for, as his diaries show, Britten was immersing himself in modernism more deeply than can have been usual in north Norfolk. He had discovered Schoenberg – 'a marvellous Schönberg concert' on the radio included *Pierrot lunaire* which he thought 'most beautiful' – and he was to perform the composer's *Six Little Pieces* for piano at an evening of 'modern music' in Lowestoft that April; he 'adored' Picasso's paintings; and he was reading *Swann's Way*, 'which I love. It is absolutely fascinating.' (He gives the title in English, so he was presumably using the Scott Moncrieff translation, but his French was good enough for him to have tackled the original.) That he should continue to lose patience with Greatorex was understandable: 'I really cannot be bothered about him any longer,' he wrote halfway through the following – and his final – term. 'He ought to have retired 50 years ago or better never have tried to teach music ever.'[72] It was as well that he confined these thoughts to his diary rather than putting them in a letter home: to fulfil the first wish, the ancient-seeming Greatorex, who was really no older than Britten's father and younger than his mother, would have had to retire at the age of three.

At some point during these two years in Holt – if it occurred at all and if it didn't occur at South Lodge – the alleged 'rape' by 'a master' may have taken place. There would certainly have been far more opportunities than ever existed in a school just down the road from home, especially as the public-school life of a musically gifted pupil tends to include such things as privileged access to secluded practice rooms, which Britten would surely have used at all possible hours and some impossible ones too. Carpenter prefers his South Lodge thesis partly because the diary Britten kept at Gresham's makes no mention of so traumatic an event; but a boy may keep secrets even from his diary, especially if he feels complicit or guilty – and if the diary lives in the not altogether secure environment of a school study. It is surely significant, too, that while the adult Britten would talk cheerfully in interviews about South Lodge, he seldom had a word to say about Gresham's: blanking out was one mental mechanism he would employ throughout his life to cope with emotional pressure, although in this case his general feelings of loneliness and unhappiness while away at school provide a more than adequate explanation. His other strategy was to retreat into illness, and this he repeatedly did during his time at Gresham's.

The spring term of 1929, his second at the school, was almost obliterated by his ill health. The trouble began on 24 January with him suffering from 'my usual bilious complaint plus a nasty feverish cold'; he remained in the school sanatorium until 6 February. Two days later, he wrote a chatty, orange-impregnated letter – he was eating oranges 'a la Pop' – to his 'darling Mummy', reporting that he was now downstairs though not yet back in school. On 23 February he was taken home to Lowestoft and stayed there until 12 March; but on his return to Holt he immediately fell ill again. He began a rambling letter-diary to his 'angelic Mummy' on Monday on 18 March, 'feeling better, but still rather sickyfied'; despite this, he was tucking into the sponge cake and biscuits she had sent – they were 'absolutely "it", you were a pet to send them'.[73] Next morning, he had a 'good breakfast, which consisted of about 7 or 8 pieces of bread and butter and honey, and two cups of tea' and, a little later, he had 'just finished the grapes, darling, which were absolutely ripping; you *were* an angel'; so there was evidently not much wrong with his appetite. Although the term didn't end until 4 April, he went home on 26 March and was declared 'out of quarantine' on 31 March.[74] There had been a nastily virulent 'bug' of some sort in the school, and it was an exceptionally cold snowy winter, yet two months is a long time for a generally fit and sporty fifteen-year-old to be knocked out of action. The fact that returning to Gresham's brought an instant deterioration in his condition suggests that the virus was augmented by emotional or psychological pressure. Summer was better, the stress mitigated by cricket and tennis, but by October he was 'absolutely rotten & sick' and off school for ten days.

'How I loathe this abominable hole,' he complained on his first day back at Gresham's in January 1930; he briefly contemplated, but rejected, suicide ('cowardly') or running away ('as bad').[75] Meanwhile, he remained observant of details which a less perceptive boy might have found merely irritating rather than intriguing, as when he overheard two boys in nearby beds snoring, one of them when 'taking breath in and out', the other 'only when breathing in': 'For about five or even six times they agreed, & then gradually they got out of time, & they took quite a time to get in again. It fascinated me so much that I could not get to sleep.'[76] He was ill in February – 'out of school, and swallowing with considerable difficulty' – and then again in July, as his School Certificate exams approached: he worried inordinately about these, having failed to distinguish himself academically at Gresham's, but when the results arrived found that he had passed with five credits. 'It is simply extraordinary the luck I am having now,' he wrote.[77] By then, in any case, he had cleared a far more important hurdle. On 19 June, he sat the open scholarship exams at the Royal College of Music, a written paper in the morning and, in the afternoon, an oral at which the assessors included Ralph Vaughan Williams and John Ireland: 'After that I have surprise of winning comp. inspite of 2 brilliant others in final.' His headmaster at Gresham's, J. R. Eccles, who may have been painfully aware that his school hadn't contributed much to this achievement, wrote to Mrs Britten with a warmth which went beyond formal congratulation:

> We are *delighted* at your boy's fine success & I congratulate you very heartily! We feel some reflected glory & realise that's a great honour to the School! I am so very glad about it all. He is such a dear boy & so modest about all his brilliant performances! I shall miss him *very* much.[78]

If that sounds slightly uncomfortable – an attempt at empathy which misses its target – it's because Britten and Gresham's had failed to understand each other. He was never going to fit in as a boarder at a public school: on the one hand, he had been too close to home for too long; on the other, he had found his teacher elsewhere, in Frank Bridge. This had irked the music staff at Gresham's from the start and some of them couldn't get over it. Miss Chapman's vinegary comment on Britten's final school report in July 1930 – 'When his intonation improves he will be a very useful viola player' – is a fairly startling example of missing the point. Eccles's remarks at the foot of the same document, while rightly praising 'A thoroughly sound & very high principled & delightful boy', go on to get him wrong in a subtly different way: 'His music has been a great joy to us all.'[79] We can imagine Britten's wry smile at that. *Joy?* Yes, sometimes and partly, but he knew that what he was doing was altogether more ambitious and complicated: he must have hoped that at least the Royal College of Music would understand what he was about.

CHAPTER 2

SOME COLLEGE

1930–34

1

At a Lowestoft tennis party during the summer of 1930, Britten was asked what career he was going to pursue. 'I told them I intended to be a composer. They were amazed! "Yes, but what else?"'[1] Auden had received a similarly doubtful response when he informed his Oxford tutor, Nevill Coghill, that he was going to be a poet, though he bumptiously replied: 'You don't understand: I'm going to be a great poet.'[2] Britten, meanwhile, knew that the alternative career of concert pianist and accompanist had to be kept in reserve, and there's every likelihood that he would have made a distinguished one: he was later to be described as the finest accompanist in the world by Gerald Moore, who by common consent *was* the finest accompanist in the world. For this his piano teacher at the Royal College of Music, Arthur Benjamin, though not a kindred spirit in terms of musical taste, deserves much credit: Britten would later recall Benjamin's kindness in nursing him 'very gently through a very, very difficult musical adolescence',[3] although at the time he ruefully recorded his piano teacher's judgement that he was 'not built for a solo pianist – how I am going to make my pennies Heaven only knows'.[4]

Nevertheless, by the time he arrived at the RCM on 22 September 1930, he had no real doubt that a composer was what he must be. Neither did his two existing teachers, Harold Samuel and Frank Bridge, and it was this certainty which oddly caused the first of his many difficulties with the college; for each of them had a firm but different idea of who would be the most suitable composition teacher for him. Samuel, writing to congratulate his pupil on his scholarship in late June, advised him 'to try for R. O. Morris', while Bridge's congratulations concluded: 'I think I might be able to get you under John Ireland for composition . . .'[5] Britten was, perhaps inevitably, inclined to take Bridge's advice and eventually told him so. Bridge's reply of 13 August contrasted the two possible teachers as backward- and forward-looking, while tactfully avoiding any mention of Morris by name, and made what he must have known to be the clinching point: 'If I were a young man I should plump for a live composer whose activities are part of the present-day outlook with a heavy leaning towards tomorrow's.'[6] But by this time Samuel, to whom Britten had been slow in responding while he dithered and discussed the matter with Bridge, had 'already fixed it for you to study with Mr R. O. Morris'. 'I feel,' he added, 'that Mr Morris is the very man for you, and particularly calculated to supply you with what you need.'[7] This, Britten noted in his diary for 22 August, was 'an upsetting letter'. He wasn't alone in being upset: through his own dilatoriness he had managed to offend both his former piano teacher and a distinguished member of the RCM's staff even before he arrived at the college.

Harold Samuel's emphatic though rejected opinion that Morris was 'the very man for you' is worth pondering for a moment. Reginald Owen Morris's former pupils included the composers Gerald Finzi and Howard Ferguson (for some time Samuel's lodger), both of whom Britten would come to know, if not especially to admire, during his London years: it was Ferguson who, in Britten's first week at the RCM, took him to a Prom at the Queen's Hall to hear a 'delicious' Mozart concerto and Mahler's Fourth Symphony, which he thought 'Much too long, but beautiful in pts';[8] they left at the interval, because 'the second part was all Elgar'.[9] Morris, who was the author of *Contrapuntal Technique in the Sixteenth Century* (1922), had 'a reputation as the country's best teacher on the stricter side',[10] as Diana McVeagh judiciously puts it in her biography of Finzi. Was Samuel therefore implying that his former pupil, whose enthusiasm for the European avant-garde was approaching its height, could do with some corrective emphasis on counterpoint and a deeper historical perspective? If so, he may have had a point, for students sometimes learn as much by reacting against their teachers as by sympathising with them. On the other hand, Morris was incurably wedded to English musical conservatism – almost literally so, for his wife's sister was married to Vaughan Williams and he shared his brother-in-law's London house in Cheyne Row – and this aspect of Morris's musical character would surely have provoked Britten, had they worked together, to something more toxic than creative disagreement. When he heard broadcast performances of Morris's compositions, he was dismissive: 'dreadful concoctions'[11] he called them on one occasion, while on another he 'struggled for about three or four minutes with R. O. Morris and then switched off'.[12]

John Ireland, who had established a reputation as one of England's leading contemporary composers and whose previous pupils included E. J. Moeran and Alan Bush, clearly seemed to be the better choice; but he was to prove troublesome in ways which greatly distressed the prim and provincial young Benjamin Britten. With a homosexual past and a failed marriage behind him, Ireland was now living alone at his dirty, chaotic house in Gunter Grove, while involved in an intense though non-sexual relationship with his star pupil, Helen Perkin. Contrary to college regulations, he did much of his teaching at home, where he was sometimes drunk. On one occasion, arriving for a lesson which had been rescheduled from 10 in the morning to 8.45 in the evening, Britten was appalled to discover his teacher in an incapable state, urinating on the carpet: this lesson, he said with characteristic understatement, was 'not a good one . . . not improved by the fact that he [Ireland] was quite drunk most of the time – foully so'.[13] Ireland was often either dreadfully late or entirely absent without notice, a trait Britten discovered during his very first week at the college: 'Waiting for J. Ireland 1½ (10–11.30), & he eventually doesn't turn up,' as he drily put it, apparently without rancour, in his diary for 25 September 1930.[14] The rancour would come later.

Although his personal life was in a mess, Ireland was at this time enjoying considerable success as a composer. His piano concerto in E flat, published in 1930 and dedicated to Helen Perkin, was so well received that he found himself dubbed 'the English Rachmaninov', an intended compliment which is unlikely to have much impressed Britten, who thought Rachmaninov's immensely popular second concerto 'vulgar' and 'old-fashioned';[15] the lustre of Ireland's concerto was such that Artur Rubinstein chose to play it at his Proms debut in 1936. It is less highly regarded today, although Grove rather surprisingly calls it 'a classic of 20th-century English music'. There is indeed some romantically Rachmaninovian piano writing in the opening movement, compromised by a jauntily infantile motif; the second movement starts well, with interesting string textures, but the solo theme lacks shape and memorability; while the lively if conventional third movement is oddly interrupted by a brief dialogue between piano and solo violin which threatens a descent into the purest Palm Court. There was little here to excite someone who had studied with Bridge and begun to take an interest in the music of the Second Viennese School, yet Britten was at first inclined to give the work, its composer and its dedicatee the benefit of the doubt: hearing it at a Prom on 2 October 1930, he found it 'very beautiful, interesting & excellently played'[16] while an RCM concert in December included 'J. Ireland pft. concerto (which I like better each time – Helen Perkin played it beautifully)'.[17] Perhaps he was just being polite. When he heard the concerto again, less than a year later, he thought it 'very loosely put together',[18] while exactly two years after that, recently graduated and no longer in awe of his former teacher, he listened to another broadcast performance of Ireland's 'meandering Pft concerto' and commented: 'The form is loose & it really is only cheap ballade music (attractive in its way) touched up.'[19]

If Britten had thought that studying with Ireland might spare him some of the contrapuntal rigours of R. O. Morris, he was swiftly disabused. Ireland, 'very nice tho' very subduing', was 'going to take me thro' a course of Palestrina; tho' to reassure me tells me that every musician, worth his salt has done this'. A week later, after a 'topping lesson', he added: 'He is *terribly* critical and enough to take the heart out of any one!'[20] 'Ireland & Benjamin are very nice still,' he said, writing home in late October, and that 'still' reminds us that a month can be a long time in the life of a sixteen-year-old. 'The former is still terribly strict & I am plodding through Counterpoint & Palestrina at the moment.'[21] His diaries repeatedly portray Ireland as fierce and discouraging – at the beginning of his second term, Britten felt that he seemed 'to be doing nothing right or worth doing nowadays'[22] – yet he doesn't actually sound disheartened, and as he came to know his teacher better he began to value him more: soon after the start of his second year, for instance, he was writing of an 'Amazingly good, & frightfully instructive lesson from Ireland'.[23] What vexed him almost beyond endurance was Ireland's appalling timekeeping, the cancelled or truncated lessons; of one, Britten complained that he spent half the time correcting proofs of his teacher's piano concerto, after which Ireland spent the rest of the lesson on the telephone, 'so I don't get much out of that!'[24] Yet even this was part of a wider vexation with the Royal College of Music, which he had swiftly decided was not much good. Ireland wasn't alone in failing to keep appointments: Britten's diaries record his repeatedly frustrated attempts to arrange meetings with the college's director, Sir Hugh Percy Allen, who was almost as afflicted by lateness and invisibility as his composition teacher. As for Dr Buck's music dictation classes, they were so 'petty' that he immediately asked to be moved up two sets and at the start of his second term dropped them altogether. On 15 May 1931, he went into the college 'to find my Comp. lesson has been moved to Thursdays, only the Coll. has not informed me of this, so that I miss a lesson this week. This Establishment!' he grumbled.[25] He sounded an identical note of contempt exactly two years later: 'Some College' – this time unpunctuated, leaving the rest unsaid.[26] It wasn't an opinion that would mellow with time. 'They don't seem very happy in retrospect,' he said of his student days in 1963. 'I feel I didn't learn very much at the Royal College of Music. I think I can say that at the Royal College not nearly enough account was taken of the exceptionally gifted musician.'[27]

His seventeenth birthday fell towards the end of his first term at the RCM and, like any other ambitious and creatively talented person of his age, he was beginning to develop a sense of his own potential place in cultural history. Perhaps by now he was quietly hoping that 1913, while more generally remembered as the last year of peace before the Great War, might one day also be remembered as the year Benjamin Britten was born. And he was now old enough to understand something which wouldn't have been clear to him earlier in his childhood: the year 1913 *was* already significant in European musical history, and in ways which specifically mattered to him. For on 31 March 1913, a concert at the Musikverein in Vienna, including works by Berg, Mahler, Schoenberg and Webern, had famously ended in a riot to which the police were called (Mahler's *Kindertotenlieder* consequently remained unheard); while almost exactly two months later, on 29 May in Paris, the first performance of Stravinsky's *The Rite of Spring* was greeted with comparable disturbances. What Britten now found frustrating was that these five composers, whose work he admired and whose stormy receptions had so aptly heralded his own birth, were still regarded as outlandish by the English musical establishment in general and the RCM in particular. But not by Frank Bridge.

The support Britten received during his time at the RCM from Bridge and his wife Ethel – though to John Ireland it looked more like the theft of his brilliant pupil's loyalty – was incalculable. Its most powerful aspect was also its simplest: they became deeply sympathetic surrogate parents who, living in Kensington Church Street, were conveniently close to the college. Again and again, particularly during his first few months in London, Britten's diaries contain artlessly telling phrases such as 'I go to see Mrs Bridge after breakfast', 'Go to see & have a second tea with Mr & Mrs Bridge', 'Go to Supper at Bridges', 'Go to see Mr Bridge after tea', 'Supper at the Bridges at 7.30',[28] and so on. They talked about music, obviously, but they also just talked. Sometimes an evening meal preceded or followed a concert which Bridge was conducting: Britten almost invariably found Bridge's concerts 'marvellous' or 'magnificent' and, in this sense at least a typical late-teenager, he conceived an equal and opposite dislike for the '*terrible execrable* conductor'[29] Adrian Boult. Hearing Bridge's *Enter Spring* at a Prom, for the first time since that momentous Norwich Festival, he was again bowled over: it was 'marvellous – that man's a genius'.[30] Soon

Bridge was off to America, where he had 'a magnificent reception', according to Britten's diary;[31] but a letter home to his
parents strikes an interestingly different note, one which was to
recur through much of his life, about the musical philistinism
of the English: 'Isn't it literally wicked,' he wrote, 'that England's
premier composer has to go out of the country (not only to the
USA but to Europe) to have any recognition what-so-jolly-well-
ever?'[32] His diary entry for 12 June 1931 both demonstrates how
much he had become part of the family and confirms his
unbounded admiration for Bridge as a conductor: 'After dinner
go to marvellous BBC concert (at 9.45) at Studio, with
Bridges . . . I have never known the orch. play better, they were
enthusiastic about his conducting, & I don't wonder.'[33]

A fortnight later, Britten spent the weekend with them at
their country home in the Sussex village of Friston (there is also
a Suffolk village of Friston, close to Aldeburgh and Snape, a
resonance which wouldn't have been lost on him). He was and
would always remain a coast-and-country boy at heart, delighted
at the end of a term to leave London and return to Lowestoft;
it must therefore have come as a pleasing surprise to discover
in Sussex that this wasn't just a matter of going 'home' but a
natural affinity with the peace, and the pace, of rural life. 'The
country around here is too superb for words,' he wrote. 'No
one about at all – lovely!'[34] There was a tennis court in the
garden, and Britten's admiration for his mentor was further
intensified by his discovery that Bridge not only played tennis
but was 'remarkably good'; he swam too and, when emerging
from the water, looked 'just like a walrus', or so Beth Britten
thought. Ben was met off the train at Eastbourne by Mrs Bridge
and Marjorie Fass, whom he described, innocently or tactfully,
as 'a friend of theirs who lives v. near & is with them most of
the day'; Beth would recall that 'Marge Fass who lived next door
seemed to be a part of the menage and adored Frank', though

this 'did not seem to worry' Ethel Bridge.[35] According to Howard Ferguson and, following him, Humphrey Carpenter, it was 'a contented *ménage à trois*'.[36] The informal way in which they were all continually in and out of each other's houses, sharing meals or listening to broadcast concerts in either place, made a notable change from the buttoned-up domestic manners to which Britten was accustomed. Marjorie Fass was quick to get the measure of young Benjy, as she called him – the Bridges were collectively the 'Brits', he 'Mr Brit' or 'Franco' – and later she would usefully puncture one or two of his grander notions. This was a relaxed, civilised and cultivated style of life away from the noise and the pressures of the city: its example would profoundly influence Britten's own choice of a permanent home.

2

'It's ghastly to think of tomorrow – of course London's marvellous but home's so good,' Britten writes in his diary for 6 January 1931, the day before setting off for his second term at the RCM.[37] This sense of something close to dread, though perfectly comprehensible, is perhaps a little disconcerting: a talented young man from the provinces, pursuing his creative ambition and discovering the capital, might have been glad to see the back of his conventional, repressive home; especially if, as in Britten's case, he happened to be a homosexual, with no chance of establishing a personal life on his respectable dentist-father's doorstep in Lowestoft. Yet there's little sign of Britten deliberately lying to himself or to his diary. The next day, insisting in a telling phrase that 'home is so beastly nice', he records how his sister Beth does most of his packing, then drives him 'with Mummy' to the station, while at Liverpool Street he is met by his sister Barbara and they go off in a taxi together; again, where another young man would have been relieved to escape from his fussing female relatives, Britten registers only loss and loneliness, as he unpacks in his digs that evening.

During his first year in London, he had only to walk across Kensington Gardens to reach the college. 51 Prince's Square, Bayswater, run by Miss Thurlow Prior, was a 'respectable boarding house': 'a nice place, but rather full of old ladies', one of whom – the landlady's sister Miss May Prior – turned out to be 'a member of the National Chorus & knew Mummy at Lowestoft'.[38] This, though evidently the connection which enabled Mrs Britten to hear of the establishment and give it her blessing, was something Britten only discovered on his arrival there; he seems to have accepted it calmly enough as a natural extension of the family cocoon on which he was still so dependent. But it set the tone for a domestic life constricted by his pleasantly dull fellow residents and recorded in crushingly bathetic diary entries such as 'The Hendersons go out after dinner' and 'Play cards with Tumpty Henderson after tea':[39] Nora and Tumpty Henderson were a pair of spinster sisters in whose company Britten spent a good deal of his leisure time. On Sundays, one or other of them sometimes accompanied him to church. He became fond of Tumpty, with whom he would occasionally go to concerts or films, but not of her sister: 'Nora Henderson is an absolute revelation to me, in how awful a person can be.'[40]

Of course, the social life of a typical student in 1930, except for the minority who enjoyed those privileges familiar from *Brideshead Revisited*, was more restricted than it would become in 1960 or 1990. Apart from the indispensable Bridges, Britten's London friendships were mostly confined to three small circles – his family and relations, his fellow lodgers and landladies, and the relatively few student musicians with whom he rehearsed and performed – which were occasionally augmented by fleeting visits from old school chums. He seems scarcely to have bumped into anyone studying another discipline at the various London colleges or to have struck up even casual acquaintances in the metropolitan world around him, about which he remained shyly incurious and unobservant. For instance, every few weeks from his arrival at the college until his departure at the end of 1933, his diary meticulously records his haircut at Whiteley's, the Bayswater department store, a fact which Donald Mitchell quite reasonably sees as evidence that the diaries offer 'vital information about almost every sphere of his activities'. This is true; yet one can't help feeling that anyone else, over this lengthy period of time, would have at least got to know the barber's name and that any other diarist would have described such a regularly recurring figure, perhaps even recording the jokes traditionally told by barbers to their captive audiences. Although Britten sometimes met his sister Barbara and one or two friends for lunch at Selfridges or an ABC and often had a meal with the Bridges before or after a concert, he drank little and seldom visited pubs: his diaries are hangover-free. While capable of admiring reckless behaviour in others, in his own conduct he remained correct, cautious, and a little prim: a habit of social remoteness, for which he would find himself censured much later on, was there from the beginning.

At the start of his second year at the college, Britten moved to Burleigh House, 173 Cromwell Road: there, as he soon discovered, his fellow residents were less tolerant of their hard-working music student than their predecessors at Prince's Square. By the beginning of December 1931 there were 'rows about my practising – people threaten to leave if it doesn't stop'; but what upset him most, according to his diary, was the way in which they would be 'moaning' behind his back while telling him to his face that they didn't mind it. 'The av. person,' he concluded, 'seems to be a dishonest fool.'[41] He tactfully decamped to the college's practice rooms for the rest of the term. When he returned to Cromwell Road after Christmas, he transferred to a top-floor room and hired a piano of his own, which fitted (he said) 'quite well'; it proved not to his taste, however, and on 22 February, accompanied by his indefatigable mother, he was off 'to see a Pft (grand) that a Mrs Audrey Melville is going to lend me here'.[42] This was duly delivered ten days later, and its predecessor taken away, all in the space of an hour: 'there really is quite a lot of room in my room now surprisingly enough', he noted; as attics go, his was a capacious one. In January, he had been joined there by his sister Beth, who was embarking on a dressmaking course in London and moved into the adjacent room. The family cocoon was re-forming around him; his term-time diary entries for the next two years usually mention time spent with Beth or Barbara or both his sisters.

Britten the college student often seems less mature than the schoolboy who had proclaimed his enthusiasm for Schoenberg, Picasso and Proust. His reading, in particular, lurched backwards in a nostalgic attempt to reinhabit the world he had left; but the attraction of the school stories he chose to read was double-edged for, while they offered comforting revisitations of child-hood, they also tended to include explorations of compromised or corrupted innocence. Among them were F. W. Farrar's *Eric, or Little by Little*, Hugh Walpole's *Jeremy at Crale* and H. A. Vachell's *The Hill*, a novel about Harrow whose homo-sexual aspects had attracted some notoriety when it first appeared in 1905; but the novel to which he returned obsessively, reading it 'for the umpteenth time' in May 1932, was *David Copperfield*, which he judged to be 'an absolutely first rate book – inspired from beginning to end'.[43] Many readers will find that praise excessive: we are more likely to regard *David Copperfield* as memorable though flawed and ultimately sentimental, inferior

to *Bleak House* and *Our Mutual Friend* or to more compact
masterpieces such as *Great Expectations* and *Hard Times*. Yet it's
easy to see why Britten should have been so attracted to it, for
some of its most powerful elements are uncannily close to themes
which were to recur in his work: there are the scenes evocatively
set in the fishing community of Great Yarmouth, the next town
up the East Anglian coast from Lowestoft; and there is young
David's appalled relationship with his sadistic stepfather
Murdstone, his hero-worship of the unreliably charismatic
Steerforth and his gradual discovery of a corrupt adult world.
Much later, Britten told Charles Osborne that he had 'seriously'
considered an opera based on *David Copperfield*, but decided that
he 'would find the overall shape almost impossible to cope with'.[44]
Then, within days of that 'umpteenth' reading, Britten found
himself listening on the radio to 'a wonderful, impressive but
terribly eerie & scary play':[45] this was a dramatisation of Henry
James's novella *The Turn of the Screw*. He read the book the
following winter and decided it was an 'incredible masterpiece'.[46]
It too would stay with him.

His reading during these years was focused not just on childhood but on the past; with such resolutely unmodernist exceptions
as W. H. Davies, Walter de la Mare and Robert Graves (each
of whose work he enjoyed and set), this was as true of poets as
it was of novelists. There is nothing to suggest that he had come
across the era-defining poem of the 1920s, *The Waste Land*; nor,
though his arrival in London in the autumn of 1930 coincided
with the publication by Faber of Auden's first commercially
produced book, *Poems*, would he yet have recognised himself as
an inhabitant of the region described by Samuel Hynes, in *The
Auden Generation*, as 'Auden Country'. Nevertheless, without
being aware of it, he was. Hynes calls *Paid on Both Sides* – the
'charade' which accompanies the thirty lyrics of *Poems* – 'an
apprehensive parable of immaturity, marked, inevitably, by

Auden's homosexuality, but in a tradition that is not overtly homosexual – the Public School, First World War tradition of the games-playing male society'.[47] Almost every word of that is exactly applicable to the young Britten. 'Auden Country', according to Hynes, was a 'dense mingling of public and private, school and war, nature and machinery, which in the poetry of the 'thirties becomes a familiar landscape'.[48] It would in due course become familiar, even intimate, to Britten, but for the time being he had no sense that these things, many of which must have been buzzing around in his head, could be the components of creative life. He hadn't properly connected with the contemporary intellectual world: for this, the curious pattern of his education – his long years at a philistine prep school followed by a relatively brief spell, without sixth-form experience, at Gresham's – was largely to blame. Consequently, his developing taste in poetry, unshaped either by an academic canon or by contact with the literary world around him, was randomly eclectic; yet the sheer oddness of the poems he grew to like would often serve him surprisingly well when he came to set them to music.

A comparable degree of randomness – and a cheerful acceptance of the middlebrow which sharply contrasts with his views on music – is evident in his visits to the theatre and the cinema, often dictated by the tastes of his fellow lodgers in London or his family in Lowestoft. Plays, including musicals, would at best prompt him to unqualified schoolboyish enthusiasm: he found *The Song of the Drum* 'absolutely sidesplitting . . . dancing & scenary were stupendous', while *Stand Up and Sing* was 'a perfectly topping, side-splitting, rolicking good show'.[49] Yet such terms already seem stretched and ill-fitting, like grown-out-of clothes, and his more interesting reactions began to include almost apologetic reservations: *The Vagabond King* was 'quite amusing – tho' of course nothing in it'[50] and, as for Paul Robeson (appearing with 'an Vaudville company'), 'He has a remarkable organ, but didn't seem able to use it.'[51] It seems extraordinary that he could have been persuaded to endure *Lilac Time*, with its dreadful reorchestrations of Schubert, although he did his best: 'Very amusing in parts, scenary v. pretty,' he conceded, before adding, 'Music arranged excruciatingly.'[52] He thought Noël Coward's *Cavalcade* 'Magnificently produced – & with some fine & moving ideas', a phrase which strikes an unexpectedly serious critical note until qualified by this quite subtle after-thought: 'Not an especially great *play* tho'.'[53]

About films, as perhaps befits the medium, he was more brashly demotic: *Charlie's Aunt* was 'Screemingly funny' and *Canaries Sometimes Sing* 'Screaminly funny',[54] two ways of not quite saying the same thing. On the other hand, he recorded seeing '2 putrid films' without even naming them and 'some utter tosh' called *Strictly Dishonourable*. Charlie Chaplin in *City Lights* received unqualified praise – 'A wonderful piece of acting' – and *Hell's Angels* had 'Marvellous photography spoilt by slop'.[55] He didn't at all care for sentimental 'slop': it represented both a sexual taste he didn't share and an aesthetic sense he would always find suspect. At the end of a summer's day in 1932, which he had cheerfully spent walking and bathing at Lowestoft before meeting a new musician friend, Christopher Gledhill, over tea, he was dragged off to the cinema in the evening: 'Go to "Mata Hari" at Palace with Beth to see Greta Garbo. She is most attractive, I suppose, but what slop!'[56] The dismissive detachment of that 'I suppose' is rather magnificent.

The film which made by far the strongest impression on Britten during his student years was *Emil und die Detektive*, which he saw for the first time in March 1933. He thought it 'the most perfect & satisfying film I have ever seen or ever hope to see. Acting as natural & fine as possible – magnificent & subtle photography – plot very amusing & imaginative – a collosal achievement.'[57] Three days later he bought Erich Kästner's 1928 novel on which the film was based, which was going to be 'very interesting – when I can understand it'; and within a week he was contemplating 'a Suite on "Emil"'. Quite apart from its inherent qualities, *Emil und die Detektive* was precisely the film to engage an imagination already captivated by *David Copperfield* and *The Turn of the Screw*. Its hero is a blond young boy – a journeying boy, indeed – who sets off on a train journey to Berlin. The compartment, which has no corridor, is crowded at first, but after the departure of other passengers Emil finds himself alone with the bowler-hatted villain, Grundeis, who robs him. On arrival in Berlin, Emil resolves to track down Grundeis with the help of some street children, the 'detectives', in order to retrieve his stolen wallet: the crucial scene takes place in a hotel bedroom with Grundeis in the bed, Emil concealed beneath it, and the vital wallet (which turns out to be empty) trapped under the mattress between them. Both the train and hotel scenes obviously place the boy in physical and, implicitly, sexual danger; yet it's also clear that Emil must be a fairly unusual sort of boy to pursue successfully such an outlandish scheme. In other words, the transaction is two-way: Emil, like the almost anagrammatical Miles in *The Turn of the Screw*, is something more strange and complicated than a mere innocent. A few months later, Britten was almost equally struck by *Poil de Carotte*, a film based on the novel (1894) by Jules Renard about a boy driven to contemplate suicide by an unloving mother: 'I was thoroughly harrowed, intensely amused, & thrilled beyond measure, the whole time,' he wrote.[58]

Britten seems only gradually to have recognised what his taste in books and films implied about him. In June 1931, he went to the Royal Tournament at nearby Olympia and 'enjoyed every minute of it. The P.T. Squads were superb, & the musical drives. It quite makes me long to be a soldier!'[59] It would be a mistake to hear the voice of a modern camp comedian (and to assume that 'be' means 'have') in that last sentence; Britten at seventeen saw only the laughable incongruity of the idea, although he may have been influenced by a nostalgic memory of the Grenadier Guards' band on the pier at Lowestoft. The conventions of his education and his genuine enthusiasm for sport combined to cloak any vestige of sexual interest in an ironic heartiness which made it invisible even to himself, especially when he returned (as he rather often did) to South Lodge. In April 1932, for instance, he went to the school's gymnasium display and noted, with an air of schoolmasterly connoisseurship, 'There are some very good boys here.'[60] He captained the old boys' cricket team, and when he described their matches it was with precisely the tone and vocabulary of those old-fashioned school stories he so enjoyed: 'I go & play cricket with South Lodge boys, up on their field. Great fun: have a glorious knock, making 33 & eventually retiring with a bust bat!'[61] And he was more than happy to spend a very physical August day with his Lowestoft neighbours' young nephew and a friend, 'the two Davids': 'Bathe before lunch & before tea. Great fun, v. rough. Rounders in aft. back by 7.0. Great fun. David (alias "Jerry") Gill is a nice boy.'[62] For the most part, this was as innocent as the jaunty style suggests, yet as the diary proceeds there's an increasingly transparent preoccupation with a single subject, or indeed a single word: boys. He must have been aware of this by the time he visited the Tate in September 1932, where he saw 'a marvellous picture of a "Dead Boy", by Alfred Stevens'.[63] The emphasis became both comical and a bit confusing in the summer of 1933: he had been working on his song setting of Graves's 'Song: Lift Boy' and on *A Boy Was Born* (which he calls, without quotation marks, 'my Boy') when in July he met and formed a lasting friendship with the music critic Henry Boys. He recorded this coincidence without a hint of amusement, which suggests that by now he understood precisely why he shouldn't be amused.

At first, when he returned to Lowestoft for vacations, life seemed to carry on much as usual, with visits to friends, tea parties, games of tennis, bathing in the sea and walking with Caesar the family dog or into town to Morlings music shop. Tennis, indeed, remained a passion to be treated with the serious commitment he otherwise reserved for music: so, on winning the Ernest Farrar Composition Prize in July 1931, he went straight to the sports shop in Lowestoft and bought 'a new tennis racquet with prize money – Austin – 75/- (paying 70/-) a superb one';[64] the following spring, awarded the Cobbett Prize, he bought himself a new suit. However, during the late summer of 1931, Mr Britten became seriously ill with what was at first assumed to be bronchitis: he consequently missed his elder son Bobby's wedding, which took place on 3 September in West Hartlepool. During his career as a dentist, Mr Britten had grown suspicious of doctors, whom he thought more likely to cause trouble than to cure it, and he was reluctant to consult one. The following May, back in Lowestoft for the Whitsun weekend, Britten noted in his diary: 'Pop isn't so well & is in bed all day.'[65] That somewhat elderly and euphemistic style is the one in which he would continue to record the progress of his father's illness, which was eventually diagnosed as lymphadenoma; it carries genuine affection and concern, but almost no warmth. This he continued to reserve for his adored mother who, over the Christmas and New Year period of 1931–2, organised two characteristic if unusually ambitious social functions, perhaps sensing that these might be among the last such occasions to be held at Kirkley Cliff Road. On 29 December, there was a dance in the dining room which 'abt. 33 people' attended (Britten, who was no dancer, observed cautiously: 'I think it goes pretty well'); Mr Britten hired records and a radiogram from Morlings, although it wasn't until the following Christmas that he finally bought one of his own. And on 9 January, the Saturday before Britten's return to college, there was a grand edition of Mrs Britten's musical evenings, loyally documented by her son:

> Besides ourselves 3 Colemans, Mrs & John Nicholson Mr & Mrs Back (who both sing) Mr & Mrs Owles. Mrs & Miss Phillips. 2 Miss Boyds. 2 Miss Astles (Miss Ethel plays.) Miss Banks. Miss Goldsmith. Sing alot of Part Songs including My variations – quite good! I play Ravel 'Jeux d'eau' & Debussy 'Reflets' & Franck. Symp. Variations. Mum sings Ireland '12 Oxen' & Armstrong Gibbs 'to one who passed Whistling'. Quite a success. They go about 11.45.[66]

Quite a success! One wonders how he put up with it, on two counts: the level of the others' musicianship was surely irksome to someone of his ability and taste (on one occasion, while accompanying a Mrs Taylor in Beethoven's 'Spring' Sonata, he did indeed slam down the piano lid and walk out); while all those middle-aged spinsters, eerily recreating the milieu of his London boarding houses, can hardly have made exciting company for an eighteen-year-old student. Home was indeed 'so beastly nice'.

3

Yet in one sense – and it was the one that mattered most – Britten's life during his student years was extraordinarily rich. He may have found the RCM disappointing, but London itself was full of music, and he immersed himself in it with all the urgent enthusiasm of a boy from East Anglia whose childhood home had lacked even a radio and a gramophone. His diaries describe his visits to concerts, as well as noting those he heard (sometimes with difficulty) on the 'wireless' and the records he began to buy, and in every case he adds appreciative or critical comments: the entries thus chart in unusual detail the development of a great composer's musical taste during his formative years. It was a complicated and at times contradictory process.

Aimez-vous Brahms . . . ? To Françoise Sagan's famous question, the young Britten would have responded with an unequivocal '*Oui*'. 'Ben was absolutely mad about Brahms,' said his Lowestoft friend Basil Reeve, who remembered him arranging the last movement of the fourth symphony for two pianos in the summer of 1930, just before he left for London. 'We used to go up and play that at Morlings.'[67] He heard Mengelberg ('superb, magnificent, great') conduct the 'thrilling' third symphony in October and, a month later, Rubinstein in the second piano concerto: 'His playing & the heavenly music makes me feel absolutely hopeless.'[68] A few months after that, in the same work, Walter Gieseking was 'simply magnificent . . . I've never heard a Concerto played so well', while Lauri Kennedy's cello solo in the slow movement was '*too* gorgeous'.[69] He was almost as keen on the first concerto. 'What a marvel that first movement is,'[70] he wrote in February 1931, after hearing it played by Wilhelm Backhaus, but he was merciless about a broadcast performance, with Ernö Dohnanyi as soloist, towards the end of the same month: 'Horrible scramble it sounded; anyway the strength of the first movement was there; but oh! the third movement.'[71] This was the time at which Britten's admiration for Brahms reached its peak, for on 9 February he 'went to get my Brahms picture framed after tea' before noticing in the *Radio Times* that a performance of the third quartet by the Hungarian String Quartet was to be broadcast that evening:

'So I borrow Miss Prior's Wireless, & have marvellous 1/2 hour listening to the purest music in the purest of possible forms. What a marvellous craze for the viola Brahms had! What a humorous theme the last movement has!'[72] That diary entry is doubly interesting, both for its prescient insistence on the supremacy of chamber over symphonic music and for its focus on the viola – Britten's instrument, and Bridge's – which, as we shall discover, was often a determining factor in his judgement of other composers' works. He was fully aware of this: listening to a broadcast of Brahms's horn trio on 28 May, he had to admit that he preferred 'our Philistine viola version, to this over-swamped horn business. Horn – Horn – nothing else.'[73] (He sounds exactly like Mrs Organ Morgan in *Under Milk Wood*.)

Britten's liking for Brahms continued, if less fulsomely, throughout his time at the RCM, but it was emphatically over soon after he graduated: by then, 'most of Brahms' was 'music which repulses me', to which he added, as an explanatory paren-thesis, '(solid, dull)'.[74] Those two words really do say it all; even committed Brahmsians might grudgingly admit that their man had been in every respect the wrong sort of composer for Britten, with his instincts for clarity and restraint, to admire. And indeed there'd been a hint of this perception in his final year when, playing through Howard Ferguson's violin sonata with the composer, he found the 'hand of Brahms heavy over it';[75] he knew that the influence of a heavy hand was just what he didn't need. Discovering this for himself was an educational process as important as anything he could learn from his teachers; mean-while, he was making equally significant discoveries of a more positive and enduring sort. Mahler, despite what Britten at first thought to be the inordinate length of the fourth symphony – at that time he had yet to hear the *really* long ones – taught him the great and astonishing lesson that it is possible to write lucidly for individual parts while using enormous orchestral forces and also made him think afresh about ways of using song in a symphonic work. The fourth was to remain his favourite among Mahler's symphonies and by April 1933, when he listened to a broadcast of Webern conducting it, he had grasped exactly what it was all about: 'This work seems a mix up of everything that one has ever heard, but it is definitely Mahler. Like a lovely spring day.'[76] It seems an especially astute comment from one who in due course would write his own *Spring Symphony*.

The music of Stravinsky prompted a parallel journey from wariness to enthusiasm. An all-Stravinsky programme conducted by Ernest Ansermet in January 1931 was 'Remarkable, puzzling'. He 'quite enjoyed' the piano concerto but found *Le sacre du printemps* (though much earlier and, of course, another spring work) 'bewildering and terrifying. I didn't really enjoy it, but I think it's incredibly marvellous and arresting.'[77] Honest puzzlement was often a positive sign with him. A year later, at the Queen's Hall, he heard Ansermet again conduct; Stravinsky himself was the soloist in the *Capriccio* for piano and orchestra of 1929 ('Amusing but not much more') and this was followed by the still more recent 'Marvellous Symphony of Psalms . . . Bits of it laboured I thought but the end was truly inspired.'[78] As with the Mahler, Britten had latched on to a work which was to be instructive and useful to him, and it was one which, by the summer of 1932, he was determined to know from all angles. On 20 July he bought the newly released Columbia records of 'Stravinsky's great Psalm Symphony',[79] conducted by the composer, while, back in Lowestoft ten days later, he had the 'vocal score of Stravinsky's great Psalm Symph, sent from Chesters';[80] there was nothing equivocal about his judgement of it now. A week after that, he summoned Basil Reeve to listen to the records, which he had evidently brought home with him to Suffolk, perhaps for that very purpose.

With contemporary British composers, as with conductors,

Britten's opinions were more likely to be coloured by extra-musical matters: he had a young man's fads and fancies as well as a young man's instinctive dislike of anything which smelt too mustily of the establishment. So, for quite some time, he couldn't abide Elgar. We may feel he protests too much: 'Elgar 2nd Symphony, (dreadful nobilmente sempre) – I come out after 3rd movement – so bored. He [Elgar] conducts – ovation beforehand (!!!!!!!!!).'[81] That's from his first term at the RCM, when it would have been unthinkable for him to admire so stuffy a figure, and it hasn't much to do with the music, in which a more mature ear might have detected some surprising kinships with Mahler. By the following spring, he had learned to sound more calmly analytical: 'I listened with an open mind' – to the Enigma Variations – 'but cannot say that I was less annoyed with them, than usual.' He even ventured comments on some of the individual variations before reaching his weary conclusion: 'I suppose it's my fault, and there is something lacking in me, that I am absolutely incapable of enjoying Elgar, for more than 2 minutes.'[82] Again, the tone is too effortful to convince; but he would begin to enjoy Elgar before his college days were over, finding in *Falstaff* 'some v. fine stuff – and also some . . . . !!!!'[83] As with Mahler and Stravinsky, the piece to win him over was one which seems to resonate with his own future as a composer, the concert overture *In the South*: 'a very beautiful work in parts';[84] that contrast between stormy sections and the tranquil interlude which was separately published as 'In Moonlight' would eventually find its echo in the 'Sea Interludes' from *Peter Grimes*.

Britten's early enthusiasm for the 'miraculous' tone poems of Delius – 'He is a wizard'[85] – looks unlikely at first sight. Although the use of orchestral colour must have appealed to him, he would soon develop reservations about the composer's formal blurriness: his *Song of the High Hills* was 'marvellously beautiful, tho' meandering & too long'.[86] He had a different sort of trouble with

Holst's *Planets*, which 'arn't very much to my taste . . . too much harp, celesta, Bells etc.',[87] a point which he repeated when next he heard the suite: 'too sugary (celeste) . . . I feel no music of that generation can be compared to works like Walton's Viola Concerto'.[88] This indeed was a huge favourite, which Britten thought 'a work of genius' – not least, of course, because of the solo instrument for which it was written. Otherwise, his response to recent British music was often lukewarm, ranging from 'mediocre' Granville Bantock to 'pleasant' Arthur Somerville; as for Bax's *November Woods*, he was 'bored . . . not much November about it'.[89] While Vaughan Williams's Tallis Fantasia was 'V. beautiful (wonderfully scored), but over long', his *Wasps* was 'apaling'.[90] For some time Britten seems to have felt wary about commenting freely on Vaughan Williams, who was not only a different sort of composer but also one of his RCM examiners; it was after his composition exam in July 1931 – described by Britten as an 'Absolute Farce . . . they look at the wrong things & make me play the wrong things' – that Vaughan Williams apparently remarked, 'Very clever but beastly music.'[91] In his final year, however, Britten went with his fellow student Grace Williams to a performance at the college of *Hugh the Drover*, on which he commented in thoughtful and revealing detail:

> It needs a larger stage, of course – even so the First Act was very exciting & the rest was a dreadful anticlimax. V.W. has shown in places apt use of chorus, in others dreadful disregard of natural movements. The music was full of folk-song, (if you like that sort of thing) – it was best so – when not (as between Scenes in Act II), it was dreadful.[92]

He was thinking very clearly in dramatic as well as musical terms – and about the relationship between the two – but he hadn't guessed that before long he too would be drawn to folk song.

He continued to revere Beethoven though was less certain about Schubert, preferences which in time would be reversed. A Bartók concert in March 1932 prompted one of his carefully balanced judgements: 'I cannot say I love this music but it is amazingly clever & descriptive.'[93] His view of the Second Viennese School subsided for a while into bafflement: 'Schönberg – Heaven only knows!! . . . his 'Erwartung' – I could not make head or tail of it',[94] he wrote after listening to a radio broadcast, although a BBC Symphony Orchestra concert performance of the *Five Orchestral Pieces*, despite being conducted 'by that worst of all conductors' Adrian Boult, contained 'some quite fine – better than I expected – Colours – no. 3 – marvellous'.[95] In Berg's *Lyric Suite*, 'The imagination & intense emotion . . . certainly amaze me if not altogether pleases me', while *Wozzeck* was 'thoroughly sincere & moving music':[96] cautious rather than ringing endorsements in early 1933 of a composer with whom Britten would shortly hope to study. This was completely in character – a somewhat qualified interest burgeoning, as with Mahler and Stravinsky, into outright admiration – but there may have been another reason for his rapidly accelerating interest in Berg: it was in July 1933 that he got to know Henry Boys, who had met Berg in 1931 and was full of praise for him. Britten had just been awarded the Octavia Travelling Scholarship which, as the RCM's Director Sir Hugh Allen encouragingly put it in a postscript to his summer report, would enable him to 'get some new experience abroad'[97] after his graduation; going to Vienna to work with Berg must have seemed just the sort of experience envisaged by the college. But this intelligent proposal was to collapse in a disapproving muddle: someone (probably Allen) told Britten's mother that Berg was 'not a good influence', reflecting what Britten himself later described as 'an almost moral prejudice against serial music'. He continued: 'I think also that there was some confusion in my parents' minds – thinking that "not a good influence" meant morally, not musically.'[98] Berg, of course, was morally irreproachable; and he was certainly to be a musical influence on Britten.

Finally, at a chronological distance from Schoenberg and Berg though appealing to a wholly compatible intellectual–aesthetic frame of mind, there remained Bach and, always and specially for Britten, the Brandenburg Concertos. He heard Henry Wood conduct them in November 1930, almost inevitably noting that the sixth, 'with a mass of violas', was 'very fine'.[99] 'Don't v. much like Wood's Bach,' he grumbled, but that didn't prevent him from going to hear the same man conduct the same concerto, 'rather a ragged Brandenburg no. 6',[100] two years later. It was a work for which Britten would feel a particularly intimate affection throughout his life; early in 1969, he conducted the English Chamber Orchestra in a recording of the Brandenburgs. There are wonderful things throughout the set, but the sixth is magical, especially the second movement: 'The haunting 3/2 tune of the Adagio,' wrote Imogen Holst at the time, 'is a reminder that the viola was Bach's favourite orchestral instrument.'[101] And, she might have added, Britten's.

4

After returning to his digs from a concert in November 1932, Britten casually noted: 'Walk back with G. Finzi & G. Holst.'[102] The pavement itself couldn't have been less impressed by the fact that it happened to be carrying three of England's finest twentieth-century composers. A couple of months later, during one of his not-sure-about-Schoenberg evenings ('What I could make of it, owing to a skin-of-its-teeth performance, was rather dull, but some good things'), Britten had what ought to have been a momentous encounter, but 'Meet Sch. in interval' was all he had to say.[103] Thanks to London and the Bridges, and even a little to the college about which he was so disparaging, he could bump into some of the greatest musicians of the age while remaining extraordinarily sanguine about it.

If the process of meeting fellow musicians – performers as much as composers – had got off to a slow start, that was his own shy fault; when urged, early on, to move into a student hostel, he had stubbornly insisted on remaining in the middle-aged security of his respectable boarding house. During his early months in London, his main regular form of shared music-making was the rather uncharacteristic one of singing as a bass with the English Madrigal Choir, to which both he and his sister Barbara belonged. It wasn't until 11 February 1931, halfway through his second term at the RCM, that he noted in his diary: 'Meet an Italian (?) Violin Scholar at College and arrange to practise duets with him.'[104] He didn't risk the Italian's name, Remo Lauricella, which he would for some time have trouble spelling, but his diary entries do sound a good deal more cheerful from this point onwards. Two days later he and his 'brilliant' new friend met to play the violin and piano reduction of Mozart's A major 'Turkish' Concerto (K219) and by 24 February his tone had relaxed to one of unaffectedly hearty, schoolboyish pleasure: 'Practise with the Italian boy in afternoon – he's jolly good.'[105] Lauricella, who was a year older than Britten, had won an open scholarship to the college at the age of fifteen; they practised together regularly on Tuesday afternoons. At the end of June, Britten composed *Two Pieces* for violin and piano for Lauricella and himself to play: the first, 'Going down Hill on a Bicycle: A Boy's Song (after H. C. Beeching)', continues the sportive theme, although he thought the second, 'By the moon we sport and play (after Shelley)', 'more satisfactory than the Bicycle one'.[106] The following winter, the duo was joined by the cellist Bernard

Richards, an exact contemporary of Britten who had arrived at the college on the same day in 1930, and became a trio: 'In afternoon I go to R.C.M. & play with Lauricella until 4.0 & then play trio (Bridge – Phantasy C min.) with the addition of a 'Cellist – Richards, who is nice & very good,' Britten wrote on 19 January 1932. 'Great fun. We mean to do this regularly.'[107] It was a neat and auspicious touch to initiate the trio's existence with that early (and not *too* difficult) work by Bridge, of whom Lauricella as well as Britten had been a composition pupil; by May they would be tackling, among other things, Bridge's more recent and demanding second trio.

Stimulated both by what he was hearing and by what he was playing, Britten had embarked on his first great flurry of adult composition, the journey which would soon lead to the *Sinfonietta*, his actual Op. 1. But before reaching this milestone he wrote, between 9 March and 4 May 1932, a work of at least equal interest, the Double Concerto for Violin and Viola, partly inspired by the Walton Viola Concerto which had so impressed him a few months earlier; perhaps he imagined Lauricella and himself as soloists. If so, the idea remained in his imagination, for the piece was never to be performed during his lifetime. It received its premiere in a concert by the Britten–Pears Orchestra under Kent Nagano, in which the soloists were Katherine Hunka and Philip Dukes, at the Aldeburgh Festival in 1997: as Colin Matthews, who edited the concerto, wrote in a festival programme note, 'the instrumentation is so carefully indicated in the draft that what will be heard is virtually 100 per cent Britten'.[108] Though this is by no means the only instance of a piece first heard long after Britten's death prompting a reassessment of the composer's development, it is arguably the most significant. He was typically self-critical as he worked on it: on 18 March he wrote 'an unsatisfactory beginning' to the second movement; by 21 March it had become 'a fatuous second movement'; and, as for the last movement, 'I shall tear *that* up soon,' he decided on 29 March.[109] 'I'm putting my Concerto away for a bit,' he said, two days after he completed the work, and he seems to have meant for ever.[110] Perhaps he abruptly found it too English and old-fashioned for his rapidly fluctuating taste; the *Sinfonietta* would be much more abrasive. But in fact the concerto, opening with a characteristic horn call which reappears as a ghostly flute echo towards the end of the third movement, possesses the clarity and transparency of mature Britten; the hauntingly quiet ending has that sense of hard-won and slightly compromised resolution after turmoil which would later be found in, for instance, the Cello Symphony.

The *Sinfonietta*, which Britten began on 20 June and completed on 9 July, is quite different: it opens with a hint of Stravinsky and a stronger whiff of Schoenberg, as if consciously designed to rebuff the Double Concerto's lingering Englishness. He started composing, without much sense of overall shape, 'a movement which might be a bit of a Chamber symphony', but by the time he finished the sketch it was a 'Symphonietta for 10 instruments'.[111] He scored it rapidly and while doing so tried it out on Ireland ('very pleased') and, next day, Bridge and Herbert Howells ('they approve'); by 16 July he was sufficiently confident to telephone Anne Macnaghten, who had recently established the Macnaghten–Lemare concerts to promote contemporary British music, and to report that 'they're probably going to do my Sinfonietta'.[112] But this jaunty confidence was to be severely tested as the *Sinfonietta* progressed towards its Macnaghten–Lemare premiere on 31 January 1933 and a performance at the RCM, conducted by the composer, six weeks later. 'I have never heard such an appalling row!' wrote Britten after a college rehearsal on 22 September. 'However when we have a flute & a 'cello & when the other players have looked at their parts, I think it will be all right.'[113] It wasn't: the autumn became a tragicomic sequence of 'the most execrable rehearsal', swiftly followed by 'the most atrocious of all rehearsals'; not until 17 November could Britten report the attendance of a full team and 'Quite an improvement'.[114] This didn't last: when Iris Lemare rehearsed the piece in January, again with missing musicians, the result was 'Not at all good'. Yet when the first performance took place – among a ragbag programme of works by H. K. Andrews, Gordon Jacob, Gerald Finzi and Grace Williams – he conceded: 'Considering amt. of rehearsal & nature of same, my work went quite well – but oh!'[115] *The Times* thought well of it, noting that Britten 'seems to be striking out on a path of his own',[116] although the *Daily Telegraph* considered him merely 'as provocative as any of the foreign exponents of the catch-as-catch-can style of composition'.[117]

The piece did seem to be jinxed. On 5 February, a scheduled BBC broadcast under Edward Clark was postponed (until June 1934) when the allotted forty-five minutes of rehearsal time proved insufficient. His own college rehearsals continued to trouble him too, until the last moment when, after a satisfactory final rehearsal, 'I conduct a show of my Sinfonietta which goes quite well.'[118] The day before the concert, he sent a charmingly modest postcard to Finzi: 'If you aren't doing anything tomorrow evening (Thursday), and you feel inclined, you might drop into the College hall and hear a show of my Sinfonietta which I shall be trying to conduct. I suddenly thought that you might like to know.'[119] It was only the second occasion on which a work of his would be publicly performed at the college during his time there and it would also be, astonishingly, the last. Nevertheless, his Op. 1 was now out in the musical world. In June, Britten told his parents that Hermann Scherchen was to conduct it in a broadcast concert from Strasbourg on 7 August ('the parts have gone off to-day'), yet the jinx persisted: due to the fallibility of radio reception in summer, he was unable to hear it and uncertain whether the performance even took place. By this time, he had completely forgotten about the Double Concerto.

Given the number and variety of projects on which he had been engaged, this isn't nearly as improbable as it may at first seem: 'Hundreds of schemes are in the air at the moment,'[120] he wrote on 3 April 1933, exaggerating just a bit. Another shelved orchestral work, the ballet score *Plymouth Town*, had its origins in a meeting with the folklorist and dance historian Violet Alford in July 1931: she supplied him with a scenario which, with uncanny prescience, involved both a nautical setting and a theme of corrupted innocence. Britten sketched the work at Lowestoft during his summer vacation and scored it in London during the autumn, completing it on 22 November; in December he submitted it to the Camargo Society – the forerunner of the Vic–Wells Ballet and the Royal Ballet – who eventually rejected it. Undeterred by this, he started a second ballet score for Violet Alford in June 1932, to be based on an eccentric scenario about Basque shepherds, at the very moment he was beginning the *Sinfonietta*; but this remained, not altogether surprisingly, incomplete.

The three most significant chamber works Britten composed during 1932 and 1933 were the *Phantasy* in F minor for string quintet, the *Phantasy*, Op. 2, for oboe and string trio, and *Alla Quartetto Serioso: 'Go play, boy, play'*. The first of these, the only work of his apart from the *Sinfonietta* to be performed at the RCM, was written specifically to satisfy the requirements of the 1932 Cobbett Chamber Music Prize, which it duly won; Britten's characteristic response to the college performance on 22 July was 'bad – but I expected worse'.[121] On 12 December it received both its first and second public performances by the Macnaghten String Quartet with Nora Wilson (viola): the composer didn't attend the lunchtime concert at All Hallows-by-the-Tower as he was meeting his mother off the train at Liverpool Street, but he did hear it in the evening, when it was part of the third

Macnaghten–Lemare concert at the Ballet Club and 'v. badly played by Anne MacN's quart. + Vla. Worse, by far, than rehearsals.'[122] *The Times*, on the contrary, thought that the quintet 'did not build up into a satisfying whole' but that it was 'very well played by Miss Macnaghten's Quintet'.[123] It was broadcast by the BBC on 17 February 1933, played by a quintet led by André Mangeot, an interesting figure in the musical and cultural life of the time. Born in 1883, he formed several London-based chamber ensembles and for a year in the mid-1920s employed Christopher Isherwood as his secretary. For Britten there was a further strong recommendation: 'I had some excellent tennis with Mangeot & his two sons out at Cobham on Tuesday,' he wrote in June 1933.[124] For a fine musician to be talented at tennis as well was always sure to win his approval.

The *Phantasy* for oboe and string trio was composed during the autumn of 1932: 'More or less satisfactory – sometimes I think it is my best work – sometimes my worst' was Britten's characteristically cautious assessment on 10 October,[125] and he continued to revise it over the following months; it was to establish his reputation as a composer of chamber music. It was written for the great oboist Leon Goossens – an early instance of Britten's lifelong habit of composing works for outstanding specific soloists – and on 6 August 1933 it was broadcast by the BBC in a studio performance given by its dedicatee with members of the International String Quartet, led by Mangeot: Britten thought that Goossens played his part 'splendidly'. Of the first concert performance at St John's Institute, Westminster, given by the same musicians on 21 November, the *Monthly Musical Record* commented: 'Benjamin Britten's oboe quartet aroused considerable interest, being uncannily stylish, inventive and securely poised for a composer reported to be still in his teens.'[126] Presumably the writer knew that the day of the concert was the last day on which this 'reported' fact would be true.

November was also the deadline for works to be submitted for the following year's International Society for Contemporary Music (ISCM) Festival and, having unsuccessfully entered both the *Sinfonietta* and the earlier *Phantasy* quintet for the 1933 festival, Britten now tried again and with better luck. The *Phantasy* for oboe and string trio was accepted for performance at the Florence ISCM Festival in April 1934.

Alla Quartetto Serioso was a different sort of project, stemming from a younger kind of compositional impulse though partially resurfacing in two later works. It began as 'an easy mov. for St. Quart.',[127] to be called *Alla Marcia*, or 'Go play, boy, play' (a quotation from *The Winter's Tale*) on 13 February 1933, although at the beginning of April – when Britten had just been bowled over by *Emil und die Detektive* – this briefly became conflated with an abortive 'Emil' suite; abandoning that, he finished three and sketched the fourth of five movements for *Alla Quartetto Serioso*. Two were given titles and dedications, 'P.T.' for David Layton from Gresham's and 'Ragging' for his South Lodge friend Francis Barton: this attempt to bring an air of adolescent, schoolboyish rough-and-tumble to serious composition was, of course, utterly in character. The three completed movements were first performed at All Hallows-by-the-Tower by the Macnaghten String Quartet on 4 December 1933 and repeated at a Macnaghten–Lemare Ballet Club concert on 11 December: 'Anne did her best with my "Go Play, Boy, Play" – but again I want 1st class instrumentalists besides enthusiasm.' Britten is said to have walked off rudely afterwards, without thanking Anne Macnaghten, which would have been a plausible way to avoid saying anything about the performance, although his diary entry continues: 'Go on to MacNaghtens for supper after.'[128] Perhaps he ate in sulky silence. The fragments were extensively revised as *Three Divertimenti* (1936), while the original version of *Alla Marcia* was to resurface in the 'Parade' section of *Les Illuminations*, Op. 18.

He was no less busy with works for voices. The *Three Two-Part Songs* of 1932 (Walter de la Mare's 'The Ride-by-nights', 'The Rainbow' and 'The Ship of Rio') and the *Two Part-Songs* of 1933 (George Wither's 'I Lov'd a Lass' and Robert Graves's 'Song: Lift-Boy') are minor compositions, undignified by opus numbers, but *A Boy Was Born*, Op. 3, is another matter altogether. Initially, Britten thought of this simply as a 'work for Chorus' and a 'Christmas work', though he seems to have had a sense from the outset that it would prove to be both ambitious and troublesome. On 12 November 1932, after his haircut at Whiteley's, he bought from Chatto & Windus in St Martin's Lane a copy of *Ancient English Carols 1400–1700* (1928), collected and arranged by Edith Rickert, and began work; but it wasn't until the Christmas holiday that he found time to choose most of the texts he would use in *A Boy Was Born*. It was to take the form of an opening – and disarmingly innocent-seeming – theme followed by six variations, in some of which two texts might be conflated: this is the kind of scheme we shall meet again in Britten's work. It took him until Easter 1933 to reach the final section, the longest and most complicated in the piece, which continued to torment him for the next two months. He completed the work in early June and played it through to Hubert Foss, the music publisher at Oxford University Press, who approved of it; but he still had to face the 'awful business'[129] of copying out the parts. Almost all the texts are 'ancient', in the rather approximate sense of dating from the fifteenth to seventeenth centuries, with the exception of Christina Rossetti's 'In the Bleak Mid-Winter' (Variation 5): unlike its more familiar carol setting, this is actually made bleak and wintry, an early example of Britten's uncanny knack of writing chilly music, and it merges into the icy calm of the anonymous fifteenth-century 'Lully, lulley, lully, lulley, / The falcon hath borne my make [mate] away'. As Christmas works go, *A Boy Was Born* seems neither very devotional nor very festive, its focus firmly on emotional drama rather than on theology.

By late 1933, when Britten's time as a student was nearing its end, he had produced successful works in the major genres of orchestral, chamber and vocal music: his achievements were widely recognised, except at the RCM. This wasn't entirely the college's fault. One of the many paradoxes about Britten is that while his 'ordinary' middle-class background in Lowestoft had equipped him to be a clear-headed and methodical businessman (as colleagues who assumed they were dealing with a scatter-brained composer sometimes discovered to their cost), his shyness and insecurity, his perfectionism and his readiness to take offence made his relationships with institutions edgy and tense: he rubbed some people up the wrong way at the RCM, just as he had at Gresham's, and just as would occasionally happen in the future with colleagues, concert promoters, festival organisers, publishers, record companies and the BBC. That, we might smugly say, is the price of creative genius, except that there's really nothing smug about it: it's simply true. And it would be a mistake to assume that creative genius isn't as capable of being delighted by quite simple things as anyone else. On 13 December 1933, Britten addressed to Mr & Mrs R. V. Britten of Lowestoft a plain postcard, on the reverse of which was written: 'BENJAMIN BRITTEN A.R.C.M. Much love.'[130] It was, as it said, for both his parents, but perhaps especially for his ailing father, to whom there must have been an implied, kindly meant subtext: 'There. Told you so.'

On New Year's Eve, after a last drive in the family car – a Humber Snipe which Mr Britten had bought only a year earlier but was now too ill to use – Britten told his diary that he was 'not sorry' to see the back of 1933. Although both he and his siblings had made good progress in their various careers during the year, 'the slur on the whole has been Pop's dreadful illness'.

'Mum's nursing & pluck has been the only bright spot in the whole dreadful time,' he added. She was indeed exemplary in this respect, despite a developing interest in Christian Science which led her to disapprove of her husband's medical treatment: 'You know all this is contrary to my C.S.,' she told Beth early in 1934, 'but I am only doing as the family wants and Pop himself!'[131] As for Ben, he ended his diary entry with an unfeasible wish: 'Let us see whether 1934 can give us back what seems to us the impossible – Pop's health.[132] He knew he was whistling in the dark.

5

'I only started enjoying myself as a human being after I left college and got down to some real work,' said Britten in 1959.[133] This simple-looking statement is a little more subtle than it seems and precisely right: 'enjoying myself' and 'real work' were always synonymous for him; moreover, he had an intuitive sense that 'work', when destined for a college's examinations or awards, wasn't quite 'real'. This new sort of work, a freelance composer's attempt to eke out a living, involved making the best of whatever was available, a process he grumblingly enjoyed. 'I cannot write a single note of anything respectable at the moment,' he told Grace Williams on 3 January 1934, 'and so – on the off chance of making some money – I am dishing up some very old stuff (written, some of it, over ten years ago) as a dear little school suite for strings – You see what I have come to . . .'[134] This 'school suite' was the *Simple Symphony*, Op. 4: it recycled material from his childhood into four movements which are wonderfully assured in everything but their coyly alliterative titles: 'Boisterous Bourrée', 'Playful Pizzicato', 'Sentimental Sarabande' and

'Frolicsome Finale'. It was first performed on 6 March at the Stuart Hall, Norwich, by the Norwich String Orchestra conducted by the composer.

The venue and the performers are significant: he had come home. Although Britten would live in cities again, and even for a while in America, Suffolk was the place to which he would always return. He had business cards printed and seems to have been perfectly content to publish his address, 21 Kirkley Cliff Road, Lowestoft. This was a matter partly of choice – he knew that a room in London would have kept him more closely in touch with the musical world and its opportunities – and partly of duty: 'Pop' was 'really pretty bad now'. Beneath both these factors lay a solid core of instinct: this was where he belonged and this was where his music came from. As it turned out, there might have been little point in paying for digs in London for he was to spend two periods of 1934 travelling in Europe: on 10 January, he learned from Hubert Foss at OUP that 'my Oboe Quart. has been accepted by international jury for Contemporary Music Festival'.[135] By the end of March, he would be on his way to Florence.

Before this, there was to be the fraught process of the rehearsal and broadcast first performance of *A Boy Was Born*: although a date in late February had been mooted, Britten had heard nothing from the BBC since the preceding September. When he wrote on 24 January to Edwin Benbow of the Wireless Singers (later the BBC Singers), it was with understandable anxiety – 'the time for preparation is getting very short, & I am rather worried'[136] – and with a request that Frank Bridge should conduct; in the event, the conductor was Leslie Woodgate, who earned the composer's warm praise and thus began a long association with his work. Britten's main worry concerned the boys of St Mark's, North Audley Street: their part, though not difficult, was probably 'not much like what they are accustomed to sing', and he was anxious to avoid the excessive smoothness of the English cathedral tradition. When he heard them at St Mark's, however, he was delighted – 'They sing like angels'[137] – but when they were transplanted to the BBC, their 'intonation, after being impeccable in their own hall, is very bad';[138] there was a lesson here for the future. Nevertheless, the performance on 23 February at the concert hall of Broadcasting House, which Britten attended with the Bridges, was a great success: 'My "Boy was Born" goes infinitely better than rehearsals, some of it really going well. It goes down pretty well.'[139] He sounds as if he could hardly believe his ears. To the same day's diary entry, above the date, he added a two-word postscript: 'Elgar dies.'

'I *am* going to Italy,' he wrote to Grace Williams, three days later.[140] It was quite an adventure, and he sensibly decided to take with him John Pounder, his loyal and trustworthy friend since their days together at South Lodge. They left Lowestoft on the morning of 27 March and were to stay overnight in London at the Wilton Hotel; during the day, Britten typically fitted in lunch with his sister Barbara, the collection of tickets from Italian State Railways, a rehearsal of his piece with the members of the Griller Quartet who were to perform it with Goossens in Florence, tea with Mrs Bridge, an early supper with Beth and a visit to the Lyric Theatre to see *Reunion in Vienna* by Robert Sherwood. The following morning, they caught the boat train from Victoria and after a rough crossing ('many people succumb') reached Paris in the early evening before taking an overnight train to Turin. By the time they got to Florence at 7.45 the next evening, they were 'pretty exhausted'. Britten's diary records somewhat dutiful-sounding visits to galleries and concerts and, as was his way, is business-like rather than evocative. Much livelier is his letter home of 30 March, which has not only a character who clearly belongs in *A Room with a View* – 'one Miss Cherry, a schoolmistress

– rather prim, but very amusing' – but also a foredoomed attempt at descriptive prose: 'Snow everywhere – lakes, mountains galore, I never seen anything like it. The light was so superb – very sunny, with occasional clouds – and it made the colouring very brilliant. As you notice, I cannot describe it.'[141] They had met a couple called Pearce – the husband had been, like Pounder, at Charterhouse; both men were to become solicitors – and there's a charming authenticity, as Forsterian as it is Brittenesque, to J. Allan Pearce's recollection of the Pension Balestri's staircase, 'down which John Pounder came tripping, very nimbly for such a tall man, watched by Ben at the elderly upright piano in the hall, who vividly described his descent on the keys'.[142] The knack of turning almost anything into musical language both recalls the party-piece imitations of Britten's childhood and anticipates his work as a composer for documentary films, particularly the 'running downstairs music' for *The King's Stamp* in 1935. Also staying at the Pension Balestri were Hermann Scherchen, who the previous summer had been scheduled to conduct the *Sinfonietta*'s European premiere, and his fourteen-year-old son Wulff.

On Thursday 5 April, Goossens and the Grillers performed Britten's quartet 'very beautifully & it's quite well received': 'Its colloquies between the oboe and the strings stamp it as music which belongs inherently to the instruments for which it is scored,'[143] the reviewer in *The Times* perceptively noted. The following day, Scherchen organised a grand excursion to Siena – the party filled five omnibuses and was given lunch by the mayor – but it poured with rain. 'Young Wulff Scherchen (son of Hermann) attaches himself to me, & I spend all the time with him,'[144] wrote Britten, and there's no reason to think him disingenuous. Wulff Scherchen's own memories happily acknowledge his pleasure at discovering a friend who seemed barely older than himself: 'I didn't feel he was seven years older than me. I thought we were much closer in age than that. We were boys together.'[145] The spirit of being 'boys together' was, of course, one into which Britten could always unselfconsciously enter. Neither Wulff's English nor Ben's German was up to much, but this didn't bother them: 'That is the beautiful thing about friendship – languages don't matter, you make signs, you can nudge one another with your elbow . . .'[146] Perhaps they managed a prototype of the 'Aldeburgh Deutsch' later invented by Britten and Mstislav Rostropovich, the Russian cellist and conductor. Anyway, the young Englishman's Englishness was in itself hugely amusing, not the least comical of his quirks being the cautious way in which he, alone of the party, had provided himself with a waterproof raincoat, just in case. When drizzle turned to deluge, he offered to share this useful garment with the shorts-and-sandals-clad Wulff: 'He opened it out, stuck his right arm into the right sleeve and got me to put my left arm in the left sleeve . . . We thought that was hilariously funny but then we had to walk along with our middle legs together, and then the outer legs, doing a three-legged march which increased general hilarity. Oh, it was wonderful!'[147] Britten's raincoat had suddenly become as magical a prop as Gene Kelly's umbrella, and if they could have managed to twirl round a lamp post together they surely would have done. Lowestoft must have seemed a world away.

Back in Florence, the new friends went for a walk on Saturday morning, but at lunchtime Britten received 'a telegram from home – come to-day, Pop not so well'. The excellent John Pounder insisted on accompanying him. They bought English newspapers on the journey, but their interests luckily didn't extend to the 'Deaths' column. When they reached Lowestoft on Monday, Britten discovered that his father had in fact died of a cerebral haemorrhage on Friday: 'A great man – with one of the finest brains I have ever come across, & what a father!'[148] That sense of awkward, bitten-off emotion remained until the end. For his part, Robert Victor Britten had left an equally stilted (and equally sincere) note for 'the 4 B's', Barbara, Bobby, Beth and Benjamin: 'Goodbye my four! My love to you all Its grand to have known you and have your love – – Comfort Mum'.[149] To his diary for the preceding Friday, when he had walked in the rain with Wulff, Britten added a postscript: 'Pop dies – see Monday.' It appears in exactly the same place, above the date, that he had recorded the death of Elgar on 23 February. Though the coincidence wouldn't have been so apparent at the time, he may have had some inkling that on both those two days, in art and in life, the death of the old had been accompanied by the arrival of the new.

The funeral took place at St John's, the 'low' church favoured by Mrs Britten, on Wednesday 11 April: it was 'a very simple and lovely service', conducted by Basil Reeve's father (the Reverend Cyril Reeve) and Britten's uncle, the Reverend Sheldon Painter. The music included 'In Tears of Grief' from the end of the *St Matthew Passion* and 'Jesu, as Thou art our Saviour', the third variation from Britten's *A Boy Was Born*: the local paper made much of this, as if there were still something quaint about the late dentist's son composing music. 'Mum is a perfect marvel, even when we go up to Kirkley Cemetary after, she has control of herself,'[150] Britten wrote; that 'control' belongs to the time and the class, but it is typical of Mrs Britten to have shown it so notably and of her son to have admired it. There was much to be done – Mrs Britten had 'everso many' letters to write – but the following week widow and younger son were able to set off for a break at Prestatyn in Wales, where Bobby and his wife Marjorie had taken over Clive House, a struggling prep school. It was an awkward time: Britten had less in common with his elder brother than with his sisters and he had never quite taken to Bobby's wife who, in the privacy of his diary, he nicknamed 'Barge'. He made himself useful, coaching the boys at singing and cricket and predictably finding them easier company than the adults; it was an apt place for him to work on the school songs which would become his Op. 7, *Friday Afternoons* – the time when the Clive House boys sang. He recorded his usual, occasionally acidic, comments on broadcast concerts, although he enthused over Frank Bridge's ability to make Greig's first *Peer Gynt* suite 'sound positively thrilling': 'What the world has lost in his not conducting enough, cannot be estimated.'[151] The idea had been to give Mrs Britten a long relaxing spell away from home, but on 7 May this came to an abrupt end: 'Mum is sent for by Aunt Queenie (her sister) who is in the middle of an attack of "melancholia". So regardless of the fact that she needs a long rest & holiday, Mum has to pack up in order to go & nurse her. What the rest of the family thinks of it I don't know.'[152] He was perhaps almost as irritated with his mother for agreeing to go as he was with his aunt for summoning her; when he wrote to her, however, it was still in the over-fulsome style of his childhood: 'I miss you most terribly, my dear . . .'[153] He stayed on for another fortnight in Wales, joined for the last few days by his sister Beth. 'I shall be sick to leave this place,' he admitted, '& am so fond of the school & the kids that I dread going back to the void at Lowestoft.'[154]

That sense of 'void' was all the more acute since 21 Kirkley Cliff Road had been Mr Britten's professional base as well as his home: his assistant, Laurence Sewell, continued the dental practice, retaining the name 'Britten & Sewell' on the brass plaque, in the ground-floor surgery. But there were compensations, among them the proximity of that other prep school,

South Lodge. Just before leaving for Florence, Britten had seen his sister Barbara off at Lowestoft station and made this laconic note: 'Walk abit back with Dunkerley of S. Lodge.'[155] His friendship with thirteen-year-old Piers Dunkerley prospered during the cricketing summer term, as he wrote on 15 July: 'In aft. Tony Jones, & Piers Dunkerley (South Lodge Boys) come. Spend aft. on beach & bathe with P.D. Back to tea in garden . . .'[156] Although Piers was only a few months younger than Wulff Scherchen, the two relationships were very different: Piers inhabited a world Britten knew in his bones, while Wulff's world was entirely foreign. One promised a fond revisitation of past experience; the other beckoned from the unvisited future.

Britten spent much of that summer retreating into safe familiar pleasures – his diaries record days of cricket, tennis and croquet, sunbathing and sea-bathing – and one can scarcely blame him: the triumphant emergence into musical adulthood, his graduation so swiftly followed by success in Florence, had been abruptly interrupted by bereavement. The task of keeping his mother company necessarily fell mostly on him: Barbara was a nurse in London, Bobby a headmaster in Wales and Beth was setting up her dressmaking business in Finchley. An outsider might have reasonably concluded that, of the four children, Ben was the one who could get on with his work in Lowestoft. But he couldn't. He was meant to be working on *Holiday Tales*, Op. 5 – subsequently *Holiday Diary* – for his new publisher, Ralph Hawkes, but listlessness kept getting in the way. 'I do odd jobs, try unsuccessfully for umpteenth time to settle down to piano pieces for Hawkes,' he wrote on 15 September and, two days later: 'To-day I make a great effort – staying in practically all day (except for a lovely rough bathe before lunch) & putting off tennis at Tamplins. The result isn't satisfactory tho' . . .'[157] Music seldom came quite such a poor third after bathing and tennis, but the happiest spell of the summer was a week in which, incredibly, he managed to do without music almost completely. This was a sailing holiday with a group of friends on the Norfolk Broads and, helped by the presence of a man named Roger and a boat called *Puddleduck*, it sounds like pure *Swallows and Amazons*: 'Attempt to take dinghy out in morning near ends in disaster, but Roger does manage to get P'duck down to Potter before lunch . . .' At the end of the week, Britten could hardly bear to go home: 'It has been a great holiday, & it is sickening to go back to civilisation again.'[158]

Yet civilisation, even in East Anglia, wasn't all bad: being based once again in Lowestoft enabled Britten to develop an important, though generally overlooked, friendship with the composer E. J. Moeran, who had recently taken a house with his mother in the south Norfolk village of Lingwood, very much within the orbit of Mrs Britten's and Audrey Alston's musical connections. Jack Moeran, born in Norfolk of Irish ancestry, was almost twenty years older than Britten; he had studied at the RCM before the war and with John Ireland after it. At this time, he was starting work on his Symphony in G minor (1937), the second movement of which, he said, 'was conceived around the sand-dunes and marshes of East Norfolk'.[159] That is in every sense close to Britten territory – the county boundary between Norfolk and Suffolk is only just north of Lowestoft – and the notion of creating a musical sound-world from 'sand-dunes and marshes' is hugely suggestive in the context of his later work. When Moeran eventually finished the symphony in 1936, he hastened to show it to Britten: 'Jack Moeran was in last night, with his new symphony.'[160] No less influential on the younger man was Moeran's interest in folk music. On 16 December 1933, returning by train from London, Britten had travelled 'as far as Beccles with Moeran, & "Harry", his folk-singer'.[161] This was Harry Cox, from Great Yarmouth, 'who went on to become a celebrated face of the traditional folk revival, recording more than 200 songs and appearing frequently on television until his death in 1971';[162] Moeran had discovered him while collecting Norfolk folk songs, of which he amassed over 150. By early 1934, Moeran had become a key part of Britten's musical life: his influence led, in February, to the Norwich Festival commissioning from Britten a work for 1936 – it would be *Our Hunting Fathers* – and he was a moving spirit behind the first performance of *Simple Symphony* on 6 March. Ten days later, Britten had a 'long telephone conversation with Moeran about various musical matters'; a week after that, 'I meet Moeran at Hawkes at 11.00 & play with him the duet version of his Suite Farrago . . .'[163] Thereafter, at frequent intervals throughout the summer, Moeran would visit Lowestoft for lunch or tea, 'much talk' and the inevitable sea-bathing. For Britten, he had two enduringly influential qualities: he was a composer who knew how to get the East Anglian coast into his music; and he was fascinated by folk song without resembling Vaughan Williams.

Britten's compositional block remained: 1934 was an alarmingly unproductive year for the prolific young composer. In July he completed, without much enthusiasm, a *Te Deum* in C which he thought 'libelous'; he meant 'plagiaristic', feeling it owed too much to Stravinsky's *Symphony of Psalms*. It was for the boys of St Mark's, North Audley Street, who had so impressed him in *A Boy Was Born*, as was the *Jubilate Deo* in E flat which he wrote in August. In October he finished *Holiday Tales*, which was played by George Loughlin to the Mendelssohn Scholarship committee (who found it 'incomprehensible') on 5 November: in keeping with the spirit of this outdoor summer, its four movements were entitled 'Early Morning Bathe', 'Sailing', 'Fun-fair' and 'Night'. The work was dedicated to Arthur Benjamin who seems, in the composer's absence, to have supplied the overall title. By this time, Britten was once more in Europe, using the still unspent funds from his Octavia Travelling Scholarship and accompanied by his mother.

The devotion and kindness Britten showed towards this increasingly tiresome lady were beyond reproach; nevertheless, some of his diary entries, as he records their travels together in Switzerland, Austria and Germany, show signs of gritted teeth. While Mrs Britten went to what her son called 'a Christian Science show', he took himself off for 'a long walk round old Basel, seeing everything'; in Vienna, she had 'a very nasty fall in her room while washing', which left her 'wobbly' for days; meanwhile, 'a Mrs Koller', who was 'a Christ. Science friend of Mum's', turned up and he found himself obliged to accompany 'this Mrs Koller' to the opera – '*Cav*' and '*Pag*' – about which 'I couldn't make myself thrilled'.[164] He had been hearing more exciting things than that, including 'a very lovely show of Zauberflöte' in Basel and a superb *Fledermaus* ('never have I heard an orchestra play like that . . . the singers too . . . inspired from the beginning to the end') which was 'A marvellous intro-duction to the Winer Oper'.[165] On a picture postcard of the Vienna Opera House which he sent to Grace Williams ('just to make you jealous'), he succumbed to Wagnerian delirium: 'I'm coming back – soon & oft. Meistersinger, Siegfried, last week & Götterdämerung to-night!!!'[166] But the most significant event during his visit to Vienna was his meeting, on 10 November, with the 'very nice & interesting' Erwin Stein of Universal Edition: both Stein, Britten's future publisher at Boosey & Hawkes, and his daughter Marion (later Harewood and, later still, Thorpe) were to become close friends of the composer.

Mother and son arrived back in London, where they were to spend a further week at Burleigh House before returning to Lowestoft, on 29 November: 'I can't say I'm pleased to be back,' Britten grumbled, but there's an unmistakable sense that re-engagement with the practicalities of musical life was neces-sary and overdue. He spent the very next day first listening to the pianist Betty Humby play through his *Holiday Tales*, then

attending a rehearsal of *A Boy Was Born*, and finally dashing to
Wigmore Hall 'to hear Betty H. play my pieces well, but the
audience doesn't like them much'.[167] He celebrated his twenty-
first birthday on Saturday 1 December – having been in Munich
on the actual day, 22 November – before setting off for a brief
visit to the Bridges in Sussex, partly to seek help in drafting his
reply to J. F. R. Stainer of the Mendelssohn Foundation, who
had offered him an insulting £50: 'I do feel,' he wrote, 'that the
title "Mendelssohn Scholar" should only go to the recipient of
the full award of £150 a year . . . I am afraid that I must respectfully refuse it.' He couldn't resist mentioning his 'regret' that
Stainer had found 'my pieces outside your comprehension',
adding somewhat disingenuously that 'when they were played
at the Wigmore Hall last Friday, the audience seemed appreciative'.[168] That isn't quite what he had told his diary. The performance of *A Boy Was Born* on 17 December, conducted by Iris
Lemare at the Mercury Theatre, was so poor that he had to
leave, 'not being able to stand the strain', after the second variation, although the boys of St Alban the Martyr were 'very, very
good and beautiful'.[169] Earlier the same day, he had heard the
'brilliant fiddler' Henri Temianka with Betty Humby play 'my
3 pieces . . . excellently' at Wigmore Hall: these were three
movements of the incomplete suite (Op. 6), which was not to
be heard in full until 1936; the fact that Britten, usually so reliable in meeting compositional deadlines, failed to complete this
work on time says much about his inability to work in the months
following his father's death.

   The family Christmas in Lowestoft 'wasn't so bad considering
the circs., but none of us felt particularly merry!'[170] Similarly
unconducive to merriment was a broadcast concert on
28 December, conducted 'atrociously' by Vaughan Williams and
including 'dreadful' works by Elizabeth Maconchy, R. O. Morris,
Robin Milford and Vaughan Williams himself: 'It is concerts

like this which make me absolutely despair of English Music and its critics.'[171] He neither attempted a summing-up of the old year nor made resolutions for the new one. He didn't need to. It was obvious that something had to change.

CHAPTER 3

MOST SURPRISING DAYS

1935–39

1

It came without warning. Throughout the early months of 1935, Britten sounds unaccountably cheerful for someone without a dependable source of income who was stuck mostly in Lowestoft and making weekly journeys along the Waveney Valley to Bungay to conduct an amateur orchestra, which he called the BBBB or 'Benj. Britten Bungay Band, alias the "Hag's Band"', an unkind reference to its founder, Mrs Kersty Chamberlain. One dreadful foggy evening in January, he grumpily decided: 'It is no use trying to rehearse them – the only advice worth giving them is "Go away & learn to play your instruments".' On the way back to Lowestoft, the car broke down, having run dry, in the dense fog. Even so, 'a good dinner, and the Mahler gram. records (Kindertodtenlieder) restores my faith in life'.[1] He was seeing old friends such as John Pounder and Francis Barton – whom he re-encountered while staying with the Bridges in Sussex – and, whenever he was in London, he had developed the slightly eccentric habit of nipping into news cinemas, even on the busiest days, to catch the Disney shorts: he was especially partial to a *Silly Symphony*. But a living had to be earned, and by April it seemed as if he would have to settle for a routine job with the

BBC, a prospect which he didn't at all relish. Then, on Saturday 27 April:

> A most surprising day. Edward Clark's secretary 'phones at breakfast saying would I get in touch with a certain film impressario, M. Cavalcanti, which I do, with the result that I lunch with him (and another director Mr Coldstream) at Blackheath – where the G.P.O. Film studio is – and that I am booked to do the music to a film on the new Jubilee Stamp – only half-serious luckily. Talk much about this – go to Lewisham for 2 hrs (see a good Mickey Mouse) then back to the studio to see some 'shooting' – but I can't get definite instructions enough out of them to start work yet.[2]

'O brave new world . . .': yet every Miranda needs her Prospero, and in this case it seems that the idea of introducing Britten to the GPO Film Unit had come from none other than Frank Bridge. It was a brilliant idea in every way. Not only was the task of writing precisely timed scores to tight deadlines the perfect medicine for Britten's creative inertia; it was also exactly suited to the orderly ways of one who so embodied the virtues, as well as some of the vices, of a traditional prep- and public-school education. And, in one move, it transplanted an outsider who had been on the edge of 1930s cultural life into its very centre.

The GPO Film Unit had been an almost accidental invention: it had grown out of the defunct Empire Marketing Board, whose founders can scarcely have imagined or intended to leave a legacy of such radical creativity. Among those involved with it were the documentary film-makers John Grierson and Basil Wright; the sound recordist, producer and director Alberto Cavalcanti; the painter William Coldstream; and, from 1935, Britten and W. H. Auden. Shortly after Britten began working for the Unit, Cavalcanti treated him to a private screening of some recent productions: *Weather Forecast* and *Spring on the Farm*, both directed by Evelyn Spice; *The Song of Ceylon*, directed by Basil Wright; and *Mr Pit and Mr Pot*, directed by Cavalcanti himself. Britten, who loved funny short films, was especially taken with the last of these, a 'work of genius – which the charming English Distributors won't buy! – it being too *silly*'.[3] Their current project, *The King's Stamp*, was about the design and printing of a stamp to commemorate George V's Silver Jubilee.

The date of the Jubilee was 6 May, a 'heavenly day' according to Britten, who otherwise didn't think much of the occasion. He was in Lowestoft and, on 4 May, 'having fights about decorating our house for Jubilee' which he thought 'too nationalistic';[4] by the following morning, he had capitulated and was 'helping Beth decorate house a bit with flags – (under duress)',[5] but the disagreement was symptomatic of his increasing resistance to his mother's views. As for his work on the film score itself, he had something to mutter about and also, far more importantly, something to do: 'I spend the whole blessed day slogging at the film music in my room – with a watch in one hand and a pencil in the other – trying to make what little ideas I have (& they are precious few on this God-forsaken subject) syncronize with the Seconds . . . I slog away until abt. 11.0 at night – trying to concoct *some* rubbish about a Jubilee Stamp.'[6] Beneath the grumbling, there's the unmistakable voice of someone rather enjoying himself; the more he worked at it the more he became delighted by this fiendishly tricky low-budget job. The available instrumentation was restricted and odd: two pianos (played by Britten himself and Howard Ferguson), flute, clarinet and percussion. On 17 May they recorded the music: 'It goes quite well – & is good fun to do . . . Considering the hurry of everything, I think it is quite effective & suits the film.' It still sounded 'quite good' when he heard the playback next morning. 'Then watch Cavalcanti & Stocks synchronising it . . . It is a marvellously clever work.'[7] In this respect, it differed from other celebrations of the Jubilee: a week later, there was 'the incredible Jubilee Concert at Albert Hall, arr. by dear Walford Davies. Needless to say, no serious musicians go.'[8] Needless to say: one effect of the Jubilee, as tends to be the case with royal occasions, was to emphasise the gulf between the conservative establishment and the intellectual-creative left, which was where Britten now found himself.

Remembering his time with the GPO Film Unit a decade later, he concentrated on the practicalities. 'I had to work quickly, to force myself to work when I didn't want to, and to get used to working in all kinds of circumstances,' he told a BBC schools audience, before describing the difficulty (which was also the fun) of creating sounds to accompany shots of an unloading ship: 'We had pails of water which we slopped everywhere, drain pipes wth coal slipping down them, model railways, whistles and every kind of paraphernalia we could think of.'[9] But the work also had a more personal revelation in store for him. After spending much of June on Cavalcanti's next documentary, a film about miners eventually called *Coal Face*, on 5 July he travelled with Basil Wright to the Worcestershire village of Colwall – where, coincidentally, his brother Bobby had taught at the Elms School – to 'talk over matters for films with Wystan Auden (who is a master at the Downs School here . . .)': 'Auden is the most amazing man, a very brilliant & attractive personality – he was at Farfield, Greshams, but before my time.'[10] They spent two days there, staying overnight at the Park Hotel in Tewkesbury. At this point, with his rather more orthodox prep-school experience, Britten was principally struck by the relaxed atmosphere at the Downs: 'they are a remarkably nice lot of boys – very free with the masters, but yet discipline is maintained'; their paintings were 'some of the most vital &

thrilling things I have ever seen in modern art'; and, to complete
a 'heavenly' Saturday, there was a cricket match in which 'One
lad (David) makes a very fine century'.[11] Britten's observant and
generous appreciation of all kinds of youthful creativity was, of
course, a lifelong characteristic. The diary entry doesn't say,
though he must surely have noticed, that the boys called their
English master 'Uncle Wiz'.

That the first meeting between the greatest poet and greatest
composer born in England during the twentieth century – as
they might quite sensibly be described – should have taken place
in such circumstances, though slightly comical, is less anachronistic than it may at first appear. School-related coincidences are
a recurring feature in English creative life and prep-school
teaching was a convenient way for young writers to make ends
meet: it was, after all, how John Betjeman came to be taught
briefly by T. S. Eliot. Moreover, Auden and Britten were both
men whose creative personalities owed much to the oddities
of their education. Yet there the similarity ends. The most
vivid portrait of Auden as a schoolboy remains the one supplied
by Isherwood in his early autobiography *Lions and Shadows*,
where he appears as 'a stodgy, podgy little boy' called Hugh
Weston:

> He was precociously clever, untidy, lazy and, with the masters,
> inclined to be insolent. His ambition was to become a mining
> engineer; and his playbox was full of thick scientific books on
> geology and metals and machines, borrowed from his father's
> library. His father was a doctor . . . I remember him chiefly for
> his naughtiness, his insolence, his smirking tantalizing air of
> knowing disreputable and exciting secrets. With his hinted
> forbidden knowledge and stock of mispronounced scientific
> words, portentously uttered, he enjoyed among us, his semi-savage
> credulous schoolfellows, the status of a kind of witch-doctor.[12]

Nothing could be less like the competitive, meticulous, athletic young composer. And that may go some way towards explaining why Wystan Auden, despite his formidable intelligence, so completely failed to understand Benjamin Britten.

For the time being, this wouldn't matter: both men were in mutual awe of something they did have in common, an astonishing ability to work with speed and brilliance at their chosen art. Their first, somewhat semi-detached, collaboration was on *Coal Face*, for which each had written his contribution before they met in July; the prose commentary was by Montague Slater, subsequently the librettist for *Peter Grimes*; the film received its first screening in London on 27 October. In July, Britten was working on *H.P.O. or 6d Telegram* – 'it is a brute, fourteen small sections of about 8–20 sec. each'[13] – although this was eventually released without his music and, during the late summer, he provided scores for three short films – *Gas Abstract, Dinner Hour, Men Behind the Meters* – made for the British Commercial Gas Association. Then, in the autumn, he collaborated with Auden on a film to be called *Negroes*, an intractible and eventually (in this form) abandoned project. On 17 September, having spent a day working on it with Auden and Coldstream, he lamented: 'I always feel very young & stupid when with these brains – I mostly sit silent when they hold forth about subjects in general. What brains!'[14] As if to rub it in, he and Auden then went off to the Westminster Theatre 'where the Group theatre are doing some of his plays' (*The Dance of Death* and *The Dog Beneath the Skin*), but he didn't stay to watch the rehearsal. For the next month or so, he struggled on with *Negroes* – even visiting the jazz specialists, Levy's of Whitechapel, to 'hear more Negro records', though he doesn't seem to have bought any – while at the same time continuing to cope with the GPO Film Unit's weirdly miscellaneous demands: 'percussion, piano (Howard Ferguson) & two extra perc. from Blackheath Conservatoire (to play chains, rewinders, sandpaper, whistles, carts, water etc.)';[15] 'telephone apparatus noises & after lunch title musics & 2 sequences for 5 documentary G.P.O. Films (Fl, Ob., Cl., Fg., Perc., Pft . . .)';[16] and 'new recording of Telegram Abstract film (Fl, Ob, Cl, Xyl. & Glock, Perc. & Pft)'.[17] By this time, he had met Rupert Doone and Robert Medley of the Group Theatre, for whose production of *Timon of Athens* he was to write the music. And there was yet another GPO Film Unit project to work on with Auden.

This was 'a new film T.P.O (Railway Post) with Cavalcanti & [Harry] Watt';[18] we know it as *Night Mail*, the most celebrated short documentary of its time. It involved not only the by now familiar combination of finicky detail and apparently endless meetings but an expedition 'to listen to trains themselves – in pouring rain & very wet grass'.[19] Meanwhile, Auden worked on his poem in a narrow corridor at the back of the GPO Film Unit in Soho Square, accompanied by whistling and card-playing messenger boys, and delivering it in instalments to the production office where anything that didn't fit was unceremoniously binned: 'He'd say, "Alright. That's quite all right. Just roll it up and throw it away."'[20] The surviving poem occupies only the closing few minutes of *Night Mail*, from the moment the night mail crosses the border into Scotland, and it is accompanied by the most ambitious music Britten had yet composed for film. When the time came to record it, on 15 January 1936, he made an unusually detailed diary entry:

> Up early & get to Soho Square at 9.45. Some bother over parts for orchestra, but I eventually get down to Blackheath at 11.0 for big T.P.O recording. A large orchestra for me – Fl. Ob. Bsn. Trpt. Harp (Marie Kotchinska – very good), Vl, Vla. Vlc. CB, Percussion & wind machine – a splendid

team. The music I wrote really comes off well – &, for what is wanted, creates quite alot of sensation! The whole trouble, & what takes so much time is that over the music has to be spoken a verse – kind of patter – written by Auden – in strict rhythm with the music. To represent the train noises. There is too much to be spoken in a single breath by the one voice (it is essential to keep to the same voice & to have no breaks) so we have to record separately – me, having to conduct both from an improvised visual metronome – flashes on the screen – a very difficult job! [Stuart] Legg speaks the stuff splendidly tho'.[21]

Night Mail was first seen at the Arts Theatre in Cambridge on 4 February 1936 and a London commercial release followed a month later; but by this time Auden had resigned from the GPO Film Unit.

2

If Britten had achieved nothing but his work on film scores during 1935, we wouldn't be able to accuse him of indolence. However, this was very far from the case. He had promised to compose a set of 'insect pieces' for the oboist Sylvia Spencer, who had given a performance of his *Phantasy* Quartet with the Grillers on 4 December 1934, and on 17 April he told her he had 'written two insect pieces – sketched three more – sketched the scoring for accompaniment of string orchestra'; the two surviving insects, 'Wasp' and 'Grasshopper', were eventually performed in 1979 and published the following year. Britten continued:

> In fact out of a simple little piece for oboe & piano has grown
> (or is growing) a large and elaborate suite for oboe & strings.
> It is all your fault, of course; I didn't want to write the blessed
> thing – I am supposed to be (a) finishing a string quartet (b)
> finishing a violin & piano suite (c) writing an orchestral work
> for Norwich Festival 1936 (d) writing an orchestral work for
> Robert Mayer . . .[22]

The suite for oboe and strings failed to appear, although Mitchell
and Reed plausibly suggest that some of the material may have
have found its way into the *Temporal Variations* for oboe and
piano; the string quartet was his revision of '*Go play, boy, play*'
into *Three Divertimenti*; the suite for violin and piano, the 'Moto
Perpetuo' which became his Op. 6, would be first performed
(and broadcast) on 13 March 1936 by Antonio Brosa and the
composer; and the orchestral work for Norwich was to become
Our Hunting Fathers, Op. 8. Only the commission for Robert
Mayer – presumably for one of his children's concerts – seems
to have sunk completely without trace. And there was other
unfinished business, such as *Friday Afternoons*, which had been
impeded by a problem of textual copyright. This was evidently
a composer with his hands full, only a week or so before that
'most surprising day' when he was suddenly invited to lunch
with Cavalcanti and Coldstream.

　　Despite the pressures of work, he still found time to attend
some concerts and to hear many more on the radio, commenting
on them in his usual forthright style. The War of the Conductors
had, if anything, increased in ferocity. 'When F.B. conducts the
chief advantage is to be able to listen to the music without
bothering about the interpretation. The shows are always "just
right",'[23] he wrote, formulating a principle which would be
crucial to his own conducting and to which he returned: 'What
is so fine about his shows are that he is content to give us the

music – without the stunts of a Mengelberg or a Koussevitsky or the ignorance of a Beecham or a Boult.'[24] On 20 January, Bridge conducted a BBC concert in which Haydn ('v. beautifully played') and his own 'thrilling' *Enter Spring* framed 'Schönberg's lovely Verklärte Nacht – which the strings play splendidly',[25] an influential work for Britten as well as an intriguing piece of programming. The mutual admiration between teacher and pupil was undimmed: a few weeks later, staying at Friston, they talked 'until past midnight', about Bridge's 'life, a matter of the Will'o the wisp character of his success both as composer & esp. as conductor', a conversation whose shape may well have influenced Britten's *Variations on a Theme of Frank Bridge*. Back in London, though, there was a 'Very deadly show – a typical, ignorant, listless Boult concert',[26] while towards the end of the year he heard 'Boult sterilize Purcell's very lovely King Arthur': 'Performance (apart from BBC Chorus) was scandalous . . . Boult at his worst & most typical.' But, he very perceptively noted, 'what a lovely style of prosody Purcell has! and fine sense of instrumental colour'.[27] Then there was the 'public menace' Henry Wood, who 'ought to be shot quickly before he does much more murdering of classics ancient & modern'[28] but who, despite this powerful wish, managed to remain alive until 1944.

Working in London meant living in London, so Britten returned without enthusiasm to his old lodgings at 173 Cromwell Road, Burleigh House, while he 'searched for a flat'. This flat-hunting had been given additional urgency by some 'great discussions with Mum on her future – oh these problems!':[29] Mrs Britten understandably disliked living alone above her late husband's dental practice in Lowestoft and was planning a move to Frinton-on-Sea, where she had Christian Science friends; but Britten, just as understandably, found this dubious in principle and undesirable in practice, since it deprived him of his Suffolk base and his childhood connections. He had also been talking at length to his elder sister Barbara about 'troubles of life – rather overwhelming at the moment – she is very good & nice on these matters',[30] which included their mother's planned move and his own sexuality. The flat he found, liberating him from Burleigh House although not from his family, was in West Cottage Road, West End Green, NW6: he was to share it with his dressmaking sister Beth and there would be a room for their mother whenever she wanted to visit London. There were, he discovered, aspects to this process which he'd never quite thought about before: 'A dreadful business when one has so much work to do, because all the furniture has to be procured,' he explained, unnecessarily, to Marjorie Fass. 'However, anything to get away from Boarding Houses.'[31] There were further domestic discoveries in store after they moved in on 6 November: 'One snag about this flat life is the time taken up by household jobs.'[32] By chance rather than by design, he had always until now lived in places where such things were done for him.

During the autumn, partly as a result of his increasing sense of independence but also thanks to the influence of his colleagues at the GPO Film Unit, Britten became for the first and last time in his life a committed political animal. The Abyssinian war, which mightn't previously have engaged his attention, was the subject of frequent diary entries. At first he viewed it with detachment – 'Great indignation & excitement in London' – but within a week he was participating in the indignation himself: 'The Italians begin to use poison gas in their "civilisation" of Abyssinia.'[33] Without necessarily reading very widely or thinking very deeply about it, he found himself trying on some second-hand communist clothes. 'I envy you most terribly going to Russia!'[34] he told the violinist Henri Temianka on 15 November, while on 23 December he wrote 'a long letter to Mrs Chamberlin (Kersty) in defence of Communism – not a difficult letter to write! It has shocked a lot of people that I am interested in the subject!'[35] Shocking musical friends in East Anglia was probably about as far as this interest was going to take him.

In Lowestoft on Christmas Eve, however, he was deeply shaken by a musical loss: 'Hear that Alban Berg dies. This makes me very miserable as I feel he is one of the most important men writing to-day. And we could do with many successors to Wozzeck, Lulu & Lyric Suite. A very great man.' Then he added, above the date, a postscript: 'Go for a very long & mysterious walk – 10.30–11.30. Think alot about Alban Berg.'[36] Henry Boys, who had done so much to foster Britten's admiration for Berg, later remembered the 'absolute desolation' of a telephone call from Britten on 28 December; the following day, in West Hampstead, the two men spent the afternoon 'talking (Berg), gramophoning (Mahler, Kindertotenlieder) & playing (Berg – Wozzeck)'.[37] One can't help noticing that Britten was more obviously moved by this death than by his own father's; and, although this is largely explained by the English middle-class habit of emotional reticence, the sense of a specifically cultural bereavement affected him profoundly. Berg was, moreover, the musical hero he had wanted but failed to meet. And neither he nor anyone else had yet heard the work of Berg's which was to affect him most.

3

'1936 finds me infinitely better off in all ways than did the beginning of 1935,' wrote Britten on New Year's Day. He sounds chirpy, and with good reason, but beyond the chirpiness lies some shrewd self-assessment. First, he noted that he was at last earning his living, 'with occasionally something to spare', and this was certainly true: in addition to his pay of £5 per week from the GPO Film Unit, he had negotiated a weekly retainer of £3 from his publishers Boosey & Hawkes; his guaranteed income of £8, excluding any freelance fees, was approximately double the national average wage. Nevertheless, he prudently reminded himself, there was nothing to be hoped from performing rights with his GPO work, since that became Crown Property. He had 'ideas for writing alot of original music' – a rather important one would start to take shape the very next day – and was enjoying 'alot of success but not a staggering amount of performances, tho' reputation (even for bad) growing steadily': he was perfectly clear about the gulf between quality and reputation, and he had already acquired the distrust of critical opinion which would last a lifetime. He was equally perceptive about his personal relationships, aware of his 'bad inferiority complex' with Auden, Coldstream and Wright, yet 'fortunate in having friends like Mr & Mrs Frank Bridge, Henry Boys, Basil Reeve (& young Piers Dunkerley – tell it not in Gath) and afar off Francis Barton'. Finally, he was happy with his 'pleasant, tho' cold' flat and the company of Beth, 'with whom I get on very well', if still mildly surprised by the notion of housework. 'So for 1936.'[38]

The lucid, organised intelligence of this progress report is something the younger Britten couldn't have quite managed: it signals a newly achieved degree of calmness and maturity. The following day, after a morning at Soho Square and an afternoon at Blackheath working on *Night Mail*, he invited Auden home for supper: 'We talk amongst many things of a new Song Cycle (probably on Animals) that I may write. Very nice and interesting & pleasant evening.'[39] This, of course, was to be *Our Hunting Fathers*, of which he would later say 'it's my op. 1 alright',[40] even though it was actually his Op. 8: that retrospective redesignation – by which he surely meant 'This is my first completely mature work' – seems exactly in accord with the new year spirit in which it was conceived. But it was inevitable that Britten's sense of newly achieved clarity should illuminate some cobwebby corners, and just as certain that Auden should interest himself in this illumination.

Concerning 'young Piers Dunkerley', we should proceed with caution, as indeed Britten himself did: it's as well to note, first of all, that while 'tell it not in Gath' is a biblical phrase about Saul and Jonathan (II Samuel 1:20), who 'in their death . . . were not divided' (1:23), it is also a phrase used habitually by Britten about other kinds of supposedly secret matters. After leaving South Lodge, Piers had gone on to Bloxham, a public school in north Oxfordshire; his parents had separated when he was much younger and Britten saw himself, not for the last time, partly fulfilling the role of an absent father, providing helpful advice and occasional treats. On the evening of 10 January, he had arranged for Piers and his sister Daphne to be among the extras required for the party scene in *Calendar of the Year* in which Auden was to appear as Father Christmas; the other participants included the Romilly brothers, Giles and Esmond, who had famously run away from Wellington to start a radical-pacifist magazine, *Out of Bounds*. Britten, looking on, found the scene 'amusing to watch . . . although I feel Auden made some mistakes in choice – some being definitely Bohemian!' It went on until 11.30, 'tho' I dispatch Piers & Daphne (who make a success) by 10.45'. His feeling of unease remained: 'Piers makes friends with Giles Romilly – not too great, I hope, tho' Giles seems nice, & may broaden Piers mind a lot – which he needs – but he is a nice lad for all that.'[41] This diary entry is important and easily misread. For instance, we may well be amused (as Auden, at this time a 'Bohemian' to his fingertips, would certainly have been) to find 'Bohemian' apparently used in such an archly disapproving tone. But this isn't quite what Britten means: the party was supposed to be that of 'a typical respectable upper-middle-class family', and his point is that some of the assembled extras failed to look the part. Moreover, his worry about the influence of Giles Romilly, though unmistakably touched with envy, was entirely understandable: he rightly felt protective of Piers, a sensitive and impressionable fifteen-year-old who wasn't having a particularly easy time at his new school.

On 16 January, a day which began in fog and ended with heavy snow, Britten spent the morning working at Soho Square before lunching with his colleagues, Auden, Coldstream, Cavalcanti and Wright. Then:

> Take afternoon off to see Piers Dunkerley – take him to a cinema (only see a very poor Tom Wallis–Ralph Lynn show – saved by two good Disneys 'Music Land' & Pluto's 'Judgment day') & out to tea. I have a lot to talk to him about – he being to all intents & purposes fatherless & obviously having a difficult time – poor lad. Giles Romilly isn't too good for him I fear. However he unburdens his soul in a long walk across Hyde Park after tea at the Criterion – & I do feel I've helped him a bit. But what a boy to help! So splendid in brain & form – and delightful company.[42]

There's both tone and undertone here: although his genuine concern and goodwill are beyond reproach, an underlying element of nostalgic voyeurism can't be denied. Britten had discovered the pleasure of giving pleasure, especially to the young, and he perfectly understood that any hint of impropriety would spoil it. When he saw Piers again at Easter (cinema and tea, followed by a long conversational walk), the undertone was more emphatic: 'Bloxham seems a queer school, & it makes one sick that they can't leave a nice lad like Piers alone – but it is understandable – good heavens!'[43] He reported on this meeting with his 'foster child Piers D.' to his friend and confidant John

Pounder: 'I had a long talk with him the other day which was a great strain on me ("the normal functions" etc. etc). You can't imagine how delightfully paternal I can be!'[44] The following day, he saw Piers again: they saw some 'lovely, witty Silly Symphonies', followed by a large tea '& walk & ping-pong with the lad after'. 'He is a nice thing,' Britten continued, 'and I am very fond of him – thank heaven not sexually, but I am getting to such a condition that I am lost without some children (of either sex) near me.'[45]

Britten, of course, could 'leave a lad alone' and he viewed adults who couldn't with distaste: rehearsing his *Te Deum* (a work he had completed on the evening of 20 January as King George V lay dying) with Reginald Goodall's choir, he found that the boy soloist had been replaced because 'the old good one has been taken off by some man to live with him – for obvious reasons – & Goodall is rightly indignant'.[46] He was anxious not only to assure himself of his own correct behaviour but also to distance himself from the 'Bohemianism' of the Auden circle. Visiting David Layton, an old friend from Gresham's, in Cambridge, he approvingly noted: 'He is a very good sort – clean, healthy, thinking & balanced.'[47] (Auden would have aspired to only one of those four qualities.) He read the recently published *Mr Norris Changes Trains* by '(Auden's friend) Christopher Isherwood', and found it 'splendidly done – & very exciting'. But: 'I feel he over accentuates the importance of the sex episodes – necessary as they are for atmosphere.'[48] And when he and Beth went to the first night of *The Dog Beneath the Skin*, he admired Auden's choruses ('the best part of the show was the speaking of them by Robert Speaight') but disliked Rupert Doone's overemphatic direction and felt that, despite being 'very much cut', the play 'even might be more so – alot of it moves to slowly I feel'.[49] Nor did he think much of Herbert Murrill's accompanying music.

Books about the Auden 'gang' by its members – such as
Isherwood's *Lions and Shadows* and *Christopher and his Kind*,
Spender's *World Within World* and *The Temple* – invariably touch
on Auden's early desire to assemble his friends as if they were
a pack of creative playing cards: the Poet (himself), the Novelist
(Isherwood), and so on. Since 'the Composer' had until recently
been a vacancy unfilled, he had been delighted to welcome
Britten into the group. However, among the younger Auden's
less admirable, though by no means uncommon, traits was an
intuitive conviction that everyone else really wanted to be like
him; Britten, with his largely unreconstructed middle-class
values, seemed to him (as estate agents used to say of derelict
houses) ripe for conversion. Accordingly, in March, he dedicated
two poems to Britten. The first of these, 'Underneath the abject
willow', is definitely a call and possibly an invitation to sexual
action; the second, 'Night covers up the rigid land', looks like an
acknowledgement of sexual rejection; but it needs to be borne
in mind that, since these both occur among a prolific sequence
of undedicated ballad-like love poems, there may be more mischief
than passion at work here. That caveat entered, the opening
stanza of the first is fairly explicit:

> Underneath the abject willow,
>   Lover, sulk no more;
> Act from thought should quickly follow.
>   What is thinking for?
> Your unique and moping station
>   Proves you cold;
>   Stand up and fold
> Your map of desolation.[50]

Fairly explicit, yet unspecific: Britten wasn't in love with Auden
and, if he was indeed a sulking 'Lover', the most obvious object

of his affection was Piers Dunkerley. Was Auden advising that Britten should take Piers to bed? He was quite subversive enough. But the poem's message is surely more general than that: Auden simply found Britten's chastity vexatious and couldn't understand how he put up with it (still less, that it might be a vital part of his creative psychology). Britten's response was a brilliant repayment in kind: he neutralised the poem by setting it as a duet for voices and piano, thereby turning it from a reproach about what he wouldn't do into an example of what he could do. As for 'Night covers up the rigid land', the crucial couplet – 'You love your life and I love you, / So I must lie alone'[51] – seems to state a simple truism if it concerns Auden's feelings for Britten, except that Auden had no intention of lying alone for very long.

As well as collaborating on *Calendar of the Year*, the two men were working on *Our Hunting Fathers* for the Norwich Festival, who had specifically asked for an orchestral piece: it was by no means the last time Britten would disregard the terms of a commission. On 18 February, in Lowestoft to help his mother with her removal to Frinton, he had lunch at the Victoria Hotel with 'the very objectionable, self-important, ignorant, bumptious & altogether despicable secretary of the Norwich Festival', Graham Goodes, whom he easily talked into 'letting me do a vocal suite (Sophie Wyss) for the Sept. festival'; Britten thought 'it was only to give himself airs that he ever queried it',[52] although as a secretary reporting to a committee Goodes perhaps had a point. Next day, he recorded that his mother had no regrets about leaving Lowestoft: she was staying with her Christian Science friend Mrs Hill Forster while her new house was sorted out and the dog Caesar seemed happy too. As for himself: 'I personally don't mind a scrap – except for the fact that one suddenly realises that now, one's youth is so to speak gone.' Yet for someone to whom childhood mattered so much, this was a much bigger 'but' than he chose to admit: 'Purely sentimental,'

he added, 'but life is coloured by sentiment.'[53] He loyally agreed
to spend most weekends with her in Frinton-on-Sea: as she went
off to her Christian Science meeting on the second Sunday, he
glumly noted that there was 'quite a little colony' of Christian
Scientists in the town; a month later, at Easter, they had their
'periodical row about going to Communion'. It was, he said,
'difficult for Mum to realise that one's opinions change at all
– tho it would be a bad outlook if they didn't'.[54] Like his communism, his atheism would eventually soften: meanwhile, in his
twenty-third year, he was at last behaving like a rebellious
teenager.

There was nothing teenage about his music and its growing
reputation. Nevertheless, the first performance of his *Three
Divertimenti*, by the Stratton Quartet at Wigmore Hall on 25
February, having gone well in the morning rehearsal, was 'a
dismal failure. Received with sniggers & pretty cold silence.'
Britten, properly unrepentant, while conceding that they were
'not great music', insisted that they were 'interesting & quite
brilliant' (and so they are). As he expected, Jack Westrup gave
them 'a stinking notice' in the *Daily Telegraph*, leaving him mainly
angry with himself: 'It's all silly, as I don't usually care a jot for
critics least of all J.A.W.'[55] But a few days later there was a BBC
broadcast of his *Te Deum* which 'made some delicious sounds'
and in early March Edric Cundell at the Aeolian Hall conducted
the *Sinfonietta* 'not badly': 'I can't help liking some of this work,'
he modestly noted. 'It is absolutely genuine at anyrate.'[56] Between
these came the premiere of 'War & Death' – later known as
Russian Funeral – at the Westminster Theatre, as part of a double
bill with Brecht's *Die Massnahme* (*The Measures Taken*). In March,
he took on two new film commissions: one was a 'rather lovely
thing about English Villages' (*Around the Village Green*); the
other, more urgently, 'a short film on peace' (*Peace of Britain*),
to be directed by Paul Rotha for Strand Films. This was rapidly

completed and at once ran into trouble with the censor, thus creating far more interest than it might otherwise have hoped to generate: '½ centre pages of Herald & New Chronicle, & Manchester Guardian – BBC. News twice. Never has a film had such good publicity!'[57] chortled Britten. Then, later in April, he was off to Barcelona – with the novel excitement of flying from the aerodrome at Croydon – for the ISCM Festival, where Antonio Brosa was to join him in a performance of his Op. 6 Suite for violin and piano.

This took place at the Casal del Metge on 21 April. 'The concert went very well – Toni played like a God, & tho' I was very nervous nothing went wrong in *my* part!' he told his mother. They were 're-called three times. People seem to approve of it.'[58] He didn't appreciate the extent of this approval until he returned to London a week later, to find himself besieged by phone calls, including one from an interviewing journalist at the *News Chronicle*: 'I seem to have had an enormous amount of publicity when away – photos & all – & everyone has seen something.'[59] He added that he couldn't help feeling gratified 'after all the blows before this – and after too I expect': a prescient note of caution. The experience of his broadcast concert with André Mangeot scheduled for the previous Friday was somewhat less gratifying: it had been cancelled at the last minute, after they had rehearsed in the studio, because of an overrunning political speech in connection with the presidential elections. There was no reason yet for him to view Spanish politics as anything other than an intrusive nuisance in his professional life.

Like its predecessor in Florence, the ISCM Festival in Barcelona was to affect Britten in unexpected ways. The first was purely musical. On Sunday 19 April, he heard the posthumous first performance of Berg's Violin Concerto, in which the soloist was Louis Krasner; it was to have been conducted by Webern, but he suffered a nervous breakdown during the Saturday-morning rehearsal and was replaced for the Berg part of the programme by Hermann Scherchen, who had one afternoon to study and rehearse the previously unseen concerto, with Ernest Ansermet stepping in to conduct the rest of the concert. These circumstances must have given an additional frisson to an already momentous occasion, but Britten confined his observations to the music: 'The first half of the programme (Borck, Gerhardt, Krenek) is completely swamped by a show of Berg's last work Violin Concerto (just shattering – very simple, & touching) & the Wozzeck pieces – which always leave me like a wet rag.'[60] To Grace Williams he wrote: 'The new Berg concerto is *great* – Best of the festival.'[61] After returning to England, he went to the work's London premiere on 1 May: this time, Webern did conduct ('not good at all') while the orchestra was 'definitely B.B.C.-ish'. Krasner was once more the soloist in the concerto, 'which is again a very moving experience': 'It certainly is a very great work, & at the end I feel pretty wet with anger about losing a genius like this.'[62] Constant Lambert agreed, sadly recording Berg's death in his preface to the second edition of *Music Ho!* and adding that the composer had 'left behind him an elegiac Violin Concerto of astonishing mastery and haunting beauty'.[63] It took time for the Berg concerto to be widely accepted as a twentieth-century masterpiece – in 1955, the authors of *The Record Guide* used two full pages (more space than for any other single work) to argue that it 'will surely be recognized as among the most deeply affecting things in modern music'[64] – but Britten's judgement now looks incontrovertible: the work's influence on his own violin concerto of 1939 would be profound.

In Barcelona, Britten also made two significant new friends: the composer Lennox Berkeley and the writer and critic Peter Burra. Together with the composer Arnold Cooke, whom he already knew, they took Britten on an unexpected post-concert excursion:

> After the concert go with L.B., Peter Burra, & AC. to a night club in Chinatown – my 1st & not particularly pleasant experience – as a young harlot is very keen on picking my pockets tho' I loose nothing. The dancing (mostly male – & dressed as females) is very lovely. But my god the sordidity – & the sexual temptations of every kind at each corner.[65]

His unease and mixed feelings make him sound very young and completely unlike Auden and Isherwood, who would have been perfectly at home. But Britten is learning: he can admit that the dancing boys in drag are 'very lovely' and he nicely catches the balance of 'sordidity' and 'temptations'. Next day, the same quartet took an afternoon walk 'round the harbour, on top of Mount Juic – a heavenly view of the town & the seaside across the aerial railway to the restaurant over the harbour' and, two days after that, they returned to Mont Juic for a festival of folk dances. Britten became fond of Burra, who was covering the ISCM Festival for *The Times*, but as the week progressed it was Berkeley to whom he became increasingly attached: 'He is a very delightful person, & with sound ideas on music.'[66] They were to meet again in the summer.

The intervening months were troubled ones for Britten, in several distinct ways. He couldn't help being depressed by events in and beyond Europe – Mussolini's annexation of Abyssinia, Hitler's invasion of the Rhineland and, in July, Franco's revolt triggering the Spanish Civil War – as well as by the 'state of music & politics in the world & in England in particular'.[67] He was struggling with *Our Hunting Fathers*, especially the recalcitrant 'Rats', although by mid-June he actually felt 'quite cheerful' about it: having played it over and described it in detail to his mother, he noted cheerfully that 'She disapproves very thoroughly of "Rats" – but that is almost an incentive'.[68] He rashly bought for £6 a second-hand Lagonda, from which various bits fell off or ceased to work before his sister Beth involved it in an expensive accident with a bus. And he began to worry with a new, if not terribly helpful, frankness about sex: 'Life is a pretty hefty struggle these days – sexually as well,' he wrote on 5 June. That weekend he had 'lots of bother with Mum – saying things . . . that arn't polite, conventional, or innocent'. An interestingly positive aspect to his unhappy state, however, was a difference in the way he heard music: after listening to the Adagietto from Mahler's fifth symphony, he went 'to bed with a nice (if erotic) taste in my mouth',[69] though he couldn't have guessed that this movement would one day be inextricably linked in the world's mind with *Death in Venice*. On 7 July, he set off for Crantock in Cornwall, where he hoped to spend a peaceful summer walking and composing in a chalet rented from Ethel Nettleship; she was Augustus John's sister-in-law and sister of the singer and singing teacher Ursula Nettleship. It was 'perfectly glorious country . . . and, o, the sea view!' he delightedly exclaimed on arriving: he foresaw 'a pretty pleasant month – working at Hunting Fathers – reading alot & walking the neighbourhood'.[70]

But terrible weather seemed to be following him around. In Frinton, he had been grumbling about dull skies and the north-east wind (which should have come as no surprise to him) and now, in Cornwall, the weather was 'just putrid'. In spite of this, he as usual walked for miles, often to Holywell Bay. Friday 17 July was 'An incredibly violent day – wind, & rain – exhilarating in a way – it would be miraculous if one could discard all ones clothes & walk miles in it'. He was rediscovering a physical relationship with the natural world in a way which Hardy, that great bad-weather poet whose work he was later to set, would have understood; so, indeed, would Crabbe. Then, on the Sunday, the weather cleared, though not before he had been disturbed by new arrivals, with a gramophone, in nearby chalets ('Too much like civilisation'). So he went for a 'terrific walk', lasting over three hours, which took him well beyond Holywell:

> I have never enjoyed a walk so much – and the climax is when I find a colossal chasm in the rocks – miles away from civilisa-tion – climb an enormous distance down to rocky shore & undress & bathe stark naked. The sheer sensual exstasy of it! – coupled with the real danger (currents & submerged rocks) & doubts whether I shall be able to climb the tortuous path to the top. Utter bliss.[71]

This is a grown-up version of his walking and bathing at Lowestoft: the experience is more intense, the response more engaged. How to get this into his music (as Mahler had in his Adagietto)? Perhaps he would find out as he neared the comple-tion of *Our Hunting Fathers*. The excitement certainly seemed to last him through Monday: 'I work hard at scoring – nearing the end of Hawking – & very excited – do 13 pages to-day. – working, morning, aft., & after dinner.'[72] By Friday 24 July he was 'exhilerated at having finished Hunting Fathers'; he spent the day on chores such as page numbering, indexing, cueing and tempo marking, all of which was 'good fun, especially as I am at the moment thrilled with the work'. In the evening, he found time to sketch part of 'a funeral march for those youthful Spanish martyrs'; he was thinking about teenage members of the Popular Front who, he read, had been shot in their hundreds by the Fascists. Writing to his mother, he contrasted their heroism with his own country's political inertia: 'Imagine English boys of 14 even knowing what Popular Front means – much less dying for it.'[73]

On Saturday, he was joined by his friend from the ISCM Festival, Lennox Berkeley, who was ten years his senior and, by a remarkable coincidence, yet another old boy of Gresham's, where he had been a contemporary of Auden: 'He is a dear and we agree on most points & it is nice to discuss things we don't agree on!'[74] Britten's use of 'dear' as code for 'sympathetic, homosexual' was a recently acquired habit. Berkeley had brought with him the scores of two recent symphonies – Walton's first and Vaughan Williams's fourth – and the pair spent 'most hysterical evenings pulling them to pieces'; Britten had already heard a broadcast of the Walton and thought it a 'definite retrogression on the Viola concerto'[75] which he so much admired. They began jointly composing a suite, *Mont Juic* (Op. 12), based on the Catalan folk music they had heard together in Barcelona, and they took photographs of each other, hunched studiously over the chalet's one writing table, pretending to work. Within a matter of days, Britten had become closer to Berkeley than to any other adult acquaintance, apart from those – such as Francis Barton and John Pounder – whom he had known since childhood. The night before Berkeley returned to London, they had 'Long talks before sleep – it is extraordinary how intimate one becomes when the lights are out!' That typically self-teasing phrase certainly doesn't exclude some degree of physical intimacy; but next day, after a sorrowful parting at the railway station, Britten returned to his diary for some firm though affectionate line drawing: 'He is an awful dear – very intelligent & kind – & I am very attached to him, even after this short time. In spite of his avowed sexual weakness for young men of my age & form – he is considerate & open, & we have come to an agreement on that subject.' He looked forward to their working together, 'especially on the Spanish tunes'.[76]

After this, he ought to have settled down to a routine of working, walking, bathing and – a new enthusiasm – surfing.

However, his mother and other family members arrived to stay nearby, together with his old viola teacher's son John Alston, and home-like distractions such as shopping and ping-pong began to intrude; soon he was arguing furiously, especially about politics, with his brother Robert, although after supper one evening they listened on the gramophone to 'some lovely Duke Ellington & J. Strauss',[77] an odd couple by any standard and an intriguing extension of Britten's usual tastes. Then, just after the soprano Sophie Wyss arrived to rehearse *Our Hunting Fathers* with him in the village hall, an occasion which must have startled any passing eavesdropper, Britten's holiday came to an abrupt end in a flurry of activity: two film score offers in one day and a summons back to London.

4

Our Hunting Fathers was meant to be a nuisance: that, among other and more respectable reasons, was why Britten felt 'thrilled' by it. Its deep roots stretched back to the infamous essay on 'Animals' which concluded his career as a schoolboy at South Lodge. In asking Auden to assemble the text – which consists of three poems (the anonymous 'Rats Away' and 'Messalina' and Thomas Ravenscroft's 'Hawking for the Partridge') topped and tailed by Auden's own prologue and epilogue – he was asking for trouble: even before he had written a note of the music, there was a deliberate mismatch between the subversive knottiness of the words and the likely taste (and, for that matter, comprehension) of an audience at the triennial Norfolk and Norwich Festival. And to this, Britten gleefully added trouble of his own.

The first performance took place at St Andrew's Hall in

Norwich on the afternoon of Friday 25 September 1936: Sophie Wyss was the soloist, with the London Philharmonic Orchestra conducted by the composer. That last phrase seems so ordinary and familiar that we may need to remind ourselves that the 22-year-old composer had never before conducted such a work, with such a large orchestra, on such an occasion. For their part, the orchestra had never seen such a score: at a rehearsal in London on the preceding Saturday, during which Britten became 'het up & desparate', there was 'fooling in the orchestra & titters at the work – the "Rats" especially brought shreaks of laughter'. Vaughan Williams, whose *Five Tudor Portraits* was receiving its premiere in the same programme, had to intervene and remind the players that they must behave professionally; but they *were* more professional than most of the musicians with whom Britten had worked, and the rehearsal 'got better & better'. Afterwards, Sophie and her husband Arnold Gyde took Ben and Beth for a meal at the Strand Palace Hotel where, despite 'Arnold's optimism and kindness', he still felt 'pretty suicidal'.[78] The following afternoon, he consulted Frank Bridge and tried to persuade him to take over the conducting – a proposal Bridge, who seems never to have put a foot wrong in his dealings with his protégé, firmly declined. On Monday, there were two rehearsals in Norwich; most of the orchestra travelled there by the same train as Britten, who was reluctant to meet them 'after Saturday's catastrophe'. The first rehearsal went well; the second, with an audience, less so, but by then the orchestra was tired. Britten noted that some people were 'very excited' about the work, which doesn't necessarily mean they liked it.

The oddly arranged Norwich concert on Friday began with a performance by the Hungarian violinist Jelly D'Arányi of the Brahms concerto, conducted by Heathcote Statham, who was the cathedral organist and conductor of the Norwich Philharmonic Society; then Vaughan Williams conducted his *Five Tudor*

Portraits, which were followed by a ninety-minute lunch interval; after this, Britten conducted *Our Hunting Fathers*. 'The Norwich audience had a bad day,' as Michael Kennedy explains in his study of Britten: 'Vaughan Williams's settings of what were then considered to be the bawdy poems of Skelton caused the elderly Countess of Albemarle to turn purple in the face and walk out, loudly exclaiming "Disgusting", while the text of Britten's work contained a dance of death indicting those – many of them among the Norfolk gentry – who killed animals for pleasure.'[79] The latter proved the less controversial only because so much of the text was unintelligible on first hearing, but *Our Hunting Fathers* certainly made its impact. According to Britten:

> I conduct 1st perf. of my Hunting Fathers with Sophie Wyss – who is excellent indeed. The orchestra plays – better than I had dared to hope – tho' one or two slips. I am *very* pleased with it & it goes down quite well – most of the audience being very interested if bewildered. A very complimentary & excited gathering in the artists' room afterwards – including F. Bridge & Mrs B., – Vaughan Williams, J. Moeran, Patrick Hadley, Ralph Hawkes, Basil Wright, J. Cheetal Rupert Doone, Robert Medley, Alstons galore Mum & Beth, Ronald Duncan etc. etc.[80]

The supporting group of just about everyone who mattered – Auden, only just back from Iceland, was the notable absentee – is impressive and touching. Frank Bridge, however, read the mood of the occasion rather differently: 'The quintessence of disappointment on your young face was so marked that had I had a few minutes alone with you, I might have consoled you with the fact "that many a good work has begun its public life in much the same indifferent way." It is extremely hard to bear, but one *must* & I suppose *does* anyway.'[81] Bridge, as it happened, didn't altogether care for the work and had the tactful good sense not to say so until later.

As with his *Sinfonietta*, Britten had chosen to present a challenging work at a moment when something less demanding might have won him more friends, but this at least enabled him to take some comfort from any reception: he would be gratified if the audience loved it; if they hated it, that would be because they were (as he had always suspected) stupid. As an additional insurance policy, he provided an unhelpful and even slightly offputting programme note, a typical young man's strategy. Its opening statement seems straightforward enough: 'Poems on animals in their relationship to humans – as pests, pets, and as a means of sport – have been chosen by W. H. Auden as a basis for this work. To these he has added a prologue and an epilogue.' After this, the paragraphs on individual movements tend to be mystifying ('quick quaver figures in the flutes and bassoons indicate a more subjective aspect of the pests'), uninformative (the fact that 'Messalina' is about the death of a pet monkey isn't mentioned) or simply evasive ('Something depressing appears to have happened . . .').[82] No wonder the audience failed to make much sense of it. A good deal of the music, with its echoes of Berg's *Wozzeck* and Shostakovich's *Lady Macbeth of Mtsensk* (Britten had heard a concert performance in March and written about it for *World Film News*), they must have found simply terrifying. Some of them may have perceived the brilliance of invention but none of them could have picked up the ways in which *Our Hunting Fathers* connects with both earlier and later works: the obsessive, pleadingly repeated 'Fie, fie, fie, fie!' at the end of 'Messalina' seems to juxtapose childishness and grief, looking back to *Quatre Chansons Françaises* and forward to *The Turn of the Screw* (and we may notice how harp, clarinet and oboe, three of Britten's favourite sounds, purify the grief); in 'Dance of Death', there's a gloriously infantile little tune ('We falconers thus make sullen kites . . .') before the hectic climax which anticipates the 'Dies Irae' of the *Sinfonia da Requiem*. The birds' curious names include 'German' and 'Jew', which are isolated and repeated together in the movement's coda, although the significance of this doesn't appear to have been noticed at the time.

If Britten was stoical about the performance, his stoicism was further tested by the reviews. While the *Daily Telegraph* and *Eastern Daily Press* both trod cautiously, *The Times* thought this was 'just a stage to be got through' and wished Britten 'safely and quickly through it'. The *Observer*'s review, by A. H. Fox Strangways, is a sharp reminder of the loathing that these clever young men, Auden and Britten, could inspire in their less gifted elders: the music was 'dire nonsense'; Auden's poems 'remain obscure after a tenth reading'; and since 'what he [Britten] had done was hardly worth doing . . . he would have served his reputation better had he remained . . . anonymous'.[83] The work clearly wasn't about to gatecrash its way into the standard concert repertoire, but it did receive a broadcast performance on 30 April 1937 under (of all people) Boult, which went surprisingly well – 'They do my Hunting Fathers very creditably – I am awfully pleased with it, I'm afraid'[84] – although Bridge gently pointed out that words which had been difficult to understand in the concert hall were wholly incomprehensible over the air; after that, it remained unperformed until June 1950 – when, at Chelsea Town Hall, Peter Pears sang it with the Chelsea Symphony Orchestra conducted by Norman Del Mar – and unrecorded during the composer's lifetime. Thus the most important and original of Britten's early works became, not greatly to his surprise, neglected and forgotten.

He returned to London and the scramble of a freelance life, which had already begun to get him down. 'My brain is getting completely fogged with so many different activities,' he wrote on 10 September, before listing the seven things he had done that day:

> (1) I write some more of the music for Travel Association Film [*Around the Village Green*] after breakfast (2). I go to Ralph Hawkes at 12.0 to arrange about Capitol film [*Love from a Stranger*] (3) I rehearse with Sophie (back from Bognor) 'Our Hunting Fathers' for Norwich – & she sings it well . . . (4). I spent aft. discussing music for Group Theatre prod. of Agamemnon with Rupert Doone & he reads the whole play (3.30.–6.30) (5). I get 'phone calls & letters about articles for World Film News (6) I try also to get together some ideas for the Ob. & piano work [*Temporal Variations*] for Hallis concerts (7) & Our H.F. proofs are to be done.[85]

After all this, he spent a 'very pleasant evening' with the Bridges: supper and then a concert conducted by Frank Bridge. Most of his days were comparably hectic, and even he had to admit that it was 'just abit too much'. And there was more to come before the year's end, such as the reworking of the Rossini arrangements he had made for Cavalcanti's *The Tocher* into *Soirées Musicales*, Op. 9, as well as music for *The Ascent of F6*, the new Auden/ Isherwood play which he received on 7 October, and Strand Films' *The Way to the Sea*. He had discovered two eternal truths about the creative freelancer's life: promising projects turn dull (the Group Theatre's *Agamemnon* would become especially tiresome) and payment seldom keeps pace with work ('There is so much to come in & nothing seems to come').[86] By October his health was affected. First, there was 'this beastly cold which is ravaging us all', he told his mother, adding, 'but of *course* you have escaped it' – a cheeky reference to the immunity supposedly conferred by her belief in Christian Science. Next came 'a very bad nose-bleed (a real pourer)', brought on by 'Overwork

& excessive nose-blowing with the cold':[87] a Dr Moberly ordered him to take a few days' complete rest and, implicitly, to take on less work.

The very next week he was back to his old ways. On Tuesday 20 October, after 'much business', he went to Blackheath to correct the parts and in the afternoon to record the incidental music for *three* GPO films (*Calendar of the Year*, *The Savings of Bill Blewitt*, *Lines to the Tschierva Hut*). The following day, when he heard the playback, he snapped: 'It is *lousy* & completely *bum* – bad recording & all that playing wasted. This is the last straw – what with all this stuff to think about & above all the Group theatre to try & organize I go then in the aft (after Boosey & Hawkes for abit) & see Rupert & really tell him I cannot do everything.' Yet, that evening, he was cheered up by recording his music for *Around the Village Green*: 'Folk & traditional tunes (some from Moeran) – lovely stuff, & I must admit my scoring comes off like hell.' It was his first proper attempt at folk-song arrangement, and his acknowledgement of Moeran's contribution is significant. Afterwards, there was 'riotous supper & ping-pong, till 12.0. Come back feeling that life is worth living inspite of Group Theatre – if one doesn't think of Spain, of course.'[88] But how could one not think of Spain?

There was domestic upheaval too: on 30 October, Ben and Beth moved house, leaving West Hampstead for a larger flat above her dress shop at 559 Finchley Road, NW3, where they soon installed a lodger called Kathleen Mead. While the removers dismantled everything around him, Britten still managed to write a section of music for *Agamemnon*, working 'on any odd bit of furniture that escapes their clutches'. He supervised the other end of the move in the afternoon, then rushed off to Liverpool Street to meet his mother, who was staying with Barbara while she helped with the new flat, before going with Antonio Brosa and Henry Boys to a concert at

Wigmore Hall, in which the Boyd Neel Orchestra performed his *Simple Symphony* ('which goes swimmingly, & gets a rousing reception!') and the 'new' (1934) Suite for Strings by Schoenberg. 'It goes down very badly,' Britten noted, without surprise; he, on the contrary, thought it 'a miracle in every way – very striking & full of deep passion & content'.[89]

Auden's new collection of poems, *Look, Stranger!*, was published in October: he thought the title, supplied by Faber during his absence in Iceland, sounded 'like the work of a vegetarian lady novelist';[90] the American edition, adapting the next three words from that famous poem's opening line, was retitled *On This Island*. Britten bought his copy (it seems extraordinary that he wasn't sent one) on 2 November, finding in it 'some splendid things' and adding, rather drily, 'He has written two for me included in it.'[91] Auden himself had spent much of the autumn working with Louis MacNeice on *Letters from Iceland*, which also included something for Britten in 'Auden and MacNeice: Their Last Will and Testament': 'For my friend Benjamin Britten, composer, I beg / That fortune send him soon a passionate affair.'[92] He arrived in person on Britten's doorstep at teatime on 1 December, 'to stay for a time while we work on the Strand Film. It will be nice having him, if I can conquer this appalling inferiority complex that I always have when with vital brains like his.'[93] Auden's turbulent reputation as a house guest evidently hadn't reached Britten's ears, and on this occasion he seems mostly to have behaved himself; Beth even recalled that 'Both Mum and I liked to have him to stay, he had such beautiful manners'.[94] That evening, Auden announced his intention of going to Spain after Christmas to fight (in the event, he drove an ambulance) and refused to be dissuaded by Britten's argument, which we shall meet again, that the pursuit of his art was of infinitely more value to the world than his probable ineffectiveness as a soldier. As it turned out, the weeks the two men spent working on *The Way to the Sea* were the most relaxed in their entire relationship: after dinner with Lennox Berkeley and Peter Burra one evening, 'Wystan & I talk late into night & he is a great comfort. He is the most charming, most vital, genuine & important person I know & if the Spanish Rebels kill him it will be a bloody atrocity.'[95] On 15 December, after a 'very rowdy & pleasant' meal with Auden and MacNeice, the three men went on to a concert at Wigmore Hall which included both Britten's new piece for oboe and piano (*Temporal Variations*) and *Two Ballads*, settings of 'Mother Courage' by Montagu Slater and Auden's 'Underneath the abject willow', performed by Sophie Wyss and Betty Bannerman; quite what Auden made of his subversive poem's transformation into an almost Victorian-style duet we can only guess.

The Way to the Sea had been commissioned by the Southern Railway to mark the electrification of their line from London to Southampton; its underlying premise is slightly odd, since crowds eager to visit the seaside were likelier to choose a more obvious resort such as Brighton. The tone of Auden's commentary is odder still, awkwardly combining travelogue pastiche with didactic nudges: in a merciless pun on the electric 'power' which is the ostensible theme, we are shown south London lineside terraces, 'the homes of those who have the least power of choice'; an exemplary white factory surrounded by fields turns out to be a Co-operative Dairy; and the apparently pacifist wishes – 'Let the intricate ferocious machinery be only amusing, / Let the nature of glory be a matter for friendly debate among all these people' – come strangely from someone intending to go off and fight.[96] As Britten had acutely noted in a parenthesis after watching *The Dog Beneath the Skin* earlier in the year, 'how W.H.A. loves his moral!'[97] He, though his sense of personal morality was far sharper than Auden's, was altogether more pragmatic when it came to public and political matters. For instance, when Edward VIII abdicated on 10 December, he thought an opportunity had been missed: 'It would have been good politically to unite England & U.S.A. – she [Wallis Simpson] would have been an excellent Queen democratically . . . they wanted to get rid of a King with too much personality & any little excuse surficed.'[98] Typically, this seems both naive and, in another way, far-sighted; typical, too, is his unfocused and half-hearted dislike of 'they', an 'establishment' he was quite keen to join. When his wealthy publisher Ralph Hawkes drove him around in one of his expensive cars, he was as delighted as Mr Toad: 'certainly wizzing thro' London in a 37 h.p. Hispano Suiza has it's points', he admitted,[99] while a few weeks later they were off to Buckinghamshire 'in his superb Cadillac (we do 85 on the Western Avenue!)'.[100] He wanted a fast car of his own and before too long he would have one. He wouldn't be following Uncle Wiz to Spain.

5

Though depressed by the 'approaching thunder clouds' of the international situation, Britten greeted the new year of 1937 with understandable optimism. He was pleased with what he had recently achieved in the two main areas of his professional life – serious new works for public performance and bread-and-butter commissions for stage and screen – and conscious of his good fortune in having Ralph Hawkes as a 'splendid publisher & general patron'. He had plenty of ideas for the future. The domestic outlook had been unsettled, however, by Beth's announcement of her engagement to Kit Welford, a friend from Peasenhall in Suffolk who was now a medical student at St Thomas's Hospital, and he unnecessarily told his diary that he had 'No prospect & little inclination for marriage' himself.[101]

But before the end of January his life was thrown into utter turmoil. The trouble began with a trip to Paris with Henry Boys and Ronald Duncan, the poet and playwright, during which he was hoodwinked into visiting a brothel before going to a scarcely more enjoyable performance at the Folies Bergères. They returned to a 'dank & dark' London to find Kathleen, the lodger, ill with flu and Beth about to go down with it; Britten himself had 'a filthy cold & I must prevent it developing into this plague'. Mrs Britten arrived from Frinton to nurse her daughter and ordered her reluctant son to stay in bed. Kathleen was soon better and Ben seemed to be escaping with nothing much more than a severe cold, but Beth showed no sign of improvement and, within a few days, Mrs Britten herself had succumbed to flu: she moved into her son's bedroom, while Ben temporarily lodged with a friend of his sister Barbara. Beth developed pneumonia and on 25 January it was confirmed that Mrs Britten too was suffering from bronchial pneumonia; in the early morning of 31 January – while her son, still dislodged from the flat by the patients and their nurses, was staying overnight in Hampstead – she died of a heart attack. Beth, in the next room, was too ill to be told at first, although next day Dr Moberly decided 'that sooner or later it must dawn on her' and 'does it very beautifully & Barbara & nurse stand by'.[102] The funeral took place in Lowestoft on 3 February: Britten could say little more than that 'It was a fitting service for darling Mum . . . & Mr Coleman plays suitable music'. When he returned to London, he was told that 'that Beth appears to be forming an Empyena – & operation is considered necessary'[103] – in fact, a minor procedure carried out successfully under a local anaesthetic by Dr Moberly two days later. It was late February before she fully recovered.

Britten's ailment was different, and so was his recovery: he had lost the most important person in his life, who had not only given birth to him and nurtured him but had invented the very idea of him as a composer. His grief in his diary entries is sincere and prolonged, yet coloured by that odd rhetoric of piety which we glimpsed in his far less fulsome response to his father's death: 'So I lose the grandest mother a person could possibly have – & I only hope she realised that I felt like it. Nothing one can do eases the terrible ache that one feels – O God Almighty –.'[104] But writing to his old friend John Pounder he sounds more like his authentic self: 'It is a terrible feeling, this loneliness, and the very happy & beautiful memories I have of Mum don't make it any easier . . .'[105] It was that *loneliness* which nagged at him over the next few months: he described himself as 'a person who has lost a beloved mother & who is going to loose a very dear sister into marriage in the near future'[106] and he increasingly lamented, as he returned to it at night, the singleness of his uncompanioned bed. Wrapped up in this was the inescapable fact that he was too scrupulous to acknowledge and too intelligent to ignore: his mother had prevented him from leading the life he must now begin to lead.

His work naturally suffered from illness and bereavement, and from a bit of bad luck: Malcolm Sargent cancelled a perform-ance of the *Sinfonietta*, pleading time pressures, although Britten suspected dirty work (his own inability to attend a Sargent rehearsal at the height of the flu outbreak can't have helped). On the same day, Wednesday 24 February, he learned that the Mercury Theatre wanted to cut the final scene of *The Ascent of F6*, 'including a lot of my best music – including the Blues', his setting of Auden's 'Stop all the clocks'. He ended up 'scoring piddling bits of music-hall stuff' for Montagu Slater's Left Theatre production, *Pageant of Empire*, the following Sunday. But in between, after Friday's first-night performance of *F6*, there was a brief respite: 'a good party at the Theatre & then feeling very cheerful we all sing (all cast & about 20 audience)

my blues two or three times as well as going thro most of the
music of the play!' Though unforeseen and gratifying, this wasn't
the end of the evening's surprises: 'Then I play & play & play,
while the whole cast dances & sings & fools, & gets generally
wild. In fact have a good & merry time (& me not far from
being the centre of attraction strange as it may seem!).'[107] But
it wasn't strange at all; on the contrary, it seems a perfect emblem
of his new-found independence.

Beth was sufficiently recovered for him to escape for a few
days at the Bridges' in Sussex. Frank Bridge, who had also been
seriously ill during the previous autumn, was now fit enough
for long argumentative walks: he must have noticed a change
in Britten, who had suddenly developed into a much more
contentious and less reverential kind of disciple. Bridge, Britten
now decided, 'has a rather precious & escapist view of art – but
that is typical of his generation – & eminently excusable', while
on the way back to London they argued 'hotly about politics'.
Afterwards, characterising himself as 'horribly intolerant in a
youthful hot-headed way', he worried that he might have been
'hurtful to people who have helped & are helping me in every
way possible'.[108] But everything one knows about Frank and
Ethel Bridge suggests that they would have perfectly understood
what was happening to Britten and why.

Auden was back from Spain, alive and uncovered in glory,
at the beginning of March, but Britten was in that state when
cheerful events serve only to accentuate one's own unhappiness.
The following Saturday was a 'miserable kind of day – as Beth
gets better & her discomfort & my worry decrease, we both feel
more & more sad', a subtle perception of the way in which
worry can actually mitigate sadness. Yet, despite his unhappiness,
it turned out to be a day of some interest. In the morning, he
attended a rehearsal of his part-songs 'I Loved a Lass' and
'Lift-Boy' by the BBC Singers and their conductor Trevor

Harvey for a broadcast that evening, to which he went with Auden, Isherwood and William Coldstream (there was an unheard performance of his *Simple Symphony* on the BBC's Midland Region that evening too); afterwards, the four men had supper together. Following the morning's rehearsal, he had lunched with 'T.H., Peter Piers, & [Basil] Douglas – at their flat – with interesting tho' snobbish & superficial arguments'.[109] Although they had almost certainly been in the same room before, this was his first proper meeting with Peter Pears; the misspelled surname is less significant than it looks, as Britten's first attempts at spelling unfamiliar names were seldom correct. His reaction against the 'snobbish' and 'superficial' aspects of the lunchtime conversation in Charlotte Street came from an enduring habit of Lowestoft common sense which never quite deserted him, even when he became honoured and ennobled. His diary entry doesn't say whether or not they spoke of Peter Burra, whom Britten had met in Barcelona and with whom Pears had been at school (and in love) at Lancing: if they did, Britten must surely have mentioned that he was to spend the very next weekend at Burra's country cottage at Bucklebury Common, near Newbury in Berkshire.

When he arrived there, his reaction was simple: it was 'grand to be in the country after all this time in London'. So grand, indeed, that he was immediately off to view 'a charming little cottage nearby – which I'm thinking of taking as it is such a heavnly part of the country'.[110] As it happened, it was Finzi rather than Britten who would make his home at nearby Ashmansworth, but the fact that he was urgently thinking of a move to the country is further evidence of his newly acquired independence. Burra taught him to play squash at which he, of course, instantly excelled, despite spraining an ankle which, he thought, added to his 'glamour'. On the Sunday, they had lunch with 'rich friends of Peters, the Behrends nearby – charming &

cultured people who have done a tremendous amount to help artists' and who would in due course do a tremendous amount to help him: sprained ankle or not, Britten was landing on his feet. That evening, in Burra's cottage, which was owned by the Behrends, they played piano and violin, 'swapping parts & making the most extraordinary noise', and then talked until midnight: 'Peter is one of the world's dears.' He spent Monday morning finishing *Reveille*, a virtuoso violin study for Antonio Brosa, while Burra 'plays with his new toy, the motor Bike which symbolises his craving for the normal or "Tough" at the moment': Britten here seems obtuse about the possible forms of homo-sexual desire, but he hadn't visited Berlin nor was there a figure such as the leather-jacketed gay poet Thom Gunn (then aged seven) to enlighten him. He was back in London in time to hear Guy Warrack conduct *Soirées Musicales*, his 'Rossini suite', then have tea with Poppy Vulliamy and Ronald Duncan, and dinner with Christopher Isherwood, 'a grand person; unaffected, extremely amusing & devastatingly intelligent'.[111] He began to springclean his life, tackling overdue correspondence and consigning the Lagonda to a scrapheap. After two dreadful months, all sorts of fresh starts seemed possible.

On 25 April, Peter Burra wrote to his twin sister Nell, a singer and actress who had worked with the Group Theatre, 'that Benjamin Britten and Lennox Berkeley were coming during the following week to view a nearby farmhouse they might share';[112] he also mentioned that he would be at the BBC performance of *Our Hunting Fathers* on 30 April. But on 27 April, he was killed in a light aircraft accident near his home – 'flying with one of his "tough" friends', noted Britten, still not quite understanding this. He was 'a darling of the 1st rank' with a 'first-rate brain, that was at the moment in great difficulties – tho' this is far too terrible a solution for them';[113] the nineteen-year-old pilot, Allan Anderson, wasn't seriously injured.

Burra's 'great difficulties' with his sexuality had been compounded by his friendship with a young German, 'Willi', who appeared to be a Nazi spy 'sent to Britain to compile a list of prominent British homosexuals'.[114] Of his 'first-rate brain' there is ample evidence: four years older than Britten, he had edited a quarterly journal, *Farrago*, at Oxford; published biographical studies of Van Gogh, Virginia Woolf and Wordsworth; and contributed to *The Nineteenth Century and After* an essay on E. M. Forster which delighted the novelist and was reprinted in the 1942 Everyman edition of *A Passage to India*. Britten, Lennox Berkeley and Peter Pears were among the mourners at the funeral at Bucklebury on 29 April; the following day, back in London (and after a rehearsal of *Our Hunting Fathers* with Boult, who 'doesn't really grasp the work', for that evening's BBC concert), Britten had dinner with Pears and Basil Douglas, partly 'to discuss what is best about Peter Burra's things'.[115] Their decision was that his oldest friend, Pears, and his newest, Britten, should go to Berkshire to spend a day 'sorting out letters, photos & other personalities preparatory to the big clean up'; the implication, of course, is that two close friends would have to sift his papers before they were seen by less sympathetic eyes. The following Thursday, they travelled on a late, dirty and packed train to Reading, arriving around midnight, and then set off for the Behrends' house in torrential rain on the motorbike Pears and Burra had shared, getting lost and not arriving until nearly two o'clock. Their hosts, fortunately, were in London. After completing their task next day, Britten commented: 'Peter Pears is a dear & a very sympathetic person. – tho' I'll admit I am not too keen on travelling on his motor bike!'[116] Britten, as we have seen, loved cars and had in fact just found another one: a Lee Francis, which he bought the following week and crashed before the month was out. Then, on 12 May, it was Coronation Day, with the obligatory weather: a dull morning followed by a continuously wet afternoon. Ben, Beth and Kit Welford tried to escape with a country picnic, but there was no avoiding it in the end: 'Listen to a coronation revue in the evening, after the coronation address by the King (the poor man masters his stutter well), & coronation news – In fact spend a coronation evening, writting coronation letters & retiring to a coronation if lonely bed.'[117]

During the spring, Britten composed music for two BBC productions, *King Arthur* (broadcast in April) and *Up the Garden Path* (June), and began his series of *Cabaret Songs* to texts by Auden, but his most important work of 1937 was unquestionably the *Variations on a Theme of Frank Bridge*, Op. 10. At the beginning of June, Boyd Neel, with whom he had worked on the music for *Love from a Stranger*, was invited to bring his string orchestra to the Salzburg Festival in late August and to include in his programme the first performance of a new English work. It was an impossible demand, given the time available, and Neel knew of only one person who could possibly meet it: 'I suddenly thought of Britten (till then hardly known outside inner musical circles) because I had noticed his extraordinary speed of composition during some film work in which we had been associated.'[118] It took Britten ten days to sketch the complete work, and a month after that it was fully scored. *Variations on a Theme of Frank Bridge* is what Wordsworth called a 'timely utterance': a composition for strings in a favourite form and a homage to the musician he most admired and loved, it satisfied an urgent inner need. He conceived the work as a series of character portraits – a method ironically similar to that of the *Enigma Variations*, except that they were all aspects of one character – which he noted on the composition sketch: thus, for instance, the first Adagio variation (after the 'Introduction and Theme') describes 'His integrity', the second March 'Presto alla marcia' 'His energy', and so on through to the 'Fugue and Finale', which represent 'His skill and Our affection'. Britten wanted to include these descriptions in the published score but the Bridges, with typical self-effacing tact, dissuaded him. By 15 July, he was able to rehearse the piece with the Boyd Neel Orchestra: 'I take them thro' the Variations, which will be successful I think . . . the work is grateful to play, & the orch. themselves (a charming crowd) are very enthusiastic.'[119]

The first broadcast performance of *Variations on a Theme of Frank Bridge*, by the Boyd Neel Orchestra, was from Radio Hilversum on 25 August; two days later, the work received its first public performance in Salzburg, where it was the centrepiece of an attractive concert of English string music (Purcell's G minor *Chaconne* and Elgar's *Introduction and Allegro* topped and tailed the programme, which also included Delius's *Two Aquarelles* and works by Rutland Boughton and Arnold Bax for oboe and strings, with Leon Goossens as soloist). Britten was unable to be there in person, but a friend of his, on holiday in Europe, was present in the Grosser Saal of the Mozarteum: 'Well, Benjie,' wrote Peter Pears, the only person in his adult life to address him thus, 'I have dashed back to the hotel so that I can write down at once something about the concert.' He was in no doubt that 'the Variations were a great success, as indeed the orchestra was and Boyd Neel – and I got a *very* strong impression that the Variations were the most *interesting* work in the programme.' He provided detailed comments on the individual movements and promised to collect press reviews as they appeared before signing off, 'Much love to you – Peter.'[120] It is entirely appropriate that the first known letter between the two men should have been packed with appreciative musical detail, for music would never cease to be the foundation on which their relationship was built.

Peter Neville Luard Pears, born in Farnham on 22 June 1910, was over three years older than Britten, but his musical career had hardly begun. At his prep school, The Grange at Crowborough in Sussex, he was, according to his own recollection, 'a bright little boy'; thereafter the brightness seemed to diminish. He was academically undistinguished at Lancing and he left Keble College, Oxford, without taking a degree. After that, like many other reasonably educated but unfocused young men of his background, he became a prep-school master and returned to The Grange: it was Nell Burra who eventually persuaded him to renounce 'a life of Grey Flannel Prep School Mastering'.[121] He thus shared with Britten – who, according to his brother Robert, sometimes regretted not having gone to Cambridge – a twinge of academic diappointment which sharpened his musical ambition. This had begun at Lancing, where he played the piano and the organ and 'produced explosive noises on a bassoon';[122] he brought these useful talents to the Lancing College Chamber Music Society, formed by Pears, Burra and friends in April 1926, and its grander successor the Lancing College Orchestral Society. He also sang, first as the leading treble in the school choir and later as a tenor. Then, while at Keble, having tried unsuccessfully for an organ scholarship at Christ Church (where Burra was), he became assistant organist at Hertford College. But it wasn't until 1933 that, with Nell Burra's encouragement, he auditioned for the Webber–Douglas School of Singing ('Your friend Peter,' she was told, 'has a marvellous *mezza voce*, but nothing much else which would earn him a living!') and then successfully applied for a singing scholarship at the RCM. He stayed only two terms, leaving to join the Wireless Vocal Octet, which in 1935 became 'BBC Singers B' and performed both in religious services and with the BBC Chorus in concerts. He also joined the English Singers, a six-strong madrigal group, with whom he toured the United States in late 1936: it was on the voyage to New York that he met the German-born Elizabeth Mayer, whose subsequent friendship was to become so important to both Britten and Pears. Britten, of course, had yet to visit America, and there was one other aspect of their musical careers in which Pears outstripped his new friend. Although he treasured his privately made discs of *A Boy Was Born*, Britten had yet to make a commercial recording; whereas, earlier in 1936, Pears had recorded Peter Warlock's *Corpus Christi Carol* as tenor soloist with the BBC Choir, conducted by Leslie Woodgate, for Decca. As his biographer Christopher Headington carefully puts it: 'we at once notice a thoughtful word delivery and a sensitive moulding of quietly flowing phrases, but also a certain whiteness of tone'.[123]

By the time *Variations on a Theme of Frank Bridge* was performed in Salzburg, the two men had become close friends. They played tennis as well as music together and on the weekend of 17–18 July were guests of the Behrends at their Berkshire home, the Grey House. On the Saturday there was 'lots of good tennis' followed by dinner ('& what a dinner') after which Britten and Pears were able to 'play & sing to a late hour'; on Sunday, however, Britten found himself having 'to stand up to the whole company to defend my (& all our set) "left" opinions', adding 'I am not at all vanquished, but maintain my points'.[124] The other weekend guests included Robert Bernays, an MP who was Parliamentary Secretary to the Minister of Health, so Britten had some reason to feel pleased with himself; the Behrends themselves would have been more likely to share many of his views. His thank-you letter to Mary Behrend – listing 'the lovely tennis, bathing, conversation, (tho' I fear I overstepped the mark *there*!), company in general, exquisite hospitality in every direction, & last but not least, the really overwhelming kindness of the hosts'[125]– is full of a warmth which anticipates his later relationship with another sympathetic and civilised surrogate mother, Elizabeth Mayer.

Britten's notion of acquiring a cottage, or even a farmhouse, near Newbury had been supplanted, after Peter Burra's death, by a much better idea. He loved Suffolk and by now must have begun to see that the absence of living parents there might be a reason to love it more rather than less; his share of his mother's estate, following the sale of her house in Frinton, came to just under £2,000. The Welfords of Peasenhall Hall, his sister Beth's future parents-in-law, were hospitable and Arthur Welford was, rather usefully, an architect; so Britten had not only a base for his house-hunting but a free, on-the-spot source of expert advice. In late June, after several disappointments, he came across 'a Mill at Snape, which seems to have possibilities – but alot of alterations to be made'.[126] By the time he went over the mill again on 11 July, with an advisory committee comprising both his sisters and his prospective brother-in-law, Kit's father had drawn up plans for its conversion: 'The place seems definitely good to-day, & I almost decide to make them an offer. The others seem impressed too.'[127] He stayed at Peasenhall until the middle of the week, by which time he had made up his mind. 'I think I have found a good spot to live in – it is an old Mill & house in a quaint old village called Snape near here,' he told Nell Burra on 14 July. 'It isn't exactly isolated, but it has a grand view and alot of land to ensure its not being built round.'[128] He would share it with Lennox Berkeley, although it would be 'ages' before they could move in. He completed the purchase in August and the Old Mill was ready for habitation by the following April.

Not all his schemes were as sensible as that one. A year earlier, on 3 July 1936, he had given tea to Harry Morris, 'the little boy Barbara found', who was 'getting on with his fiddle, & sings very nicely, & seems very intelligent'; he was also keen on gym and showed Britten 'some of his especial tricks'.[129] The combination of musicianship and sportsmanship was always a winning one, but Harry differed from Britten's other young protégés in coming from a poor north London background;

Barbara had 'found' him in the course of her work as matron and health visitor at a medical centre in Kilburn. The two met again in the spring of 1937 and on 26 June spent 'a very enjoyable afternoon' on Hampstead Heath, followed by tea and talk: 'he is a splendid little boy & I hope I'll be able to do something for him', Britten wrote.[130] This 'something' had by mid-July formed into the idea that Harry should accompany him on holiday to Cornwall, a suggestion Britten very properly discussed with Harry's parents, who were 'charming & terribly keen for him to come with me'.[131] The holiday was to begin on 13 August. Harry spent the previous night at the flat in Finchley Road where he was already 'very homesick' (a possibility which, since the boy had never before left home, may not have occurred to anyone), but he cheered up next morning with the prospect of a train journey on the Cornish Riviera from Paddington: 'it is exhilerating to see his face when he sees things for the first time', wrote Britten, noting with extra pleasure that 'the meal in the dining car is the most tremendous experience'. But this pleasure was somewhat dented by their reception on the station platform at Newquay, where they were met by his brother Robert and his wife Marjorie, already installed at Crantock, who 'don't seem too pleased to see us'.[132]

For a while, despite Robert's habit of 'asking his newly made & very intimate friends in', the holiday went reasonably well: 'Harry is terribly struck by his first visit to a theatre!' Britten wrote on 18 August. 'He is getting on very well with us.' On 23 August, he had to attend the Boyd Neel Orchestra's final rehearsal of *Variations on a Theme of Frank Bridge* in London; his brother, who had other business there, accompanied him on an early train, leaving Harry in the care of his sister Beth, who had arrived in Cornwall with her future husband Kit a fortnight earlier. After the rehearsal and dinner with the Bridges, who were 'very excited' by the work, Britten went to meet Robert at Barbara's flat, 'to find them all wild with "in loco parentis" wrath at my so-called conceit and bumptiousness . . . we have (R. & I) a first-rate bust up, & part for rest of evening'.[133] The two brothers reunited to catch the 2 a.m. train from Paddington although by the time they reached Cornwall they were at opposite ends of it: Robert at the back and Ben, having charmed his way into riding with the driver and fireman, in the cab for the last stage; the latter, as if in a scene from *Night Mail*, cheerfully showed him how the boiler worked. The next day he noted that the 'split is very marked', but added stoically: 'Personally I'm not distressed.' Harry, however, *was* distressed by something on or soon after 25 August – the evening Britten tuned in to Hilversum to hear his *Bridge* premiere – although we may never know quite what: the diary is uncharacteristically silent for five days. The boy returned to London, presumably accompanied on the train journey by one of the adults, and the holiday staggered miserably on until the end of the month.

What went wrong? Harry later told his wife and son that 'he had been alarmed by what he understood as a sexual approach from Britten in his bedroom'.[134] Those are the film-maker and writer John Bridcut's words, of which the careful and crucial ones are 'what he understood as'. It seems unlikely that the scrupulous Britten would have made 'a sexual approach' and almost inconceivable that he would have done so while sharing a small holiday bungalow with, among others, Robert and Beth; moreover, such behaviour would have run directly counter to the basis of his relationships with boys, which were founded on providing and sharing essentially innocent pleasures. Two possible explanations spring to mind. The likelier one is that Britten was indulging in some sort of horseplay, forgetful of the fact that Harry's experience didn't include the odd antics of prep-school boys and their eccentric masters; he had just heard the successful first broadcast of his splendid new work and may have been in a foolishly cheerful mood. A remoter possibility is that Harry had overheard the brothers arguing about the inadvisability of Ben travelling around the country with otherwise unaccompanied small boys – perhaps with some vivid expression of why this was such a bad idea – and, feeling in any case homesick and unhappy in the tense atmosphere, saw this as a way of enabling his departure. We know that the matter had been raised between Robert and Ben well before their London 'bust up' from a later diary entry: on 17 October, Britten records his lasting anger that 'such things were said by a comparative stranger',[135] which implies one of those 'newly made & very intimate friends' from the second day of the holiday had been involved too. Harry himself curiously 'suggested that the episode, whatever it was, happened on the second day of the holiday';[136] if it had actually been 'a sexual approach', he is unlikely to have waited until the thirteenth day before he reacted to it.

A good intention had badly misfired, and on such occasions the author of the intention may be hurt at least as deeply as the recipient. But it's worth sparing a moment's sympathy for the third party in the affair, Robert Britten. As the headmaster of a prep school, for whom any taint of sexual scandal involving a boy would have been professionally disastrous, he had reason to be appalled by his younger brother's recklessness: he knew precisely what 'in loco parentis' meant and can hardly be blamed for feeling that Ben had been either cavalier or obtuse. Ben certainly seemed to have become emboldened, perhaps partly on account of his developing friendship with Christopher Isherwood who, like Auden (though in a less hectoring style), was keen that Britten should sort out his sexuality. As Isherwood wrote later: 'We were extraordinarily interfering in this respect – as bossy as a pair of self-assured young psychiatrists.'[137] On 25 June, Britten and Isherwood met for a meal and 'a grand evening': 'He gives me sound advice about many things, & he being a grand person I shall possibly take it.'[138] This advice, we can only guess, was *carpe diem*; by way of reinforcing it, the following week, Isherwood took Britten on what looks like a carefully planned nocturnal expedition:

> After dinner I go out with Christopher Isherwood, sit for ages in Regent's Park & talk very pleasantly & then on to Oddenino's & Café Royal – get slightly drunk, & then at mid-night go to Jermyn St & have a turkish Bath. Very pleasant sensations – completely sensuous, but very healthy. It is extraordinary to find one's resistance to anything gradually weakening. The trouble was that we spent the night there – couldn't sleep a wink on the hard beds, in the perpetual restlessness of the surroundings.[139]

This does look obtuse: the Savoy Turkish Baths in Jermyn Street 'was a commercial space in which men felt safe enough to have sex relatively openly – a public space which was, in effect, private'.[140] But Britten's apparent point-missing is teasingly deliberate: that wasn't quite what he wanted and, rather to his credit, he resisted Isherwood's attempt to badger him into it. They had evidently talked about Harry Morris during their long conversations for, a few days later, Britten invited them both to tea: he thought this a success – Harry 'is a charming boy, & C. wanted to meet him'[141] – but Isherwood may well have felt a bit puzzled. About this time, he rather helplessly asked Basil Wright: 'Well, have we convinced Ben he's queer, or haven't we?'[142]

Two postscripts to the Harry Morris episode seemed to confirm Britten in his belief that he had nothing to be ashamed of. On 11 October, Harry came to tea: 'I am surprised to find that after the slight over-dose of him in the summer, I am pleased to see him.'[143] And on 24 February 1938, Britten visited the

Morrises to discuss Harry's future: noticing that the boy was a keen draughtsman, he thought he might be able (with Arthur Welford's help) to guide him towards a career in architecture. 'I go & see the Morris family about Harry's future – architect or butcher – butcher wins. Take Harry to Film.'[144] With 'butcher wins', he graciously admits defeat: he had done his best.

6

Mrs Britten's death had enabled her son to buy the Old Mill; Peter Burra's death had led to Britten's friendship with Peter Pears. One signalled his intention to make his permanent home in Suffolk and eventually to reject London; the other, his emotional commitment to someone outside the flamboyantly bohemian Auden–Isherwood set. These were life-defining events, and their consequences were lifelong.

Immediately after the unhappy end of the Cornish holiday, Britten and Pears decided to share a London flat – 'He's a dear – & I'm glad I'm going to live with him'[145] – although they weren't to move in to 43 Nevern Square, SW5, until 16 March 1938. In any case, Beth's forthcoming marriage meant leaving 559 Finchley Road and, as far as Ben was concerned, this couldn't happen soon enough, even though it involved a complicated division of his belongings between Peasenhall (where they were both to be temporarily based), an outbuilding at the Old Mill and the room in Hampstead which he was to use when he had to be in London: 'Beth & I are in such a state that we almost want to pack each other,'[146] he told Mary Behrend on 17 October. They actually moved out three days later: 'I am heartily glad to be rid of 559 Finchley Road – it might have been a nice house, but all these memories are too bitter – The loss of Mum & Pop, instead of lessening, seems to be more & more apparent every day.'[147] Houses and their ghosts: it was a theme to which he would return, more than once. Pears, meanwhile, was about to leave for America for another two-month tour with the New English Singers. Writing from Peasenhall on 24 October, Britten (in his earliest extant letter to Pears) not only wished him well on his travels but, very significantly, resolved to make the same journey: 'I envy you alot going all over America – it would be good fun to go – In fact I must go myself before long – One of the thousand & one things I'm going to do before long.' He forecast a winter of great compositional activity in his friend's absence: he was 'on first-rate terms with the Muse', he said, and he promised 'More songs, & with luck a piano concerto'. And there was another resolution: 'Next year must be the beginning of grand things. Singing & life in general.' In signing off with 'All my love & Bon Voyage', he styled himself, as Pears had done, 'Benjie'.[148]

The songs Britten mentioned were the ongoing series of Auden settings, of which *On This Island*, Op. 11, was conceived as a first instalment: Sophie Wyss performed them, accompanied by the composer, in a BBC contemporary music concert on 19 November. The piano concerto was, at this point, little more than a vague ambition – though one strong enough for him to speak of it to Ralph Hawkes. Britten had recently completed a BBC commission, the incidental music for a religious programme, *The Company of Heaven*, broadcast on 29 September: it was performed by Sophie Wyss, Peter Pears and the BBC Chorus and Orchestra, conducted by Trevor Harvey. Although it contains the first music written by him specifically for Pears, a setting of 'A thousand gleaming fires' by Emily Brontë, Britten had become 'bored' with the rest of it: when he went over the score with Robin Whitworth, the programme's producer, he rather sourly remarked that he seemed 'pleased – so I suppose it's the kind of stuff he wants'.[149] But as the rehearsals progressed, he warmed to the work, until on the evening of the transmission he had to admit: 'My side of it goes marvellously – & I do like some of it.' He admitted that he didn't really understand the programme, adding: 'What interests me is that I have nice words to set.'[150] A week later – having in the meantime been to Paris with the Bridges and returned to hear Boyd Neel give the London premiere of his *Bridge* variations at Wigmore Hall – he visited the Leeds Festival with the Behrends, who took him off to Haworth to see the Brontë parsonage: 'Appallingly dark & bleak country – all stones are black – no wonder that Wuthering Heights ensued!'[151] That evening they heard Lennox Berkeley conduct the first performance of his oratorio *Jonah*; Britten was to see a good deal of Berkeley during the remainder of 1937, as he completed the scoring of their 'Catalan suite', *Mont Juic*, which received its first performance in a BBC light music concert, conducted by Joseph Lewis, on 8 January 1938. He was also, at John Pudney's request, writing the incidental music (which he thought 'awful muck') for a BBC series called *Lines on the Map*.

In much of this work, there's a sense of loose ends being tied up, as if in preparation for some big new undertaking. On 14 December, Ralph Hawkes told Kenneth Wright at the BBC that Britten was keen to write a piano concerto for the following year's Proms. Wright didn't hesitate: he immediately invited Britten not only to produce the concerto but to perform it as soloist. Britten, however, did hesitate: he was in Peasenhall, suffering from the aftermath of dental problems combined with overwork and his usual winter cold, while preparing for his sister's wedding; so he had excuses to cover what may well have been an attack of paralysing nervousness. On 16 January, he replied to Wright in a tone of transparently feigned lightness: 'Anyhow of course I should be honoured to play the old Concerto at the Proms. next season. So far there's not an awful lot written, but what there is in my head seems to me pretty satisfactory.'[152]

Beth Britten married Kit Welford at St Michael's Church in Peasenhall on 22 January 1938. She was adamant that Ben should give her away, 'as he had looked after me when I was ill and supported me through all the dreadful years when he and I had lost both our parents', but Robert was equally convinced that he should do so: 'there was practically a fight outside the Yoxford Arms where all the Britten contingent stayed the night before the wedding'.[153] Perhaps this ludicrous scene came back to him later, when he was envisaging social mayhem in the not greatly dissimilar Loxford for *Albert Herring*. The bride had her way. The photographs taken on the day show Britten looking perfectly turned out, as he always was on such formal occasions, and wearing that enigmatic, slightly amused smile which would so often appear on his public face. Beth and Kit, not keen to stay on indefinitely at Peasenhall, were to have use of the Old Mill when they were not in London and would become its effective caretakers during Ben's absence in America. This building, with its associated pleasures and traumas, was one of Britten's two major concerns – the other was the piano concerto – during the first half of the year.

The previous July, just after he decided to buy the Old Mill, he had written of his prospective tenant, Lennox Berkeley: 'He is a dear & I'm glad I'm going to live with him.'[154] Those are exactly the words he would use, only five weeks later, about Pears and the flat in Nevern Square. The cynical reader will suspect him of a kind of Bunburyism, with one lover for the town and another for the country, but that wasn't the case: for one thing, neither man was Britten's lover, though each hoped to be; for another, Berkeley and Pears were perfectly good if not close friends with each other. Britten already had reservations about Berkeley: 'I always feel better towards L.B. when I am with him,'[155] he wrote on 20 September, a subtle remark which implies that he had doubts about his friend *in absentia* which were charmed away by his good company. These doubts had to do less with his music, about which Britten was generous, than with his unreciprocated sexual interest in Britten and his Catholicism. Berkeley spent Christmas 1937 in retreat at the Benedictine monastery of Solesmes in France and was in Paris, staying with his friend Jean Françaix, when he heard of Ravel's death on 28 December; he attended the funeral on 30 December before returning to work on *The Judgement of Paris*, an uncommissioned ballet score which he tried unsuccessfully to place with the Ballet Russe de Monte Carlo. However, after his return to London in February – with Françaix, who was to rehearse his *Le roi nu* with the Vic–Wells Ballet – he played through *The Judgement of Paris* at Sadler's Wells to the company's director Ninette de Valois, chief choreographer Frederick Ashton and music director Constant Lambert: Ashton agreed to choreograph it and a first performance was scheduled for 10 May.

Meanwhile, conversion of the Old Mill continued and the day when Britten could take possession neared. The sails and other apparatus had already been removed from the main round section and the roof lowered; the two circular rooms were to be his bedroom on the first floor and his studio beneath. The mill cottages were turned into Berkeley's studio, bedrooms and a living room; these rooms were connected to the mill by a new single-storey construction housing boiler and bathroom with (an odd school-like feature) two adjacent shower heads. Britten was to have his piano in the round studio, while Berkeley's would be at one end of the former cottages, as audibly distant as possible. But on 12 March, as Hitler invaded Austria, Britten thought it might never happen: 'War within a month at least, I suppose & end to all this pleasure – end of Snape, end of Concerto, friends, work, love – oh, blast, blast, damn . . .'[156] His pessimism was, for the time being, unjustified. The 'great move' began on 9 April and on 13 April Berkeley's much-needed furniture and silver arrived; next day, Britten bought 'a 2nd hand Morris 8 – for tootling about the place'[157] and the rest of his own furniture arrived from store. But the building didn't give up its past without a struggle: Beth remembered her brother trying to work in his studio accompanied by the resident insects, 'sitting at his table with a ruler at his side and as the various creatures dropped he swotted them'.[158]

Almost at once, there was trouble at the Mill. Britten had engaged not only a housekeeper, Mrs Hearn, but an entire family, the Byes, to look after the place: Mrs Bye (ten shillings a week) helped the housekeeper, Mr Bye (another ten shillings) worked in the garden and Master Bye tended the boiler for five bob. Beth's mother-in-law Mrs Welford, who had more experience of domestic management, quickly saw that the Byes were doing next to nothing for their £1 5s a week and advised Britten to sack the lot of them, which he did on 28 April. Meanwhile, his friend Poppy Vulliamy had persuaded him to take on a boy from her Basque refugee camp, Andoni Barrutia, who soon became bored and unhappy and upset Mrs Hearn: as with Harry Morris, he had assumed that a boy from a very different background would be like him, and the arrangement ended after a fortnight. Britten summarised these events in an exasperated letter to John Pounder, who had been staying at the Nevern Square flat while Pears was singing at Glyndebourne: 'Briefly; the crisis has been: sacking of a complete family working here: reorganising of whole house: notice of housekeeper: pacifying of ditto: Andoni is going – which bleeds my heart but it better on the whole: And the moods & temperaments connected with all these.'[159] 'It's been hard to work on top of it all,' he told Ralph Hawkes on 5 May, 'but I have been hard at the big B.B.C. Holy show & nearly got that off my chest.' This was *The World of the Spirit*, to be broadcast at Whitsun. 'I have had to put the old Concerto aside for a bit,' he added, despite the fact that Henry Wood was impatient to see and hear it. 'I wonder if you could use your proverbial tact & keep him quiet for a week or two to give me time to finish the sketch, prepare the two-piano version, & practise the damn thing.'[160]

On 10 May, as planned, Berkeley's *The Judgement of Paris* received its premiere at Sadler's Wells as part of a fund-raising gala programme which also included Arthur Bliss's *Checkmate*, Constant Lambert's *Horoscope* and the Meyebeer/Lambert *Les Patineurs*: Britten thought it 'very good' and enjoyed the party afterwards 'with Freddy Ashton – the dancers – & C. Lambert'.[161] Berkeley's former partner José Raffalli had come over from Paris for the occasion and subsequently went with him to the Old Mill; John Pounder was staying at Nevern Square; a few days later, another old schoolfriend of Britten's, the 'decidedly bearable' Francis Barton, arrived for a visit. When Pears returned from Glyndebourne he observed, correctly and a shade suspiciously, that their flat 'looked as though you might have been entertaining someone'.[162] One way and another, it was obviously a time for rediscovering old friends. In June, the sixteenth ISCM Festival – at which the Boyd Neel String Orchestra performed *Variations on a Theme of Frank Bridge* – was held in London, and there Britten bumped into another old friend, the conductor Hermann Scherchen, who enjoyed the *Variations* and wanted to programme the piece. From him Britten learned that Scherchen's son Wulff, with whom he had so memorably shared a raincoat during an earlier ISCM Festival, was now living in Cambridge with his mother Gustel; he was studying at the Perse School and hoping to win a scholarship to Christ's College. Perhaps Britten, with his East Anglian base, would care to get in touch with him?

He wasted no time. On 25 June, the day after the festival ended, he wrote to Wulff. 'I do not know whether you will remember me or not,' he began, before reminding him of 'one day in Siena' and making it clear that he was writing at Wulff's father's suggestion. Although he now had a flat in London, he lived 'mostly in a windmill in Suffolk', a slightly misleading description of the saucepan-shaped building which the Old Mill had become, and hoped he might either 'come & fetch you in a car' from Cambridge; alternatively, they could meet in London.[163] Windmill apart, it is a scrupulous letter, both proper and persuasive, and its author can hardly have anticipated Wulff's return-of-post reply (which he was not, in fact, at home to receive, having gone to visit the Bridges in Sussex). Wulff began, winningly, 'Dear ?', going on to explain that he was 'quite at a loss whether to address you "Dear Sir", "Benjamin", "Britten", or just "Hello, old chap . . ."' He remembered their previous meeting very well:

> Wasn't that day in Sienna a whole 'family' outing, with the whole orchestra and that wonderful saxophonist Rascher, who is by now professor in Sweden or somewhere? We two went tramping to the piazza something or other and explored the 'guildahalla'. Nein? I was in shorts and sandals (as I am now) and it started to rain. I got thoroughly wet, but it was worth it! – pleasant reminiscences of a glorious past! (Excuse my poetic strain).
>
> At the moment, I am basking in the sun, only the sun doesn't appear to be there somehow. Curious fact, but there it is. It is very nice of you to ask me to come and see you sometimes (rather apt quotation from Mae West don't you think?) I should just love to come and have a look at your windmill. I have always wanted to do that, since reading Daudet's 'lettres de mon moulin'.
>
> I am usually free on Saturday afternoons and Sundays and I hope you will be able to manage a week-end.[164]

As a postscript on forms of address, Wulff wondered about 'Dearest' or 'Darling Benjamin'; Britten had his 'full permission to make me eat my words – with a three course dinner preferably'. Altogether, it is an extraordinary letter, affectionate, mischievous, knowing and seductive: the references to wearing shorts and sandals ('as I am now') and to Mae West, the ingenious way in which a Saturday afternoon expands into a weekend and the postscript's hint that a hungry young man likes to be fed are all exactly targeted. When shown the letter sixty-five years later by John Bridcut, who was making the television film *Britten's Children*, the octogenarian Wulff laughingly exclaimed: 'Full marks for that boy!'[165]

In his reply of 30 June, Britten, while cheerfully insisting that 'if you dared to call me anything more formal than "Benjamin" I should be very angry',[166] sounds slightly wrong-footed. Nevertheless, he suggested that Wulff should visit Snape on the weekend of 9 July and might perhaps take a train to Bury St Edmunds or Stowmarket (Bridcut suggests that he more resourcefully travelled all the way to Saxmundham) where Britten would meet him in the car: 'it would save alot of time', he said, but he probably wanted to exclude Wulff's mother from this potentially fraught reunion. In fact, the moment passed off easily: they recognised each other at once and were immediately relaxed. Ben, said Wulff later, hadn't changed at all; Wulff, on the other hand, had become a tall, self-asssured eighteen-year-old who had spent the past four years growing up fast, with his broken home – his father was based in Switzerland – spread across a troubled Europe. The age difference which had seemed slight when they met in Florence now dwindled into irrelevance; and Britten, more accustomed to befriending adolescent boys and to being befriended by somewhat older men, found himself on the brink of an altogether new kind of relationship.

In Bridcut's documentary, Wulff – by this time an elderly,

handsome Australian who adopted his English wife's surname and is called John Woolford – returns at last to the Old Mill and sits on the exact spot on the studio floor where, that July weekend in 1938, he listened to Britten playing Beethoven for him on the piano. 'The music just overwhelmed me – the feeling that music arouses, the fact that Ben was playing for *me*, not for anyone else,' he says. 'This was a personal performance. I was taken out of myself, and I had an outpouring of emotions – the tears were streaming down my face, and I couldn't stop. I was blissfully happy. Ben stopped, terribly concerned, and found a handkerchief for me to dry my tears with. He said, "Anything I can do? Are you all right?" and I said, "I'm perfectly all right, I'm so happy I can't explain it to you."'[167] That, as Wulff young and old both knew, is a feeling people have when they have just fallen in love; and Ben was, if anything, the more astonished of the pair. It was he who, writing to Wulff the following week, struggled to find the right tone: 'Well, old thing, I did enjoy having you for the weekend. It was grand to see that you hadn't altered from that kid in Florence & Siena (I hope you take that as a compliment!).'[168] Genies are, of course, notoriously averse to being put back into bottles. But Britten is being both artfully and transparently – for it is meant to be seen through – duplicitous: it's seldom a compliment to tell a grown-up youth of eighteen that he resembles his thirteen-year-old self and, in any case, Wulff *had* changed. That was precisely the point. Theirs was now a powerfully different relationship, even though he wouldn't visit the Old Mill again until the autumn, partly on account of his own complicated summer arrangements and partly because Britten had another urgent commitment: 'The Concerto is not nearly done yet – quite desperate is the situation . . . Here I am – wasting my time writing rot to you & the world is champing for my masterpiece . . .'[169]

It was, indeed, horribly behind schedule. At the end of May, he had assured the BBC's Kenneth Wright that it was 'going fine': it would 'be done soon after Whit & I'll be along at once to show it you'.[170] A month later, Whitsun having come and gone, he told Ralph Hawkes: 'The Concerto is now forging ahead.'[171] By 4 July, 'The old Concerto is now finished, & I feel quite elated about it,' but he had yet to score it and was about to be interrupted by, among other things, his first weekend with Wulff. He could, however, provide Hawkes and, through him, Boosey & Hawkes's publicist Carl Rosen with information including title ('Pianoforte Concerto no. 1 in D major'), duration ('roughly 30 mins.'), instrumentation, titles of movements ('1. Toccata 2. Waltz 3. Recitative & Aria leading to: 4, March') and a wry postscript: 'Re publicity, I can't think of anything to say – except it's damn difficult to play!'[172] The manuscript full score is dated 'Snape – July 26th 1938' which, if not quite Beethovenian in its last-minuteness, was cutting things fine for a Proms premiere on 18 August. When he wrote to Wulff on 1 August, he was in the middle of writing the programme note: 'Mind you listen in hard – it is a thousand pities that you can't be there – at least I think it is!'[173] This extensive note, less off-putting than the one he supplied for *Our Hunting Fathers* but still rather humourless, is reproduced with the concert details in *Pictures from a Life*.[174] As Wulff would be abroad during August, Britten invited Piers Dunkerley, now in the sixth form at Bloxham, to stay with him in London and 'hold his hand' as he prepared for the performance. Piers, entering into the spirit, replied that he wanted to 'hold your paw – dirty or not' but wondered, with irrefutable logic: 'By the way, if I'm to hold your hand, how are you going to tickle the ivories?'[175]

The Piano Concerto, Op. 13, as we now know it, differs from the work heard in the Queen's Hall and on BBC London Regional that August evening: in 1945, Britten replaced the original third movement with an Impromptu – incorporating

material from some of his incidental music of the late 1930s –
which, for an eerie moment, sounds like a cousin of Finzi's
Eclogue. In either version, the most striking movement is the
astonishingly dextrous opening Toccata, with its étude-like
cadenza leading to an unexpectedly gentle slow section of orchestral writing; the Waltz which follows is haunted by slightly
sinister voicings, though without the parodic overtones of the
Wiener Walzer in the *Bridge Variations*; the concluding March is
unsettling too, though surely with comic overtones (it feels
almost like a cartoon march, which might have accompanied
the mock-military antics of those Disney characters so enjoyed
by Britten). If all this suggests a work of mood swings, unsure
of its own seriousness, that wouldn't have disconcerted anyone
who had heard the Prokofiev concertos or Shostakovich's first
piano concerto of 1933. And indeed the audience in the hall
seemed to enjoy it, although critical opinion was mixed: an
otherwise intelligent piece in *The Times* failed to see the funny
side of the finale, while William McNaught in the *Musical Times*
returned to the familiar complaint about 'Mr Britten's cleverness'
which had 'got the better of him and let him into all sorts of
errors'.[176] This must have been especially frustrating since exactly
the same objection which had been made against his 'difficult'
works (such as *Our Hunting Fathers*) was now being lobbed at
a 'popular' one: a clear case of being damned if you do and
damned if you don't. Most worrying of all, however, may have
been the reaction of the Bridges and of Marjorie Fass, who
heartily detested the piece (and thought 'he was overworked &
tired & played much worse at the show than at the rehearsal');
when he played them the off-air records made of it, 'we all sat
with shut faces'.[177] Auden, in Brussels, failed to find a radio
which would pick up London Regional but saw the 'rather
snooty' notice in *The Times* and gathered that the work 'had an
enthusiastic reception': he wondered 'about its effect on a certain

person of importance'.[178] This important person was in Strasbourg, where he did manage to hear the broadcast and bravely wrote that he thought the finale 'pompous'. Britten, never good at receiving even light-hearted criticism, did his best: 'I was pleased to hear that you listened-in to the Concerto, & sorry that it came over badly – as it must have done if the Finale sounded "pompous" – which I can assure you it is not, whatever else it may be!' Yet Wulff wasn't so far wrong: if he had written 'mock-pompous', he would have been precisely right. 'I had a tremendous amount of press, which is the best thing of all,' Britten continued. 'What annoyed one or two critics was that it went down so well with the obviously "lay" audience!'[179] Although audiences have continued to enjoy it, the concerto hasn't become a popular repertoire piece – probably, as Michael Kennedy suggested, because the first movement so outshines the others: 'After the Toccata the temperature drops; the musical interest, stimulated by an unusually compelling concerto first-movement, is dissipated by the suite-like sequence.'[180] Though billed as the composer's piano concerto 'No. 1', it was to have no successors.

When Britten played his concerto records to the stony-faced Bridges and their friends, he was also able to bring with him the records of *Variations on a Theme of Frank Bridge* which the Boyd Neel String Orchestra had made on 15 July for Decca. As Marjorie Fass put it, 'when we had the variations at last we cld smile'. These were the first commercially issued records of Britten's music – a surprising fact, in view of the amount which had been broadcast by the BBC – and although he had some contact with Walter Yeomans at Decca, events intervened before any further recordings could be made; Britten's long association with the label, which lasted until his death, would resume in May 1943. However, on 14 July he had accompanied Hedli Anderson in recording four of his *Cabaret Songs* for Columbia:

'Johnny', 'Funeral Blues' and two subsequently lost pieces, 'Give up love' and 'Jam Tart' (the latter a parody of Cole Porter's 'You're the Top'). These must have been deemed in some way unsatisfactory, because on 18 January 1939 Anderson and Britten re-recorded 'Johnny', together with 'Tell me the truth about love'; the producer was Walter Legge. All the poems were, of course, by Auden who, in an undated letter early in 1939, demanded: 'Where are the records?'[181] That question remains unanswerable, for they were never issued; the masters were subsequently destroyed and with them the only commercially made pre-war recordings by Benjamin Britten.

After his stressful August, Britten promised himself a music-free month in September. He went sailing with Ralph Hawkes on his Stravinskian yacht *Firebird*; he spent time 'wandering the country in a small Morris 8'; and he attempted to write letters on an old typewriter he'd been given, with results which might have impressed Don Marquis: 'i hope you have had a good hphliday . . . widl horses arnr'nt going to make me xxx do any work . . . best wishes (signed) Benjimih Brittedn.!'[182] The lucky recipient of that one was Edwina Jackson at Boosey & Hawkes. Wulff came for a weekend at Snape, just before the start of his new term, and Berkeley was there too: the atmosphere was polite but tense. By early October, Britten was back at work. There was the incidental music for the new Auden–Isherwood play, *On the Frontier*, first produced by the Group Theatre at the Arts Theatre, Cambridge, on 14 November; some organ music for *They Walk Alone* by Max Catto, first produced by Bertold Viertel (the Friedrich Bergmann of Isherwood's *Prater Violet*) at the Q Theatre, London, on 21 November; and a much more substantial score for J. B. Priestley's *Johnson Over Jordan*, which had its premiere at the New Theatre, London, on 22 February 1939. Then there was 'the Co-op part song',[183] *Advance Democracy*, a setting of words by Randall Swingler for unaccompanied chorus. And by late November he had started work on a violin concerto.

Peter Pears took the part of the Ostnian Announcer and Britten himself played the piano during the short Cambridge run of *On the Frontier*. This latter task, a modest one for someone who had recently been the soloist in his taxing new concerto at the Queen's Hall, was clearly made more congenial by the proximity of Wulff; Britten, indeed, stayed with the Scherchens both during the play's run from 14 to 19 November and for several weekends during the autumn. Gustel evidently approved of him sufficiently to allow her son to accept an invitation to stay at the Old Mill for Christmas and New Year.

7

Wulff was musical but not a musician, and he wasn't much good at either tennis or swimming: these deficiencies made him an unlikely recipient of Britten's friendship. But he was literary, with a particular enthusiasm for European romanticism and – in poets such as Keats and Shelley – its English equivalent. So why didn't he try writing poetry of his own? 'There seems to be something at the back of that silly old head of yours – & it might help in getting it out – nicht wahr?'[184] It need never be shown to anyone, Britten added, except him. This sounds like a pardonable ruse designed to tempt Wulff into baring his soul, but Britten can't have anticipated an immediate response of four or five pieces, two of which were unmistakably love poems addressed to himself (one was called 'Sturm & Drang'). He wrote a wonderfully sensible and judicious reply, with helpfully detailed comments on the poems which were not about him and the advice to 'Write lots more. Read lots more.' Auden's *Look, Stranger!*, he continued, was 'the finest book of poetry published these twenty years':[185] a piece of cronyism and perhaps, given the dedications in the book, teasing self-advertisement, but also a perfectly sound judgement about what an intelligent young man should be reading. All this advice-giving was making him feel '*very* depressed' about his own great age: 'The strain of becoming a quarter of a century is bearing hard upon me,' he wrote on his twenty-fifth birthday, 22 November. 'It's a horrible thing to feel one's youth slipping o – so surely away from one & I had such a damn good youth too. I wish you were here to comfort me!'[186] Although he wasn't being entirely serious, this is a long way from the childishly celebrated birthdays of his quite recent past. He didn't mention that Lennox had given him a rather lovely birthday present: a set of miniature scores of the complete Haydn String Quartets, bound in marbled boards with white leather spines.

At the beginning of December, Wulff was sitting his scholarship exams at Christ's, where he hoped to read Modern Languages. As these approached, he may have realised that he wouldn't be successful, and this may partly explain the tone of his letter dated 6 December which begins 'Darling Ben' and ends 'Wish me luck darling, all the best, Wulff'. In a postscript he looked forward to his Christmas visit to Snape: 'I shall need a rest. My nerves are getting frayed . . . Till Xmas dearest. All my love.' And then:

> Love, love, love. I'm going to go sentimental & cry if I continue this letter. Try & change Xmas to next Sunday. Oh my darling, I love you. Yours ever, Wulff. Love, love, love, love. (Give my love to Peter & Lennox). Please send a post-card every day till end of week. I'm feeling absolutely desolate. Don't ever leave me darling. xxxx[187]

We can't quite blame it on the exams, nor is it just an adolescent crush, though there are elements of both these things. In a way, the letter's most remarkable aspect is its sending of love to Peter and Lennox, both of whom he had by now met: this quite clearly asserts Wulff's status as part of an emotionally engaged quartet, perhaps even adding a touch of condescension towards his two rivals for Ben's affection. He and Lennox had met for the second time a fortnight earlier, at a party before the last night of *On the Frontier*, an uneasy occasion at his mother's house; in a misguided attempt at rapprochement, Wulff suggested that the three of them should spend Christmas together at Snape. Berkeley, who had returned with Britten to the Old Mill, replied with a frankness which must have disconcerted Wulff (and may well have contributed to the altered tone of *his* letters to Ben): 'I don't think it would be any fun at all the three of us being here together. It's a pity, because, strangely enough, I like you. You mustn't worry yourself about me. That side of it is a matter between Ben and me, and so long as we have settled it, it is not your responsibility or even your concern.'[188] It was, he said, 'uncommonly nice' of Wulff to have felt and thought as he had; all the same, that 'strangely enough' must have stung, while the idea that this was entirely a matter for him and Ben was nonsensical, since for him Wulff was the problem. For Ben, however, Lennox was the problem.

Lennox, who had spent much of the autumn living at the Old Mill (and doing the usefully practical things around house and garden which were beyond Ben), took himself off to old friends in Gloucestershire for Christmas. On Christmas Eve, he wrote a letter as emotionally overwrought as Wulff's earlier in the month: 'Darling, I must write because I can't think of anything but you, everything seems drab and uninteresting except you, so I'm writing in dispair, hoping to feel better after,' he began. He sent his love to Wulff, 'though I can't feel quite so well disposed towards him at the moment as I shd like to'.[189] Ben telephoned as soon as he received this, but Lennox couldn't speak freely in his host's presence, so that evening he wrote again: 'It's almost impossible for me not to be haunted by the green-eyed monster when Wulff is with you . . . I feel an awful fool to have let myself fall in love so violently – I really ought to know better at my age.' He seems to sense (and so perhaps do we) the presence of a mischievous Puck making fools of them all. All the same, he was going to spend January in Paris, which partly explains the bucking-up tone of Ben's reply: 'A very happy New Year to you! I am sure you're feeling fine now that you're in Paris & with José & all those friends of yours.'[190] Of Christmas in Snape, he merely said that it had been 'definitely good, in spite of the very thick snow'. Wulff remembered it as one of those magical times when he and Ben had the Old Mill to themselves: 'Just the two of us walking, talking, trying to add pieces to the huge jigsaw puzzle on the table by the entrance; stoking the boiler before showering in the morning in that little outhouse . . .' There seemed to be 'Christmas dinner every night at one or another of Ben's friends' houses nearby' and he told Tony Scotland that it 'was a time when Ben and I cemented our relationship'.[191] That is a slightly tricky phrase which may, with all the other evidence of their intimacy, suggest that during the winter of 1938–9 the relationship was sexually consummated, but it needs to be read against one of Wulff's more guarded remarks to John Bridcut: 'Oh yes, hugs and kisses – any time! The hugs, of course, were easy to accept, but kisses were more difficult. It was pleasant enough, but this isn't quite what boys do!'[192]

If that were indeed the extent of their physical contact, it may explain Britten's otherwise out-of-character behaviour in January. He was going to Brussels, to perform his piano concerto with the Belgian Radio Symphony Orchestra conducted by Franz André on the 5th, and while there he would stay with Auden and Isherwood. Auden shrewdly or naughtily offered to fix him up with a sixteen-year-old boy who would 'make you crazy . . . Such eyes. O la la.'[193] Although this was just the sort of proposal to bring out the East Anglian puritan in Britten, on this occasion he not only looked forward to it but told his intimate friends, including Berkeley, who reacted with dismay: 'I think you must try and behave nicely there in spite of being in the possession of mysterious addresses. I hate to think of you doing – I mean – oh damn, well you know what I mean.' He went on to insist that this wasn't 'jealousy this time, but a sort of respect for you and a really deep kind of affection that makes me want you to be everything that's marvellous and good'.[194] There is no evidence that Britten actually took up Auden's offer. On the day of the performance, he sent a picture postcard of the Maison du Roi to Wulff: 'Having a v.g. time – the rehearsal was a wow this morning.'[195] The card was also signed by Isherwood (who added a sentence: 'Hoping to see you again before we sail for America') and by Isherwood's unreliable on–off lover Jackie Hewitt, who would later be unwisely installed as caretaker-lodger in Britten and Pears's new London flat; after less than a year at Nevern Square, they had moved to 67 Hallam Street, W1, conveniently close to the BBC.

The party they gave there on 17 January was both a house-warming for them and a farewell for Auden and Isherwood, who were sailing from Southampton on the following day. William Coldstream, one of the guests, noted that the others present included 'Christopher's new boy friend, a German boy friend of Benjamin's, and Hedli Anderson'.[196] Britten himself was both flattered and alarmed by the way in which his relationship with Wulff was now regarded: 'our little friendship seems to be rumoured all over the continent'. 'I personally don't care what people say,' he claimed, a little disingenuously, 'but it might react badly on you – a foreigner in England. *I* should love to shout it to the skies – as you know.'[197] This, given the prevailing

legal position, would have been most unwise, although his sense
that in early 1939 a German in England should tread carefully
was sound enough; either way, the party and his casual introductions ('This is Wulff', 'You've heard me talk about Wulff') did
nothing to quash the rumours. Hedli Anderson sang Britten's
Cabaret Songs and Pears a subsequently lost setting of Stephen
Spender's 'Not to you I sighed', while Britten played the piano
'with great gusto . . . He likes doing what he does well all the
time.' Spender himself was among the appreciative guests and
Wulff, writing after his return to Cambridge, was appreciative
too: 'I'm beginning to fall in love with Peter in the way one
falls in love with a friend and not a sex-maniac like you . . . Tell
Peter he's a darling & tell Jackie I hope to see him again soon.
"Tell me the truth about love" & the Spender song have
completely obsessed me since I returned.'[198] Britten replied that
he was glad Wulff *liked* Peter but that he *disliked* 'being called
a s.-m – even by *your* fairy lips. See? T'aint true – Oim a good
boy, Oi am.'[199] It reads like an artful double bluff: the switch
into urchin dialect seems to imply that he isn't at all a good boy,
yet an impression of badness is just what the tediously virtuous
might wish to give. Roger Nichols connects this with Miles's
'You see, I am bad, I am bad, aren't I?' in *The Turn of the Screw*,
and the register is indeed strikingly similar.[200]

   At the beginning of February, Berkeley returned to Snape.
While love letters (and love poems) continually arrived from
Cambridge, and while Britten replied in terms of almost equal
passion – and began, with Wulff in mind, to work on *Les
Illuminations* – Lennox tried desperately to rebuild his relationship with Ben. It was hopeless, of course, as a letter from Britten
to Pears in mid-March makes clear: 'we've had a bit of a crisis
and I'm only too thankful to be going away. I had the most
fearful feeling of revulsion the other day – conscience and all
that – just like old days. He's been very upset, poor dear – but

that makes it worse!'[201] Among Berkeley's peace offerings was a splendid fast car, 'a heavenly thing – 16 h.p. A.C. Coupé & goes like the wind'.[202] It belonged to Lennox, but even when he was away from the Old Mill he left it there for Ben to drive. And drive it he certainly did, reporting to its absent owner that he had taken it on the Newmarket road at 85 mph 'just to show that the wheels were going round properly',[203] while Wulff remembered that 'we buzzed down the long straight stretch of the new Brighton road at over 90 mph'.[204] By this time, Lennox had gone back to Paris, and Ben seems to have given Wulff the impression that the car was a delayed twenty-fifth birthday present: there is a photograph, taken by Britten at the Old Mill, of the AC with its headlights blazing and Wulff in the passenger seat, a trophy within a trophy. This remained for Wulff, like 'a sudden cold shower down the back of the neck', the one troubling feature of an otherwise idyllic period: he knew that Lennox had been given 'a definite and brutal brush off' and couldn't understand 'why Ben had not returned his present when making the break'.[205] The answer – that it wasn't a present and anyway it couldn't be returned to an owner who was out of the country – doesn't quite exonerate Britten.

'How shall we find the concord of this discord?' It is worth remembering that concord *was* found: that all four men – Ben, Peter, Lennox and Wulff – were to spend their later years in exceptionally long and stable partnerships (Wulff Scherchen married Pauline Woolford on 10 October 1943; Lennox Berkeley married Freda Bernstein on 14 December 1946). However, in the spring of 1939, it was a mathematical inevitability that two of them would be hurt. During the previous year's happier spring, Britten and Berkeley had discussed the idea of a joint visit to America, but nothing had come of it. Now, the possibility recurred to Britten in rather different terms, partly because, as he told Wulff on 7 February, 'I *may* have an offer from Holywood for a film':[206] the subject was to have been King Arthur and the director Lewis Milestone. He could no longer stand the thought of Lennox as his travelling companion and he obviously couldn't take Wulff (ironically, it was the British authorities who would in due course export him to Canada as an enemy alien); but in Peter Pears he had a close friend for whom he had begun to write songs and whom he could accompany at the piano. They were both pacifists who would be not only useless but conceivably imprisoned in the event of a European war; their friends Auden and Isherwood were already in the States. By early March they had settled on a plan which involved first of all sailing to Canada at the end of April. Britten told Mary Behrend that 'the real reason is to do some really intensive thinking & for me personally to do some work to please *myself*'. At this stage, they anticipated that Peter would be 'back at the end of the summer', although Ben had 'other ideas & may stay on abit or go to the U.S.A.'[207] And, apart from all the other excellent reasons for going, an indefinite stay in America would solve both the actual problem of Lennox and the potential problem of Wulff.

In these circumstances, Pears's later account of their departure, in Tony Palmer's film *A Time There Was*, may look evasive or euphemistic: 'Ben began to feel that he wasn't doing much good, although he had actually done quite well . . . And in '39, Ben and I decided that he was not getting anywhere fast enough, as it were . . .'[208] But Britten's (for him) meagre output in the early months of 1939 confirms this. His one substantial work was *Ballad of Heroes*, Op. 14, for tenor, chorus and orchestra, composed in early March and first performed by Walter Widdup, the London Co-operative Chorus and the London Symphony Orchestra, conducted by Constant Lambert, at the Queen's Hall on 5 April: conceived as a memorial to British members of the International Brigade killed in Spain, it sets two poems by

Randall Swingler and one by Auden. The Swingler texts, 'You who stand at your doors' and 'Still though the scene of possible Summer recedes', are solemnly didactic and entirely apt; the Auden, a truncated version of his 'Danse Macabre' ('It's farewell to the drawing-room's civilized cry . . .'), apparently used without the poet's consent, is more problematical, largely because the combination of faster tempo and denser language renders it incomprehensible. The work is undeniably powerful, with echoes of Mahler and Shostakovich, and was well received; yet it marks the end of an era, of a decade and of a period in the composer's life, a sense confirmed by the fact that the Spanish Civil War officially ended just four days before its first performance.

By contrast, the work-in-progress which looked forward to Britten's future was *Les Illuminations*. Sophie Wyss remembered returning from a recital with him by train in 1938: 'he came over to me very excitedly as we were unable to sit together, and said that he had just read the most wonderful poetry by Rimbaud and was so eager to set it to music'.[209] She thought that he had 'seen a copy of Rimbaud's works while he was recently staying with Auden in Birmingham', a likelihood corroborated by Auden's sonnet 'Rimbaud',[210] written in December 1938. When, about this time, Britten started to think seriously about the songs, the relationship between the transgressive young poet and his older friend Verlaine would have acquired a special resonance for him. Indeed, it was to Wulff that he excitedly wrote on 19 March, having just composed 'Being Beauteous' and 'Marine': 'Written two good (!) songs this week – French words. Arthur Rimbaud – marvellous poems. I'll show you them later.'[211] These two songs were first performed by Sophie Wyss in a BBC midday concert from Birmingham on 21 April, together with the *Bridge Variations, Simple Symphony*, three songs from *On This Island* and one from *Friday Afternoons*, the first occasion on which an all-Britten programme had been broadcast. When he discovered that Wulff hadn't bothered to tune in, Britten erupted in fury, first by telephone and then by letter, in a manner which was less tirade-and-apology than serve-and-volley:

> I'm sorry I was such a pig on the 'phone tonight but I felt so damn sick that you hadn't taken the trouble to listen to my concert. You see – the first *complete* concert of one's music is a pretty good trial – & the fact that it was a great success makes one rather bucked – BUT the fact that you didn't hear it – especially as I was thinking about you so much during it (especially in the new Rimbaud songs) – is very gruelling. However one looks at it it is beastly. But I was writing this just to comfort you, but it doesn't seem to do it – perhaps it is a good thing I'm going away. Blast it. – Anyhow Lennox will have listened.[212]

Perhaps it was a good thing, too, for Wulff who, despite being in love with Ben and flirtatiously fond of his friends' admiration, had become increasingly ill at ease when he found himself among the London gay clique – but then so was Britten, who would never really return to it. *Les Illuminations* would be finished on a different continent, almost in a different life.

On 28 April, there was another farewell party at Hallam Street; among those present were Barbara Britten, Beth and Kit Welford (with their month-old son Thomas, Britten's nephew), Hedli Anderson, John Pounder, Trevor Harvey and Antonio Brosa. Next morning, Britten and Pears took the train – 'the way to the sea' – to Southampton, from where they were to sail aboard the Cunard White Star *Ausonia* to Quebec. At the quayside, they were greeted by two unexpected friends, Frank and Ethel Bridge, who had driven over from Friston to see them off. As they exchanged farewells, Bridge suddenly produced a parting gift for Britten, his own Giussani viola, accompanied by a note:

> So that a bit of us accompanies you on your adventure.
> We are all 'revelations' as you know. Just go on expanding.
> Ever your affectionate
> & devoted
> Ethel & Frank
> Bon voyage & bon retour.[213]

Thus a symbolic baton was passed from the outstandingly gifted English musician of one generation to his still more brilliant protégé. They would never meet again.

CHAPTER 4

AMERICAN OVERTURES
1939–42

1

'What a fool one is to come away,' wrote Britten, aboard the
Ausonia, on 3 May: he was missing Snape and missing Wulff;
there was nothing to do except 'Eat, sleep, ping-pong, eat, walk,
decks, eat, eat, deck-tennis, eat, read, sleep'; and 'the last two
days [during which there had been 'a terrific gale'] have been
unadulterated misery'.[1] Then things began to improve: he discovered 'nice people' on board – including R. J. Yeatman, the
co-author of *1066 and All That* – and some of them recognised
Britten from his photograph which had appeared in a London
periodical, the *Bystander*. He and Pears were persuaded to give
a recital, which pleased 'the old ladies' but must have pleased
them too. A small boy had 'attached himself – a nice kid of 14,
but inclined to cling rather', he told Lennox Berkeley, and
there was a 'nice Purser who's terrifically hot at ping-pong':
Britten was determined to beat him at it 'before this interminable
week is out'.[2] In contrast to his letters to friends in England was
one to the composer Aaron Copland, whom he had met in
London at the 1938 ISCM Festival and who had visited Snape
one hot weekend, written amid icebergs on 8 May: 'At last, &
look where I am! On the way to Canada, & surrounded by ice.

A thousand reasons – mostly "problems" – have brought me away, & I've come to stay in your continent for the Summer.' One of those 'problems' was that he'd become 'heavily tied up in a certain direction': Wulff or Lennox or the problematical combination of the two. He outlined his tentative plans, emphasised that nothing was settled, and added: 'I've come with the guy I share a flat with in London. Nice person, & I know you'd approve.'³

That is beautifully and tactfully put: one especially notices the flatteringly adoptive Americanism of 'guy'. He was indeed fortunate in his travelling companion, and would remain so; for now, there were practical advantages (such as giving impromptu recitals) in being with a singer, rather than with a composer or a student just turning nineteen. And Pears was clear about his own position as the junior partner: 'I realised that I was much less important . . . I was perfectly aware of his [Ben's] stature and how great he was, there's no doubt about that.'⁴ They reached Quebec on 9 May and went first to Montreal, where they visited the Canadian Broadcasting Corporation who 'treated us like kings';⁵ a performance of the *Bridge Variations*, introduced (though not conducted) by the composer, and a song recital by Britten and Pears were to be broadcast from Toronto in June, and there would also be a commission for a new work from the CBC. Then they travelled on to Gray Rocks Inn at St Jovite Station in the Laurentian Mountains, where they stayed for three weeks in a hillside log cabin overlooking a lake among forests. It was a working holiday, with ironic echoes of the one Britten and Berkeley had spent in their Cornish chalet, but this time the personal chemistry was very different. 'We are getting on well together & no fights,'⁶ Ben told Beth, with magnificent understatement. He was finishing off a BBC commission (incidental music for *The Sword in the Stone*, broadcast between 11 June and 16 July that year), as well as working on *Les Illuminations* and the violin concerto while Peter practised his singing: 'We usually work it that when he wants to make noises I go out for a walk & he walks when I want to work.'[7]

They spent the second and third weeks of June partly in Toronto – where the CBC had studios and Boosey & Hawkes an office – and partly in Grand Rapids, Michigan, some 250 miles further west, where they stayed with the organist of Park (First) Congregational Church, Harold Einecke, and his wife Mary, whom Pears had met when on tour with the New English Singers. From its name, or even from an uninstructed glance at a map, Grand Rapids may appear to be more exotic than the medium-sized industrial city it is; but, as Philip Larkin once said of Coventry, 'Nothing, like something, happens anywhere', and in this case something happened. It was at Grand Rapids in June 1939 that Britten and Pears consummated their relationship – given Ben's background and personality, it is entirely possible that this was his first full sexual experience – and formed a 'pact': a very civil partnership that would last a lifetime. From Toronto on 19 June, Ben dashed off a clutch of letters to catch a sailing of the *Queen Mary* for England. To Wulff, he wrote excitedly that he was 'thinking hard about the future' and that America, which was 'tremendously large & beautiful' and 'enterprising & vital', might be the place to stay. To Lennox, he more carefully said that 'things are going fine out here', rather enigmatically adding: 'We had a terrific time in Grand Rapids.'[8] His commissioned work for CBC began to take shape, a toccata for piano and string orchestra: with its rapturous glissandos, it would be the most ecstatic piece he had ever written and it would be called *Young Apollo*, Op. 16. When, a month later, it was complete, he described it to the photographer Enid Slater as 'founded on the end of Hyperion "from all his limbs celestial . . ." It is very bright & brilliant music – rather inspired by such sunshine as I've never seen before. But I'm pleased with it – may call it "The Young Apollo", if that doesn't sound too lush! But it *is* lush!'⁹ Even though Wulff was certainly the Young Apollo he had in mind (and Keats, we will remember, was among Wulff's favourite poets), the piece's sensual energy also springs from his transformed relationship with Peter and the 'sunshine' this had brought into his life.

Next, they travelled to New York, staying briefly at the inexpensive, Auden-recommended George Washington Hotel. Although Pears had been to the city before, Britten obviously hadn't; when given a guided tour of the sights, including Broadway, by Boosey & Hawkes's representative Hans Heinsheimer, he tried to look as if he was enjoying himself. He subsequently told Wulff that New York was 'a staggering place – very beautiful in some ways – intensely alive & doing',¹⁰ but he didn't fool Heinsheimer: 'It was absolutely awful. I still remember this unbelievably polite smile Ben had – really Ben always smiled nicely – but really it was a flop.'¹¹ They stayed only four days in the city, though this was long enough for Pears to re-establish contact with his friend Elizabeth Mayer, and on 1 July Britten and Pears went north as a self-acknowledged couple to visit Aaron Copland and his partner Victor Kraft at Woodstock: indeed, the example of Copland and Kraft must have given them confidence in defining their own partnership. They liked Woodstock so much – the Hudson and the Catskills were more to Britten's taste than Broadway – that they decided to rent a studio there for a month: here they established a domestic routine, including time allotted to housework (a concept Ben never quite grasped); after that, their working day was interrupted only by a light lunch until six, when they would set out for Copland's cottage, bathe in a stream, play tennis and finally eat their main meal of the day at a snack bar which was called the Trolley Car. Apart from finishing *Les Illuminations* and *Young Apollo*, Britten worked on *A.M.D.G.* (*Ad Majorem Dei Gloriam*), choral settings of seven poems by Gerard Manley

Hopkins. On 12 July, he returned briefly to New York for a
very successful open-air performance of his *Bridge Variations* by
the New York Philharmonic Orchestra, conducted by Frieder
Weissmann: 'I had to go twice onto the platform to bow – the
orchestra was very pleased & so was the audience (about 5000!),'
he told Beth. 'The write-ups have been marvellous – so I feel
rather "started" in New York now!'[12] He assured his sister that
she would 'adore this city' and seems to have fallen momentarily
in love with it himself – as who wouldn't, with all that applause
ringing in his ears? But his description in the same letter of
'Woodstock in the Kingston District of the Hudson River (look
it up on the map) near the Catskills Mts' as 'very beautiful'
strikes a more authentic note: in New York, as in London, he
couldn't wait to get back to the country. It was from Woodstock,
two days earlier, that he had cabled to Ralph Hawkes: 'JUST
FINISHED TWO NEW RIMBAUD SONGS SUITABLE
WITH OTHERS FOR PROMENADE PERFORMANCE
STOP SENDING SCORES THIS WEEK CONCERTO
FOLLOWING'.[13]

The two new songs were 'Royauté' and 'Antique'; but in the
event only 'Being Beauteous' and 'Marine' were to be performed
by Sophie Wyss at Queen's Hall on 17 August and the version
of *Les Illuminations* with which we are familiar today wasn't
completed until 25 October. Given that Britten had started
thinking about the cycle before the end of 1938, this is by his
standards an unusually long gestation period, covering a momentous period in the composer's life, for a piece lasting around
twenty-five minutes; Ian Bostridge, who is among its finest
modern interpreters, describes it as 'a work of transition'. One
of the several ways in which this is true concerns its actual
structure, which altered considerably from the outline Britten
sent to Hawkes on 3 June, most strikingly in the placement of
'Being Beauteous', which he moved from third to seventh

position – or eighth, if we count IIIa ('Phrase') and IIIb ('Antique') as separate items. This song provides a cautionary example of the danger involved in too easily linking composition with biography. It now follows the dreamily introspective 'Interlude' for strings (where, as in the opening 'Fanfare', we seem temporarily to be in the more innocent world of the *Bridge Variations*), which concludes with a disconcertingly gentle, anything but 'sauvage', reappearance of the cycle's thrice-repeated motto, 'J'ai seul la clef de cette parade sauvage'. Then comes 'Being Beauteous': 'an erotic vision dedicated to P.N.L.P., Peter Pears, it was also professionally the work which represented Britten's allegiance to his companion', says Bostridge, correctly noting that, although written for Sophie Wyss, 'it became part of Pears's repertoire and Wyss disappeared from Britten's life'.[14] The song's placing and its dedication seem unambiguous, until we recall that it was written in March (the manuscript full score is dated 11 April) and that the 'Being Beauteous' Britten had in mind when composing it was not Peter but Wulff, who neglected to listen to the first broadcast performance and so forfeited his claim to it. On the other hand, the later 'Antique' – 'Gracieux fils de Pan . . .' – *is* dedicated to K.H.W.S.

We might be tempted to accuse Britten of having it both ways; but the temptation should be resisted because, although that is just what he is doing, accusation would be out of place. Peter was not a substitute or a replacement for Wulff: they were different kinds of love and so capable of coexistence. Peter was, among other things, a mother to Britten; Wulff, among other things, a son. This, indeed, is something Peter seemed unnervingly to grasp when he wrote to Wulff in June: 'I am looking after Ben as well as he deserves . . .'[15] (Britten's childhood friend Basil Reeve told Donald Mitchell, even more disconcertingly, that 'His mother's voice and Peter Pears's voice were fantastically similar',[16] and the same point was made, presumably by the same person, to Beth Britten: 'A close friend of Ben's who had known my mother well and heard her voice, remarked to me recently, that Peter's voice was very like my mother's, and she had just died.')[17] So *Les Illuminations* is also 'a work of transition' in this second sense: when it began, Britten's emotional needs were confused and unsatisfied; by the time it was finished, he had found a permanent and, as we shall see, remarkably resilient solution to this problem. And that, surely, is why the piece has its false ending. When the phrase we hear at the start, 'J'ai seul la clef de cette parade sauvage', appears for the third time at the close of the eighth movement, 'Parade', it seems to complete the work; but it is followed by 'Départ':

Assez vu. La vision s'est rencontrée à tous les airs.
Assez eu. Rumeurs de villes, le soir, et au soleil, et toujours.
Assez connu. Les arrêts de la vie. Ô Rumeurs et Visions!
Départ dans le'affection et le bruit neufs!

Britten too has had 'enough' – especially of noisy towns and life's setbacks – and here finds the more reflective, elegiac voice of his later song cycles, the new sound to celebrate his new affection.

The effect of 'Départ' is thus brilliantly to qualify and modify the force of the backward-looking 'Parade', a march whose musical source is the 'alla marcia' movement from '*Go play, boy, play*'. The textual source of 'Parade', with its adoring depiction of rough young men, is the most explicitly and violently homoerotic of all the passages Britten chose to set from Rimbaud, from which he tactfully omitted the sentence 'On les envoie prendre du dos en ville, affublés d'un *luxe* dégoûtant' (though the translation he used, Helen Rootham's, evades the 'take from behind' implication of 'prendre du dos'). Was Rimbaud recalling his alleged rape by the Communards in 1871 here? Given his sadomasochistic aspect – his knife games with Verlaine, for instance – it seems altogether possible that he would have enjoyed being sexually assaulted by some 'drôles très solides'. And was Britten, in turn, recalling his own alleged rape at school? That would certainly give an additional – and quite characteristically ironic – bite to his reuse of music from '*Go play, boy, play*'. Such connections can't be proved and would seem fanciful were it not for the recurrence of this juxtaposition of sexual violence and oblique references to school in Britten's later compositions. Here again, *Les Illuminations* can be seen as a remarkable 'work of transition'.

'Woodstock has been very successful,' Britten reported to Ralph Hawkes; it had been 'nice & hot (not broiling like New York)' and he had done 'lots of work'.[18] Britten and Pears planned to stay there, with the congenial company and landscape, until mid-August. Then Ben would accompany Peter to New York, before seeing him off on the *Queen Mary* on the 23rd: he had singing engagements planned for the autumn in England, including the first performance of *A.M.D.G.* As for himself, he told Beth he had no plans for the future, although he had to go to Toronto to perform *Young Apollo* for CBC and he thought he might travel to New Mexico, which Auden was visiting with his new boyfriend Chester Kallman; he more than once hinted that he might remain in America indefinitely. Despite his deep forebodings, he had no clear sense yet that war in Europe was imminent. Having arrived in New York, Britten and Pears paid what was intended to be, for Ben, an introduction and, for Peter, a farewell visit to his old friend Elizabeth Mayer at Amityville, Long Island, where her husband, Dr William Mayer, worked as a psychiatrist at Long Island Home. Here, something extraordinary happened: it may be simplest to say that both men fell under Mrs Mayer's benign spell. They signed the Mayers' visitors' book on 21 August 1939. It was just two days before

Edith Britten with her four children, 1914

Benjamin and his father aboard *HMS Burslem*, 1921

The cast of *The Water Babies* with Benjamin on his mother's knee, 1918

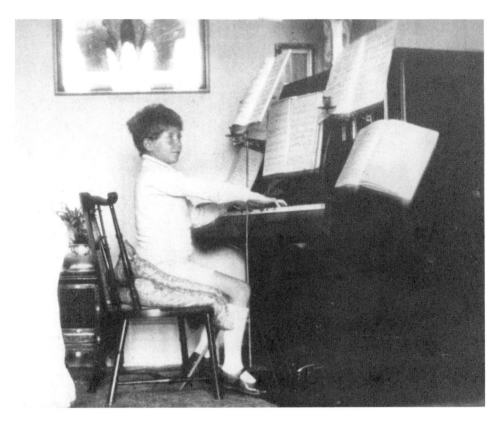

Above: The prodigy: Benjamin with multiple scores, *c.* 1921

Prep schoolboy: with Francis Barton, 1928

Public schoolboy: reading by a river, *c.* 1929

Britten with Ethel and Frank Bridge, *c.*1930

Wulff Scherchen, Britten and John Alston in Snape, *c.* 1938–9

Britten with his sister Beth at her wedding, 1938

Peggy Brosa, Antonio Brosa, Victor Kraft, Britten and Aaron Copland picnicking in America; Peter Pears behind the camera, *c.* 1939–40

Above: Pears and Britten in Brooklyn Heights, New York, where they shared a house with, among others, W. H. Auden, 1940

Auden and Britten in New York at the time of rehearsals for *Paul Bunyan*, 1941

Pears and Britten with his sister, Beth Welford, and his niece and nephew on Snape Bridge, 1943

Britten at the gate of the Old Mill, Snape, 1946

Britten and Eric Crozier with the set model for *Peter Grimes*, 1945

'Now the Great Bear and Pleiades...': the scene in The Boar from *Peter Grimes* with Pears in the title role, Sadler's Wells, 1945

Britten, Pears and the English Opera Group at Glyndebourne during rehearsals for *Albert Herring*, 1947

Britten, Pears, Joan Cross, Otakar Kraus, Lesley Duff and Anna Pollak on tour across Europe with *The Rape of Lucretia*, 1947

Britten in his Rolls with children from the cast of *Let's Make an Opera*, 1949

Pears planned to sail for England but, as he later said, 'We went down there for what was supposed to be a weekend and in fact . . . we stayed for three years.'[19]

2

The Mayers had lived at Amityville since May 1937, when Dr William Mayer was appointed Medical Director at Long Island Home. The family – the parents and their four children – had emigrated from Germany in stages during the preceding troubled decade: Beata, Elizabeth's eldest daughter from a previous marriage, and Michael both left in 1933, she to train as a nurse in Italy and he to continue his education in England; then, in November 1936, Elizabeth joined her husband, who was already working in the USA, travelling with their two remaining children, Ulrica and Christopher. This was the journey on which she and Pears first met; she had been alerted to his presence aboard the *Washington* by a letter from his former flatmate Basil Douglas, who also happened to have been a pupil of Elizabeth Mayer's in Munich, where she had taught German and singing. Though she had abandoned earlier thoughts of a musical career for herself, she remained intensely sympathetic to music and musicians: her husband seems to have happily accepted that she was the dominant intellectual force in the household and her four children, whose talents lay elsewhere, were miraculously unresentful when she filled their little home with brilliantly creative people by way of compensation. There are obvious echoes here of the Britten family in Lowestoft, but with a major difference: Mrs Britten was blessed with a musically talented son, while Mrs Mayer would have liked to have been blessed with one. For Britten, Elizabeth Mayer became the latest in a series of surrogate mothers who already included Ethel Bridge, Marjorie Fass and Mary Behrend. To understand how soon and how fully he appreciated her, one can't do better than to quote from his letter of 7 November 1939 to Enid Slater:

> Peter & I have found some wonderful friends – who are (luckily) devoted to us – & on no account will let us depart. They are German émigrés (from Munich). He – is a Psychiatrist & an assistant at this mental Home. She – is one of those grand people who have been essential through the ages for the production of art; really sympathetic & enthusiastic, with instinctive good taste (in all the arts) & a great friend of thousands of those poor fish – artists. She is never happy unless she has them all round her – living here or round about at the moment are lots of them – many refugees. Wystan comes here from New York nearly every weekend – an excellent German painter lives here too, – Scharl – friends include the Manns, Borgesi, Einstein. That's the kind of person she is. She did wonderful work under Hitler; incredibly brave things. I think she's one of the few really good people in the world – & I find her essential in these times when one has rather lost faith in human nature.[20]

Stanton Cottage, where the Mayers lived in the grounds of Long Island Home, was far from large. 'I don't know how we all fitted in,' said Beata Sauerlander; '. . . there was a big middle room, a huge dining room table where we all ate; and then there was the living room with a Bechstein piano. That was Peter and Ben's domain.'[21] When Auden was working in another room – filling it with cigarette smoke and continually being brought cups of tea by Elizabeth Mayer – there can have been hardly any space left for the family.

Although Britten and Pears had decided to remain in America

by late August, the outbreak of war on 3 September troubled
them deeply. Barbara cabled to her brother, evidently telling
him not to return, and he immediately replied by letter. He
urged her to get away from London if possible – concern for
his sisters and a wish for them to make full use of the Old Mill
at Snape are recurring themes in his wartime letters home – and
continued: 'So far I am taking your advice because (a) I hear
that we are not wanted back (b) if I come I should only be put
in prison – which seems silly, just to do nothing & eat up food.'[22]
Though it wasn't true that as a pacifist he would necessarily end
up in prison, his instinct was surely right; but this was by no
means a lightly taken decision, and his anxiety about what he
really ought to do certainly contributed to his serious health
problems over the following two years. On the same day, he
wrote to Ralph Hawkes, to whom he gave the simplest explanation for remaining 'out here for a bit still': 'I have lots of things
to do, & am at the moment staying with friends on Long Island,
and inspite of everything working very hard.'[23] He certainly had
several projects to keep him fully occupied: there was the final
shaping of *Les Illuminations* and the violin concerto; there was
a new fifteen-minute orchestral piece which he wanted to call
'Kermesse Canadienne' (it became *Canadian Carnival*, Op. 19);
and he was about to start work with Auden on the 'school operetta',
Paul Bunyan. Businesslike as ever, he lost no time in establishing
a close professional relationship with Max Winkler, of Boosey
Hawkes Belwin Incorporated in New York, for whom he planned
to write 'simple marketable works' and whose financial support
would become invaluable when the transfer of funds from London
became impossible; and he wrote, enclosing a warmly affectionate
letter of introduction from Frank Bridge, to Elizabeth Sprague
Coolidge, the great musical benefactor, who was in due course to
commission his first string quartet.

A few weeks later, Hawkes passed on a slightly bizarre

proposal from the British Council. It began as an enigmatic cable on 21 September, in which Hawkes, who had in effect already accepted the invitation on his composer's behalf ('I SAID YES'), wanted to know if he would be interested in a commission 'FOR FULL SCALE ORCHESTRAL WORK SYMPHONIC POEM SYMPHONY SUITE OVERTURE UNDERSTAND FEE SUBSTANTIAL EVEN HUNDREDS'. Britten replied that he was 'ABLE AND WILLING PROVIDED NO JINGO',[24] understandably feeling that it was neither the time nor the place for him to compose an overtly patriotic piece. Only when Hawkes had made further enquiries did 'all the surprising details' (as Britten mildly put it) become clear: the ultimate client was the Japanese government and they wanted a work, for which they provided a rather odd specification, to celebrate the 2,600th anniversary of the Japanese Empire. 'SOUNDS CRAZY BUT WILL DO', Britten replied. In an undated letter of October 1939, he explained that he had an idea for a short symphonic work, to be called *Sinfonia da Requiem*, 'which sounds rather what they would like' – although, even at that early stage, it appeared to be neither celebratory nor imperial. It was to be delivered by May 1940.

Yet all the work in hand and all the kindness of the Mayers couldn't disguise an underlying truth: 'I feel *terribly* homesick, my dear,' he told Beth. 'Yearning for things to get all right & so that we could meet again, & go on living as before.'[25] He veered between wanting everyone he loved in Europe to cross the Atlantic to safety – 'you [Wulff] & Gustel, & if possible Barbara & the family too'[26] – and longing to return to them, and to Suffolk, himself. The informal tenancies of both his English homes had turned out disastrously: Jackie Hewitt had left the Hallam Street flat in a filthy state, with rent and bills unpaid, and had even robbed the gas meter; while at Snape, Lennox Berkeley dithered, first declining a proposal that Ralph

Hawkes should occupy the Old Mill, then decamping to stay with the critic John Davenport. There were times when Britten's unhappiness erupted in understandable frustration: 'Sometimes I feel a bomb on Snape might not be a terrible thing – but I *don't* want to sell it.'[27] Similarly, his fury with Berkeley – who 'writes letters about conscience & duty (King & Country etc.) & complains about neglect . . . He's just NO GOOD'[28] – was essentially a reflection of his own inner turmoil and an acknow-ledgement that Berkeley's unresolved dilemmas weren't so very far from his. When the Mayers provided Ben and Peter with a wonderful Christmas in the German style – the main celebration taking place on Christmas Eve – it could only emphasise how far they were from home.

On New Year's Day, Ralph Hawkes was to arrive from England: he and Britten planned to travel together to Chicago, where on the 15th the American premiere of his piano concerto would take place, with the Illinois Symphony Orchestra, conducted by Albert Goldberg, and the composer as soloist; but Hawkes was delayed until the middle of the month, so Britten travelled alone. He went first to Champaign, Illinois, where he 'heard lots of wind-bands & met conductors' for an article he was writing for the *New York Times*; next to Chicago to rehearse; then on to Grand Rapids; and finally back to Chicago for the perfor-mance. He assured Elizabeth Mayer that 'when I'm by myself I'm pretty efficient at arranging matters – booking rooms, tickets etc. & getting about. It's only when Peter's around that I become so shy & retiring . . .'[29] He had left behind at Amityville two people who loved him. 'Everything here awaits you patiently,' wrote Mrs Mayer. 'Your table at the window, the little piece of red blotting paper, which made me cry silently, the ruler . . . Here is your home now.'[30] For Pears, it was their first substantial time apart while they had been in America, and Britten's itinerary couldn't help triggering memories: 'I shall never forget a certain night in Grand Rapids,' he wrote. 'Ich liebe dich, io t'amo, jeg elske dyg (?), je t'aime, in fact, my little white-thighed beauty, I'm terribly in love with you.'[31] We should notice not the archness but the passionate expression, committed to the headed notepaper of Boosey Hawkes Belwin Incorporated, of a love that still hardly dared to speak its name.

The Chicago performance of the concerto wasn't without mishap. During the first movement, the piano keyboard's fixings came adrift and Britten had to stop the orchestra, apologise and start again. Albert Goldberg recalled that, just as he had his arms raised for the recommencement, 'Britten stood up looked at the audience and said, "I hope you don't think it was I who was to blame." And that won the audience you know.'[32] The evening was indeed, as Britten said, 'a great success' both in the hall and with the critics: Edward Barry, in the *Chicago Tribune*, thought that 'Mr Britten – tall, slim, and 26 – is as English as rain' and Eugene Stinson, in the *Chicago Daily News*, predicted that Britten would be 'vigorously applauded . . . wherever he plays in America' while shrewdly observing that the concerto 'is not as strong as it is bold and not as deep as it is entertaining'.[33] The winter was severe in the Midwest: fourteen degrees below freezing one day, according to Britten, who had 'vile cold and flu' in Chicago, felt 'completely dead' on his return to Amityville, but within a few days was 'fine now – Mrs Mayer is such an angel & looks after me like a mother'.[34] That optimism about his recovery (for the benefit of his sister Beth) was, however, misplaced. It was another month before either of his sisters heard of him again and, when news came, it was in the worrying form of a letter to Beth from Peter, who had a series of medical crises to report. After staying in bed for a few days to shake off the flu, Ben 'had a long and horrible nose-bleed which left him pretty weakish, and it seems that a streptococcus of some sort seized upon that moment to attack him'. His temperature increased to 104 degrees ('you can guess it was a bit alarming') and then, four days later, to 107 degrees; his tonsils were 'quite rotten apparently and must come out at the first suitable moment'. He was, as Pears wryly pointed out, surrounded by a surfeit of doctors as well as – and more usefully – by Beata, who was a professional nurse, had done 'night duty for about a week, and now she stays with him for most of the day'. She had been, he added, 'quite marvellous'.[35]

The unfolding, sequential nature of this illness will sound familiar; it is exactly the sort of thing that had happened to Britten at Gresham's. The fact that America affected him in the same way as public school wasn't lost on Auden, who liked to attribute all maladies to psychosomatic causes, and he may have had a point: in each case, Britten found deracination intolerably stressful, longed to return home and became more seriously and lengthily unwell than might have been expected. Meanwhile, in London, at the Aeolian Hall on 30 January, Sophie Wyss with the Boyd Neel Orchestra had given the first complete perform-ance of *Les Illuminations*, in a concert at which Britten would have dearly loved to be present. He wasn't even well enough to write to her about it until 15 March, when he hoarsely dictated a letter to his 'amiable nurse-secretary', the indefatig-able Beata: 'I hear you have never sung better and I know what that means.'[36] He had only been sent parts of the reviews which dealt with the composition rather than the performance, but he hoped the 'snarky old critics' had been kind to her; in fact, both *The Times* and the *Daily Telegraph* were remarkably unsnarky, the latter noting that 'Sophie Wyss's soprano voice did perfect justice to Benjamin Britten's delightful song cycle'.[37] London musical life was entering its wartime semi-hibernation and England was also enduring a dreadful winter; the Bridges, snowbound in Sussex, were unable to get to the concert. But Lennox Berkeley was there, as generously appreciative as ever of his friend's music:

'The "Illuminations" are marvellous – even better than I had expected . . . I think it's an absolute knock-out, and the best thing you've done (of what I've heard).'[38]

It was still a struggle, even at the end of the month, for Britten to get to the premiere of his Violin Concerto, Op. 15, which was given by Antonio Brosa with the New York Philharmonic Orchestra conducted by John Barbirolli at Carnegie Hall on 28 March. The performance, the first of two on consecutive days, was both a huge success in its own right and the happy conclusion to a chapter of accidents: Barbirolli had originally engaged Brosa to play the Berg concerto, under the impression that they would be giving the piece its American premiere (which had in fact taken place in the same hall three years earlier); it was Brosa who suggested Britten's new concerto as an alternative and the invaluable Hawkes who arranged for Barbirolli to hear Brosa play it through in London with Henry Boys at the piano. 'The work will never be better played or more completely understood than it was by you on Thursday & Friday, & I am more than grateful to you for having spent so much time & energy in learning it,' Britten told Brosa on 31 March.[39] He was also able to congratulate him on 'the rapturous notices you had from all the critics', modestly omitting to mention that his own share of the reviews – especially Olin Downes's in the *New York Times* – hadn't been so far from rapturous either. The piece subtly acknowledges the fact that, after Berg's reinvention of the form, the violin concerto would never be quite the same again: it is more conservative, certainly (if not as conservative as Samuel Barber's, also written in 1939 and also perhaps a kind of reply to Berg), yet the rhythmic motif with which it begins suggests a respectful nod towards the opening of the earlier work, from which Britten has learned a thing or two about orchestral colour and the use of percussion. Its most puzzling and rather English characteristic is that its virtuosic demands, including an enormous central cadenza, never seem at all showy. There is much dancing and dazzling, and for a while a mildly exotic whiff of the Eastern Mediterranean, before the concerto settles into its concluding mood of resolution which, like the ending of *A Midsummer Night's Dream*, is also one of disenchantment. After all the energetic invention which has preceded it, this episode seems strangely drawn out, as if the expected final cadence keeps clambering onto a slippery rock, falling off and trying again until it eventually succeeds.

That a work receiving its first performance in March 1940 should be so unsure of its own ending is entirely appropriate. A few days later, Britten replied to a cable from Boosey & Hawkes, who had been asked by the Japanese Embassy to confirm details of his commission for them: 'TITLE SINFONIA DA REQUIEM OR FIRST SYMPHONY SUBTITLE TO MEMORY OF MY PARENTS THREE INTERLINKED MOVEMENTS ABOUT TWENTY MINUTES'.[40] He was, as so often, cutting things fine. On 28 April he wrote to Beth: 'I now find myself faced with the proposition of writing a Symphony in about 3 weeks!' He had only, he said, just had official confirmation – the earlier exchange of cables being apparently insufficient for him – and was relieved that the fee (7,000 yen or approximately $1,650) would temporarily ease his financial worries; wartime restrictions had made it impossible to transfer money from England. But, he added, 'I should have written the work anyhow – it is a Sinfonia da Requiem, combining my ideas on war & a memorial for Mum & Pop.'[41] This pacifist element makes it sound even less like anything the Japanese government would want and, as with *Our Hunting Fathers*, Britten seems to have been intent on fulfilling his commission in a manner guaranteed to displease its sponsors: his description of it to Enid Slater as 'a work with plenty of "peace propaganda" in it – if they will accept it' suggests that he knew what he was doing.

At the same time, he developed 'a sudden craze for Michael Angelo Sonnetts & have set about half a dozen of them'[42] – his *Seven Sonnets of Michelangelo*, Op. 22, would be finished by the end of October – and he was thinking about a string quartet. In July, he met Paul Wittgenstein, the philosopher's pianist brother who had lost his right arm during the First World War and who now commissioned from him the *Diversions*, Op. 21, for piano (left hand) and orchestra. Having completed the *Sinfonia da Requiem*, he learned from the British Embassy in Tokyo that he was expected to attend its first performance, but thought that the rapidly deteriorating relations between the USA and Japan made this trip unlikely. 'Anyhow,' he told Barbara, 'I don't want to go – they have too much rice, earthquakes and hari-kari (or mata-hari, whatever that is).'[43]

No matter how hard he tried to sound jauntily encouraging in his letters to Barbara, Beth and Kit Welford, Britten had assorted causes for unhappiness. On a simple practical level, his financial affairs were in a mess: overdrawn at his English bank, despite his quarterly retainer from Boosey & Hawkes, he instructed Beth to cash in his life insurance policy, 'leave a little to keep the account going & pinch the rest – see? Have a good time yourselves – buy some rum & forget for abit – the same for Barbara!'[44] He continued to urge the Welfords to live in the Old Mill (when he wasn't reiterating his wish to get rid of the place) or, conversely, to come to America: he even made enquiries about a job for Kit, who was by this time a locum GP at Swaffham in Norfolk, and sent a formal promise to 'guarantee your maintenance in this country – & that of any young relations or friends you know of who can get away'.[45] Yet, as he wrote more frankly to other friends, 'America is a great disappointment'; it was 'so narrow, so self-satisfied, so chauvanistic, so superficial, so reactionary, & above all so *ugly*'.[46] Meanwhile, there had been troubling news – followed by lack of news – about Wulff

Scherchen, who had first been interned as an enemy alien and then shipped with other internees to Canada: it seemed that he might have been aboard the *Arandora Star*, torpedoed and sunk on 2 July with the loss of some six hundred internees and prisoners of war. Finally, after much frantic sending of cables and letters (including Britten's kind and supportive ones to Gustel Scherchen), Wulff was located at an internment camp near Ottawa: 'At last we have traced you! . . . now I can start sending you things – if I can think of anything besides the lists of things I am *not* allowed to send you!'[47] He was, at least, on the safer side of the Atlantic. 'My dear Gustel,' Britten wrote on 26 August, 'I know how you feel. It is tragic for the dear boy, but we must, & he must, just regard it as a period of "marking-time" (as it is for everybody else).'[48]

Thus he identified the underlying cause of his own private malaise: 'marking time' was something Britten always found intolerable and, despite an astonishing level of creativity, he couldn't avoid the sense of being trapped, in his own words 'stuck here', waiting for the end of something. To try and achieve some illusion of freedom, he bought himself a cheap car, a 1931 Ford, in which he and Pears set off for a late summer holiday in New England. They ended up, after a series of breakdowns and garage visits, at Owl's Head in Maine; the car's trouble, he told Copland, 'was probably neurotic – being associated with loupy musicians' (surely a gentle swipe at Auden's theory of illness), but they had arrived at 'the most glorious spot' and were 'working like the dickens & happy as kings'.[49] Among the other guests at the Owl's Head Inn was Kurt Weill, who was 'awfully nice & sympathetic, and it was remarkable how many friends we had in common, both in Europe & here':[50] wartime America, for all its faults, had become the meeting ground for cultural émigrés, a place where Schoenberg and Stravinsky could end up as Californian near neighbours. While at Owl's Head,

Britten finished his Wittgenstein commission before he and Pears set off again to Massachusetts, visiting Auden at Williamsburg and Lincoln Kirstein at Ashfield. 'I find it very easy to work up here,' he told Ralph Hawkes, '& as we are having grand hospitality the going is very cheap!'[51] Money remained a constant worry: he approached an agent, Abe Meyer at MCA, about the possibility of getting some film music work (rather to the displeasure of Hawkes, whose firm was setting up its own agency division) and he contemplated going to Mexico or Canada and re-entering the USA as an immigrant, a step which might have had both financial advantages and less desirable consequences if America entered the war.

In a long and rambling letter written from the Owl's Head Inn to Beth – its stream-of-consciousness style perhaps connected with a brief recurrence of his throat infection and a temperature peaking at 103 degrees – Britten hinted that he and Pears might be moving on from Amityville, where they had been the Mayers' guests for exactly a year, sometimes sleeping at the house of Dr Titley, the director of Long Island Home, but eating and working at Stanton Cottage. The Home, he said, was 'really a small village where everyone knows everyone & everyone's business, & the intrigues and scandals are unbelievable'. There had been 'a certain amount of friction' about when and where people were asked to meals: it was 'impossible for people to be shut up together without squabbling'.[52] In fact, there seems to have been less tension than one might expect in a small professional community: a recent patch of coolness, according to Elizabeth Mayer, had actually been caused by Britten borrowing Dr Titley's tennis racket and forgetting to return it. A fortnight later, although it was 'grand to be back with the family' who were 'such dears & a comfort in these bloody times', he told Beth that 'We feel we have to be nearer the big city where things go on & jobs are born'. So, although he admitted that he loathed the idea, 'Peter & I are going to take a flat with Wystan Auden for the winter in Brooklyn – one of the districts of New York City'.[53]

3

What Britten tactfully called a 'flat' and Pears, writing to his mother, described as 'rooms' in a house 'just bought' by 'a friend of ours'[54] was in fact one room on the top floor of a four-storey brownstone house owned by George Davis, the writer and literary editor of *Harper's Bazaar*, at 7 Middagh Street, Brooklyn Heights. It seems unlikely that either Beth Britten or Jessie Pears would have recognised the place from the information they had been given nor, probably, would they have approved of it. 'Auden was proxy landlord,' as the Britten scholars Donald Mitchell and Philip Reed put it, 'to a household that surely must have been among the most remarkable ever to have been gathered together under one roof.'[55] This is scarcely an exaggeration. Among its residents for longer or shorter spells – apart from Auden, Britten and Pears, and sometimes Davis himself – were the writers Paul and Jane Bowles, Carson McCullers, Louis MacNeice, and Golo and Klaus Mann; the stripper and actress Gypsy Rose Lee; and the theatrical designer Oliver Smith. As Klaus Mann noted in his diary, 'What an epic one could write about this!'[56] There are, it hardly needs to be said, two sharply distinct ways of reacting to such a ménage. In the opinion of Denis de Rougemont, the author of *Passion and Society*, 'all that was new in America in music, painting, or choreography emanated from that house, the only center of thought and art that I found in any large city of the country'; whereas for Caroline Seebohm, it was 'a huge, rambling society of creative eccentrics, living in varieties of squalor' in which 'Auden ruled the roost after a fashion; he collected rents, paid bills, organized food, calling meal times'.[57] The fashion in which Auden ruled was recalled by Paul Bowles: 'Our communal living worked well largely because Auden ran it. He would preface a meal by announcing: "We've got roast and two veg, salad and savory, and there will be no political discussion."'[58] But Auden's orderly mealtimes were calm interludes in the general chaos: MacNeice, who stayed briefly when a visiting lecturer at Cornell, remembered 'Auden writing in one room, a girl novelist [McCullers] writing with a cup of sherry in another, a composer [Britten] composing, a singer [Pears] hitting a high note and holding it, and Gypsy Rose Lee coming round for meals like a whirlwind of laughter and sex. It was the way the populace once liked to think of artists – ever so bohemian, raiding the icebox at midnight and eating the cat food by mistake.'[59]

'It was a marvellous house,' said Michael Mayer, in an interview with Mitchell and Reed, recalling a house-warming celebration on 22 November which doubled as Britten's 27th birthday party. 'We played children's games most of the evening: charades, and "ghosts" and games like that . . . I always tell people, Gypsy Rose Lee once sat on my lap with a gin bottle in her hand! . . . I had to act out "You can't take it with you" and I did it by trying to carry Carson McCullers across the threshold . . .'[60] When Britten described the same occasion to Antonio and Peggy Brosa on 20 December, it was in a tone of tolerant if rather weary irony:

We gave a housewarming party two or three weeks ago, at which Gypsie Rose Lee was a feature and we played murder all over the house and you could not imagine a better setting for it. The evening or rather morning ended with Peter and George Davis, owner of the house, doing a ballet to Petrushka,

up the curtains and the hot water pipes – an impressive if
destructive sight. Living is quite pleasant here when it is not
too exciting, but I find it almost impossible to work, and retire
to Amityville at least once a week.[61]

There was another party for Chester Kallman's twentieth
birthday on 7 January: his stepmother, Dorothy J. Farnan,
remembered that 'Lincoln Kirstein, cofounder of the New York
City Ballet, and Marc Blitzstein, the composer, dropped in . . .
Peter Pears sang "Make Believe" from *Show Boat*, and Wystan
wrote a poem for the occasion.'[62]

Britten had decided that he must be 'where things go on'
and there he was; but he didn't really fit in and nor, one imagines,
did the Steinway he imported into the communal living room.
He seems to have made himself almost invisible to some of his
fellow residents: Bowles found him 'not talkative' and Golo
Mann thought vaguely that he 'soon left Brooklyn and returned
to England'.[63] Pears, though happier about joining in (it was he
who climbed the curtains and sang Jerome Kern), didn't care
for the place either: it was 'a bohemian household, too wild,
too uncertain . . . I don't mind a bit of grubbiness, but not
downright dirt . . . it didn't suit us.'[64] There were contacts to
be made in the city – especially for Pears who, as the performing
half of the partnership, needed them most – but by the following
spring, Britten was retreating more and more to Amityville. 'A
winter in New York is just about the limit for me,' he wrote to
Beth on 12 May. 'However, I have very good friends & of course
Amityville I can flee to, if it gets too much for me – such as this
present moment.'[65] The experience of the preceding six months
had perhaps been more valuable than he knew, in finally establishing beyond all doubt that urban bohemian life wasn't for
him.

In the meantime, the story of the *Sinfonia da Requiem*'s

commission had reached its inevitable conclusion. Prince Fuminaro Konoye, president of the Committee for the 2,600th Anniversary, wrote in November to declare Britten's composition 'unsuitable for performance on such an occasion as our national ceremony': his committee was 'puzzled' because the piece failed to express 'felicitations', it was 'religious music of a Christian nature', and it had a 'melancholy tone both in its melodic pattern and rhythm'.[66] These are reasonable points, or at least they would have been if Britten had not already supplied details of the work, including title and dedication. But the dedication seems not to have been passed on to the Japanese Embassy by the British Council and a good deal of nuance may have been lost in translation on both sides. Britten, of course, was mightily relieved by the disappearance of his summons to Tokyo and wrote rather too jauntily, in a reply partly drafted by Auden, to the Japanese vice consul in New York, referring to the Prince as 'Mr'; Ralph Hawkes sternly remarked that this letter 'does not appear to have helped the situation with the British Council here and I must say that I think you might have addressed Prince Konoye with his correct title'. Otherwise, Hawkes was his usual acute and supportive self, observing that 'it is the Festival itself which is the point and not the actual character of the work written for it. If they had wanted 20 minutes of trumpeting, they should have said so . . .'[67] There was, he added, 'no question of refunding the money'. This, said Britten, he had already spent, while 'the publicity of having a work rejected by the Japanese Consulate for being Christian is a wow'.[68]

It was an inelegant solution to the problem, but Britten had two reasons, apart from the money, to be satisfied with it: the *Sinfonia da Requiem* was far too important a work to have been squandered on a politically compromised occasion; and the first performance would now by given by the New York Philharmonic Orchestra under John Barbirolli at Carnegie Hall, on 29 March

1941. This was a Saturday, which severely limited the press coverage, but the concert was repeated on the following Sunday afternoon and broadcast by CBS to an estimated audience of nine million listeners. Britten was quietly pleased: Barbirolli had taken a lot of trouble over it, the orchestra enjoyed playing it, the audience were friendly, 'the show was a good one'. To Peggy Brosa he added this interesting if enigmatic comment: 'Personally, I think it is the best so far, & since it's the last opus, it's as it should be – although to me it is so personal & intimate a piece, that it is rather like those awful dreams where one parades about the place naked – slightly embarrassing!'[69] The thunderous drumbeats which open the Lacrymosa, and return at the end of the movement, seem bellicose for an avowedly pacifist work, until we recall (as Britten surely did) those processional drums in the music Purcell wrote for Queen Mary's funeral in 1695. The Morse-code motif at the start of the Dies Irae has distant military overtones too; then there's a sudden burst of proto-'Sea Interlude', some stuttering brass exchanges and a plangent viola melody before the whole thing builds to a climax which brilliantly fragments into its component parts (the effect is the aural equivalent, in reverse, of that early Channel 4 logo in which jagged multicoloured bits of the figure 4 converged from every direction). Out of this chaos, the majestically serene Requiem Aeternam emerges: here a sombre, stately flute tune gives way to one of Britten's most rapturous reaching-for-eternity themes before the piece ends in a mood of resigned tranquillity. The *Sinfonia da Requiem* lasts only twenty minutes, but it encompasses a world as vast as that of a Mahler symphony; indeed, when it is sometimes programmed with one of the larger Mahler symphonies, one can have a strange sense of it being nowhere near as long yet somehow just as *big* a work.

Britten's vulnerable sense of walking naked in the *Sinfonia da Requiem* may strike us as odd until we reflect that his exposure in the song cycles is shared with both poet and singer, whereas the orchestra expresses the composer's unmediated self. Pears's role as the sharer of Britten's compositional life, whenever words were involved, had now become unassailable. During 1940 he had taken singing lessons in New York, first with Therese Behr-Schnabel and then with Clytie Mundy: 'The improvement in his voice after only a month is quite staggering,'[70] Britten had written in March, and by April he was 'singing 100% better'.[71] The composition of the Michelangelo sonnets, dedicated 'to Peter', was predicated on this improvement, but although they were finished in the autumn of 1940 they were not to be performed in public until 23 September 1942 at Wigmore Hall. This delay was mainly because Pears didn't yet feel ready to do them justice, although Mitchell and Reed suggest that there may also have been, on Britten's part, 'a certain reluctance to bring these passionate avowals of love – for his singer, for his singer's voice above all – into the public domain'.[72] They performed the songs for friends at Amityville and made a private recording of them in New York, of which Christopher Headington provides a typically sympathetic, detailed analysis: he notes that the voice 'is a young one, yet it has authority and purpose'; the intonation 'is secure and the words clear both in diction and in the projection of their meaning'; but there are 'some weaknesses' such as a problematical high E and a mannered downward portamento at the end of the fifth song.[73] However, Pears did sing – and Britten, after a tussle with the Musicians' Union, did conduct – the first American performance of *Les Illuminations* on 18 May 1941 in a concert broadcast by CBS as part of the eighteenth ISCM Festival. This work, which had only been lent to Sophie Wyss, now belonged to Pears.

Paul Bunyan, the Britten–Auden collaboration which its creators had once dreamed of seeing staged on Broadway, received its rather more modest first production, billed as 'A New

Operetta in 2 Acts', at the Brander Matthews Hall of Columbia University during the week beginning 5 May. The audience liked it well enough, but the critical reaction was largely unfavourable: Olin Downes, in the *New York Times*, felt that both Britten ('a very clever young man' who 'scores with astonishing expertness and fluency') and Auden had failed to do themselves justice, while Virgil Thomson, in the *New York Herald Tribune*, thought that Britten's contribution was 'sort of witty at its best' and agreed that 'Mr Britten can do better'.[74] The work was problematical in two particular respects. Firstly, the notion of a work whose titular hero, a legendary giant, never appears onstage belonged much more obviously to the surreal-fantastical world of the earlier Auden–Isherwood dramas than to the New York of 1941. Secondly, the spectacle of two young Englishmen in exile tackling so specifically American a theme could hardly fail to seem impertinent: *Paul Bunyan*, according to *Time*, was an 'anemic operetta put up by two British expatriates'.[75] For Britten, the production of *Paul Bunyan* and his departure from Middagh Street signalled the beginning of a gradual estrangement from Auden in both life and work: their collaborations had provided invaluable experience for him, but they had represented an uncomfortable kind of fancy dress for a composer who was always more at ease in his ordinary clothes, even when these were somewhat formal.

To earn a little money, and to maintain his hands-on involvement in music-making, Britten accepted the position of Conductor for the 1941 season of the Suffolk Friends of Music Symphony Orchestra: this was Suffolk County on Long Island, a coincidence which prompted both amusement and homesickness. His appointment had been encouraged by the Mayers' friend David Rothman, a member of the orchestra's committee who kept the hardware store at Southold, an almost-Suffolk name which had shed a consonant in crossing the Atlantic. The orchestra's membership consisted of 'professional musicians, adult amateurs, and advanced students of high school age' – a step up from the 'Benj. Britten Bungay Band', though not a huge one – and the job of conducting them required 'a great deal of energy, a certain amount of skill and an infinite amount of tact'.[76] Britten clearly possessed the first two qualities; the third he found trickier, sometimes resorting to a mode of school-masterly English irony. 'Gentlemen,' he remarked on one occasion, 'what I hear sounds vaguely familiar, but I find nothing like it in my score!'[77] Perfectionism, not vanity, made it a dispiriting experience for him, and there was worse to come. In Tony Palmer's film *A Time There Was*, David Rothman recalled Britten's inconsolable misery after a concert at which there were more people on the stage than in the audience: he wondered whether he should give up music altogether and take a job at the hardware store instead. It may sound like a theatrical gesture, but it was a reflection both of his genuine loss of confidence and of the creative artist's frequent desire to do something more obviously useful. His delight in simple things had been re-awakened by the Rothmans' fourteen-year-old son Bobby who, to the dismay of his father (who thought such common pleasures would be beneath the composer's dignity), took Britten bowling; nothing, of course, could have been better calculated to please the competitive schoolboy in him. As so often in England, Britten found he could talk more easily to an intelligent teenager than to most adults. Walking along the shore of Long Island Sound, David Rothman once suggested to Britten that the sound of the gulls might inspire him, a mildly tactless remark though, given the subject of his next opera, an almost prophetic one. Britten waited until Rothman was out of earshot and then said to Bobby: 'You know, those seagulls don't give me any inspiration. It all just comes to me up here – I really don't need the seagulls for it!'[78] There was a family picnic at Orient Point on Long Island, filmed for posterity by David Rothman, during which Britten's unaffected boyishness is splendidly evident – 'You are such a delightful family,' he told his host, 'I have scarcely ever felt so easy and at home with people, as I do with you all'[79] – and on one occasion he and Bobby shared a twin-bedded room at the Rothmans' house. Britten, Bobby remembered, gave him a hug before they went to sleep: 'It was just a certain fondness, a certain kindness. Nothing took place that I would have been upset about if anyone else was watching. There was at one time a tender hug, and that was about it.'[80]

At the end of May, Britten and Pears set off in their neurotic Ford for Escondido, California: 'I have lots of work to do & have a nice long invitation to stay in a grand house near the sea & in an orange grove!'[81] The invitation, for the whole summer, was from the married pianists Ethel Bartlett and Rae Robertson, for whom Britten had composed the *Introduction and Rondo alla Burlesca*, Op. 23, No. 1, the previous autumn (Bartlett and Robertson gave the first performance on 5 January 1941). The 'lots of work' was to include a companion piece for two pianos – *Mazurka Elegiaca*, Op. 23, No. 2 (In Memoriam I. J. Paderewski) – as well as a second set of Rossini arrangements, *Matinées Musicales*, Op. 24, and, most importantly, the first String Quartet, Op. 25, commissioned by Elizabeth Sprague Coolidge. At Escondido, the two men established a working routine which, as usual, accommodated Britten's need for silence and Pears's need to make a noise: the latter would spend each morning practising in the nearby house of a sympathetic Englishwoman. The Robertsons, said Pears, were 'very, very sweet people',[82] although Britten had to put up with some unwanted attention from Ethel Bartlett which her husband irritatingly failed to discourage: 'the personal relationships got in such a deplorable mess that any normal life was impossible', he later told Beth, after spending '3 months living on an emotional volcano'.[83]

The summer's most momentous event came wrapped in an insignificant disguise. Someone, in mid-July, thought Britten might be interested in an article in the *Listener* of 29 May by E. M. Forster, based on a talk he had given for the BBC Overseas Service on 'George Crabbe: The Poet and the Man', since Crabbe had come from and written about the Suffolk coast. Forster's essay – which opens with the memorable sentence 'To talk about Crabbe is to talk about England' – might have been designed to be read by a homesick exaptriate East Anglian. It contains both an evocative description of Crabbe's birthplace, Aldeburgh ('. . . a bleak little place: not beautiful. It huddles round a flint-towered church and sprawls down to the North Sea – and what a wallop the sea makes as it pounds the shingle!') and a brilliant summary of the poet's peculiar attractiveness: 'I like him and read him again and again: and his tartness, his acid humour, his honesty, his feeling for certain English types and certain English scenery, do appeal to me very much.'[84] Forster then goes on to quote from the most haunting of all Crabbe's narrative poems, 'Peter Grimes' from *The Borough*. Britten wrote with understandable delight to Elizabeth Mayer on 29 July: 'We've just re-discovered the poetry of George Crabbe (all about Suffolk!) & are very excited – maybe an opera one day . . . !'[85] They had moved on from Forster's piece to the poems them-selves, thanks to Pears's habit of browsing in 'a marvellous Rare Book shop' which he thought the 'only good thing' in Los Angeles;[86] it was there that he and Britten found an 1851 copy of *The Poetical Works of the Rev. George Crabbe*. In his speech on receiving the first Aspen Award in 1964, Britten recalled that life-changing moment:

But the thing I am *most* grateful to your country for is this: it was in California, in the unhappy summer of 1941, that, coming across a copy of the Poetical Works of George Crabbe in a Los

Angeles bookshop, I first read his poem, *Peter Grimes*; and, at the same time, reading a most perceptive and revealing article about it by E. M. Forster, I suddenly realised where I belonged and what I lacked. I had become without roots, and when I got back to England six months later I was ready to put them down.[87]

4

During the previous two years, Britten and Pears had often sought advice, from the British Embassy and from friends, about whether or not they should return home, and the reply was always the same: stay where you are. The authorities in England, they were told, were happy for them to remain 'artistic ambassadors', and in this admittedly ill-defined role they had some success. Britten's work was now much more widely performed and broadcast in the United States than in his own country: this was partly due to the fact that an ambassador is by definition absent and unable to look after his interests at home, but there were other and trickier reasons for his reputation to have taken a tumble in London.

His article 'An English Composer Sees America' in the April 1940 issue of the American music magazine *Tempo* had, as he remarked to Ralph Hawkes, 'caused a rumpus in London'[88] when it appeared there later in the year. It's an odd mixture of part-truths flattering to his host nation and sound common sense. His attack on the BBC for its policy of broadcasting monthly concerts of music by 'contemporary composers (generally of the most formidable and unattractive kind)' comes strangely from one who had so notably benefited from the BBC's support of young composers at a time when even his own college seemed to find his work unperformable; while his opposing vision of America as a land in which 'the composer has a chance of obtaining commissions from radio and phonograph companies' errs on the side of rose-tinted optimism. On the other hand, his argument that contemporary music is best served when placed 'in concert programs side by side with the well-tried master-pieces' so that it may be 'judged solely on its merits as music' is sensible (and would become standard post-war BBC practice). Most interesting of all is his definition of two contrasting responses to 'the preponderating German influence which had been stifling English music for 150 years':

> There were two reactions to this: one on the part of practising musicians like Elgar and Frank Bridge, who realized the value of the classical tradition yet whose utterances were character-istically English; the other, and temporarily more influential, reaction was that of the folksong group. This group adopted English folksong as the chief influence in their work, and disregarded most of the lessons Europe had to give. It held up the progress for twenty-five years, but it has now entirely subsided, since audiences found it monotonous melodically and harmonically.[89]

That sweeping gesture with which Britten consigns composers such as Vaughan Williams to the dustbin of musical history is breathtaking, but hardly less astonishing is his praise of the once-detested Elgar. In a second article for American readers, 'England and the Folk-Art Problem' (*Modern Music*, January/ February 1941), he went further. Elgar, he wrote, represented the 'professional' approach to music, as opposed to the amateurism of 'Parry and his followers', and was moreover 'a most eclectic composer, his most obvious influences being Wagner, Tchaikovsky, and Franck'.[90] One reason for this change of heart was that Britten's own musical language had become more conservative, but another and far more significant one was his recognition that Elgar – like Bridge, like Britten himself – was a composer who had learned from Europe while fashioning a modern English music.

It was inevitable that some members of the musical establishment at home would regard these articles as instances of sniping ingratitude from someone who was safely out of the country at a troubled time. Matters were made worse when news seeped out that the absent composer had accepted a commission from the government of Japan. When Ralph Hawkes returned to London after his own extended visit to America, in September 1940, he wrote glumly to Britten of the 'difficulty' in getting his work performed and the 'caustic comment' passed on his absence abroad. Most of the comment had been directed at Auden and Isherwood, until the first performance in England of the Violin Concerto, given by Thomas Matthews, with the LPO conducted by Basil Cameron, at the Queen's Hall on 6 April 1941. This had the unanticipated effect of shifting the attack, on two fronts, to Britten. The first of these began with an enthusiastic review in the *Sunday Times* of 4 May by Ernest Newman: 'If anything had been required to strengthen my former feeling that Mr Britten is a thoroughbred, this fine piece of writing would be enough.' It was the word 'thoroughbred' which incensed readers to such an extent that on 8 June Newman returned to it: 'A few weeks ago I used the word thoroughbred in connection with Benjamin Britten's new violin concerto; and ever since then I have been fighting single-handed the battle of Britten.' This in turn prompted a furious letter from George Baker, which concluded: 'I would like to remind Mr Newman that most of our musical "thoroughbreds" are stabled in or near London and are directing all their endeavours towards winning the City and Suburban and the Victory Stakes, two classic events that form part of a programme called the Battle of Britain; a programme in which Mr Britten has no part.'[91]

Meanwhile, the *Musical Times* of June 1941 carried a letter from Pilot-Officer E. R. Lewis about 'a young English composer now in America' who, the writer erroneously asserted, had taken American citizenship. Lewis was particularly vexed by the 'particular favour shown by concert-givers, particularly the B.B.C.' towards the unnamed composer: 'The one justification of such prominence is overwhelming merit, and this composer's reputation hardly fulfils that condition.' By simultaneously belittling Britten's reputation and exaggerating the meagre number of performances his work was now receiving, Lewis prepared the ground for a rhetorical question: 'Why should special favour be given to works which are not of the first rank when they come from men who have avoided national service, and when so many British artists have suffered inroads upon their work so as to preserve that freedom which, musically, they have not yet enjoyed to the full?'[92] Though based on misapprehensions, in its muddled way this expresses a widely held resentment. In the ensuing correspondence, two writers (both, as it happens, with East Anglian connections) made important points. Gerald Cockshott – a schoolmaster, writer and composer from Norwich – drew attention to musical casualties of the previous war, such as Ivor Gurney and George Butterworth, and argued that although Britten might not be making 'any immediate contribution to the national cause', it was 'by its cultural achievements that a nation will be judged'.[93] And Jack Moeran wrote to dispel the illusion that Britten had fled at the outbreak of war: 'I would point out that he left this country many weeks [actually months] earlier, and that at the time of the outbreak he was already fulfilling engagements in the U.S.A.'[94]

There was a subtext to these attacks on Britten and Pears, which would remain a nuisance for some years to come: the unspoken assumption that pacifism and homosexuality were inextricably linked and perhaps even amounted to much the same thing, commonly expressed in a phrase such as 'Nancy Boys'. Anyone who ever met Britten and Pears would have realised how ludicrously wide of the mark this was, but their indignant detractors hadn't met them. Another false assumption was that these musical absentees were lolling about and enjoying themselves abroad while their countrymen fought; whereas, of course, they were working hard, earning little, and feeling desperately homesick. It wasn't only reading Crabbe that had made Britten long for home: his Californian summer had turned sour. In letters to his sisters, he tried hard to sound cheerful and reassuring, with travellers' tales about hitchhikers, the blue Pacific and the extraordinary heat, but on 19 August he admitted to Beth that he was 'abit sick of California – there is a feeling of unreality about it which is not so pleasant as you'd think'.[95] In early September, he told Barbara that he was fed up with Americans generally: 'Their driving – their incessant radio – their fat and pampered children – their yearning for culture (to be absorbed in afternoon lectures, now that they can't "do" Europe) – and above all their blasted stomachs . . .'[96] But it was to Wulff, now back in England and in the Pioneer Corps, that he really let rip: 'In many ways this summer has been terrible for us – I have never felt so completely out of harmony with America . . . All the weaknesses of the civilised world, all the lack of direction, find their epitome in California.'[97] Even New York was preferable to Los Angeles, which he thought 'the ugliest and most sprawling city on earth'.

The day before he and Pears began their return journey east, however, Britten had an important engagement in Los Angeles: the first performance, by the Coolidge Quartet on 21 September at Thorne Hall, Occidental College, of his first String Quartet, Op. 25. He had completed it on 28 July, a few days after hearing from its sponsor that he had been awarded the Coolidge Medal, whose previous recipients included Frank Bridge, for 1941. 'Our quartet,' he told Mrs Coolidge on 24 July, 'is progressing very well'; he thought it 'my best piece so far, which is rather extra-ordinary for me, since at this period of work I usually am in a deep depression'.[98] This wasn't strictly true: he was often elated as he neared the end of a composition – though not always by its performance or reviews – and he had an enviable knack of immersing himself in work when depressed by other matters. But he was right to be pleased with the quartet and delighted by the performance it received from the players led by William Kroll, subsequently the founder of the Kroll Quartet; he even managed to describe the review in the *Los Angeles Times* as 'quite friendly'. Though appreciative of the third movement ('the most important movement in point of achievement') and the fourth ('a brilliant success'), it was obtuse about the piece's memorably haunted opening ('The idea was all right but the music was not effective'), a reminder that what may strike us now as charac-teristically Brittenesque was still puzzling and unfamiliar to some listeners. The same artists gave several subsequent performances of the work, including one in New York on 28 December attended by the composer, who reported to Mrs Coolidge that they 'played it wonderfully'.

The String Quartet was by far the most important work Britten completed during the second half of 1941. Back at Amityville, he had two other commissions to finish: the *Scottish Ballad*, Op. 26, for two pianos and orchestra, and *An Occasional Overture*, Op. 27. The first of these was written for his Californian hosts, Ethel Bartlett and Rae Robertson (who was Scottish), and first performed by them with the Cincinnati Symphony Orchestra conducted by Eugene Goossens on 28 November 1941. After an unpromisingly bombastic start, it has an attractively dreamlike central episode before rather losing its way again; unlike Britten's major works of the period, it doesn't seem to have anything to say. The second, although commissioned by Artur Rodzinski and the Cleveland Orchestra, seems not to have been performed at the time; the manuscript, which Britten left behind in the USA when he returned to England, was only rediscovered shortly before the composer's death. By then, both title and opus number had been reused, and the work – a more obviously engaging piece than the *Scottish Ballad* – was renamed *An American Overture* for its first performance by the City of Birmingham Symphony Orchestra under Simon Rattle in 1983.

The troublesome summer was followed by an unhappy autumn, during which Britten experienced one of his rare composing blocks; this was when he seriously thought about giving up music for a job in David Rothman's hardware store. Although he told Peggy Brosa in early November that he had been 'working very very hard', what he really meant was that he'd been very busy: after finishing the overture for Rodzinksi ('which I don't think he's going to play after all – disappointing after the hurry'), he'd been to Boston to see Koussevitzky about performances of his *Sinfonia*, 'had a fearful scare over Peter's papers' after an initial refusal to extend his work permit and been awarded his Coolidge Medal in Washington ('Mrs C. caused quite a stir by calling me Benjy in front of the assembled audience!').[99] Then he was off to Chicago, to conduct the Illinois Symphony Orchestra in performances of the *Sinfonia* and, with Pears as soloist, *Les Illuminations*, on 24 November. His own estimate of this concert was positive – 'the orchestra played well, Peter sang splendidly & had a good reception, & I wasn't too bad (except for 2 up-beats in one spot!) with the stick' – although he thought the reviews were 'pretty catty'.[100] That was putting it mildly: though cautious about the Rimbaud songs, they were extraordinarily hostile to the *Sinfonia*. 'Seldom does one encounter a new piece so thoroughly incomprehensible,' said

Edward Barry in the *Chicago Tribune*. 'The ear is baffled by its instrumental texture and passes nothing on to the mind.' Remi Gassmann in the *Chicago Daily Times* agreed: 'Mr Britten does not write for the orchestra in the sense that he provides it with music to play. He merely uses the orchestra to produce a variety of instrumental sound-effects.'[101] By now, Britten had learned to be – or, at least, to appear to be – amused by this sort of nonsense. To a postcard of Picasso's 'Study for *Guernica*' sent to Albert Goldberg, the Illinois orchestra's conductor who had arranged the concert, he added a parenthetical question: '(Is the Sinfonia as obscure as this??)'.[102]

Next day, Britten and Pears went on to Grand Rapids, where they performed a voice-and-piano reduction of *Les Illuminations*, together with some of the folk-song arrangements on which Britten had been intermittently working. Then they stayed for a few days at Ann Arbor, where Auden was teaching for a year as an associate professor of English and sharing a house with a student, Charles H. Miller, who remembered how 'Peter, handsome and irresponsible, loomed large over his Benjy, and I didn't need Wystan to tell me, as he did in a murmured aside, "Now there's a happy married couple."'[103] Auden must have felt this the more keenly since his own relationship with Chester Kallman, which had at first seemed so idyllic, was marred by their sexual incompatibility and Chester's promiscuity. His sense of exclusion from this evidently successful partnership – as well as the abandonment of a planned collaboration on an oratorio – marked a further stage in the gradual process of drawing apart from Britten.

The USA declared war on Japan on 8 December, after the previous day's attack on Pearl Harbor. The following week, Britten and Pears gave a recital under the auspices of the American Women's Hospitals Reserve Corps at Southold High School on Long Island. Britten played Beethoven's F major

Sonata, Op. 10, No. 2, and Chopin's B flat minor Scherzo ('His performance of these works was truly electrifying,' said the local paper) and accompanied Pears in a quartet of operatic arias. But it was the three groups of English songs which must have been most affecting for the homesick performers themselves: Purcell and Bridge among the composers in the first set; after the interval, four of Britten's folk-song settings; and, at the end, Lisa Lehman's *Three Cautionary Tales* and a pair of Britten cabaret songs ('Funeral Blues' and 'Calypso'). Their decision to return home remained unshaken, despite the increased danger: 'We have already our priority on the boat,' he told Antonio and Peggy Brosa on 31 December, 'but we still haven't got our exit permits, and when we get them, we've got to wait for a boat . . .' He thought, optimistically, that this might take 'at least a fortnight or so'. The Brosas were in America and in on the secret, but he didn't want to alarm his family in England. 'By the way,' he added, 'you won't mention to anyone that we're going back, will you, please – because I think Beth & Barbara would have forty fits if they knew I was sailing at this time.'[104]

Meanwhile, Britten's work was receiving some significant performances. Pears sang *Les Illuminations* in New York on 22 December, to great acclaim both in the hall – 'At the conclusion, the audience cheered, shouted "Bravi!" and generally carried on,' reported the *New York World-Telegram*[105] – and from the press. At Symphony Hall, Boston, on 2 and 3 January, Serge Koussevitzky conducted the *Sinfonia da Requiem* with the Boston Symphony Orchestra in 'a wonderful show', according to Britten, who was there. Following the death of his wife on 11 January, the conductor established the Koussevitsky Music Foundation in her memory and immediately commissioned from Britten the opera which would eventually be *Peter Grimes*. Then there was the first performance of *Diversions*, Op. 21, by Paul Wittgenstein and the Philadelphia Orchestra under Eugene Ormandy, which pleased the composer less: he had been to Philadelphia, he told Albert Goldberg, 'to hear Wittgenstein wreck my diversions'.[106] Isherwood was at the concert and afterwards met 'Benjy and his friend Peter Pears . . . They are leaving soon for England where Benjy has decided to register as a C.O. We all got sadder and sadder and drunker and drunker.'[107] Yet, despite the wreckage of his *Diversions*, Britten's reputation was growing: at this of all moments he might, had he felt so inclined, have opted to become an American composer, in the sense that Auden became an American poet (and Isherwood an American novelist). The fact that he had absolutely no intention of doing so, even when there was substantial money involved – a few months earlier, he had turned down the chance of becoming Professor of Music at the University of New Mexico, at the huge salary of $32,000 – is further evidence of an unbridgeable distance between the two men. If Auden aspired to be, as he lightly put it later, 'a minor atlantic Goethe', what might an Americanised Britten have been like? A minor atlantic Schubert? No, it wasn't for him.

For Auden, the determination of Britten and Pears to return home was, among other things, a personal affront. 'I need scarcely say, my dear, how much I shall miss you and Peter, or how much I love you both,' he wrote from Ann Arbor on 31 January. Such an opening must sooner or later be followed by 'but . . .'. After praise of Britten as 'the white hope of music' and a rash of grandly capitalised abstractions (Goodness, Beauty, Order, Chaos, Bohemianism, Bourgeois Convention) come these two paragraphs:

> For middle-class Englishmen like you and me, the danger is
> of course the second [bourgeois convention]. Your attraction
> to thin-as-a-board juveniles, i.e. to the sexless and innocent,
> is a symptom of this. And I am certain too that it is your denial
> and evasion of the demands of disorder that is responsible for

your attacks of ill-health, ie sickness is your substitute for
the Bohemian.

Wherever you go you are and probably always will be
surrounded by people who adore you, nurse you, and praise
everything you do, eg Elisabeth, Peter (Please show this to P
to whom all this is also addressed). Up to a certain point this
is fine for you, but beware. You see, Bengy dear, you are always
tempted to make things too easy for yourself in this way, ie
to build yourself a warm nest of love (of course when you get
it, you find it a little stifling) by playing the lovable talented
little boy.[108]

This is clumsily hectoring even for Auden, who must by now
have had some inkling of his friend's sensitivity; it is, moreover,
wrong on several counts. Auden had never understood Britten's
relationship with younger boys, in which the principal elements
were a prep-school-masterish enjoyment of fun and games, a
nostalgic wish to re-experience the happier part of his own
childhood and a touchingly simple desire to do good. As we
have seen and will see, the boys he valued tended to be sturdy
and athletic, keen on tennis and swimming, rather than 'thin-
as-a-board juveniles'. In the only case where there may have
been sexual contact, the boy (Wulff) was eighteen years old: the
same age, in fact, as Chester Kallman when he embarked on his
relationship with Auden. Then there is the point about Britten
surrounding himself with friends such as Elizabeth and Peter,
creating 'a warm nest of love': this is true if staggeringly tactless,
yet what Auden doesn't see is that – given Britten's combination
of intense creative energy, orderly working habits, erratic health
and domestic incompetence – it was a practical necessity. And
there's an appalling irony in writing 'you are always tempted to
make things too easy for yourself' to someone who was about
to cross the Atlantic in a cargo ship in the middle of a world

war. Britten replied, but since Auden threw away all personal correspondence, we can only guess what he might have said. Unsurprisingly (and despite a short semi-apologetic note from Auden), this exchange of letters effectively marked the end of their friendship.

Even as late as 1 March 1942, Britten was still evasively telling his brother-in-law Kit Welford: 'I am not quite sure what will happen to me . . . I have certain things I want to do & which I may or may not be able to do – when I know I'll let you & Beth know, of course.'[109] He didn't let them know, and by failing to anticipate that he and Pears would have to spend five weeks aboard ship, during which time his family heard nothing from him, he risked causing at least as much worry as he had hoped to spare them. To the Brosas, ten days later, Pears could at last write: 'Our draft board has graciously permitted us to be off, and off we go early next week.' They were overjoyed at the prospect: 'April is such a marvellous month. Think of seeing real spring again – Oh! Peggy and Toni, when shall we all see it together again.'[110] That determination to look forward was positive and sustaining, but there was also, inevitably, the sense of an ending: it was, as Britten wrote in the Mayers' visitors' book on 6 March, 'The end of the week-end (see Aug. 21st 1939).'[111] At last, on 16 March, the two men boarded a Swedish cargo ship, the MS *Axel Johnson*, at New York. 'I bring B. and P. to the boat at 3 p.m.,' noted Elizabeth Mayer in her diary, adding in the margin: 'The Ides of March.'[112]

CHAPTER 5

WHERE I BELONG

1942–47

1

The *Axel Johnson* wasn't a bit like the *Ausonia*. It was, as Britten later told Bobby Rothman in a lively account of the voyage, 'a rather decrepid old boat (a Swedish freighter) and everything went wrong with her'. First, they 'sat for four days just off the Statue of Liberty while the steering was being repaired'.[1] Then they travelled slowly up the east coast, calling at various ports: by 25 March they had only reached Boston, where they spent several days during further repairs to the steering. After that, the ship went on to Halifax, Nova Scotia, from where Pears sent a postcard (of the bandstand in the public gardens) to Beata: 'So far so good though God how slow & boring! This town is the bottom of the pit . . .'.[2] They eventually set sail for England on 4 April. The customs authorities in New York had confiscated Britten's manuscripts of work-in-progress – his setting of Auden's *Hymn to St Cecilia* and the first movement of a possible clarinet concerto for Benny Goodman – on the grounds that they might contain coded information, although this may have been a blessing, as it kept him busily engaged in reconstructing the former from memory as well as working on *A Ceremony of Carols*; Pears, meanwhile, was drafting a number-by-number synopsis of

Peter Grimes, of which at this early stage he had some thought of writing the libretto. They had a cramped two-berth cabin opposite the ship's refrigerator, which Pears found faintly disconcerting; nor did he think much of the company, which included some 'callow, foul mouthed, witless recruits',³ although there was a French professor on whom they could practise their spoken (but not sung) French. They crossed the Atlantic in a convoy, by which they were temporarily abandoned when the ship's funnel caught fire: 'we stood quite still for ages, attracting all the submarines for miles – so we expected!'⁴ On 17 April, the *Axel Johnson* docked in Liverpool, where the two men disembarked and sent telegrams to their astonished relatives announcing that they were safely home.

Exactly where home might now be was another matter. They had relinquished the Hallam Street flat after the disastrous experience of Jackie Hewitt's caretaking, so for the time being Pears had to stay with his parents in Barnes while Britten was based at the Old Mill or at his sister Barbara's flat in Chelsea or at Northwood, Middlesex, where Beth and her husband Kit were now living in a house large enough to accommodate Barbara and her friend Helen Hurst as well if they needed to get out of central London; it was from there that Beth dashed into town when Barbara rang to say that she had received a telegram from their brother in Liverpool, asking whether she could put him up for the night. Beth remembered that Ben 'looked much older' and that he and Peter 'were both very shocked to see the effects of the Blitz on London':⁵ among the most shocking of these, from a musical point of view, had been the destruction of the Queen's Hall, hitherto the home of the annual Promenade Concerts which now transferred to the Royal Albert Hall. The Welfords had looked after Britten's Morris 8 for him, but petrol shortages severely curtailed the use he could make of it; instead, when he needed to get from Snape to London, he cycled to the railway station at Campsea Ashe, pedalling through Tunstall, where the village shop by the crossroads was called 'Herring's', a name he stored away for future use.

Was he glad to be back? For quite some time, he wouldn't be sure. He found that, while people hadn't essentially changed, they had somehow become more like themselves, 'the nice ones, much nicer, & the unpleasant ones, a little worse'; there had been 'no suggestion of vindictiveness' but (a shrewd observation) one or two instances of '*over*-kindness, which makes one suspicious'.[6] In May, he wrote to Elizabeth Mayer that he was 'horribly homesick for my American home': he had been poring over a map with the Welfords, showing them 'where you all lived, where we went, & what we did when we got there', and he felt that 'the greater part of my life *must* be spent with you all on your side of the Atlantic'. Yet no sooner had he written those words than he inadvertently demonstrated why they would never be true: 'Snape is just heaven. I couldn't believe that a place could be so lovely. The garden was looking so neat & intentional, & the house is so comfortable and so lovely to look at – & the *view* . . . over the village to the river & marshes beyond.'[7] That is the authentic voice of belonging, and we shall hear it again.

A major reason for his vacillating emotions about England was the fraught process of registering as a conscientious objector. The decision of his first tribunal, on 28 May, was that he be registered 'as a person liable under the Act to be called-up for service but employed only in non-combatant duties'; however, after a successful appeal to the Appellate Tribunal, he was granted complete exemption. Mitchell and Reed point out that the chairman of this second tribunal was Sir Francis Floud, whose son Peter had been at Gresham's with Britten – which made him more appreciative than others might have been of the appellant's outstanding musical talent – and also that 'if Britten had not declared himself a pacifist and had been called up for military service, he would almost certainly have been found medically unfit'.[8] In this respect, he may have chosen, as he often did, to do things the hard way. Certainly, the fulsome protestations of Christian belief in his statements may strike us now as embarrassingly awkward for a man of uncertain religious convictions; in preparing these, and in his tribunal appearances, he was assisted by Canon Stuart Morris, General Secretary of the Peace Pledge Union, for whom he had composed his *Pacifist March* in 1937. Although he felt typically guilty about it, there was no denying that he had 'got the best possible result', as he told Elizabeth Mayer in September: 'I am now left completely free to go on with my work . . . Stuart Morris who was my council was very good, & both Montagu Slater & William Walton were excellent witnesses . . .'[9] By this time Pears too had successfully registered.

Both Britten and Pears lost no time in immersing themselves in work as soon as possible after their return home. For Britten, this included tidying up the *Hymn to St Cecilia* and the *Ceremony of Carols*, writing music for two BBC/CBS radio series (*Britain to America* and *An American in England*), toying with abortive projects (a harp concerto and a sonata for orchestra) and, above all, planning *Peter Grimes*: the libretto was to be by Montagu Slater who, by early June, was 'steaming ahead' with it. Pears, meanwhile, had been offered the title role in Offenbach's *The Tales of Hoffman* at the Strand Theatre within days of arriving back in London: when it opened on 6 May, 'Peter sang so well, acted so delightfully, and was such a ravishing personality on stage . . . that everyone was delighted & more than surprised.'[10] During the latter part of the month and throughout June, the production toured the north of England and Scotland, with great success, but Britten was devastated to be separated from his partner for so long; when Peter managed to get a couple of days off, catching an overnight train from Glasgow, Ben 'walked five miles to the station (Chelsea to King's Cross) by 7.10 in the morning (started at 5.50) to meet him – I'm pretty proud of that!'[11] The letters between them, though discreetly signed with initials, are unreservedly passionate and, in one case, hysterically angry. This was on 1 June, when a little drama of missed telephone calls led to a furious outburst from Britten: 'Why the hell can't you organise your times abit – why the hell don't you do what you say, be in till 10.15 – why the hell – well, & so on. And all because I wanted to speak to you so badly. Boohoo. Boohoo.'[12] But there was another reason for his unhappiness, for he had just spent a disastrous afternoon with Wulff: 'Poor dear, he's had such a hell of a time – but it's accentuated the old hard, vindictive side of him; the old conventional communist, materialist side; the boasting, garrulous side too – so that he's completely unbearable.'[13] They went to see a film, John Ford's *How Green Was My Valley*, which was 'easier than talking to him – but a *lousy* picture'.[14] A few days later, writing to Elizabeth Mayer, he could put the matter more calmly: Wulff was 'rather altered', 'rather vindictive, and hard', but 'underneath he is an awfully sweet boy. Perhaps if he could find the right girl whom he could marry . . .'[15] In being hard on Wulff, he was really being hard on himself: what he hadn't quite appreciated was how far he too had been changed (he was 'much older', as Beth had noted) by the experience of the past three years. They did meet again in September when, at Boosey & Hawkes in Regent Street, Britten gave him a miniature score of *Les Illuminations* inscribed: 'For Wulff of course – Benjamin B. September 1942, i.e. 3 years too late.'[16]

Despite a summer of anxiety and illness – he blamed overwork and lack of vitamins, but his 'nice new doctor, a Norwegian' was taking him 'very seriously' and prescribing 'bottle after bottle of the most revolting medicines'[17] – Britten had cause for satisfaction in the way his work was at last being appreciated. On

22 July, the first English performance of the *Sinfonia da Requiem* was given at the Proms by the LPO under Basil Cameron, an occasion preceded by articles in the BBC's two weeklies ('The Virtuosity of Benjamin Britten' by Jack Westrup in the *Listener* and 'Britten's New Symphony' by Ralph Hill in the *Radio Times*) and followed by positive reviews, among which William Glock's in the *Observer* was especially perceptive. Glock saw the *Sinfonia* as deriving from Liszt and Fauré but also from Mahler and Berg. Like other critics, he rather undervalued the transcendental power of the third movement – although this may have been due to the performance – but he greatly admired the first: 'And although we can take Britten's orchestral imagination for granted by now,' he wrote, 'the invention here is on the Berlioz–Mahler level.'[18] Britten told his old friend Mary Behrend that he was 'happy about the show – with all its defects it was a much better performance than I had expected, a grand reception, & on the whole kind criticisms'.[19] Further performances were scheduled for London, Manchester, Liverpool and, as Britten wonderingly noted, Stockholm.

A still more significant occasion followed on 23 September at Wigmore Hall, when the first public performance of *Seven Sonnets of Michelangelo* was given by Pears, the work's dedicatee, accompanied by Britten at the piano. Although Pears's vocal technique and confidence had improved immeasurably in the two years since the cycle's completion, this remained a very special challenge, while Britten, who suffered appalling stage fright before performing, was terrified: 'I was dreadfully nervous . . . it was rather like parading naked in public.'[20] He knew, nevertheless, that it had to be done and done well and, no less crucially, seen to be done well: in an uncharacteristically confident piece of self-promotion, he told Ernest Newman, chief music critic of the *Sunday Times*, 'I am so keen for you to hear them [the *Sonnets*], as I am pleased with them myself – a very

rare occurrence with me!'[21] Newman was indeed in the audience
and thought that the songs were 'evidently of exceptional quality,
but the style is so unexpectedly different from that of Mr Britten's
other recent works . . . that one can record only the general
impression made by the first performance'. *The Times* gratify-
ingly noted that Pears's 'pleasing voice' had 'grown more robust
and his skill consolidated by experience', while Ferruccio Bonavia
in the *Telegraph* nicely caught the distinction of Britten's setting:
'The writing is lyrical and, at the same time, utterly unconventional.' It was, however, Edward Sackville-West in the *New
Statesman and Nation* who made the largest and most memorable
claim: 'I suggest that these are the finest chamber songs England
has had to show since the seventeenth century, and the best any
country has produced since the death of Wolf.'[22] The audience
response was rapturous, although a later *Telegraph* critic, Peter
Stadlen, remembered that it was preceded by 'a second or two
of tense silence':[23] the two men on the stage were, after all,
well known as pacifists in wartime, but were they also – in these
settings of homoerotic poems dedicated by one to the other –
quietly yet firmly declaring something else? An elderly Wigmore
Hall stagehand, congratulating Britten on the performance,
'added that he hadn't been aware of their "particular (hm) friendship"'.[24] That Britten and Pears were announcing a more than
musical partnership seems to have been tacitly understood and
accepted with tactful generosity by many, perhaps most, of those
present.

Immediately after the performance, they were approached
with an offer to record the *Sonnets* commercially, which they
did at EMI's Abbey Road studios on 20 November. The records,
produced by Walter Legge and released as a pair of plum-label
HMV 78s (one 10″ and one 12″), were an immediate success
and they remain astonishing: Pears's declamatory confidence is
balanced by wry hints of intimacy, and the unaccompanied

paragraph at the start of the final sonnet has never sounded more glorious. Pears and Britten gave further performances of the cycle at a National Gallery lunchtime concert on 22 October and at Charlton House, Greenwich, on 2 May 1943, in aid of the Friends War Relief Service. But they also included the work in the recitals they gave, sometimes in improbably remote venues, for CEMA, the recently established Council for the Encouragement of Music and the Arts (and forerunner of the Arts Council): William Glock wrote in the *Observer* that Britten 'had introduced his *Michelangelo Sonnets* to an audience in Bishop's Stortford, who fell completely in love with them'[25] on 18 November. These recitals were undertaken as a contribution to the war effort and would have daunted or depressed many professional musicians, but Britten, who always enjoyed bringing music to non-specialist audiences, enthusiastically described them to Elizabeth Mayer:

> We go all over the place, under the strangest conditions – playing on awful old pianos – singing easy, but always good, programmes – & really have the greatest successes with the simplest audiences . . . I feel it is absolutely worth it, because, as we have so often agreed, it does get music really to the people, finds out what they want & puts the emphasis on the music, & not the personality of the artist, or their previous fame. One starts completely from 'scratch' as it were, since more often than not, they haven't even heard of Schubert – much less, Britten or Pears![26]

To Bobby Rothman, he added that he had to 'play on pianos all out of tune, when some of the notes won't go down & those that do won't come up'.[27] On one occasion, after performing for CEMA at Melksham in Wiltshire, Britten and Pears went on to give a shorter recital at a school three miles away; an admiring pupil, Claire Purdie, having walked to hear them in Melksham, walked back to the school to hear them again. But by the time she arrived on foot, their second programme was over: 'I was so upset that I marched in without thinking and told them what had happened. Whereupon BB opened the piano lid and PP sang "Down by the Salley Gardens" just for me.'[28]

In August, Britten and Pears had moved to 104a Cheyne Walk, SW10, the house of their old friend Ursula Nettleship, who was working as an administrator for CEMA and responsible for organising many of their recitals; but, although she was out of London much of the time, the arrangement could only be a temporary one. 'We still haven't found a nice place to live in London, though we have tried everywhere,' Britten told Elizabeth Mayer in November, quite reasonably adding: 'It's very difficult not being able to unpack one's things.'[29] And there were other, more personal difficulties: the lack of a permanent London home, combined with Pears's increasingly hectic touring schedule, led to misery when they were apart and rows when they were together. Their letters and telephone calls were filled with affectionate attempts to repair the damage inflicted by 'our miserable tiffs', as Pears called them. Early in December, Britten wrote to him – somewhere in the West Midlands, where he was singing to factory audiences – to apologise for an 'uncommunicative' phone conversation: 'Ursula was in the room & I couldn't say much. We have patched up our little scrap, but I find living here very difficult. She has been in bed all day & had to be waited on abit.'[30] It's possible that Ursula Nettleship didn't realise her tenants were lovers, though likelier that the reticent Britten simply didn't wish an emotional conversation to be overheard. She certainly treated them as formal tenants: *Letters from a Life* reproduces her signed and intemised receipt for the eight weeks to 31 January 1943, with a fairly hefty total of £27 (rent £16, light and heat £2, telephone £9).[31]

Since their return to England, Britten and Pears had made some important new friends. One was Clifford Curzon, probably the finest and certainly the most fastidious English pianist of his generation, with whom Britten was to perform and record the two-piano works written for 'the two gizzards' or 'the little owls', as he called the Robertsons. Another was Michael Tippett, who had been in the audience at the National Gallery performance of the *Michelangelo Sonnets*; when Britten was shown Tippett's *A Child of Our Time* (not to receive its premiere until March 1944) in December, he thought it 'a grand work', and in 1943 Tippett was to compose *Boyhood's End* for Pears and Britten. There is a clear shift of emphasis here, away from the left-wing documentary-makers and literati who had figured so largely in Britten's pre-war London life and towards relationships solidly underpinned by shared musical values. But a third new friendship, though creatively productive, was emotionally rather more complicated. This was with the music critic Edward Sackville-West, who had written with such enthusiasm about the *Michelangelo Sonnets*. By that time, he and Britten had already met and discussed the possibility of incidental music for a two-part radio drama, to be called *The Rescue*, based on the *Odyssey* of Homer. When shown a draft version of the opening pages in October, Britten was delighted: 'It has quite a terrifying atmosphere, & grand opportunities for juicy music!'[32] The following month, on 16 November, there was a private concert at 96 Cheyne Walk, a few steps from 104a. James Lees-Milne was there, in his driest Casca-esque mood:

Rick [Stewart-Jones] and John Russell organized a concert at Whistler's House, 96, in which Eddy and young Benjamin Britten played on two pianos Schubert and Chopin, and a tenor, Peter Pears, sang extremely competently the Dichterliebe of Schumann as well as Seven Sonnets of Michelangelo, composed by Britten himself. Everyone said what a good concert this was. I am so ignorant I can only judge music emotionally, not intellectually.[33]

Then, at the beginning of December, Britten received from Sackville-West an overwrought letter, which began 'Dear White Child' (an allusion to Auden's 'dear white children' in the *Hymn to St Cecilia*) and, after a glancing reference to *The Rescue*, continued: 'How foolish I am to be writing to you like this! how foolish ever to have told you how much – how unspeakably I love you! For I know from experience how unwelcome and embarrassing it is to be loved by someone for whom you cannot care.'[34] Britten replied with calming kindness and 'real affection', wanting their friendship to survive (as it did), not least because 'I love being with you & picking your brains'.

The first public performance of the *Michelangelo Sonnets* at Wigmore Hall was followed on 28 November by that of the confiscated and reconstructed *Hymn to St Cecilia*, given by the BBC Singers conducted by Leslie Woodgate; it had already been broadcast on 22 November, which was both the saint's day and the composer's twenty-ninth birthday. This benignly approachable piece, Britten's final collaboration with Auden and dedicated to their mutual friend Elizabeth Mayer, was also well received. Although Britten sometimes seemed unable to 'distinguish between the divine spark and the spark of the firework manufacturer', in this work he had 'not invoked St Cecilia in vain', said Gerald Abraham in the *Observer*. 'It is not merely that the "Hymn" sounds well; Britten's music almost always does. This is music that will probably last when Mr Britten's Roman candles are long burnt out.'[35] A week later, *A Ceremony of Carols* (subsequently revised by the composer) was performed at Norwich Castle by the women's voices of the Fleet Street Choir, who also gave the first London performance on 21

December at the National Gallery: neither the forces nor the venues were ideal for a work written with boy trebles in mind and, with its processional opening and recessional conclusion, intended to be heard in a church. On 13 December, Pears gave the first performance of four folk-song arrangements ('The Bonny Earl o' Moray', 'Little Sir William', 'The Salley Gardens' and that encore favourite 'Oliver Cromwell') in their orchestral versions, with the New London Orchestra conducted by Alex Sherman; two days after this, he successfully auditioned for Sadler's Wells Opera Company and at once embarked on a hectic sequence of operatic roles, starting with Tamino in *The Magic Flute*. And on 22 December, the BBC Midland Light Orchestra under Rae Jenkins gave, as a BBC Forces Service broadcast, the first English performance of *Matinées Musicales*.

So the year was ending with more in the way of performance and praise for both Britten and Pears than they would have dared to imagine when it began. Nevertheless, an otherwise happy Christmas was 'blighted' by the unexplained arrest of their friend and advocate Canon Stuart Morris on a charge under the Official Secrets Act; after a trial held *in camera*, he was sentenced to nine months in prison. More cheerfully, Beth Welford, who was imminently expecting her second child, had moved to the safety of Snape, where Sally – Britten's niece and Pears's god-daughter – was born on 13 January 1943. At Wigmore Hall on 30 January, Walter Goehr conducted the first English performance of *Les Illuminations* in its orchestral version, with Pears as soloist; a few days later, Britten and Pears left Cheyne Walk and moved to a maisonette at 45a St John's Wood High Street, NW8. This time, it was Pears who wrote to their common confidante Elizabeth Mayer in terms which neatly illustrate his and Britten's differing approaches to domestic life: 'It was very exciting going round choosing curtain materials – I wish you had been there. You can imagine how I enjoyed it and

Ben loathed it! They are nice curtains . . .'[36] At least Britten
now had somewhere to unpack his things.

He had hardly done so when once again, following a recurrent late-winter pattern, he became seriously ill: it seemed
possible that overuse of the proprietary drug usually called M&B
(sulphonamide, manufactured by May & Baker) had weakened
his long-term resistance to seasonal bugs. This year, however,
he developed measles and was sent to Grove Hospital in Tooting,
a circumstance which he managed to find ludicrous: 'Yes – isn't
this a major bore? – at *my* age too – Measles at Tooting!'[37] He
had plenty to think about musically and, thanks to Enid Slater,
plenty of books to read. She had sent him a life of Constable,
in whom he detected a kindred spirit: 'Apart from having an
almost sexy love for his paintings, I admire his extraordinary
oneness of purpose, & character to go on with lack of success.'[38]
Ralph Hawkes, indulging the invalid's passing fancy, gave him
a score of Richard Strauss's *Der Rosenkavalier*, as he was 'impatient to see how the old magician makes his effects'. Possibly to
Hawkes's relief (as well as ours), Britten assured him that his
own forthcoming opera wouldn't be 'as lush or glittering as this
one – after all there *is* a difference between Vienna & Suffolk!'[39]
Once out of Grove Hospital, he would need to go somewhere
quiet and rural for a few weeks to recuperate; fortunately, he
knew just the place.

2

The Old Mill stands on rising ground, just north of the village
centre in Snape, with views across the River Alde to the marshes
and reed beds beyond. At the crossroads is the Crown, on whose
main bar, with its curved high-backed settles, Britten and his

designer Kenneth Green would base the Boar in *Peter Grimes*; in 1943, there were several village shops, now mostly compressed into one small modern 'convenience store' on the site of a former garage. A few hundred yards beyond the Crown, a narrow railing-fenced bridge, demolished in 1959, crossed the Alde to the 'commodious wharf and warehouse'[40] founded by Newson Garrett and the handsome range of nineteenth-century industrial buildings known – despite actually being in the neighbouring parish of Tunstall – as Snape Maltings. Along the northern bank of the river, the Sailor's Path leads to the coast, four miles away at Aldeburgh. This is Crabbe's country, and Britten's: he may not have been a true local, but neither was he an 'incomer'. He was indisputably a Suffolk man, with relatives in the county (some of whom had lived at the Old Mill in his absence), so he could justifiably feel that he was back where he belonged. 'We are so happy here in Snape,' he wrote, 'Beth & the children, Kit, when he can get away, & the same for Peter . . .'[41] It was a good place for him to recuperate: he was at home and with a family around him.

Beth remembered that, in the months following his return to Snape, her brother struck 'a bad patch' and became 'convinced he would never write anything again'; but this time, instead of contemplating an alternative career in hardware, he spent his days 'walking across the marshes, walking in fact anywhere, everywhere'.[42] In doing so, he discovered the missing element in his creative routine: for almost the rest of his life, he would rise early, work through the morning until lunch at one o'clock, walk in the afternoon, work from tea until dinner and, after dinner, read or talk or listen to music. During one of these walks, he was passing the Maltings, 'singing at the top of his voice and waving his stick in the air, when he suddenly realised that a group of people were staring at him'. 'They must have thought I was mad,' he told his sister, an impression doubtless reinforced by the fact that, according to Oliver Knussen, 'Britten had one of the most appalling singing voices of any composer I've ever come across . . . no pitch to speak of – just a kind of *Sprechstimme* drone.'[43] His routine wasn't, however, quite as puritanically rigid as it may seem. 'Sometimes,' Beth said, 'when I went to take him his coffee, I found Ben reading a "who-dunnit". When I looked surprised, he would look up guiltily and say that it relaxed him,'[44] just as potboilers and cartoons had done a decade earlier.

While working on the incidental music for the radio series *An American in England*, which was broadcast weekly to America at 3 a.m. London time during the summer of 1942, Britten had been astonished by the brilliance of the RAF Orchestra's 21-year-old principal horn, Dennis Brain, for whom he 'took every opportunity to write elaborate horn solos'. Then, during the feverish leisure of his stay at Grove Hospital, he found that he was 'intrigued by the Nocturne idea for Voice & Horn';[45] not, of course, for any old voice and horn, but specifically for Pears and Brain. It was to be Britten's first major composition since returning to England but, as he worked on it at Snape, he was cautiously if knowingly modest. Writing to Pears on 21 March, and regretting that he'd been unable to accompany him in recitals, he casually mentioned that 'at least I've been able to write things for you',[46] while in early April he told Elizabeth Mayer that he had 'practically completed a new work (6 Nocturnes) for Peter [and] a lovely young horn player Dennis Brain, & Strings'. 'It is not important stuff,' he added, 'but quite pleasant, I think.'[47] This unimportant stuff would be dedicated, as an elegant acknowledgement of the love he couldn't return, to Edward Sackville-West, who had advised him in choosing the poems to be set, and it would be called the *Serenade*, Op. 31, for tenor, horn and strings.

Britten's selection of texts for this work is of special interest because – unlike those for *Les Illuminations* and the *Michelangelo Sonnets*, which were in languages likely to be safely incomprehensible to an audience (at least on first hearing) – they were in English. In discussing the *Serenade*, Humphrey Carpenter drew attention to the composer's engaging habit of 'wandering about the house and picking books from the shelves at random',[48] when he was having trouble with his work, as an explanation for his wide and eclectic knowledge of poetry; but this belongs to a slightly later period, when he had a more established home and a larger library. In fact, he found all but two of the poems in the *Serenade* in the copy of Quiller-Couch's *Oxford Book of English Verse* which he won as a school prize in 1930. He listed sixteen possibilities on the back flyleaf, of which he was to set five: 'Blow, Bugle, Blow' (Tennyson), the anonymous 'Lyke-Wake Dirge', 'Hymn to Diana' (Jonson) and 'Sonnet: To Sleep' (Keats) were included in the *Serenade*, although Britten discarded his posthumously published setting of Tennyson's 'Summer Night' ('Now sleeps the crimson petal . . .'), partly on musical grounds but also, Donald Mitchell suggests, 'perhaps because so overt an affirmation of the composer's love for his soloist might have generated problems in the early 1940s'. This would have mattered less if the poem had been in French or Italian. Of the two remaining poems in the *Serenade*, Blake's 'The Sick Rose' would probably have been known to Britten, but the stanzas from Cotton's 'Evening Quatrains' ('The day's grown old, the fainting sun / Has but a little way to run . . .'), which so magically follow the horn's Prologue, may well have been unfamiliar to him: Mitchell suspects 'that it was exactly here where Sackville-West may have stepped in, perhaps with more suggestions among which were Blake's and Cotton's texts'.[49] If so, and even if his influence were confined to the scene-setting Cotton, Sackville-West's role in shaping the *Serenade* was a crucial one. In fact, the cycle's final shape follows the kind of pattern which becomes increasingly familiar in Britten's settings of English poetry: outer movements evoking night and sleep surround a dark centre, here provided by Blake's 'O Rose, thou art sick!' and the terrifying fifteenth-century dirge.

Pears, however, at first had reservations. 'How are the songs?' he asked in an undated letter from Blackpool Opera House, where he was about to sing the Duke in Sadler's Wells's production of *Rigoletto*. 'I do hope I didn't damp your poor old enthusiasm too much about them . . .'[50] They had evidently had one of their quite frequent (and neither shocking nor surprising) disagreements the previous weekend during Pears's visit to Snape: it's conceivable that Pears felt some jealousy or resentment about Sackville-West's involvement with the work. On 1 April, Britten reassured him: '[D]on't worry, the Nocturnes will be worthy of you by the time I've finished!'[51] As indeed they were when Pears and Brain gave the first performance later that year.

Illness had forced Britten to cancel scheduled appearances – William Glock had to deputise for him at a Wigmore Hall performance of the *Michelangelo Sonnets* in March – although what irritated him most was that a recording for Decca of the *Hymn to St Cecilia* by the Fleet Street Choir had gone ahead without his permission or supervision. He tried to get it withdrawn and managed to have it re-recorded, yet he remained unhappy: 'It is a pity,' he told Hawkes, 'but the moral is, don't get measles!'[52] At least he recovered in time to give a concert with Pears and Clifford Curzon, at the Arts Theatre in Cambridge on 25 April, which included the first British performances of his two-piano pieces. He also accepted a slightly eccentric invitation from the Revd Walter Hussey, of St Matthew's Church, Northampton, which reached him via Hawkes, 'to write some music for our Jubilee celebrations next September'. Throughout his church career at Northampton and later as Dean of Chichester, Hussey was energetic and successful in commissioning work both from composers and from visual artists; what almost certainly clinched the matter for Britten was the postscript added to his letter of 22 March, in which he apologised for seeming 'impertinent' but hoped 'you will forgive me and put it down to enthusiasm for a great "bee" of mine – closer association between the arts and the Church'.[53] Britten replied that he shared Hussey's 'bee' and was sure he could manage an anthem: 'Something lively for such an occasion, don't you think?' The result would be *Rejoice in the Lamb*, Op. 30. A more modest anniversary was the tenth birthday of the Boyd Neel Orchestra in June: many of its regular members were now servicemen, but it proved possible to assemble eighteen players for a celebratory concert at Wigmore Hall on 23 June and for this occasion Britten composed his *Prelude and Fugue*, Op. 29. The typically unsettled, questing violin melody of the prelude is followed by a dazzlingly energetic fugue and an elegant reprise of the opening theme: it's a mystery that this enjoyable little work (of just under ten minutes) is so seldom heard.

'One great new friend Peter & I have made, an *excellent* composer, & most delightful man, Michael Tippett is having a bad time & may have to go to prison (you can guess what for),'[54] Britten told Elizabeth Mayer on 22 May. Shortly after he and Pears gave the first performance of Tippett's *Boyhood's End* at Morley College on 5 June – the first work written specifically for them by another composer – Tippett was indeed sentenced to three months' imprisonment in Wormwood Scrubs, having refused to undertake non-combatant military duties. He was, however, amused to be given charge of the prison orchestra in succession to Ivor Novello, who had been convicted of petrol-coupon fraud. On 11 July, Britten and Pears gave a recital in the prison, at which John Amis contrived to be present in the guise of page-turner:

> But when we got inside I explained to the chaplain that the
> turning over was so complicated that we needed an extra person
> to help, someone who could read music. The chaplain replied
> he had no one on the staff who could read music. I asked if we
> could borrow prisoner No. 5832, Tippett, M., who was known
> to us and could read music. The chaplain said it was against all
> the rules but he would see what he could do. So Michael came
> on to the platform with us and we turned alternate pages. It
> was a very moving occasion.[55]

With remission, Tippett was released from Wormwood Scrubs
on 21 August. He went straight to have breakfast with Britten
and Pears at St John's Wood High Street and then on to an
afternoon concert at Wigmore Hall, at which the Zorian Quartet
performed his second String Quartet.

For *Rejoice in the Lamb*, Britten chose to set extracts from
Christopher Smart's marvellous though extremely strange
Jubilate Agno, a decision which may have slightly alarmed Walter
Hussey, to whom he wrote on 28 May: 'I am afraid I have gone
ahead, and used abit about the cat Jeffrey, but I don't see how
it could hurt anyone – he is such a nice cat.'[56] In fact, the two
men established an easy rapport before they met, through letters
which display a charming lightness of touch on both sides. These
culminated in Hussey's list of queries about the work, sent in
late August, which he arranged as a typed questionnaire, with
blanks to be completed and phrases to be deleted, and headed
with the following rubric: 'Five minutes only – I hope – are
necessary for this paper. Candidates should attempt all ques-
tions.' Britten dealt with this in the appropriate spirit, signing
it 'E. B. Britten (minor) *(School Certificate – 5 credits)' and
adding a footnote: '*In addition to this startling qualification,
it might interest you to know I was also a valuable member of
all the elevens, Victor Ludorum, held record for several years

for Throwing the Cricket Ball (until broken by a beastly boy in a gale), apart from my highly distinguished career in the Junior Tennis World. So now you know the stature of the composer you're dealing with – !'[57] On the day of the performance, Britten was accompanied by Michael Tippett, who at his instigation had composed a *Fanfare for Brass* for the same occasion, and with whom he processed in surplice and cassock to the choir stalls: Britten, Hussey remembered, had 'slight hesitations' but Tippett 'encouraged him and they walked together and sat in the choir in like style'.[58] After the performance, Britten wrote to Hussey to say that it had been 'a great experience' and to thank the choir and the soloists, as well as the organist, Charles Barker, who had played 'most intelligently & sensitively'.[59]

By then, he added, he was busy with 'horribly-boring "incidentals"', by which he meant the music – some eighty cues lasting almost seventy-five minutes – for Edward Sackville-West's *The Rescue*. It was his most substantial work for radio, broadcast on 25 and 26 November and on several later occasions; the BBC Symphony Orchestra was conducted by Clarence Raybould. Meanwhile Britten, who had been scheduled to conduct, was in Devon, pretending to be ill and staying with Christopher Martin, the Arts Department Administrator at Dartington Hall, and his wife Cicely: his absence from Broadcasting House was the result of a furious row with Arthur Bliss, the BBC's Director of Music, over his status as a conscientious objector. The programme was well received, although Britten, in one of his frank updates to his transatlantic friend, confided that while Sackville-West was 'a friend of mine, sensitive & with good taste', he was 'not a great poet, and, after all this does need a great poet to stand up to one's memories of Homer'.[60] After that, he had to write *The Ballad of Little Musgrave and Lady Barnard*, for male voices and piano, dedicated to 'Richard Wood and the musicians of Oflag VIIB – Germany – 1943': the dedicatee, a prisoner of war at

Eichstätt, was the brother of the contralto Anne Wood, who had been a friend of Britten and Pears since the late 1930s. Britten finished the piece on 13 December.

The most critically important occasion of the autumn was unquestionably the first performance of the *Serenade*, given by Pears and Brain with strings conducted by Walter Goehr, at Wigmore Hall on 15 October: 'a lovely show, with wonderful enthusiasm and lovely notices'. Probably the loveliest was in the *Observer* by William Glock who, after recalling how his predecessor, A. H. Fox Strangways, had been able to hear new works by the mature Brahms, wrote: 'in Benjamin Britten we have at last a composer who offers us visions as great as those'. He described three of the songs – the Cotton, Tennyson and Keats – in some detail and concluded with the wish that 'HMV or Columbia or Decca should record this Serenade as soon as possible and the BBC should see that the country is made aware of its new masterpiece'.[61] The work received a second performance at Friends House, Euston Road, on 11 January 1944 and (in partial fulfilment of Glock's hopes) was recorded by Decca with Pears, Brain and the Boyd Neel Orchestra on 25 May and 8 October: Britten urged Pears to 'do a superb Serenade', and he did. This was one of a clutch of Britten recordings made by the company after their unsatisfactory effort with the *Hymn to St Cecilia*. The others included *A Ceremony of Carols*, with the Morriston Boys Choir, after the first performance of the revised version at Wigmore Hall on 4 December; three folk-song arrangements, performed by Pears and Britten, in January; and, also in January, the two-piano pieces, *Introduction and Rondo alla Burlesca* and *Mazurka Elegiaca*, with Clifford Curzon. Although Pears and Britten made some further recordings for HMV, such as the *Holy Sonnets of John Donne* in 1947, this marked the real beginning of Britten's lifelong relationship with Decca, which would grow into an unprecedented collection of recordings performed, conducted or supervised by a major composer, rivalled only by Stravinsky's association with Columbia.

In a letter to Elizabeth Mayer on 8 December 1943, Britten listed several aspects of his busy summer and autumn – at that point, he was 'quickly scribbling a short choral work' – before concluding triumphantly: 'And THEN I start the OPERA . . . Isn't that exciting?'[62]

3

When Britten first envisaged *Peter Grimes* as an opera, he thought of Christopher Isherwood as librettist. Isherwood gracefully declined the invitation on 18 February 1942: although he saw (or thought he saw) how it could be done, 'the real point is that I am quite sure I shan't have the time for such work for months or maybe years ahead; and frankly the subject doesn't excite me so much that I want to *make* time for it . . .'[63] Then Pears thought he might have a go but decided 'I hadn't the skill or the time, really'.[64] What neither man quite said was that, given the strangely charged relationship between Grimes and his apprentices, it was something of a hot potato: it's surely significant that, on arriving in England, Britten immediately passed it to the heterosexual, happily married Montagu Slater. No less significant is the fact that Slater was at best a second-rate literary talent, for Britten didn't want to be dominated again by a more powerful creative personality, as he had been by Auden. It was during his measles confinement at Grove Hospital that he began to experience doubts about Slater's ability – 'I'm beginning to feel that Montagu may not be the ideal librettist' – but he immediately rejected Auden as an alternative: 'Wystan, well – there are the old objections, & besides, he's not to hand.'[65]

Chief among his 'old objections', we may suspect, was that he found Auden an intellectual bully.

Yet there were two further reasons why the *Grimes* libretto was bound to be problematical: no one concerned had fully appreciated either the human range or the tragic ambition of Crabbe's poem, and Britten hadn't quite decided what he wanted to do with it. Isherwood, to return to him for a moment, thought the poem 'good melodramatic material'; as late as 1963, Britten himself insisted that *their* Grimes was 'a character of vision and conflict' and a 'tortured idealist, rather than the villain he was in Crabbe',[66] while, according to Pears in 1965, 'In the original poem by George Crabbe (from *The Borough*) Grimes is quite simply an unattractive and brutal ruffian';[67] and Philip Brett, in 1996, still thought Crabbe's Grimes 'an unmitigated ruffian'.[68] By embracing two common misconceptions – that the poem is 'melodramatic' and its tragic hero a 'villain' or a 'ruffian' – Britten, Pears and Slater created, and then proceeded to solve, imaginary problems. Of course, changes had to be made: as it stands, Crabbe's narrative might have translated, rather interestingly, into a different sort of musical work, something for a solo voice (Grimes) and an answering, commenting chorus, as in a Greek tragedy. Slater was right to see that, as an opera, it must be opened up: several villagers are given names and identities, while the schoolmistress Ellen Orford is imported from a quite separate poem in *The Borough*. Yet the problem with Ellen is that, although her love for Grimes is just about plausible, there's little reason to suppose that Grimes is in love with her: his attachment to her looks too much like a pacifying strategy and his repeated 'I'll marry Ellen' carries undertones of 'if I must' and (to the villagers) 'if that'll shut you up'. Consequently, we might begin to suspect Grimes of an emotional insincerity which seems at odds with the character in Crabbe's poem. More troubling, and less necessary, is Slater's altered ending: Crabbe clearly thinks of Grimes, who dies surrounded by villagers and tormented by demons, as a properly tragic figure, a point which he underlines with several allusions to *Macbeth*; Slater turns him into a suicide who goes out in his boat and drowns himself. Although this has the positive effect of reasserting the sea's role as almost a character in itself, it diminishes Grimes's tragic stature and gives the opera its disconcertingly muted conclusion.

Crabbe had the same advantage over Britten and Slater that Henry James had over Alan Hollinghurst: the very fact that there were things he couldn't say in brutal modern terms enabled him to write about them in other, more subtly nuanced ways. Crabbe seems to have understood that Grimes's sadism is an expression of unhappiness, disappointment, sexual rage and frustrated love: Grimes is the most inwardly realised of all the characters in *The Borough* – not least because, as I've suggested in 'In Search of Peter Grimes',[69] he is substantially based on the poet's own father. Moreover, he engages our sympathy in descriptive passages which find no direct equivalent in the opera, such as the unforgettable one beginning 'When tides were neap . . .' which conveys both Grimes's melancholic solitude and his consolatory identification with nature. Pears was initially tempted to make Crabbe's understated 'some, on hearing cries, / Said calmly, "Grimes is at his exercise"' more explicit: Slater had access to the material he had produced during the voyage home and, says Philip Brett, 'appears rather to have relished the hints of loose-living and sadism in Pears's drafts, even those of homoeroticism', but his own attempt at depicting Grimes's sexually charged violence towards his apprentice (of which a vestige remains in the hut scene) was disastrous.[70] It was Pears himself who then most clearly realised that their Grimes mustn't, after all, be seen as a sexual outsider: 'The more I hear of it,' he wrote, after Britten had played through to him as much as he'd written in March 1944, 'the more I feel that the queerness is unimportant & doesn't really exist in the music (or at any rate obtrude) so it mustn't do so in the words. P.G. is an introspective, an artist, a neurotic, his real problem is expression, self-expression.'[71] Ironically, this at last brings Grimes back closer to the character Pears had earlier misunderstood. Both he and Britten would later take the slightly disingenuous line that they sympathised with Grimes-the-outsider because they too were outsiders, but as pacifists rather than as homosexuals. In Tony Palmer's film *A Time There Was*, Pears says that Britten wrote the opera 'as a confrontation between an individual and society, which in fact was part of our own predicament at the time. We had obviously felt very much that we were in a very small minority of pacifists in a world of war.'[72] By 1980, this evasion wasn't really necessary; it was, however, too ingrained a habit for Pears to break.

At first Britten thought that *Peter Grimes*, commissioned by Koussevitzky, would receive its first production at the Berkshire Music Festival in Tanglewood, Massachusetts, in the summer of 1944, and he envisaged the title role as an operatic villain sung by a baritone; in any case, it was by no means certain that Pears would or could travel back to America in wartime. When the festival was suspended for the duration of the war, Koussevitzky generously allowed the premiere to take place in England; but long before then, as Pears continued to gain operatic experience while touring with Sadler's Wells, Britten had begun to think of Grimes being sung by a tenor. Thus the task of writing an opera for Koussevitzky steadily metamorphosed into the rather different task of writing an opera for Peter. Already weighted with sexual and geographical subtexts, it now acquired the special collaborative intensity of the *Michelangelo Sonnets* and the *Serenade*, in which the composer was writing specifically for a performer who was also his lover: we may sense this at moments of emotional vulnerability as different as the spellbinding aria

'Now the Great Bear and Pleiades' and the terrifying later 'mad scene'. But a creative relationship which could be natural and enriching for a single-voiced song cycle was likely to prove more problematical for a three-act opera. Pears, whose hectic touring schedule continued through 1944, took to viewing *Grimes* as his destiny: having just sung the 'dirty music' of *La Bohème* 'to the Queen & the Princesses (their first opera – most unsuitable I should have thought)', he consoled himself with the reflection that 'it's all good training for Peter Grimes, which is after all what I was born for, nicht-whar?'[73] Yet Britten's self-confidence was as fragile as ever. In January 1944, having 'broken the spell and got down to work' on *Grimes*, he was reaching for the safety of modest expectations: 'I don't know whether I shall ever be a good opera composer, but it's wonderful fun to try once in a way!' In April, he told Pears that 'Grimes is being such a brute at the moment', and in June: 'My bloody opera stinks, & that's all there is to it.'[74] To which Pears splendidly replied: 'I don't believe your opera stinks. I just don't believe it; anyway if it does, by all means be-Jeyes it, and have it as sweet as its writer for me when I see it.'[75]

But, if not at Tanglewood, where was it to be performed? Boosey & Hawkes had taken a lease on the Royal Opera House and would have liked it to be staged there; Pears's connections, on the other hand, were with Sadler's Wells, who hoped to reopen their closed London theatre the following spring. On 12 July, Britten spent 'a hectic day in London – those things around *all* day, with bumps & sirens galore – had lots to arrange, saw Ralph & fixed about P.G. at the Wells (I've written to Joan [Cross])'.[76] Although this sounds reassuringly definite, by the autumn it looked as if Sadler's Wells wouldn't be ready in time: its governing body had decided to extend their lease on the Prince's Theatre in Shaftesbury Avenue and proposed to stage *Grimes* there, an idea strongly opposed both by Britten and his

producer, Eric Crozier. There was also still the outside possibility of the Royal Opera House: 'I gather things are moving
towards Covent Garden abit,' wrote Britten in late November,
'but the betting's on P.G. at Sadler's Wells, I think now.'[77]
Meanwhile, working for the first time with an amanuensis, the
nineteen-year-old Arthur Oldham, he had begun the scoring,
which he completed on 10 February 1945: 'I have actually just
written "End" to the opera score,' he told Mary Behrend,[78]
although what he had actually written at the end of the score
was, more usefully, the date. Oldham, who stayed with Britten
at the Old Mill, happily settled into the composer's routine: 'He
would score all the morning, and then we'd go for long walks
in the afternoon, talking about music, and then in the evening
he'd do some more scoring and then after dinner we'd relax and
listen to music.' Britten, he told Humphrey Carpenter, believed
in a Michelangelo-like apprenticeship, 'learning (and he quoted
this) to "mix the paint" first, working together with a master,
and from that something would rub off'. His first task was ruling
bar lines, but he moved on to 'more constructive jobs' such as
making a two-piano arrangement of the *Simple Symphony*. When
Carpenter asked him whether the 'master' wasn't getting the
better of this deal, Oldham replied: 'I would say it was beneficial
five per cent to him and ninety-five per cent to me!' Britten, he
added, was 'an immensely good man'.[79] After the scoring was
finished, Britten and Pears developed further reservations about
aspects of Slater's libretto – especially the 'mad scene' in Act 3
– and enlisted the surreptitious help of Ronald Duncan in revising
it; as Duncan himself later pointed out, this 'wasn't easy' as it
'entailed finding lines to fit the precise run and stress of the
music'.[80] Although Slater grudgingly accepted the revisions, he
nevertheless published 'his' version in *Peter Grimes and other
poems* the following year.

That *Peter Grimes* was, in the end, the opera with which

Sadler's Wells reopened on 7 June 1945 was largely due to the determination of the company's director, the soprano Joan Cross, who also sang the role of Ellen Orford. Yet, as her successor as director, Tyrone Guthrie, pointed out to her in a letter of 23 December 1944, Cross's combination of administrator and performer created two difficulties. 'If you are – & while you are – Director you must not sing if there is any one else reasonably adequate available,' he wrote, partly because she wouldn't have the time and energy to do both but also because 'it gives the impression that so long as you are director, no leading soprano [he mentioned Joan Hammond] need apply'.[81] Guthrie was right to foresee trouble ahead. When rehearsals with the conductor, Reginald Goodall, got under way in March, it became clear that not everyone shared Joan Cross's enthusiasm for the work; the Welsh baritone who was to have taken the part of Balstrode actually withdrew. According to Pears, there was hostility from 'the older generation' both of governors and of singers, who would have preferred *Il Trovatore* or even *Merrie England*: a feeling, misguided though not incomprehensible, that the house's reopening at the end of a long war should be marked by something conservative or patriotic. Moreover, it could hardly escape the attention of the opera's enemies that its composer, star performer and producer, Eric Crozier, had all been conscientious objectors. Pears, as the opera's most public face, found himself attacked and derided, almost as if he were indeed Peter Grimes.

Because the company was touring, they had to rehearse wherever they happened to be: on 9 May, VE Day, they were in Wolverhampton and had no time to celebrate. Then, at Wigmore Hall on 31 May, there was a 'Concert-Introduction' to *Peter Grimes*, as part of the Boosey & Hawkes season: an introduction by Guthrie and an 'Outline of the Opera' by Crozier, with the musical illustrations provided by members of the cast and 'At the piano . . . Benjamin Britten'. In its more modest way, it must have been as extraordinary an evening as the opening night at Sadler's Wells a week later: the musical public's first inkling of the experience that awaited them. When that experience arrived, despite some imperfections in the performance, it was rapturously received, although the ovations were preceded by some moments of stunned silence, as was so often the case with Britten premieres. That reception was vividly described to Humphrey Carpenter by Leonard Thompson, who took the almost-silent part of the apprentice but, because his voice was breaking, couldn't manage the scream:

> When the curtain came down, for I imagine something like – well, it seemed like minutes, but it must have been about thirty seconds – there was *nothing*. Absolutely nothing. And then it broke out. And it went on and on. I think there were something like fourteen curtain calls. And Ben, of course, came on immaculate, in white tie and tails, looking like a matinee idol. And he just *folded* in the middle. That's the only way I can describe it – the deepest bow I've ever seen from anybody![82]

As ever on such occasions, Britten's composure was perfect; as ever, it was a mask. Throughout the performance, he had been pacing to and fro at the back of the theatre, too nervous to sit down; afterwards, amid the backstage congratulations, he was stony-faced. Only later, during the celebratory party given by Ralph Hawkes at the Savoy, did he begin to relax. Even so, it would take time for him to realise what he had just achieved.

Britten's achievement in *Peter Grimes* is characteristically paradoxical. The work is at once old-fashioned in its construction of linked set pieces and radical in its borrowing of montage techniques from the composer's experience in film and radio. From the opening moments, when Grimes is summoned to appear not only in court (to explain the death of his apprentice) but also in his own opera, it's clear that Britten is going to work hard on behalf of his central character. Peter Grimes's replies are surrounded by a halo of strings, almost as if he were Christ before Pontius Pilate in a Bach Passion; after this, his subsequent transitions from rough belligerence to aching introspection will be astonishing but not absurd. The pub scene which closes Act 1 – introduced, punctuated and concluded by the storm outside – is an especially bold exercise in juxtaposition: its edgy jollity and violent undercurrents are first disrupted by Peter, who enters and unexpectedly launches into his achingly inward aria 'Now the Great Bear and Pleiades' before this is swept away by the supposedly cathartic round 'Old Joe has gone fishing'; yet it too will be upset by Peter's own subversive version of the song, before Hobson the carrier arrives with the new apprentice and the storm licks round the act's end. Britten's sense of the cinematic is equally evident in the Sunday-morning scene which opens Act 2, in which the useless pieties of the offstage church service, complete with choir and organ, repeatedly nudge against the evolving human drama of Peter and Ellen on the street outside. This scene is the pivot on which the opera turns: by the end of it, the townsfolk are self-righteously setting off in pursuit of Peter in his hut. Two scenes packed with event, energy and development thus necessarily give way to the more sombre half of the opera: the by now inevitable sequence of the new apprentice's accidental death – not at his employer's hands but in a terrified fall – followed by Peter's descent into madness and his eventual suicide by drowning.

The critical reception was not one of unqualified praise; it was better than that. Because the opera was treated seriously, often at length, as a masterpiece, there was room for the reservations which form part of intelligent analysis. For instance, Frank Howes in *The Times* was worried about that anti-climactic final scene while, writing in *Time and Tide*, Philip Hope-Wallace detected 'some failure . . . in solving the problem of operatic tempo' and suggested that there was a problem with Grimes himself: 'We never really meet the man. His death breaks no heart. His suicide is a mere item of police court news.'[83] Though harsh and arguably misguided, Hope-Wallace's objections are all the more interesting because they would be so exactly answered by Britten in *Billy Budd*. Several reviewers were puzzled by the unresolved tension between sadistic villain and sympathetic outsider in Grimes (to which one possible reply is that it can be resolved only by his death), but almost everyone agreed that Pears was magnificent in the role. Scott Goddard, in the *News Chronicle*, thought that he 'gave a profoundly sympathetic rendering of the part for which he will be remembered' and concluded that the opera 'is a work that must not be ignored by those who admire originality and take the art of opera seriously'.[84] The following year, when Goddard contributed the chapter on Britten to A. L. Bacharach's *British Music of Our Time*, he dealt with the furore which had preceded the first night before adding: 'When at length *Peter Grimes* was heard, it was found to be finer as a work of art, less tendentious as a vehicle for ideas, less portentous as a manifesto than friends or enemies had implied.'[85] Among the most thoughtful of the first reviewers were William Glock in the *Observer* and Desmond Shawe-Taylor in the *New Statesman*, both of whom wrote twice and in some musical detail on *Peter Grimes*. Glock, who found 'the most masterly writing of all' in the church scene at the start of Act 2, returned to the subject a fortnight later in indignation, not with the opera but with those who had described it as 'fierce and challenging': 'What spoiled babies we have become. I should have thought that the most noticeable thing about Britten was his gift for making statements of undoubted originality in terms which everyone could understand.' He also added 'a last comment on Britten's treatment of words', insisting that

'Nowhere in "Peter Grimes" is there anything stiff or self-conscious'.[86]

Those last two points would have especially pleased the composer. In his own introduction to the opera, published in the *Sadler's Wells Opera Book* to accompany the production, he wrote: 'One of my chief aims is to try and restore to the musical setting of the English language a brilliance, freedom and vitality that have been curiously rare since the death of Purcell.'[87] It's a large and justified claim, made with persuasive modesty and indicating the special importance of Purcell for Britten during the 1940s; it may also slyly remind us that Purcell too could create a major opera from a poor libretto (Britten's own realisation of *Dido and Aeneas* would be produced in 1951). More intentionally sly were his gracious acknowledgements to Sadler's Wells, whose 'existence has been an incentive to complete *Peter Grimes*' and where 'the qualities of the Opera Company have considerably influenced both the shape and the characterization of the opera'. He hoped that 'the willingness of the Company to undertake the presentation of new operas' would 'encourage other composers to write works in what is, in my opinion, the most exciting of musical forms'.[88] This was a hope shared by William Walton, who wrote Britten a self-confessed '"fan" letter', praising his 'quite extraordinary achievement': 'It is just what English opera wants and it will I hope put the whole thing on its feet and give people at large quite another outlook about it.'[89] It's a handsome letter from the older composer, even if it doesn't quite square with Walton's reported lack of enthusiasm at the first night and his vote against a recording of *Peter Grimes* to be supported by the British Council, of whose Music Committee he was a member. By the time he received it in the third week of June, Britten himself had begun ruefully to admit that he might have achieved something special. Writing to an appreciative audience member, the mother of his 1930s colleague Basil Wright, he was 'awfully glad' that she had liked it and 'excited that it is going so well': 'It looks as if the old spell on British opera may be broken at last!'[90] If one spell had been broken, another had been created: 'I do not remember ever to have seen, at any performance of opera, an audience so steadily intent, so petrified and held in suspense as the audience of *Peter Grimes*,'[91] wrote Edmund Wilson. And the spell spread beyond the theatre: a bus conductor would shout to his passengers in Rosebery Avenue, 'Sadler's Wells! Any more for Peter Grimes, the sadistic fisherman?'

A week after the Sadler's Wells premiere of *Grimes*, Britten conducted the LSO in the first performance of *Four Sea Interludes from 'Peter Grimes'* at the inaugural Cheltenham Festival. These interludes, which were destined to have a separate life as one of Britten's most popular orchestral works, had originated in the practical necessity of having music to cover scene changes and to indicate time passing: they were in part a homage to his mentor Frank Bridge, who had died in 1941 and whose episodic, impressionistic *The Sea* had 'knocked sideways' the ten-year-old Britten when he heard it in Norwich. But they also seem to be – even more than the rest of the opera – music that couldn't have been written anywhere but the Suffolk coast. Their unmistakable sense of *spiritus loci* goes well beyond the mimetic recreations of storm and calm and distant church bells: while their focus is self-evidently the sea at Aldeburgh, they are also redolent of Snape, with its marshes and mudflats, its curlews and skylarks, and its huge shifting sky. Goddard, rounding off his 1946 essay on Britten (with a clear sense that the composer was likely to render it out of date by the time it reached print), added a final sentence to his comments on *Peter Grimes*: 'And when the *Four Interludes* from the opera were played at the Cheltenham Festival a few months [*sic*] later, there was no questioning the quality of vision Britten had experienced nor his remarkable success in expressing that vision in music of great emotional power, penetrating beauty and a completely individual manner of writing.'[92] Also at Cheltenham was another senior composer, Rutland Boughton, who, having heard the *Interludes*, found himself 'compelled to run to town for the complete work, and I rejoice in it even though my old ears cannot always accept your dissonances . . .'[93] Boughton, who was to lecture on opera in London on 1 September, wanted to refer to *Grimes* and wondered whether there might be further performances at Sadler's Wells in the autumn. But that, as Britten told him, was not to be: 'I am afraid that there won't be any performances in London in the near future: there has been a big bust-up in the company, & the Governors of the Wells have sided with the "opposition" to Grimes, & so it doesn't seem likely that it will be revived there.'[94] There were in fact to be ten further performances of the opera at Sadler's Wells the following spring – Pears and Cross, having by this time resigned from the company, appeared as guest artists – and on 13 March it was broadcast live from the theatre, though apparently not without technical problems, by the BBC.

Peter Grimes is a great – for many, the greatest – English opera; yet it deals with themes which were controversial and ambiguous and, moreover, places them in a setting which must have seemed intractably unfamiliar to most of its London audience. Its triumphant success speaks well for the intelligent receptiveness of both critics and public – though not, alas, of the management at Sadler's Wells. In July 1945, having irrevocably altered the course of music in England, it would have been more than understandable if Britten had decided that he deserved a relaxing holiday.

4

At a party given by Boosey & Hawkes while *Peter Grimes* was in repertoire at Sadler's Wells, Britten found himself talking to the violinist Yehudi Menuhin, who told him that he was about to undertake a tour of Germany, performing at venues which would include the former concentration camp at Belsen and taking with him Gerald Moore as accompanist. Like Menuhin, Britten had been 'casting about for some commitment to the human condition whose terrible depths had been so newly revealed' and begged to take Moore's place. In the few days remaining before their departure, 'Ben and I made an attempt at rehearsing a repertoire,' Menuhin remembered, 'only, after five minutes, to abandon it . . . we put our trust in luck and musical compatibility . . .' Their trust was not misplaced. They took with them 'more or less the whole standard violin literature' and they played 'without rehearsal, two or three times a day for ten days in the saddest ruins of the Third Reich'.[95] On 27 July, at Belsen, they performed twice in one afternoon; there, among the audience, was a twenty-year-old cellist, Anita Lasker (the future Mrs Peter Wallfisch and member of Aldeburgh's 'house band', the English Chamber Orchestra). She had heard of Menuhin but not of the pianist, who found himself inadvertently renamed 'Mr Button, Mr Menuhin's secretary', and shortly after the concert she described this mysterious individual in a letter to an aunt: 'Concerning the accompanist, I can only say that I just can not imagine anything more beautiful (wonderful). Somehow one never noticed that there was any accompanying going on at all, and yet I had to stare at this man like one transfixed as he sat seemingly suspended between chair and keyboard, playing so beautifully.' Also present was an English nurse who recalled 'two compassionate men clad simply in shirt and shorts creating glorious melody and moving amongst the people'.[96] Back home at the Old Mill on 1 August, Britten in his usual self-deprecating way told Pears that 'Yehudi was nice, & under the circumstances the music was as good as it could be', before adding: 'We stayed the night in Belsen, & saw over the hospital – & I needn't describe *that* to you.'[97] Not only 'needn't', but 'couldn't': both Menuhin and Pears agreed that Britten never again spoke about Belsen until very near the end of his life when, Pears told Tony Palmer, he said 'that the experience had coloured everything he had written subsequently'.[98]

What did this actually mean? It may remind us of Theodor Adorno's hauntingly memorable, though now clearly misguided, maxim that to write poetry after Auschwitz is barbaric; of course, if he had subscribed to that, Britten would never have written another note. Presumably he meant that the unclouded childlike optimism for which he had sometimes striven was no longer an option in his music, although (and quite logically) he would come to value it even more in children. Creatively, a time when 'all went well' was from now on only available to him as a barely accessible memory. There are very few easy resolutions in Britten's later work; and ease, when it is attempted, is always troubled by ambiguity. His increasing preference for leaner forms and smaller forces, though also shaped by practical circumstances, was precisely consistent with this altered view of art. And so was his choice of habitat: the bleakly chastening landscape of coastal Suffolk is plainly conducive to a musical language as ruthless and clear as winter light over the reed beds.

On his return from Germany, Britten became feverishly ill: this was possibly a reaction to the vaccination ordered by his doctor, but it was also his usual reaction to stress and, in a pattern stretching back to *Quatre Chansons Françaises*, it provided the creative incubation period for a new song cycle, *The Holy Sonnets of John Donne*, Op. 35, which he completed on 19 August. Although he had been thinking about setting Donne for at least two years, the task now became different and urgent. The result is perhaps the most abrasive and least amenable of his major song cycles: it opens mercilessly, with an accompaniment of pared-down chromaticism, and although it ends with the defiant

'Death be not proud . . .', it does so without any sense of triumph. The cycle's emotional centre of gravity comes at the end of the third sonnet where, over a simple rocking two-note figure in the accompaniment, the tenor sings on almost a single note (like a pendant to 'Now the Great Bear and Pleiades'): 'To poore me is allow'd / No ease, for long, yet vehement griefe hath beene / Th'effect and cause, the punishment and sinne.' One problem for the literary-minded listener is that Donne's great sonnets are exceptionally dependent on metrical checks and balances within each line, which Britten often overrides (this habit is naturally less intrusive in his settings of obscure or minor poems); in Pears and Britten's 1949 HMV recording, which is the closest we have to their original intentions, Pears sounds strained or pushed at some of the more awkward moments. Yet one might with equal justice describe the cycle as courageous and uncompromising, noting too that its bleak angularities seem to belong as unmistakably as *Peter Grimes* to the unforgiving Suffolk coast. Behind it, neither for the first time nor the last, stands Purcell and, in this case, his *Divine Hymns*. The work received its premiere, performed by Pears and Britten, in a concert marking the 250th anniversary of Purcell's death, at Wigmore Hall on 22 November 1945, which was also Britten's thirty-second birthday.

The same venue had already hosted one Purcell anniversary concert, on the previous evening, which included the first performance, by the Zorian String Quartet, of a work completed even more recently by Britten: his Second String Quartet, Op. 36. This had been commissioned by Mary Behrend, to whom he presented the manuscript score in December: 'I am so glad you got pleasure from it because to my mind it is the greatest advance that I have yet made, & altho' it is far from perfect, it has given me encouragement to continue on new lines.'[99] Its most striking novelty is the extended, eighteen-minute-long passacaglia or 'Chacony' – a favourite form of Purcell's and of Britten's – which concludes the work, a troubled and haunting movement made instantly memorable by the bold unison statement of the theme with which it begins. The equally spaced strokes with which this movement ends seem to hint at physical violence, a memory of South Lodge or of Grimes 'at his exercise'. John Amis, who was married to the quartet's leader, Olive Zorian, recalled Britten attending rehearsals at their flat, 'advising, encouraging, strict but tactful, the model of composer behaviour'. He also noticed a characteristic of Britten's, endearing at a distance, which could be difficult to decode: his knack of being utterly serious about music without appearing to take himself at all seriously. Amis would occasionally ask about a detail or make an admiring remark such as, '"Oh, I see, this new tune is really the old one upside down" . . . at which Ben would look hard at his score and say '"Oh, is it? Fancy that!" Sometimes he would wink as he said it.'[100] *The Times*, reviewing both Purcell concerts, was slightly cautious about the quartet ('pungent without being aggressive, original without strain') but keener on the song cycle which 'triumphs by its sustained intensity'.[101]

Britten composed a third Purcell-inspired work in the autumn of 1945, the music for a Ministry of Education film – *Instruments of the Orchestra*, directed by Muir Matheson – which he completed on New Year's Eve; in its concert version, the score would become known as *The Young Person's Guide to the Orchestra*, Op. 34, subtitled 'Variations and Fugue on a Theme of Henry Purcell'. The theme, from Purcell's music for *Abdelazar* (it also exists in a keyboard version), is used as the basis for variations by each section of the orchestra in turn before it shoulders its way back into the fugue. Some writers on Britten pass swiftly over the piece as if its clarity and popularity make it beneath notice; but the work is remarkable for at least two reasons. Firstly, it achieves its stated and tricky aim of providing an introduction to the symphony orchestra without either longeurs or condescension. But secondly, and perhaps more intriguingly, something very particular happens when the Purcell theme makes its magnificent reappearance in the closing fugue. I remember that some years ago, at the Aldeburgh Festival, I found myself talking to a distinguished twentieth-century music specialist in the Cross Keys: when the conversation turned to that puzzling topic of music which moves the listener beyond measure, I expected my friend to nominate something difficult and obscure. No, he said, the moment when the Purcell theme re-emerges in the *Young Person's Guide* is the one that does it every time. And in John Bridcut's film *Britten's Children*, there's a touching interview in which David Hemmings makes a similar point: after humming and pomming the theme, with tears in his eyes, he says, '*That*'s the champagne moment.' So it is, and it is also something else: the Elgar moment. For it will surely remind us of the way in which the opening theme returns, similarly transformed by its altered context, at the end of Elgar's first symphony. Britten had already made his peace with Elgar, as we have seen, and by thus nodding towards him in the *Young Person's Guide* he acknowledged two of his greatest English predecessors in a single work.

The composer had one young person especially in mind: eleven-year-old Humphrey Maud, son of his friends John Maud, at that time Permanent Secretary at the Ministry of Education, and his wife Jean (née Hamilton), a concert pianist. Britten had stayed with the Mauds in London in the peripatetic period following his return from America, and Humphrey remembered him 'playing through the first drafts of Peter Grimes on their piano'.[102] Later, the Maud family visited the Old Mill. Britten, Jean Maud recalled, 'was absolutely delightful with children and happy with them and they were happy with him in the most unaffected way – I mean, when we went (before he moved to

Aldeburgh) to Snape, to the Lighthouse, wasn't it?'[103] She was especially touched that the published score's dedication – 'This work is affectionately inscribed to the children of John and Jean Maud: Humphrey, Pamela, Caroline and Virginia, for their edification and entertainment' – included their eldest daughter, who had died in 1941. Humphrey, who played the cello and at the age of thirteen went on to Eton, would in due course become a regular guest at Britten and Pears's Aldeburgh home.

Their London home, meanwhile, had become unexpectedly crowded. Erwin Stein, whom Britten first met in Vienna in 1934, had four years later moved with his wife Sophie and daughter Marion to London, where he joined Boosey & Hawkes as an editor. When, in November 1944, their London flat was destroyed by fire, Britten's first concern was for the manuscript of *Peter Grimes*: 'Erwin's flat has been drenched as the house caught fire, but luckily the P.G. score is safe,'[104] he told Pears. They invited the Steins to share the maisonette in St John's Wood, where they remained until August 1946, when Pears was able to buy a leasehold house in Bayswater: this quite substantial property (3 Oxford Square, W2) was large enough to provide – as well as living space for Britten and Pears – rooms for the Steins, a small self-contained flat for Pears's parents and a third-floor attic for Eric Crozier.

By the end of January 1946, Britten had begun work on his next opera: 'I've taken the plunge and old Lucretia is now on the way. I started last night and I've now written most of the first recitative before the drinking song. I think it'll be all right but I always have cold feet at this point.'[105] The idea for *The Rape of Lucretia*, Op. 37, had come from Crozier when, late in 1944, he gave Britten his copy of *Le Viol de Lucrèce* (1931) by André Obey, 'as a possible subject for his next opera after *Grimes*'; Crozier had seen the play performed while still a schoolboy and liked it so much that he translated it into English. During the autumn of 1945, Ronald Duncan, for whose 'poetic masque' *This Way to the Tomb* Britten had just composed the music, worked at the libretto: on 19 December Britten could report to Ralph Hawkes, by then running the New York branch of Boosey & Hawkes, that 'Ronnie Duncan is half-way thro' the libretto which I think terrific'.[106] The original plan was for a tentatively named 'New Opera Company' to present the opera at Dartington, where Imogen Holst was Director of Music, in April 1946; but, when this ran into financial and practical difficulties, it was agreed with Glyndebourne's owner John Christie and general manager Rudolf Bing that *The Rape of Lucretia* should be staged at the post-war reopening of the opera house on 12 July 1946. Eric Crozier was to be the producer and John Piper the designer; and, because the opera would be performed for a run of consecutive nights before going on tour – it received a total of eighty-three performances between July and October – there would have to be two casts and two conductors. The first cast included Kathleen Ferrier (Lucretia) and Otakar Kraus (Tarquinius) with Pears and Joan Cross as the Male and Female Chorus; while among the second cast were Nancy Evans (Lucretia), Frank Rogier (Tarquinius) and Aksel Schiøtz and Flora Nielsen as the choruses. The conductors were Ernest Ansermet – who thought, in idiosyncratic but telling English, that Britten could do with 'a little joke then and now. Yes, very, sometimes'[107] – and Reginald Goodall. It was recorded in an abridged version by HMV the following year, with a cast including Pears, Cross and Evans conducted by Goodall.

'I am keen to develop a new art form (the chamber-opera, or what you will) which will stand beside the grand opera as the quartet stands beside the orchestra,' Britten told Hawkes on 30 June, an ambition which exactly anticipates his preference for Aldeburgh-sized projects over London-sized ones. He continued: 'I hope to write many works for it, & to be interested in this company for many years.'[108] He was anxious to insist that, despite Christie's financial support and Bing's management, this was 'our' company, not Glyndebourne's; however, a few weeks later, he had to write to *The Times*, clarifying a contrary mis-apprehension, that Glyndebourne was somehow '"lending" or "letting" its opera house for the production of *The Rape of Lucretia*'.[109] His apparently finnicky line drawing here was firmly based on a practical consideration: CEMA's successor, the recently formed Arts Council of Great Britain, had offered Glyndebourne a guarantee against loss for *Lucretia*'s tour (but their original figure of £5,000 had been reduced to £3,000) and Britten shrewdly guessed that they might need every penny. Although Glyndebourne must have seemed an ideal, if temporary, safe haven for what was to become the English Opera Group, the relationship between Christie and Britten was a predictably difficult one. Not only did Christie dislike *Lucretia*, remarking that there was 'no music in it'; he also 'took against Britten and his budding entourage, who understandably felt a mutual loyalty to each other' and he 'found homosexuality in general distasteful'.[110] On a more practical level, he was 'startled' to discover the extent of the losses incurred by Glyndebourne, beyond the Arts Council's guarantee, when the opera went on tour.

Lucretia is a mass of paradoxes. It is a piece in which Britten's scoring is more subtly nuanced than ever before – the woodwind colours are especially beguiling – and one which does indeed reinvent the form of the chamber opera. Yet it tends to win admirers rather than friends. It has flaws, for which Duncan usually takes most of the blame: it is too literary and too static, a point emphasised rather than diminished by the decision to incorporate Obey's two narrative chorus figures, and it is encum-bered by an anachronistic Christian epilogue, which Britten seems to have thought would mitigate its excessive bleakness (a consideration which hadn't seemed to bother him with *Grimes*).

The Male Chorus neatly solves the problem of providing a role for Pears which doesn't cast him as a heterosexual Roman; the danger is that we may sense this neatness and, with it, the extent to which Britten too has stepped to one side of the action. His heart, we may feel, isn't in *Lucretia* as it was in *Grimes* and yet – one last paradox – that detachment might in part account for the inventive fluency of his music.

Ernest Newman, in a *Sunday Times* review the composer thought 'simply puerile', felt that 'Mr Britten's second opera does not fulfil all the expectations set up by his first, and most of the blame for this I would lay on the libretto'; he went on to wonder 'what had become of Mr Britten's sense of the theatre and his feeling for his tragic subject'.[111] Cecil Gray in the *Observer* found in the libretto 'a feeling of pastiche, in which moreover, the elements do not coalesce',[112] and for Philip Hope-Wallace in the *Manchester Guardian* it 'tries but fails to make the best of many styles'.[113] However, Desmond Shawe-Taylor in the *New Statesman and Nation*, while noting the libretto's shortcomings, saw beyond them: for him, the first act was an 'unquestionable masterpiece' and the second contained 'musical and dramatic beauties of the highest order'. He had special praise for Ansermet's conducting, as well as for Crozier's production and Piper's scenery which 'raise the dramatic tension as surely as they delight the eye; how strange that we should have had to wait all this time to see a stage decorated by so evidently dramatic a painter!'[114] It was the beginning of an association between composer and artist which was to endure beyond Britten's death, in the form of Piper's magnificent memorial window in Aldeburgh Church.

While *Lucretia* was proving critically contentious and financially disastrous, *Grimes* was becoming an international success. Closely following the Sadler's Wells revival and the BBC broadcast early in 1946, it received its first performance outside

England on 21 March in Stockholm. In May, there were productions in Antwerp and in Basel and Zurich: Britten and Pears, who had actually managed a week's holiday before a fortnight's recital tour of Switzerland, attended a performance in Basel on 23 May. 'Everyone is amazed at what that theatre has achieved,' Britten wrote to Erwin Stein, although the Grimes was for his taste 'far *too* dotty, & not sympathetic enough'. He went on to note that 'the opera came off even with quite another (& wrong) kind of Peter', a point still insufficiently acknowledged by those who continue to expect all his interpreters to sound exactly like Pears. The reception was 'terrific': 'after being given laurels (!), and bowing from the box, I was *literally* hauled onto the stage . . . & carried around in quite an embarrassing manner – but very touching'.[115] Then on 6 August it received its delayed American premiere at Koussevitzky's Berkshire Music Center, Tanglewood, where it was conducted by Leonard Bernstein. Britten rushed there from Manchester, where *Lucretia* was by then on tour, having been urged by Eric Crozier *not* to come because the production was going so badly. Crozier told Humphrey Burton, in a conversation at the Aldeburgh Cinema during the 1991 Festival, that the last night of *Grimes* at Tanglewood was 'the only time I saw Ben so upset'. Although he seldom smoked, he begged a cigarette; after which, he 'took a cap from a hatstand, pulled it down as if to disguise his full appearance and had the cigarette in his mouth. Then he went on and took our call.' Crozier thought the performance 'not of a high standard', but Olin Downes in the *New York Times* wrote: 'The performance of a modern and very difficult score was astonishingly brilliant on the part of the orchestra, the chorus and, in the sum of it, the gifted and intelligent solo interpreters . . .'[116] Britten, together with Crozier and Clare and Ralph Hawkes, sent a joint telegram from Tanglewood to Joan Cross in England: 'PETER [*Grimes*] VERY NEARLY SUFFERED AWFUL FATE

LUCRETIA. MURDER MOST FOUL IT WAS BUT VERDICT UNANIMOUS ACQUITTAL.'[117]

5

Since John Christie disliked Britten personally and *Lucretia* musically (and had lost a great deal of money on the latter), it seems hardly likely that the two men would have looked forward to collaborating again. But the pragmatic truth was that the English Opera Group, as the company would be known by the end of 1946, needed a stage while Glyndebourne, for its part, needed a new opera to be produced at its 1947 festival. What it got was *Albert Herring*. As with *Our Hunting Fathers* and the *Sinfonia da Requiem*, one can't quite eliminate the lurking suspicion that Britten, intentionally or not, designed a work to be conspicuously at odds with its occasion.

Work on *Albert Herring* began in the autumn of 1946, immediately after the end of *Lucretia*'s tour. The idea for the opera came from Eric Crozier, who thought that Maupassant's story *Le Rosier de Madam Husson* – translated by Marjorie Laurie in the 1940 Penguin edition he lent to Britten as *Madame Husson's Rose-King* – would make 'an excellent companion-piece to *The Rape of Lucretia* and also provide splendid parts for Joan Cross and Peter Pears'. Tragic grandeur would be balanced by rustic comedy, with Maupassant's tale transposed to a Suffolk village and peppered with private jokes: Loxford was a version of Yoxford, Herring was the shopkeeper at Tunstall, and Lady Billows borrowed her surname from Britten's friend Lionel Billows, who worked for the British Council in Switzerland and who later suggested, with modest bemusement, that Britten had 'wanted some other name than Jones or Smith, and my rather unusual name came to his notice'.[118] Mr Gedge was the South London vicar who had discovered Leonard Thompson, the apprentice in *Grimes*; while, among those described in the cast list as 'tiresome village children', Cissie Woodger was a girl from Snape and Harold Wood a railway station on the line to Liverpool Street. Even before a word or note had been written, the notion of presenting such a farcical affair at a pompous stately home in Sussex must have tickled both men. The plot concerns the hunt for a May King – there being no girl in the village sufficiently virtuous to be May Queen – and the choice of Albert, the boy from the greengrocer's, who on the night following his coronation goes missing and magnificently discovers the grown-up delights of alcohol and sex. The comical conceit of a young man, rather than a young woman, being 'virtuous' has a long pedigree – the obvious example in English is Fielding's *Joseph Andrews* – but it also had a particular edge for Britten, whose own sexuality gave an additionally absurd twist to Albert's predicament and to Pears's portrayal of it.

Just as Montagu Slater had been surprised to find himself replaced as Britten's librettist after *Peter Grimes* by Ronald Duncan, so Duncan – who had been thinking about an opera based on *Mansfield Park*, to be called *Letters to William* – was surprised to discover that Crozier was writing the libretto for *Albert Herring*. Much has been made of Britten's cavalier approach to the dismissal and replacement of close colleagues, which often resulted from his horror of confrontational arguments, but in this case practical convenience was a major factor: Crozier, having suggested the story, was living at 3 Oxford Square, available to work with Britten in Snape and planning to marry Nancy Evans, who was a member of the company. This was simply the most efficient way of getting on with the opera, which Crozier also intended to produce. But here the project ran into further difficulties. John Christie was adamant that Glyndebourne's new artistic director, Carl Ebert, should be in charge of the production, which – as Britten pointed out – was scarcely possible since Ebert was not due to be in England until April, by which time 'the production of the new opera will be largely settled'. And Glyndebourne was constitutionally inhospitable towards visiting companies, especially when they were as spikily independent as this one. In a joint letter to Christie on 10 November 1946, Britten and Crozier set out a five-point plan for their still nameless company:

1) We shall appoint a General Manager to form a new non-profit-making company for us. This will have a board of five trustees and an assessor from the Arts Council, if they will collaborate with us. Our manager will organise the collection of capital to launch our 1947 season.

2) The management of the new company will be in the hands of –
   Music Director – Benjamin Britten
   Artistic Director – Eric Crozier
   Scenic Director – John Piper

3) Next summer, we shall stage *Albert*, a new comic opera, and *Lucretia* – the latter certainly on the Continent, and in England either before or after October 1st, according to Glyndebourne's decision about the exclusive rights which they hold till that date.

4) We should like to negotiate with you for the loan or purchase of the *Lucretia* production. Alternatively, we may build the production afresh for our company. There will be extensive alterations to the music and text of the opera before its next production.

5) Our work in 1947 will include a Continental tour, a London season and a short provincial tour. It could also perhaps include an opening season at Glyndebourne if you wished to preserve an association with us, and if an arrangement

could be made that would satisfy the artistic and financial demands of both Glyndebourne and of our new company.[119]

Christie was unpersuaded by Britten and Crozier's proposals, and on 23 November Britten wrote to him to say that the new company's programme would have to go ahead without Glyndebourne. If this was brinkmanship, it worked: Christie came back with an offer of ten days' performances after Glyndebourne's own *Orfeo ed Euridice*, though with plainly insufficient rehearsal time.

In December, the English Opera Group was formally constituted, with a board of directors chaired by Oliver Lyttelton; the other board members were Sir Kenneth Clark, Tyrone Guthrie, Ralph Hawkes, Mervyn Horder, Denis Rickett, James F. A. Smith and Erwin Stein; the artistic directors were Britten, Crozier and John Piper. A public announcement, in the form of a fund-raising brochure, followed early in the new year: 'We believe the time has come when England, which has never had a tradition of native opera, but has always depended on a repertory of foreign works, can create its own operas,'[120] it began. The Group intended to present a revival of *Lucretia* and Britten's new opera, *Albert Herring*, at Glyndebourne and hoped 'to give a short season at the Royal Opera House, Covent Garden, in early October', as well as provincial and Continental tours. By mid-January, writing from Zermatt (he and Pears were again combining concerts and holiday in Switzerland), Britten was still cautiously telling Ernest Ansermet that 'a season at Glyndebourne *may* after all take place – but you may imagine with considerable concessions of either side'.[121] Among these concessions was the appointment of Ebert and Crozier as joint – although, it seems, mutually uncomprehending – producers, an arrangement which came to an abrupt end when Ebert withdrew and Crozier found he was 'too tired to take the job on lightly at the present time'.[122]

In the event, *Albert Herring* was produced at Glyndebourne by Frederick Ashton.

Ashton, born in 1904, was the finest English choreographer of his time. He and Britten had so much in common that one might have expected them to have collaborated sooner or more often; but Britten was as wary of the outstandingly talented as of the conspicuously homosexual; and Ashton, like Auden, was both. He too had Suffolk connections: his mother's family came from Yaxley, where in 1948 he bought a cottage close to his ancestral graves. He had met Britten before the war, at a dinner given by William Walton, and afterwards wrote to him on a postcard of Bronzino's Don Garcia de' Medici: 'Is this *really* your adorable self?'[123] They had contemplated a ballet using *Variations on a Theme of Frank Bridge*. Now, while Ashton's new London home in Yeoman's Row was being redecorated, he looked forward to at last working with Britten in what he imagined would be tranquil and pleasant surroundings. He was in for a shock. 'Ben wouldn't speak to Christie or allow him inside his own theatre,' he told Julie Kavanagh. 'We weren't allowed to stay in Glyndebourne or go into the bar. The moment the rehearsal was over, we got into a bus and went to a house on the cliff somewhere.'[124] He may have exaggerated the details, but he was right about the tension: Christie was to greet members of the audience with the encouraging words, 'This isn't our sort of thing, you know.'[125] And there was also friction between Ashton and Crozier, who had a subtly delineated idea of how the opera should be: he had already disagreed with Ebert, who thought it was about 'social criticism' and 'mendacious prudery' instead of being 'a simple lyrical comedy',[126] but now he found Ashton's exuberantly comic approach too farcical for his taste. Crozier's disapproval pushed Ashton to the brink of resignation yet despite this, and although he thought the stressed personal relationships at Glyndebourne both 'small-minded' and beyond his comprehension, he did enjoy working on *Albert Herring*, from which he took away two enduring rewards: with his fee he bought an enormous Aubusson rug for the drawing room at Yeoman's Row, greatly astonishing his new housekeeper, Mrs Lily Lloyd (who was, as it happens, my grandmother), while the opera itself sowed the seeds of his own masterpiece, *La Fille mal gardée*.

'Freddie Ashton has done an excellent production and the sets look delightful,'[127] Crozier told the conductor Hans Oppenheim after the first night on 20 June 1947. He had forgiven Ashton, but not Glyndebourne's owner or the opera's early critics. The receptive audience at the dress rehearsal, he reported, had dared to laugh 'loud and long at all the things they were intended to think funny', causing Christie to describe them as 'a very *vulgar* audience'. The first-night audience were much stuffier, and so were the reviews. 'A salacious French story of Maupassant is translated by Eric Crozier into a rustic English comedy of the way a bumpkin kicks over the traces, and the result is a charade,' wrote Frank Howes in *The Times*; while Richard Capell in the *Daily Telegraph* thought that 'all these [Britten's] talents have gone to no more purpose than the raising of a snigger'. But other reviewers were more sympathetic, and one – Charles Stuart in the *Observer* – made a crucial three-way connection: 'Britten has never given us a lovelier, wittier or defter score than *Albert Herring*, which makes the perfect pendant to *Peter Grimes* and comforts many who had diagnosed a falling-off in *The Rape of Lucretia*.'[128] For a pendant to *Grimes*, even more than a counter-balance to *Lucretia*, is precisely what *Albert Herring* is: another man set apart by his oddity in a Suffolk village, this time viewed through a comic rather than a tragic lens, with the connection slyly emphasised by moments of self-parody (compare, for instance, the 'Good morning' exchanges of Mrs Sedley, her 'nieces' and Swallow in Act 1 of *Grimes* with those of Lady

Billows, the Vicar and the Mayor in Act 1 of *Herring*). It is often helpful to see Britten's compositions in terms of their inter-connectedness, as in the group of Purcell-related works, rather than in isolation.

The Glyndebourne cast included Pears as Herring, Joan Cross as Lady Billows, with Frederick Sharp and Nancy Evans as the corruptive pair of lovers, Sid from the butcher's and Nancy from the bakery; the English Opera Group Chamber Orchestra, a forerunner of the ECO, was conducted by the composer. Pears, who celebrated his thirty-seventh birthday during the run, was on the elderly side as Albert, though he would be in his fifties by the time he recorded the work in 1964 (the young John Graham-Hall, who made his Glyndebourne debut in Peter Hall's 1985 production, looked much more convincing in the part). Also among the cast were three 'children': Emmie and Cis were sung by adult sopranos, but the part of Harry was taken by thirteen-year-old David Spenser, an experienced boy actor suggested by Nancy Evans. It was the first time in an opera that Britten had created a singing role for a boy. 'He treated me with a lot of humour, which made it easy for me, because every time I opened my mouth to sing he would give me a look of utter astonishment which made us both laugh,' Spenser remembered. 'His eyebrows would go up, up, up, and there was a quiver of a smile on his face, as if he was surprised I'd even attempted the last phrase.'[129] It was a hugely enjoyable experience for a boy whose parents had split up when he was five: his father was in Ceylon and he lived with his mother, the breadwinner, for whom he had to do most of the cooking and housework. Britten, he found, was more than just a father-substitute: he was approachable on equal terms, 'a lovely listener, a soother . . . one of the few people in the world, at that time, that I could talk to'.[130] After Glyndebourne and the English

Opera Group's subsequent European tour with *Lucretia* and *Herring*, Britten invited the boy to stay at his new home in Aldeburgh.

He completed the purchase and moved in during late August. Crag House, a substantial pink-stuccoed building, lies between Crabbe Street (on its inland side) and Crag Path, the town's modest promenade, its rear windows and garden directly over-looking the shingle beach with its huts and fishing boats. One of Britten's first acts on acquiring the property was to have the postal address altered to the less pompous '4 Crabbe Street'; it was Crabbe, after all, who had brought him there. At last he could really feel he was back where he belonged, living and working within sight of the North Sea, just as in his Lowestoft childhood: both the ground-floor sitting room and his first-floor study – with a grand piano in each – had big windows facing the beach. For Pears, although he interested himself as usual in the choosing of carpets and curtains, the place had no such resonance: this was a simple fact of difference between them. Both men were by this time, as creative artists go, relatively well off: Pears had bought their London house and had begun to collect valuable paintings; Britten owned both the Old Mill (which he had let) and the house in Aldeburgh, as well as a 1929 Rolls-Royce Shooting Brake which he had acquired in the previous year. That their enthusiasms were so different, though mutually enjoyed, was one of the strengths of their relationship: in many respects – including the great married tradition of bickering over breakfast – they behaved just like any other couple. A series of photographs taken in 1948 shows them buying vege-tables from Jonah Baggott's stall outside the post office in Aldeburgh's High Street: the ease and normality of the scene is impressive even today. They managed to seem superbly unaware of the fact that, in social terms, they were doing something extraordinary.

David Spenser came to stay in Crabbe Street at the very end of August, the day after Britten had returned to Aldeburgh from London, where he had been recording the *Donne Sonnets* with Pears for HMV. Pears, meanwhile, had travelled north to sing at the inaugural Edinburgh Festival, to which Britten had also been invited (they would have performed *Die Schöne Mullerin* together) but, wanting to get down to some composing, had declined; nevertheless, he told Ralph Hawkes in his 'first letter from the new house', 'I'm fairly well represented with Y.P.'s Guide, Illuminations (Peter) & P.G. Interludes'.[131] The move was hardly complete and there was no guest bedroom ready, so David had to share Britten's double bed. But any anxiety on the boy's behalf would be misplaced: he was enjoying a holiday by the sea with a kind friend, with whom he swam every morning and walked in the afternoons, who played the piano for him each evening after supper, and whose housekeeper, Barbara Parker, made 'the most lovely apple pies' which he recalled half a lifetime later. David, at thirteen, knew about homosexuality and recognised it in the 'slightly camp' Ashton, but the issue simply didn't arise for him with Britten: 'There was no hanky-panky or I would have certainly told my mother. It was a very big bed, and I just went to sleep. The next time I came to visit, not long after, I had the spare room, which by then was ready.' For his part, Britten even put up with David's fondness for Chopin and Brahms and his dislike of Mozart, merely remarking: 'One day you will realise that Mozart was the greatest composer who ever lived, and Brahms was the worst.' After his first visit, David wrote in his thank-you letter: 'I don't think I have ever been happier in my life.'[132] His host felt this too: 'Little David went off yesterday morning – rather sadly, poor little thing,' he told Pears on 4 September. 'His home life is hell, but I think his existence has been made a little brighter by being treated properly for a few days.'[133] He sounds rather pleased with himself, and not without cause: it was what he had wanted for Harry Morris, but this time he had got it right.

Although Britten's recent life had been dominated by the production of three operas in three successive years, he had continued to fit in other work, such as the *Occasional Overture*, for the opening of the BBC Third Programme in September 1946, and the *Prelude and Fugue on a Theme of Vittoria* for Walter Hussey at St Matthew's, Northampton. With Pears, there had been concert tours of the Netherlands in October–November 1946; of Switzerland, Belgium, the Netherlands, Sweden and Denmark in January–February 1947; and of Italy in April–May. Then, in July and the first part of August, there was the EOG's European tour with *Lucretia* and *Herring*, ending in Lucerne: they had an Arts Council grant against loss of £3,000, but they lost the same again. It was while they were en route from the Holland Festival to the Lucerne Festival – the scenery was in three lorries, while most of the singers and musicians went by train – that the Group's founding friends, who were travelling in Britten's Rolls, began to confront the glum fact that touring on this scale was, for a small company, unsustainable. Then, as Eric Crozier later recalled, one of them made a ridiculous and brilliant suggestion. "'Why not,' said Peter Pears, "make our own Festival? A modest Festival with a few concerts given by friends? Why not have an Aldeburgh Festival?"'[134]

CHAPTER 6

A MODEST FESTIVAL

1947–55

1

Why not have an Aldeburgh Festival? Where to start? The town is small and, as festival locations go, remote: on the bulge of the East Anglian coast, at the end of the road. Until 1963, it was marginally more accessible than Southwold or Orford, since it still had a branch railway which connected with the not especially main line at Saxmundham and a local train humorously known as 'The Aldeburgh Flyer', but the timetable definitely hadn't been arranged with concert-goers in mind. Aldeburgh had hotels and guest houses for summer visitors, though these couldn't begin to cope with the numbers a music festival might generate. Its only suitable venues were the parish church, the cinema and the tiny 300-seat Jubilee Hall – also between Crabbe Street and the beach, a hundred yards from Britten and Pears's home – unless you were to count (and they would) the Baptist chapel in the High Street. Yet it's strange that, even now, beginning to list the reasons why a festival in Aldeburgh couldn't work seems to make the idea all the more irresistible.

Britten, Pears and Crozier must have tried hard to banish the first act of *Albert Herring* from their memories as they assembled their committee of the locally great and good. Among the first of these was Margery Spring-Rice, of Iken Hall, near Snape: she was the granddaughter of Newson Garrett, who had built the local Maltings, and she would live to see the Aldeburgh Festival's eventual transformation of the redundant malthouse into its main concert hall. 'I think the "Festival Idea" has cheered her,' Britten reported to Pears in September; 'she thinks it is the idea of the century, & is full of plans and schemes.'[1] She proposed an initial meeting at Iken Hall and suggested the involvement of the Countess of Cranbrook, who lived nearby at Great Glemham, where Crabbe had once been rector. Crozier remembered calling on 'Colonel Colbeck, the Mayor, and Mr Godfrey, the Vicar, for their advice' and then giving 'a tea-party for local friends and acquaintances'.[2] Resembling *Albert Herring*'s Lady Billows only in her determination, Fidelity Cranbrook chaired the first formal meeting of the Executive Committee, held on 27 October at Thellusson Lodge in Aldeburgh: among those present were the rector, the Revd R. C. R. Godfrey, and (a sound strategic choice) G. L. Ashby Pritt, the owner of the Wentworth Hotel; Anne Wood was there, 'representing the English Opera Group', and 'Mrs C. E. Welford' – Ben's sister Beth – tactfully represented the Britten family. Apart from describing the festival's quite promising financial basis and registering such interesting details as the Bishop's insistence that two hundred free seats should be available at any performance in the church, the minutes of this initial meeting record what would prove to be a momentous decision: 'It was AGREED that the Festival be called "The Aldeburgh Festival", but the question as to whether the words "Music" and/or "Drama", and a reference to Mr Britten's name be included, was left open.'[3] The significance of this is threefold: the festival was named to reflect its roots in the town and the community (as, for instance, 'East Suffolk Festival' wouldn't have done); the 'Music and . . .' formula, which became 'Music and the Arts', allowed it to embrace exhibitions and literary talks; and the wise reluctance of 'Mr Britten' to have his name included in the title indicated that this wasn't to be focused on one composer in the manner of Salzburg or Bayreuth.

It was typical of Britten that, having invented a new form of opera, he should now invent a new shorter form of work for voice or voices and piano as his first composition in Aldeburgh. The name he chose for what would eventually be a set of five pieces, 'Canticles', has a perfectly straightforward musical-liturgical sense, but in the case of *Canticle I: My Beloved is Mine*, Op. 40, there is more specific allusion. The text is by the early-seventeenth-century poet Francis Quarles (Britten had already set his Christmas carol in *A Boy Was Born*), who had in turn based it on a verse from *The Song of Solomon*, also known as *The Canticle of Canticles*: 'My beloved is mine, and I am his: he feedeth among the lilies.' The composer's manuscript is dated 12 September 1947 and the work was first performed by Pears and Britten at a concert in memory of Dick Sheppard, a founder of the Peace Pledge Union, on 1 November. Quarles's poem – which, like its source, uses strikingly homoerotic language – here becomes another barely encoded love song shared between its performers: the opening lines of the second stanza ('Ev'n so we met, and after long pursuit, / Ev'n so we joined; we both became entire') might aptly describe their journey to Grand Rapids, Michigan, in 1939 and they are rapturously treated. The concluding lento section, beginning 'He is my altar, I his holy place', achieves a balance of eloquence and restraint unsurpassed in Britten's word setting.

Within a week of *Canticle I*'s premiere, *Peter Grimes* opened at Covent Garden in a new production by Tyrone Guthrie, designed by Tanya Moiseiwitsch and conducted by Karl Rankl; Pears and Cross returned to their original roles for the first three performances but were replaced by Richard Lewis and

Doris Dorée for the rest of the run and the European subsequent tour, in which Reginald Goodall alternated with Rankl. Although welcomed by some of the 'dear old critics' who 'follow along three or four years behind as usual – what bores they are',[4] the production, less realistic and indeed less Suffolky than the earlier one, was disliked by Britten, who blamed the size of the house and concluded that 'small opera is the thing – in spite of the nice noises one can make with an orchestra of 85 & chorus of 60!'[5] With the Jubilee Hall in Aldeburgh soon to become his operatic venue, this was just as well. But he can't have failed to be delighted by Neville Cardus's review in the *Manchester Guardian*, which precisely summed up his own ambition for *Grimes*: 'Here, at last, are a work and a production fit to stand four-square anywhere in the world – and not because of lofty emulation of a foreign masterpiece. *Peter Grimes* is English through and through, without trustful resort to folklore.'[6]

November 1947 turned out to be an astonishingly busy month for Britten – who, only a few weeks earlier, had been promising himself some quiet composing time in his new home. On 9 November, he introduced and, with members of the Zorian String Quartet, performed two works by Frank Bridge on the BBC Third Programme. His broadcast introduction contains a deliciously mischievous summary of the musical environment into which Bridge grew:

> . . . the school of chamber music was really in the doldrums. The headmaster was Brahms, chief assistant masters, Schumann and Mendelssohn; the dancing-master, Dvorak, and of course above all, the Chairman of the Governors – Beethoven. Not much notice was taken of those rather dull, superannuated professors Haydn and Mozart – and though the occasional visits of the Art Master Schubert gave pleasure, his character was highly suspect.[7]

Ten days later, Britten and Pears gave a recital in Huddersfield of works by Purcell, Bridge and Berkeley as well as his own *Donne Sonnets*, while on 20 November they were in Chester performing Purcell, Schubert and Britten: just as in his CEMA days, he thought 'dashing over the country giving recitals' was 'a far finer & more rewarding way of making music'[8] than losing his temper at Covent Garden. On 24 November, there was a joint Third Programme recital with the Zorians, in which Britten and Pears performed four Mahler songs and two of Britten's Purcell realisations; two days after that, they broadcast *On This Island* and *Canticle I* in a programme called *Songs of Benjamin Britten*. On 29 November, they took part in a broadcast of seventeenth- and eighteenth-century duets and cantatas, and then they rounded off the month with a recital of Purcell and Schubert plus Britten's *Donne Sonnets* and folk-song arrangements in Cranleigh. Their appearances on the Third Programme had now become so frequent that Herbert Murrill, the BBC's assistant director of music, felt he had to raise the matter with the Music Booking Manager.

After this flurry of activity, Britten took a short break in Dublin before he returned to Aldeburgh and to composing. His first tasks were the incidental music for a BBC programme, *Men of Goodwill: The Reunion of Christmas*, and a long-promised song cycle for Nancy Evans, *A Charm of Lullabies*, Op. 41, which he completed on 17 December. The following day he wrote to Pears: 'Well – all my chores are done – the BBC have got their score, & yesterday we posted off to Nancy a "Charm of Lullabies" (??) all nicely washed & brushed, & quite charming & successful I think now – five of them.'[9] He had found the texts in *A Book of Lullabies*, edited by F. E. Budd; the work was first performed in The Hague by its dedicatee on 3 January 1948. Next, there was *Saint Nicolas*, Op. 42, a commission for the centenary of Pears's old school, Lancing; Crozier had been working on the text since September. The original proposal (and a cheque for £100) had come from Esther Neville-Smith, who was married to a member of staff, but it was the school's sixth-form master and historian Basil Handford who suggested, as a counterpart to the *Hymn to St Cecilia*, a work celebrating the patron saint of children, seamen and travellers and of Lancing College itself. The school is part of the Woodard Corporation, a fact that, as Handford explained in *Lancing College: History and Memories*, had rather special consequences for the commissioned work, which 'would be performed by the joint choirs of Lancing, Hurst, Ardingly and St Michael's with perhaps contingents from other schools'. Moreover, there had to be 'a special part for female voices, to be sung from the western gallery' and a movement in which the choir 'is divided into several sections so that each school could have its own short section to sing'.[10] This was, of course, the kind of fiendish challenge Britten relished, just as he relished the chance to create surprising effects: on a visit to the school, he was discovered, according to Handford, 'in Chapel walking round saying "how can I make a noise like bath water running out?"'[11] For Britten, the most resonant movement would surely have been the seventh, 'Nicolas and the Stolen Boys', with its refrain 'Timothy, Mark and John / Are gone! Are gone! Are gone!' and their mysterious resurrection from a pickled and preserved state, an image of the frozen child within himself.

The work was performed at Lancing, with Pears as Nicolas and Britten conducting, on 24 July, but the school gave permission for two earlier performances to take place during the first Aldeburgh Festival, where it formed part of the inaugural concert in the parish church. 'In return for this kindness,' said the programme note, 'it is asked that the two Aldeburgh performances shall be regarded as privileged occasions, and that public criticism of the Cantata shall be reserved for the Centenary performance at Lancing College.' It was well received: 'it testified yet again to the composer's genius for securing the most telling effects by the simplest of means', said *The Times*; Charles Stuart in the *Observer* found the 'keynote' was 'gaiety' and 'shamelessly enjoyed' the storm music; for Desmond Shawe-Taylor in the *New Statesman and Nation*, the first three episodes were 'meltingly beautiful' and there was 'great beauty' later on too. But Shawe-Taylor, perhaps drawing on undeclared personal knowledge (he was a close friend of Edward Sackville-West, with whom he shared a house in Dorset), added a telling codicil: 'Though it may be presumptuous to say so, I feel strongly that what Britten needs at this moment is a rest from occasional commissions, a rest from concert-giving and accompanying, a rest from peripatetic chamber opera, and a long period of renewed exploration into the depths of his extraordinary genius.'[12] Part of Britten must have ruefully assented to this wish, while the rest of him knew that it wasn't in his nature to grant it for long.

His one remaining compositional 'chore' during the early months of 1948 was his realisation, Op. 43, of *The Beggar's Opera* (1728) by John Gay and John Christopher Pepusch, for the English Opera Group: it was first performed at the Arts Theatre, Cambridge, on 24 May, with Pears as Macheath and Nancy Evans as Polly Peachum, conducted by Britten. He worked on the composition during his concert tour with Pears of Switzerland, Italy and the Netherlands, which lasted from late January until early March. However, writing to Ralph Hawkes from the American Hotel in Amsterdam, he cancelled a proposed American tour in terms which anticipate Desmond Shawe-Taylor's advice: 'In future I am planning only the shortest concert trips with Peter, a week or two here & there . . . 6 weeks, or 2 months more, away entirely without work is now unthinkable.' Meanwhile, the New York Met production of *Peter Grimes* had opened on 12 February: it was 'certainly the talk of the town',

Hawkes assured him and, to prove it, his picture was on the cover of *Time*, against an incongruous background of fishing nets and ropes. While grudgingly admitting that the publicity was useful, he found it 'not exactly to my taste', and he was irritated by errors in the accompanying profile – above all by the comment that he, an indefatigable correspondent, 'doesn't answer letters'. He also formed a clear opinion of the Met's production: 'It does seem to have been catastrophic! I am only too thankful I wasn't there . . .'[13] But he *was* 'there' to see Covent Garden's second cast, before their version went on tour in May: 'I must frankly say I was shocked by it,' he told David Webster, the Royal Opera House's general administrator. Richard Lewis, he thought, might have made an adequate Grimes with more rehearsal, but Doris Dorée as Ellen Orford was 'an unsympathetic character both in voice and acting' and was 'quite obviously temperamentally unsuited for the part'.[14]

As usual, Britten had been undertaking more than enough composing and performing work to exhaust anyone else – even he described it as 'a particularly worrying patch of life, overwork & depression'[15] – without taking into account the small matter of planning the inaugural Aldeburgh Festival. Fortunately, he was a natural organiser with a firm grasp of detail and a clear head for figures: he once said that if he hadn't been a composer he might have been an accountant. (But it was Oliver Knussen who shrewdly pointed out that Britten 'could have been anything that involved the effective deployment of small components within big masses', rather mischievously offering 'a general . . . or at least a chess master'[16] as examples; he would also, of course, have made an excellent schoolmaster.) Another useful and possibly unexpected talent was his ability to deploy a light touch as when, just before Christmas in 1947, he was invited to talk about the planned festival during the interval of a concert in Ipswich. The next day's *East Anglian Daily Times* reported:

Mr Britten, having affirmed his affection for the county in which he was born, said that Aldeburgh seemed to him to be the ideal place for the type of festival he had in mind. The festival he liked was not the kind which concentrated everything on music, but the sort of thing 'where one can wander about'. For several years past, he said, he had been writing large-scale musical works, not a single one of which had ever been performed in Suffolk. In these days of universal suffering, he did not see why this should be so. (Laughter.)[17]

Britten could make people laugh because he initially seemed so buttoned-up – he was his own straight man – and also because, despite his slightly mannered speech, there wasn't a hint of self-aggrandisement about him. At the same time, he was quietly confident about his festival's ambitions: it 'would steadily expand, and in ten years' time, perhaps, it might be possible to build a Suffolk Opera House in Aldeburgh'.

Now the founders' earlier tactical planning began to pay off. The cachet of Lady Cranbrook's title proved invaluable in securing the support of the golfing and yachting sets, whom she privately referred to as 'the Antibodies'. Lyn Pritt of the Wentworth Hotel provided an office and telephone for the festival's newly installed general manager, Elizabeth Sweeting, who had previously worked at Glyndebourne and more recently joined the English Opera Group as Anne Wood's assistant. On a torrentially wet January night, a well-attended public meeting at the Jubilee Hall heard about the proposals; by the end of the evening, those present had subscribed several hundred pounds as a guarantee against loss. By the beginning of February the first Aldeburgh Festival had dates – 5–13 June – and a draft programme which Britten outlined with gleeful enthusiasm to Elizabeth Mayer: 'We are planning 3 performances of "Albert Herring" – many concerts in the Church (including, Peter &

me, Clifford Curzon, two choral concerts including my new St Nicolas Cantata etc.), lectures (including E. M. Forster, Kenneth Clark, Guthrie), exhibitions of modern paintings as well as the local painters Constable & Gainsborough! & Popular concerts, & bus excursions around the district, as well as a Festival dance!'[18] Booking opened in mid-March and a few days later Britten could report to Pears that about a quarter of the tickets had already been sold. Soon there was a handsome poster announcing that the festival ('in association with THE ARTS COUNCIL OF GREAT BRITAIN') would include the following attractions:

THE ENGLISH OPERA GROUP
in
'ALBERT HERRING'
*

PETER PEARS AND BENJAMIN BRITTEN
*

CLIFFORD CURZON
*

The ZORIAN STRING QUARTET
*

SAINT NICOLAS
a new cantata by Benjamin Britten
*

LECTURES AND EXHIBITIONS OF PAINTINGS

Perhaps the most brilliant and astonishing thing about this programme is the way in which it remains entirely true to Pears's original formula of 'A modest festival with a few concerts given by friends'.

Among these friends, none was more remarkable than E. M. Forster who, although he hadn't published a novel since *A Passage to India* in 1924, was widely regarded as England's greatest living novelist until his death in 1970. He had first met Britten in 1937, at a dress rehearsal of *The Ascent of F6*, where 'he witnessed an angry scene' between the composer and the director, Rupert Doone. He had been at the National Gallery performance of the *Michelangelo Sonnets* in 1944 and had subsequently bought the HMV records, although he had no equipment on which to play them; hearing of this, Britten sent him a gramophone. He arrived to stay in Crabbe Street and to explore Crabbe's landscape some days before the start of the festival: 'in the evenings', says his biographer, P. N. Furbank, 'Britten and Pears played and sang for him and improvised parodies at the piano'; he thought them 'the sweetest people'.[19] The lecture he gave, on 'George Crabbe and Peter Grimes', is full of quirky observations and disarmingly modest about his own role in bringing Britten and Pears back to England (he merely says that they read Crabbe 'with nostalgia'), but it is also, as was his way, just a little naughty. 'It amuses me to think what an opera on Peter Grimes would have been like if I had written it,' he says, mock-innocently; it turns out that his version would have 'starred the murdered apprentices' and had 'their ghosts in the last scene' before 'blood and fire would have been thrown in the tenor's face, hell would have opened, and on a mixture of *Don Juan* and the *Freischütz* I should have lowered my final curtain'.[20] While he praises the Britten/Slater version, he hints that it wasn't quite operatic enough for his taste. His chance would come soon enough.

For many, the highlight of the festival was *Albert Herring*, which received three performances in the Jubilee Hall: having been heard in differently unsuitable venues such as Glyndebourne and Covent Garden, Albert had come home to a small Suffolk town, which was where he belonged. It was Forster, in his retrospective essay 'Looking Back on the First Aldeburgh Festival', who caught the magic of this occasion:

The full company of the English Opera Group, and its orchestra, had come down from London, and much fitting into the Jubilee Hall had to be contrived. There was not room for the harp and percussion amongst the other instruments. The harp had to be up in the auditorium with a screen in front, and the percussion on the opposite side was blanketed by gaily coloured eiderdowns to deaden the sound. The stage too was congested. The naughty children had to bounce with discretion, and Albert's sack of turnips to be dumped where no one would trip. I had seen the opera before in the immensities of Covent Garden, where the problem was not so much to avoid collisions as to get into touch. I preferred the Aldeburgh performance. It was lively and intimate. The audience, after a little hesitation, started laughing, and Joan Cross, in the part of a dictatorial lady, seemed inspired to every sort of drollery. The music kept going, balance between voices and instruments was attained and maintained, but the feeling in the Hall was not so much 'Here we are at last having an opera in Aldeburgh' as 'Here we are happy'.[21]

There is of course no room for a bar in the Jubilee Hall: during the interval the audience either spilled out onto the adjacent beach or went for a drink in the Cross Keys which – only a couple of doors away along Crabbe Street – is actually no further from the auditorium than the bar is at Snape Maltings. One member of the audience who went to the pub in the interval famously said: 'I took a ticket for this show because it is local and I felt I had to. I'd have sold it to anyone for sixpence earlier on. I wouldn't part with it now for ten pounds.' Forster reports the story, so Britten would have heard it and been delighted by it. Three days after the festival ended, he described his pleasure to Edward Dent: 'We have just come out from a most interesting experimental Festival here, in Aldeburgh; hundreds of people came – and Albert Herring was received with joy in the Jubilee Hall! What we seem to have proved without a doubt is that local people react strongly and encouragingly to this kind of local festival.'[22]

2

By the summer of 1948, Britten's international reputation as a major composer was assured; he and his partner were settled in an attractive and comfortable house in the place where he knew he belonged; and he had triumphantly created in Aldeburgh a festival which exemplified his most deeply held principles about music and community. So why wasn't he happy? One reason, not to be underestimated, is the fact that, for anyone prone to depression, the moment when accumulated successes naggingly insist 'Now you *should* be happy' can be the most depressing of all. And Britten hated the incidental consequences of his increasing fame: among the most vexatious of these was over-hearing people talking about him when he travelled by train between Suffolk and London. 'What do you do then?' his sister Beth asked. 'I go outside and stand in the corridor, or move into another carriage.'[23] But there were other reasons too.

Living in Crabbe Street wasn't turning out quite as planned. One early scheme was that Crozier, who was awaiting a divorce from his first wife, should have rooms at the top of the house, as at Oxford Square, which in due course might be converted into a self-contained flat when he was able to marry Nancy Evans; but this left insufficient space for Pears when he and Britten needed to be out of musical earshot of each other. Early in 1948, Britten told a disappointed Crozier that the idea was off, generously suggesting to Nancy Evans that he might instead buy them a cottage in Aldeburgh (there were two for sale) to use as their own local base. But in February, the divorce itself ran into legal difficulties and was indefinitely postponed. Pears, meanwhile, had familial troubles of his own: his mother died in October 1947 and his father early in 1948. Consequently, he and Britten decided to give up the house in Oxford Square, which had become unnecessarily large for them – 'we were never there much', Britten airily told Elizabeth Mayer, meaning *he* was never there much, and it was 'incredibly expensive' – although selling what was by then a very short lease proved tricky and time-consuming. Their erstwhile London tenants the Steins were moving to 22 Melbury Road, W14 (off Kensington High Street), where, reversing their previous arrangement, Britten and Pears sublet two rooms from them.

They would 'concentrate on the Aldeburgh house', Britten continued. 'Peter has taken a great interest in the house & has many ideas re furnishings & curtaining – but these are very, very difficult & expensive these days. Still we manage – & with our new Constable & Turner, & several John Pipers we feel very grand!'[24] Here, the distinctness of their enthusiasms, which were at best happily complementary, begins to seem more pointedly marked: Britten makes it clear that he isn't greatly bothered about soft furnishings, while 'very grand' comes with built-in irony from someone not keen on grandeur, least of all in Aldeburgh. There is an inescapable clash of outlooks here between Britten, who had come home to the Suffolk coast with its simple childhood pleasures of swimming and walking and good plain food, and Pears, whose instinct was to import more in the way of metropolitan sophistication into their lives. 'Little by little . . . his home had become Suffolk rather than London,'[25] writes Pears's biographer Christopher Headington, of the decision to sell Oxford Square; yet the question of how far Pears really felt at home in Crabbe Street is far from straightforward. Humphrey Carpenter points out how little time he actually spent in Aldeburgh in these years: 'for example during 1951 he was there for only six visits of a few days each, including the Festival'.[26] Soon after Kurt Hutton had photographed Britten and Pears buying vegetables in the High Street, he took some equally famous pictures of them in Billy Burrell's fishing boat, with Burrell, his lad Robin Long ('the Nipper') and E. M. Forster. Britten, next to the boy, appears easy and avuncular as he usually did when near children; Forster is wearing the attentive old codger face which came so naturally to him and, in one shot, the flat cap to go with it; only Pears, his arms more stiffly braced against the edge of the vessel, looks as if he would really rather be somewhere else. In many published versions of these photographs, including those in Carpenter's biography, Pears (on the left of the picture) has been cropped out altogether. It seems an oddly symbolic absence.[27]

Pears was definitely and distantly absent during the autumn of 1948, when he went to America: this wasn't, for once, a matter of professional engagements but a holiday spent revisiting old friends, such as the Mayers, and taking some lessons from his old singing teacher, Clytie Mundy. He travelled by air to New York on 17 October: it was his first transatlantic flight. Britten saw him off at the airport ('I loathed, more than any moment of my silly life, leaving you'), then wept in the car back to London, accidentally scattered £5 notes over Liverpool Street Station, and had to be met and comforted at Saxmundham by his sister Beth. After he had stayed overnight with the Welfords at Hasketon, Beth took him into Ipswich to try on a new suit, presumably as a diversion, but there he caught sight of a newspaper headline, "'. . . believed lost" – & immediately feared the worst'.[28] In the afternoon, after his sister had taken him back to Aldeburgh, a telegram arrived from Pears to confirm his safe arrival, and after supper Britten settled down to try and hear the first broadcast performance by Nancy Evans and Ernest Lush of *A Charm of Lullabies* 'thro' a mixture of Latvian Brass-bands, & Viennese Commentary' on the Third Programme, whose medium-wave signal was notoriously interference-prone on the east coast. The following day, Pears wrote from the Mayers' New York home in terms whose jauntiness seems almost unkind. 'The aeroplane is a great modern invention . . . not wholly uncomfortable . . . entirely safe and ever so hospitable,' he told Britten. 'The hostess was graciousness itself, the sherry was fair, the steak at Shannon was enormous, the nightcap soothed . . . I wasn't frightened at all – not at all.'[29]

But Britten's anxieties weren't to be so easily assuaged. A few days later, it was the New York traffic which troubled him: 'Please, darling, remember to look left when stepping off pavements,' he wrote, and drew a little diagram to illustrate the point.[30] The following week, writing to tell Pears that they were at last on the telephone (though he probably wouldn't use it for 'a hectic 3 minutes of transatlantic call, with fading, & not daring to say what I really feel'), he described the 'terrific sea today, most wonderfully beautiful; big racing clouds, lots of bright sun, & the gigantic waves all white', adding: 'Don't be jealous, because you'll be home soon . . .'[31] Then he spent a day in Lowestoft, where there were 'some remarkably fine-looking fishermen & boys, terrifically tanned & strong, in their curiously attractive clothes. You'd have loved it!'[32] And in early November: 'It is really heavenly here, & I can't wait for you to enjoy it with me.'[33] It sounds as if he realised he had yet to convince Pears that Suffolk was the place to be.

Britten, of course, was an incurable worrier; he was also just starting work on a major composition, the *Spring Symphony*, Op. 44, which already had a complicated history. It had been commissioned, as 'a symphony with voice' and at a fee of $1,000, by Serge Koussevitzky in March 1946. At the beginning of 1947, Britten was 'planning it for chorus & soloists' while emphasising that it would be 'a real symphony (the emphasis is on the orchestra) & consequently I am using Latin words':[34] he presumably had Stravinsky's *Symphony of Psalms* in mind as a precedent. But by August 1948, when he told Erwin Stein that he was reading possible poems for his 'Spring piece', he had evidently changed his mind about Latin texts: he may well have been influenced in this decision by Forster, who was again staying in Crabbe Street and, following the broad hint in his festival lecture, pursuing the idea of becoming Britten's next librettist, although the opera's subject had yet to be chosen. His new plan for the symphony was to create a small anthology of English poems which would chart the transition from winter to spring, and his initial resource was a battered copy of *Elizabethan Lyrics from the Original Texts*, edited by Norman Ault, which he had possessed since 1932. 'The work started abysmally slowly & badly, & I got in a real state,' he wrote to Pears in New York (he was in a real state already). 'But I think it's better now. I'm half way thro' the sketch of the 1st movement, deliberately not hurrying it, fighting every inch of the way. It is terribly hard to do, but I think it shows signs of being a piece at last.' He was finding the first part of this movement, setting anonymous sixteenth-century words about a bleak winter's night, 'such cold music that it is depressing to write';[35] it is indeed eerily chilled, the chorus singing a cappella with icy percussive interjections. For a couple of minutes, we may wonder whether this is going to be an orchestral work at all, let alone a symphony; even by the end, despite its organisation into four parts corresponding to four symphonic movements, many listeners will understandably have heard it as a cycle of twelve songs.

In Pears's absence, which in this sense may have been beneficial, Britten began to make good progress. He had sketched out six of the songs by 5 November: 'the Winter one (Orch. & Chorus), the Spenser (3 trumpets & you!), the Nashe (everyone), the Clare driving-boy (with soprano solo), a Herrick Violet (for Kathleen), and a lovely Vaughan one about a shower for you'.[36] Pears returned briefly in mid-November before setting off again to sing the *Serenade* in Lausanne, after which Britten took a break to meet him in Holland. Back in Aldeburgh early in December, he sent a confident telegram to Koussevitzky: 'SYMPHONY WELL ON WAY TO COMPLETION.'[37] But it wasn't. His 'tummy' had gone '*all* wrong again' and he thought he had a stomach ulcer; for three months, despite spending three weeks with Pears in Italy early in the new year, he suffered from his usual lingeringly unspecific winter illness, accompanied by exhaustion and depression, and the *Spring Symphony* had to await an actual spring for its resumption. In mid-March, he was back at work and pleased with it, 'apart from one still beastly bit that I *can't, can't, can't* get right'.[38] It was finished by May and received its first performance not from Koussevitzky but at the Concertgebouw in Amsterdam on 14 July, as part of the Holland Festival, where it was conducted by Eduard van Beinum; the soloists were Jo Vincent, Kathleen Ferrier and Peter Pears. This was the second time Britten had denied Koussevitzky the premiere of a work commissioned by him, and the conductor was much displeased, relenting only when the composer had explained about his illness and his inability to get to America to hear the work at Tanglewood. He was, however, able to get to Amsterdam from where he sent Koussevitzky a not altogether tactful telegram beginning 'DELIGHTED TO TELL YOU SYMPHONY GREAT SUCCESS IN HOLLAND'.[39]

The *Spring Symphony* is a more subversive work than it seems. The obvious precedent, after Latin and Stravinsky had been jettisoned, is Mahler, in works such as his second ('Resurrection') symphony and *Das Lied von der Erde* (and whose fourth feels

like a 'spring' symphony); but Britten seems determined to
disrupt any expectations raised by this thought, as when the
decorous boys' chorus of Mahler's Third Symphony is ironically
echoed by the cheery mob in 'The Driving Boy'. What we don't
get in this work, for all its avowedly celebratory intent, is tranquillity or happiness or Mahlerian expansiveness: ominously, the
longest song (just under nine minutes in the composer's own
recording) is the wintry first one. As for tranquillity, the second,
slow 'movement' seems to be moving towards it in Auden's 'Out
on the lawn I lie in bed', which belongs to his prep-school-teacher
days; but this is violently disrupted by lines which by 1949 had
become startlingly anachronistic: 'And, gentle, do not care to
know, / Where Poland draws her Eastern bow, / What violence
is done . . .' When we reach the finale, setting words from
Beaumont and Fletcher's *The Knight of the Burning Pestle*, we at
last seem to enter a world of unselfconscious rustic jollity, a May
Day celebration, complete with mooing cow horn, which ends
on an apparently optimistic C major; yet, on the words 'I cease',
it does just that, vanishing into silence like an interrupted dream.
It's a musical joke of which Haydn would have been proud,
except for its blackness. But it does confirm one's sense that the
Arcadian ideal towards which the *Spring Symphony* strives is now
out of reach, partly because this is a composition by the altered,
post-Belsen Britten and partly because his implicit hope that a
return to the east coast might enable him to recapture some of
his childhood joys and innocence hadn't been fully realised.

So he turned to the next best thing: writing a work for actual
children which would be both socially useful and emotionally
therapeutic. This was *Let's Make an Opera!*, a sort of do-it-
yourself kit for the English Opera Group to stage at the 1949
Aldeburgh Festival: it would comprise a short, musically illustrated play about the writing and rehearsal of the piece, followed
by a performance of a one-act opera, *The Little Sweep*. Although

Britten had begun thinking about 'a new Children's Opera' in October 1948, it wasn't until April 1949, with his librettist Eric Crozier now installed not too far away in Southwold, that he had the time and energy to compose the piece. Writing to Ralph Hawkes in March, he provided a point-by-point account of his various projects and plans; 'The Children's Opera' comes fifth in his list. It's worth quoting the two paragraphs he devotes to it, because they perfectly illustrate his combination of focused creativity and hard-headed practicality:

> Eric has written a charming little libretto for a one-act children's opera and is in the process of writing an introductory act in play form showing the preparation by the children of this one-act piece. The cast consists of five professional singers and six children, and the audience constitutes the chorus (a neat device for saving money, don't you think?) I have left myself ten days for composing this, but I do not anticipate any difficulties arising.
>
> The first performance will take place in Aldeburgh, in the Aldeburgh Festival in June, then in Wolverhampton and Cheltenham, and we are hoping to arrange a tour in the autumn. We have already picked some startlingly good children to take part. They all come from Ipswich, where they are at various schools.[40]

In fact, Britten wrote the piece during the first three weeks of April; on the 7th, Crozier reported that he had 'seldom seen Ben so cheerful . . . He is loving writing the children's opera and goes about with a beaming smile.'[41] Yet, the very next day, Britten told Pears: 'It's funny writing an opera without you in it – don't really like it much, I confess, but I'll admit that it makes my vocal demands less extravagant!'[42] This was a kind and tactful half-truth: he was enjoying himself partly because he was for once free of the complicated emotional baggage which accompanied writing for Pears. In its place was a simpler emotion: his inextinguishable pleasure in childhood. As with the *Young Person's Guide*, he had particular children, besides the performers, in mind; and, as with *Albert Herring*, the piece is sprinkled with local allusions. These particular children were Lady Cranbrook's, along with her two nephews, who supplied names for the children in the opera; the nineteenth-century setting was Iken Hall, the home of Margery Spring-Rice; and the housekeeper was called Miss Baggott, after the Aldeburgh grocer. Beyond these specific references, *Let's Make an Opera!* was a crucial part of Britten's contract with Suffolk: his recognition that he must give something back to the place which (on the whole) had proved friendlier to him than he might have dared to expect.

At the same time, there was another, and grander, opera to be made: the one for which Forster was to be, with Crozier's assistance, the librettist. Forster was full of enthusiasm, after his visit to Aldeburgh in August 1948, but he had no idea about a suitable story. In October, Britten and Crozier proposed *The History of Margaret Catchpole: A Suffolk Girl*, a mid-nineteenth-century novel by Richard Cobbold, which Forster rather damply told Crozier had 'attracted' him 'at first', adding: 'There seems to me good reason that Ben should not write yet again about the sea.'[43] A few weeks later, however, Britten suggested Herman Melville's late novella, *Billy Budd, Foretopman*, which he had first read about in Forster's *Aspects of the Novel*: '*Billy Budd* is a remote unearthly episode, but it is a song not without words . . . Evil is labelled and personified instead of slipping over the ocean and round the world . . . Melville – after the initial roughness of his realism – reaches straight back into the universal, to a blackness and sadness so transcending our own that they are undistinguishable from glory.'[44] One can easily see how Britten would have been drawn to this account of a work which makes it sound like a first cousin to Crabbe's *Peter Grimes* (and also how this poses an immediate problem). 'I *have* read *Billy Budd*,'[45] Forster cautiously conceded on 11 November; and, indeed, a footnote in *Aspects of the Novel* recording his indebtedness 'to Mr John Freeman's admirable monograph on Melville' almost implies that he hadn't. Anyway, he read it now: there happened to be a convenient recent edition, published by John Lehmann in 1947, with a preface by his old friend William Plomer. At the heart of Melville's tale, which is narrated with a good deal of moral philosophy and historical circumstance, is the disastrous relationship between three characters: Budd, the beautiful but stammering press-ganged sailor; Claggart, the master-at-arms whose thwarted love can only be expressed by destroying Billy; and Vere, the virtuous and scholarly though ultimately helpless captain of the *Indomitable*. Forster was taken with the story's dramatic possibilities and, no doubt, its sexual implications, but Crozier was initially unconvinced.

Early in the new year, the three collaborators met in Aldeburgh and made rapid progress: they decided on the overall shape of the work, including its framing prologue and epilogue, and the allocation of Captain Vere as a tenor role for Pears; a synopsis and a sketch of the *Indomitable*, both in Britten's hand, survive from the meeting and, within a few days, Forster had sent Crozier 'a rough-out for Vere's opening speech'. They reassembled at Crabbe Street for three weeks in March: the two librettists divided their responsibilities – 'Morgan is in charge of the drama, I am in command of the ship, and we share matters out between us,'[46] wrote Crozier – while Britten finished his *Spring Symphony*. They seemed to be getting on splendidly; Crozier was especially delighted by Forster's insistence that he should have equal billing as co-author. It was Britten who began to have misgivings. He thought the libretto 'astonishing' and Forster 'at the height of his form' yet, as he told Ralph Hawkes,

'I am afraid the subject and the treatment will be controversial.'[47] This caution seems out of character from someone who had previously enjoyed taking risks with sexually charged texts and giving the public not quite what it expected, but Britten had changed: he was almost forty and steadily becoming an establishment figure at a time of increasing hostility towards homosexuals and, in America, towards those with past or present left-wing political allegiances. Despite his fame and his festival, there were ways in which he had seldom felt less secure.

Troubling undercurrents began to develop within the team working on *Billy Budd*. The mercurial Crozier recorded the changing weather, which on a good day might seem impossibly sunny: 'I do not think there ever was a happier collaboration than this one between Ben, Morgan and me,' he wrote to Nancy Evans in August. 'We are thrilled by the work, we like each other, we respect each other's viewpoints, and yet we are all so entirely different in our experience and gifts.'[48] But only a month earlier, he more gloomily (and more accurately) noted that Britten had 'jokingly' told him that 'one day I would join the ranks of his "corpses"', the procession of discarded former colleagues which already included Slater and Duncan: 'I have known since early this year that Ben was done with me, and that we could not work together again – for some years, anyway.'[49] Britten was, in fact, furious with Crozier who, without consulting him, had sought from Boosey & Hawkes a guarantee against future royalties: 'I *cannot* feel myself bound always to use him as my librettist. I must pick & choose according to my ideas.'[50] Forster, meanwhile, was becoming increasingly frustrated by Britten's habit of working on at least three things at once and disappearing to give recitals with Pears; during April and May, they performed in Milan, Rome, Genoa, Turin, Vienna, Brussels and The Hague. From the middle of October until early December, they were in North America for their first recital tour, giving twenty concerts in the USA and Canada; Britten was unconvinced by Pears's enthusiasm for transatlantic air travel, so they sailed on the *Queen Mary*. 'How we *hate* this place,' Britten grumbled, perhaps forgetting that he always had done in the days when he could retreat to the Mayers' sanctuary on Long Island. Now it was his turn to be frustrated: he wanted to start work on composing the opera, but hadn't been sent the finished libretto: 'WHERE is BILLY BUDD?? I am getting desperate about it,'[51] he wailed to Erwin Stein.

'Where is *Billy Budd* to be staged?' would have been an equally pertinent question. The uncertainty which had preceded the first performances of *Grimes* and *Lucretia* – and fuelled Britten's preference for small-scale operas in the Jubilee Hall – returned to haunt *Budd*: on the one hand, there was a plan for Sadler's Wells to present it at the 1951 Edinburgh Festival; on the other, a suggestion from David Webster at Covent Garden that the new opera should be staged there as part of the 1951 Festival of Britain. When the Sadler's Wells proposal faltered, for financial reasons, at the end of 1949, Ian Hunter at Edinburgh innocently approached Glyndebourne as an alternative partner; but that, of course, was impossible for Britten. The opera remained homeless, while Arts Council sponsorship was sought and obtained, until November of the following year: then the dilemma was finally resolved in favour of Covent Garden, where *Billy Budd* would be first produced, rather later than originally intended, in December 1951.

When Britten and Pears returned from their American tour, they were looking forward to a quiet Christmas: Ben would get down to work on the opera, while Peter might even take some rest before they set off for another series of recitals, this time in Scotland, during February. Crozier, whose divorce had come through and with whom Britten remained on cordial terms, was at last able to marry Nancy Evans on 'what I know will be the happiest Boxing Day of both your lives'.[52] But this winter, it was

Pears's turn to be ill, and with shingles; afterwards, he went off to a clinic in Switzerland to convalesce, where Britten imagined his 'quick eye roving round for the blonds' and assured him that 'here' – he was staying with their old friends the Behrends at Burghclere – the weather was 'ideal mountain weather – you really needn't have gone away!' Britten had been to a meeting of the English Opera Group's directors to appoint a new general manager, and they had chosen Henry Foy, 'a flowery cove, moustache & curly hair (how I *hate* curls)'.[53] Foy was to prove financially disastrous and would be gone within a year. But another appointment, closer to home, was altogether more successful and enduring. Their housekeeper, Barbara Parker, had left in February 1949, to be replaced by a 'footman' (Britten's term) called Mr Robinson who had taken to behaving very oddly: his habit of nocturnal piano-thumping proved especially irksome. He was now succeeded by Nellie Hudson, a homely and straightforward spinster in her early fifties, from whose uncle Britten had bought the Old Mill at Snape. For almost a quarter of a century, until she retired on her seventy-fifth birthday, Miss Hudson expertly ran the Britten–Pears domestic establishment and its kitchen: at first, she said, she had been wary about 'concert people' and their friends, perhaps having some vague image of unwashed bohemians, but she was greatly impressed by their much-bathed cleanliness and she enjoyed cooking the traditional 'nursery food' so relished by 'Mr Britten'. She mothered him, of course, and he loved it.

3

This is where the Britten myths, and the anti-Britten myths, really begin. Eric Walter White's pioneering study, which first appeared in German as *Benjamin Britten: eine Skizze von Leben und Werk*, was published in English by Boosey & Hawkes in 1949 as *Benjamin Britten: A Sketch of his Life and Works* (and in subsequent editions by Faber as *Benjamin Britten: His Life and Operas*); this was followed by a special Britten Number of *Music Survey*, edited by Donald Mitchell and Hans Keller, in spring 1950. These generous tributes to a composer still in his thirties did not find universal favour. In particular, the anonymous *TLS* review of White's book, noting that 'every religion' develops 'a canon of sacred writings' and mentioning Karl Marx and Mary Baker Eddy as examples, continued: 'It was, therefore, to be foreseen that the latest and most flourishing of our musical sects would furnish itself with a written account of the life and works of its hero, a neat and unpretentious gospel discreetly combining the qualities of hagiography with those of a modern publicity agency.' The reviewer, Martin Cooper, may conceivably have been misled by the imprimatur of Britten's music publisher on the title page, whereas the book had in fact been commissioned by Atlantis Verlag in Zurich; but that hardly begins to excuse the tone of his review. Cooper found it 'incongruous' that 'the central character, and indeed the hero' of *Peter Grimes* should be, in White's words, 'a maladjusted aggressive psychopath', which suggests that he would have had trouble understanding *Macbeth*, and he also found incomprehensible some comparatively lucid remarks by Ronald Duncan about *Lucretia*. But perhaps the most barbed section of his review dealt with the absence, in *Grimes*, of convincing female characters which, he thought, 'accentuates the extraordinary emotional unbalance of the whole plot'.[54] In the climate of the time, this would have been very widely read as a coded reference to the 'emotional unbalance' of Britten's sexuality.

The two mid-century myths about Britten, closely linked and equally untrue, were that he had surrounded himself in Aldeburgh with a homosexual coterie and that he had betrayed his social principles by sycophantic fawning on members of the aristocracy. But, as we have already seen, he had no taste for what would later be called the gay scene and he tended to distance himself from men such as Auden and Ashton. On the other hand, while most of his 'corpses' were male, he enjoyed long and stable friendships with numerous women, including Elizabeth Mayer, Mary Behrend, Imogen Holst and Marion Stein. It was Marion Stein's marriage in September 1949 to the Earl of Harewood, a first cousin of Queen Elizabeth II (an occasion to which Britten contributed and conducted a 'Wedding Anthem' with text by Ronald Duncan), which fuelled the second myth. But Britten's connections with both were firmly grounded in music: George Harewood was president of the Aldeburgh Festival, a writer on opera and a music administrator; Marion was the daughter of Boosey & Hawkes's Erwin Stein, whom Britten had first met in pre-war Vienna and whose London house he and Pears now shared. Wilfully misinterpreting these quite straightforward facts, the American critic Virgil Thomson would claim that the musical establishment in England was 'chiefly controlled by Britten and his publisher, the latter linked by marriage to the throne'.[55]

Although a prolific letter writer, Britten was cautious about public utterance: he trod carefully in interviews and he seldom committed himself to print except on very specific occasions such as short programme notes on his own works or brief introductions (as, for example, to a history of the Boyd Neel Orchestra in 1950). So when, rarely, an opportunity occurred for him to explain what he was about, in a clear putting-the-record-straight way, he tended to seize it: his speech of acceptance on being made a Freeman of the Borough of Lowestoft in July 1951, an honour which genuinely touched him, was just such an occasion. The local dignitaries and townspeople, assembled in the theatre where the six-year-old composer had once appeared in *The Water*

Babies, might seem an improbable audience for Britten's most passionately lucid statement of his artistic credo, but for him this would have been half the point: as with his wartime CEMA concerts and his post-war provincial recitals with Pears, he believed that anything presented outside the capital must be at least as good as that offered to privileged Londoners. After thanking the Borough of Lowestoft 'for the great and rare compliment it pays to Art generally, by so honouring me, a humble composer', he gave a succinct explanation of his own cultural rootedness in Suffolk:

> Suffolk, the birthplace and inspiration of Constable and Gainsborough, the loveliest of English painters; the home of Crabbe, that most English of poets; Suffolk, with its rolling, intimate countryside; its heavenly Gothic churches, big and small; its marshes, with those wild sea-birds; its grand ports and its little fishing villages. I am firmly rooted in this glorious county. And I proved this to myself when I once tried to live somewhere else. Even when I visit countries as glorious as Italy, as friendly as Denmark or Holland – I am always home-sick, and glad to get back to Suffolk.

Here – and by pointing out, in his next paragraph, that *Peter Grimes*, *Albert Herring* and *Let's Make an Opera!* are all set in Suffolk – Britten is staking his claim as a very particular kind of artist: one whose work, like that of Constable and Gainsborough and Crabbe, is inseparable from its creator's birthplace and preferred habitat; Hardy in Wessex and Elgar in Worcestershire are also like this, but such figures became increasingly rare during the mobile, deracinated twentieth century. And of course with Britten the Suffolk landscape and seascape become implicit in everything he wrote after his post-war return there: we will recall him saying to Bobby Rothman that he didn't need to hear the gulls – because the sound of gulls had been part of his inner being from the day he was born.

This logically leads Britten to describe the kind of artist he is in practical terms: he wants 'to serve the community'. 'And the artist today has become the servant of the whole community . . . It is not a bad thing for an artist to try to serve all sorts of different people.' Nor, he adds, is it a bad thing for 'an artist to work to order', instancing *Dido and Aeneas*, the *St Matthew Passion*, *The Marriage of Figaro* and *Aida* as examples of commissions which turned out to be masterpieces. Yet, despite this apparent pragmatism, he reminds his audience that artists 'have an extra sensitivity – a skin less, perhaps, than other people'. They may do things which are 'strange or unpopular' and they may suffer for that: 'Remember for a moment Mozart in his pauper's grave; Dostoievsky sent to Siberia; Blake ridiculed as a madman; Lorca shot by the Fascists in Spain.' After this, he tactfully returns to the more grateful and reassuring image of the 'very small boy, dressed in skin-coloured tights, with madly curly hair' who 'never dreamed that he would ever appear again, on the stage of the Sparrows' Nest, and be honoured like this by his own townspeople'.[56] But there are serious subtexts buried, not too deeply, in this speech: his implication that the artist who invests in his own locality, as he had with the Aldeburgh Festival, deserves some local support in return; his clear identification with other persecuted or ridiculed creative artists while he was working on what he suspected might be his most vulnerably controversial opera, *Billy Budd*; his implicit plea for some critical generosity in the reception of new and unfamiliar works, a subject to which he would more explicitly return a few months later in an article called 'Variations on a Critical Theme' for Harewood's magazine *Opera*. It is no coincidence that these two unusually frank public reflections on the relationship between the composer and his public should flank *Budd*'s premiere.

Forster's tetchy sense of Britten's inability to focus on the main work in hand is scarcely borne out by the meagre tally of his other compositions during the period of their collaboration: these comprise the *Five Flower Songs*, Op. 47, *Lachrymae*, Op. 48, *Six Metamorphoses after Ovid*, Op. 49, and his realisation with Imogen Holst of Purcell's *Dido and Aeneas. Lachrymae*, composed in May 1950, was especially close to Britten's heart in two respects: it is a work for his own two instruments, viola and piano, and, as its subtitle 'Reflections on a Song of Dowland' suggests, it is founded on material by one of the greatest composers of the English Renaissance. Britten bases his ten variations on the first eight bars of Dowland's 'If my complaints could passions move', incorporating in the sixth a reference to 'Flow, my tears' and returning to an almost unadorned version of the original song's final strain at the end of the piece; he would use a similar strategy of ingeniously delayed gratification in a later Dowland-based piece, the *Nocturnal*, written for Julian Bream. *Lachrymae* was first performed, by William Primrose and the composer, as part of the third Aldeburgh Festival, on 20 June 1950. *Six Metamorphoses after Ovid*, a solo work for the oboist Joy Boughton, received its premiere at the following year's festival, when it was performed, somewhat eccentrically, from a boat on Thorpeness Meare; almost inevitably, the score was caught by the wind and blown into the water, from which it had to be swiftly fished out and dried.

The Purcell realisation, a harbinger of things to come, was largely the result of remote collaboration: Imogen Holst was still Director of Music at Dartington. Pears, working there as a resident tutor in February 1951, couldn't praise her highly enough: 'She is quite *brilliant* – revealing, exciting,'[57] he wrote. With the tireless dedication which she would soon bring to Aldeburgh, she had copied out a manuscript full score of *Dido and Aeneas* for Britten to work on: the Britten–Holst edition would add three numbers borrowed from elsewhere in Purcell to complete Act 2 (although Geoffrey Bush contended in a letter to *The Times* that it didn't need completing) as well as a realisation of the continuo part. It was first performed by the English Opera Group, in a double bill with Monteverdi's *Il combattimento di Tancredi e Clorinda*, at the Lyric Theatre, Hammersmith, on 1 May 1951; two differently cast performances at the Aldeburgh Festival followed in June with, respectively, Joan Cross and Nancy Evans as Dido and with George Malcolm and Britten directing from the harpsichord. Although the Britten–Holst *Dido and Aeneas* was destined to fall from favour as early music became increasingly concerned with period authenticity, Steuart Bedford conducted an undervalued recording of it in 1978, with Janet Baker an older and wiser Dido than in her celebrated earlier version and Pears as Aeneas, just as he had been at Aldeburgh twenty-seven years before.

All these works were minor undertakings in comparison with *Billy Budd*, which was turning out to be the most time-consuming and exhausting project Britten had ever attempted. One cause of his exhaustion was Forster who, at the start of 1950, had a prostate operation and in March came to Aldeburgh to convalesce. At first things went well: there were visitors at weekends, including the Steins and the Harewoods ('What a nice chap he is – so gay, friendly, and straight,' Forster enthused), and a good deal of mutual admiration exchanged. But by the end of April, 'Poor old Morgan' had been 'taken bad again' and was packed off once more to the nursing home in London. 'It's a great curse for the poor old man – & he's madly depressed,' Britten told his sister Barbara. 'But I think it's best he should go & get it all coped with as we're all getting a bit worn!'[58] In fact, they were falling out over Britten's treatment of the libretto: Forster admitted to his friend Bob Buckingham that he had had his 'first difference of opinion' with Britten 'over the dirge for the

Novice': 'He has done dry contrapuntal stuff, no doubt original and excellent from the musician's point of view, but not at all appropriate from mine.'[59] This impossible distinction dismayed and infuriated Britten, who Forster mistakenly believed had taken his criticism in good part. Nor was Britten the ideal host for an elderly convalescent: since both his parents had died while comparatively young, he had no experience of caring for the infirm old; and he was impatient with illness, his own or anyone else's. Later in the year, when Britten and Crozier visited Forster in Cambridge, the earlier 'difference' exploded into a full-scale row: Forster was 'chilly but polite' to Crozier, but 'To Britten he was outrageous: he spoke to him like some low-class servant who deserves to be whipped.'[60] This time the contentious passage was Claggart's monologue, 'O beauty, o handsomeness, good-ness'. In a subsequent letter to Britten, Forster resorted to his least helpful tone: 'It is my most important part of writing and I did not, at my first hearings, feel it sufficiently important musically,' he said. He wanted 'a sexual discharge gone evil' rather than 'soggy depression or growling remorse'; he found himself 'turning from one musical discomfort to another, and was dissatisfied'.[61] His readers are used to these lapses – in which he seems high-handed, petulant and defensive – and forgive him for them; but the critically vulnerable Britten was devastated and it was left to Crozier to repair the damage. Forster, at any rate, had regained his balance in an end-of-year diary entry: 'I am rather a fierce old man at the moment, and he is rather a spoilt boy, and certainly a busy one.'[62] He returned to Aldeburgh for several visits during 1951, and in June injured his ankle while climbing the church tower: it may well have been this injury (rather than any further quarrel) that led him to stay at Billy Burrell's bungalow in Linden Road instead of at 4 Crabbe Street. As Furbank makes clear, he was not an amenable patient.

Britten himself was ill with cystitis during July and was

further slowed down by taking the antibiotic sulphonamide M&B, apparently heedless of his earlier overreliance on the drug; but he at last finished the composition draft of *Billy Budd* on 10 August 1951. To celebrate this and to thank the festival's helpers and supporters, he and Pears held a grand party, 'a gay & incredibly mixed affair – from the local Squire (Vernon Wentworth) to the girl from the telephone exchange, & my little fisherboy friend (the "Nipper")'. A few days later, Britten played through the whole opera for the Harewoods, who compared its emotional impact to that of Verdi's *Otello*, and then for Forster, who wrote to Bob Buckingham that it was 'very fine'. But Britten wasn't taken in. He found Forster to be 'in a funny abstracted mood' and told Stein that he 'demanded to have the work played to him – but cannot remember at all what he's previously heard of it! . . . He doesn't seem to grasp it at all – or [be] really interested in the musical side of the opera!'[63] It was a relief to take a break from the *Indomitable* and to get aboard an actual boat, which he and Pears did in September, when they were joined by Basil Coleman, who was to direct the first production of *Billy Budd*, and Arthur Oldham as passengers on a thirteen-ton launch captained by Billy Burrell (with Robin Long, the Nipper, as cabin boy): they sailed across the North Sea and up the Rhine, and Robin, who didn't as a rule care much about education, wrote a careful account of the trip for his school magazine, *The Leistonian*. Britten, with his recurrent wish to help a disadvantaged youngster, floated the idea of his paying for Robin to go to a public school, but Burrell – the *other* Billy B., as Britten would affectionately refer to him – knew better: 'You want to forget that! That's the biggest mistake you'll ever make.'[64]

As with *Grimes*, the relationship between *Billy Budd* and its source is complex. Melville supplies a detailed historical context: the story is set in the summer of 1797, soon after the Nore

Mutiny which, for 'the British Empire', he explains, 'was what a strike in the fire brigade would be to London threatened by general arson';[65] thereafter, he interrupts with references and supposedly personal anecdotes to support the tale's historical veracity. His Captain Vere is wounded at the end of the *Indomitable*'s voyage and dies, 'cut off too early for the Nile and Trafalgar'.[66] Britten and his librettists, by contrast, allow him to survive into old age so that he can provide a framing prologue and epilogue which, in a quite different way, also serve to push the events back into the past. To their credit, Forster and Crozier retain almost verbatim many of the story's most memorable moments, such as Billy's ambiguous farewell to his old merchant ship the *Rights of Man*, Dansker's warning about Claggart ('Baby Budd, *Jimmy Legs* . . . is down on you')[67] and the ballad 'Billy in the Darbies' which ends the novella. There are inevitable losses in the transition from one medium to another. In the moment after Claggart has been felled, when Vere and Billy try to prop up the body, Melville adds a shocking short sentence: 'It was like handling a dead snake.'[68] By contrast, Melville describes Billy's execution in prose of extraordinary rhapsodic power: 'At the same moment it chanced that the vapory fleece hanging low in the East was shot through with a soft glory as of the fleece of the Lamb of God seen in a mystical vision, and simultaneously therewith, watched by the wedged mass of upturned faces, Billy ascended, and, ascending, took the full rose of the dawn.'[69] Other changes are simply practical. In Melville, Claggart's ominous 'Handsomely done, my lad! And handsome is as handsome did it too!'[70] is prompted by Billy spilling soup over a newly scrubbed deck; spilled soup, however, is hard to manage onstage and so the fight with Squeak has to provide a more logical, though less ironically menacing, pretext for Claggart's remark.

But one particular change threatens to skew the entire work:

in the opening scene, the flogging takes on a troubling new significance. In Melville, the culprit is 'a little fellow, young, a novice, an after-guardsman absent from his assigned post when the ship was being put about', an insignificant character guilty of a 'rather serious' lapse; Billy is 'horrified' and resolves never to 'make himself liable to such a visitation'.[71] Britten, Forster and Crozier seize on the word 'Novice' and turn him into a recurring character: after the Bosun has him flogged, offstage, for two trivial onstage offences, he becomes Claggart's chosen instrument for tempting Billy to mutiny. (Claggart, we might almost say, has found 'A feeling being subject to his blow', except that this line isn't Melville's about Claggart but Crabbe's about Grimes.) Yet there is more to it than that. The Novice's response when the punishment is ordered is 'Sir, no! – not me!' and 'Don't have me flogged – I can't bear it! – not flogging!'; and, when Claggart threatens him later, 'No! No! Don't hurt me again!' This is not the language of the man-of-war but of the prep school; we half expect the Novice to shout 'Yarroo!' or 'Cripes!' The traumatic memories lurking here are Britten's of hearing a boy being beaten at South Lodge and Forster's of his unhappy schooldays at Tonbridge. Moreover, the Bosun's irascibility seems at odds with the happy ship presided over by its mild, civilised captain who, hearing a shanty sung below decks, insists: 'Where there is happiness there cannot be harm.' This is a view to which we are meant broadly to assent and from which Claggart represents a monstrous deviation.

During the autumn, while Britten worked on the full score, arrangements had to be made for *Budd*'s premiere at Covent Garden, designed by John Piper and produced by Basil Coleman. As usual, in solving some problems he had created others. For instance, it had been an entirely sensible decision to make the benign, introspective Captain Vere a tenor role for Pears: Billy, the object of desire, and the predatory Claggart would have been, in different ways, equally inappropriate for him. But Billy had thus become, rather surprisingly, a baritone who had also to be (despite the suspension of disbelief usually inherent in opera) young and attractive. Britten's first choice was Geraint Evans, who withdrew after discovering that the role's tessitura lay too high for him and instead sang the part of Mr Flint, the Sailing Master. Fortunately, during a visit to the States, Covent Garden's David Webster discovered the Californian baritone Theodor Uppman who was, in his own words, 'very blond and curly-haired . . . I had been working a good deal of the summer out of doors, rolling great barrels of oil, my shirt off, and I had a pretty good set of muscles and I was nice and tanned.' And he could sing. Not only was Uppman the perfect Billy Budd; he also – being unconnected with the composer or Aldeburgh or even England – usefully rebutted any suggestion that Britten wrote only for members of his own clique. The opera was to have been conducted by Josef Krips but, not for the first or the last time, Britten's completion of the full score ran perilously close to its deadline: the famously myopic Krips, presented with blurry greyish photocopies, found them unread-able and withdrew. So Britten himself stepped in. 'We all know that Ben went through great turmoils,' said Uppman, 'but once he was there and doing it, there was nobody who could do it better – just the little looks and the coaxings that you could see from his hand as he was conducting; you knew what he wanted. He was a great conductor.'[72]

The first public performance of *Billy Budd* took place on Saturday, 1 December 1951. In its original version, the opera was in four acts and there were two intervals (when Britten revised *Billy Budd* into two acts in 1960, he deleted material which Ernest Newman, in an obtuse review for the *Sunday Times*, unkindly compared to *HMS Pinafore* and, with it, the initial appearance of Captain Vere). It made a long evening, and the critical reaction was both muted and confused. Britten's old friend Lennox Berkeley, who wrote to congratulate him 'on a splendid work that you alone could have written – full of beauty and in places deeply moving', pointed out that according to the *Sunday Times* he had been 'ill served by his librettists' whereas in the *Listener* he had been 'well served by his librettists'. Desmond Shawe-Taylor, in the *New Statesman*, wrote two pieces: one largely favourable, after reading the score, the other more cautious, when he had seen and heard it. Reviewers seemed even more than usually nervous about praising Britten, although Colin Mason in the *Spectator* was clear about his 'masterly solution of the technical problems' and justly concluded that the opera had 'a consistency and concentration of musical language such as are not to be found in anything Britten has previously written'.[73] John Ireland, while privately expressing reservations, wrote to tell his former student that *Billy Budd* was 'a masterpiece' in which 'The clarity, the economy of means – the invariable certainty of touch – the spontaneity, the invention – all constituted a perfect joy to me'.[74] But Michael Tippett, whose principled aversion to violence was less ambiguous and conflicted than Britten's, '"wasn't good" at enjoying the opera, especially the moment "when the Novice is brought on and he's been flogged, like a Crucifixion. It wasn't me."'[75]

Yet *Billy Budd* is indeed a masterpiece, arguably the supreme achievement among Britten's operas. Where *Grimes* suffers from a sense of irresolution and *Lucretia* from its tacked-on Christian morality, here the framing prologue and epilogue provide an entirely satisfying structure. The libretto, despite its quirks, is dramatically superb and faultlessly set. The music is Britten's finest: there are shrewd characterisations – a yearning saxophone for the Novice, a panicky side drum for stammering Billy and (as Michael Kennedy neatly puts it) 'the trombones which stalk around with Claggart';[76] there are audacities such as the sequence of thirty-four triadic chords, covering not only Vere's interview with Billy but also Claggart's burial, which then re-appears beneath Billy's final words; there is the brilliant use of the chorus – divided between Main Deck, Quarter Deck, Gunners, Afterguardsmen and Marines – whose shantyish inter-jections at times recall another anthem for doomed youth, Tippett's *A Child of Our Time*; above all, there is incomparably rich orchestral colour. Is it possible that music of such intensity is better appreciated without the distraction of a staged produc-tion? This arguably heretical suggestion is made by Ian Bostridge, who sang (and recorded) the role of Vere at the Barbican in 2007: '*Billy Budd* benefits from a degree of musical concentration on the part of the audience which may be missing in the opera house. A certain metaphysical poetry, a symphonic level of abstraction, is released which the literal representation of details of maritime life can inhibit.'[77] It's a provocative and almost paradoxical idea – an opera whose music is too good for its own good? – but it goes some way towards explaining why *Billy Budd*, unusually among Britten's or anyone else's operas, retains and even gains power when heard on record in one's study, which may be an appropriate enough setting for a work whose non-titular hero is the bookish Captain Vere.

For those who sought to perpetuate the anti-Britten myths, *Billy Budd* was a godsend: it was anonymously nicknamed 'The Bugger's Opera' and, by the reliably idiotic Thomas Beecham, 'Twilight of the Sods'. Three years later, and rather more amiably, the poet Henry Reed wrote a radio play for the Third Programme, *The Private Life of Hilda Tablet*, about the fictitious composer of an opera entitled *Emily Butter* (it was originally to have been called *Milly Mudd*), set in a department store and with an all-female cast including one Clara Taggart. The revue *Airs on a Shoestring* (1953–5) included 'A Guide to Britten' by Michael Flanders and Donald Swann, a brisk and witty musical tour of the composer's operas and several of his other works; interestingly, the show's producer, Laurier Lister, worried that the item would prove too highbrow for audiences on a pre-London tour but, as its authors later recalled, 'This actually didn't happen, and the very first time when it was played, which wasn't a sort of cultural centre, by any means, everybody loved it.'[78] Deceptively gentle in tone, the piece nevertheless makes some neat points about Britten's debts to Purcell and 'olde English' folk songs, the 'Doggy Doggy Few' (such as the Harewoods), and *Albert Herring*, who is said to have 'got pickled, and cured'. Britten, with that 'extra sensitivity – a skin less, perhaps, than other people', seldom found jokes against himself anything other than deeply hurtful, and it would have been small comfort to him to reflect that scurrilous witticisms and satirical parodies were among the surest indications of his extraordinary success.

4

Billy Budd ends in redemption. 'I'd die for you,' Billy tells Captain Vere halfway through Act 2; and, as he goes to his death, he cries, 'Starry Vere, God bless you!' Vere himself, in his epilogue, reflects: 'I could have saved him . . . But he has saved me, and the love that passes understanding has come to me.' We have to accept that in the terms of the opera Billy is a Christlike sacrificial victim, even if, in a more sceptical mood, we might question Vere's transformation of his guilt into blessing: in failing to save Billy, he has enabled Billy to save him from being 'lost on the infinite sea'. It seems logical, and in retrospect almost inevitable, that Britten's thoughts should have turned from this conundrum to the Old Testament story of Abraham and Isaac and that he should have composed, as a pendant to the opera, his *Canticle II: Abraham and Isaac*, Op. 51. He wrote the work – using a text taken, edited and slightly rearranged, from the fourth of the Chester Miracle Plays, *Histories of Lot and Abraham* – at the very start of 1952, telling Basil Coleman on 8 January that he had a 'piece of music for Kath & Peter to write'.[79] The ink hardly dry, it received its first public performance from Kathleen Ferrier, Pears and Britten in Nottingham on 21 January, as part of a recital tour which also included Birmingham (broadcast on the Midland Region Home Service), Liverpool and Manchester. There were further concert performances during 1952, including a Third Programme broadcast, but a planned recording for Decca the following year was abandoned because of Ferrier's deteriorating condition; she died of cancer on 8 October 1953.

Abraham and Isaac has become the best known and most performed of Britten's five *Canticles* – usually with a countertenor in the role of Isaac, originally sung by Ferrier – and it is easy to see why. Although it runs for little more than a quarter of an hour, it shares the mysteriously coiled-up emotional force of *Billy Budd*; and, like the opera, it demands of the secular listener (who will be appalled by this whimsically vindictive God) an imaginative acceptance of its own terms. The crucial difference, of course, is that Isaac's life, unlike Billy's, will be spared; yet, since neither Abraham nor Isaac knows this until the text's closing passages, the tension is undiminished. For once, the work received some intelligent critical responses: John W. Waterhouse in the *Birmingham Post* noted how the 'entire setting, from its Schütz-like opening device of giving God to two singers, builds and completes a wholly satisfying musical entity', while the anonymous critic of *The Times* found the 'spirit of Purcell . . . in the flowing interchange of recitative, arioso, and duet; most effective is the dovetailing of solo passages, when one voice takes over from another'.[80]

Britten and Pears's recital tour was followed by concerts in Salzburg and Vienna; after these, they took a well-deserved skiing holiday with their friends the Harewoods at Gargellen. Here the conversation turned to English opera or, more precisely, to opera about England: it was Harewood who proposed the subject of Elizabeth I and her relationship with Robert Devereux, Earl of Essex, from whom he was distantly descended. The proposal had acquired a special significance following the death of George VI on 6 February: a new Elizabethan age was beginning, so it was said, and what could be more fitting than an opera on the new Queen's great predecessor by England's finest living composer, given at a royal gala performance to celebrate the Coronation? It was a terrible idea but also an inescapable one. The imaginary headline 'BRITTEN REFUSES CORONATION OPERA' was unthinkable even though, given the discretion of all concerned, it would never actually have appeared. Britten, moreover, found the project musically attractive: his interest in Elizabethan composers such as Dowland was well known and recently attested by his *Lachrymae*, and the celebratory opera would allude to the madrigalist John Wilbye as well as to the chronologically anachronistic Purcell. It would be a 'number opera', almost a sort of pageant, which fitted well with his instinct that it must be quite unlike *Billy Budd*, and it would be called *Gloriana*. Britten assigned to it the opus number 53, to match the year of the Coronation, even though he had yet to compose his Op. 52.

For his librettist, Britten turned to William Plomer, an accomplished writer of fiction and a witty poet, with whom he had hoped to collaborate on two abortive works for children: *The Tale of Mr Tod*, which would have been based on Beatrix Potter's rabbit-roasting badger, and a science-fiction piece which was to have been called *Tyco the Vegan*. Plomer lived quietly with his partner Charles Erdmann in Bayswater, and they were shortly to move to a modest bungalow on the Sussex coast at Rustington: this kind of respectably unobtrusive homosexual life was far more to Britten's taste than bohemian flamboyance, and the two men got on well. However, when Britten returned from Austria, his schedule became characteristically hectic (it included conducting *Billy Budd* in Birmingham) and it wasn't until 27 April that he could put the proposal for his royal opera to Plomer. He did so with evident excitement and mysterious urgency: 'it is imperative that I see you', he wrote; 'about what I can only explain when I see you'.[81] When they met, Plomer was hesitant, suspecting that this was just the sort of publicity-engendering enterprise he most disliked, but a week or só later Britten pressed him: 'The Queen has graciously given her OK to the scheme I told you about . . . Everything seems set, therefore; only with the librettist, there is a doubt still . . . ?'[82] The following day, Plomer wrote to accept the commission, enclosing a copy of J. E. Neale's *Queen Elizabeth* as 'a sort of corrective' to Lytton Strachey's *Elizabeth and Essex*, which had prompted Harewood's original suggestion. Before the end of May, an official announcement had named the date of 'the gala performance of the Coronation opera as (probably) 8 June of the following year'.[83] Britten, at this stage, had only the vaguest sense of the work: 'I want the opera to be crystal clear, with lovely pageantry (however you spell it) but linked by a strong story about the Queen & Essex – strong & simple.'[84] Plomer already knew from their mutual friend Forster that Britten's demands, though strong, were unlikely to remain simple.

The collaborative evolution of *Gloriana* is traced in entertaining detail by Peter F. Alexander in his biography of Plomer.[85] Despite the tight and self-evidently non-negotiable deadline, it was an intermittent business, complicated not only by Britten's summer concert schedule – which involved festival appearances in Aix-en-Provence, Menton and Salzburg as well as Aldeburgh

– but by Plomer's dislike of the telephone and lack of a car. Like almost everyone who collaborated with him, Plomer was astonished and occasionally terrified by the speed at which the composer worked. So was Britten's newly appointed music assistant, Imogen Holst. Having left Dartington with the intention of pursuing a freelance career, she moved to Aldeburgh in September 1952 to work as Britten's amanuensis and to share some of the festival's administrative work with Elizabeth Sweeting: the latter role was to prove a turbulent one since, quite apart from disagreeing over policy and being unable to share decision-making, the two women simply didn't get on. Her first task was to make fair copies of Britten's sketches as he produced them: 'He was able to say in the middle of October, when he was just beginning Act I, that he would have finished the second act before the end of January,' she wrote. 'When he began work on the full score of the opera, he wrote at such tremendous speed that I thought I should never keep pace with him. He managed to get through at least twenty vast pages a day, and it seemed as if he never had to stop and think.'[86] He kept to his demanding schedule, despite Plomer's spell in a London nursing home during November, after a minor operation, and also despite the east coast floods of 31 January 1953, when the sea invaded the ground floor of 4 Crabbe Street.

While Plomer was recuperating, George Harewood and David Webster visited Aldeburgh, partly to see how *Gloriana* was getting on but also, more urgently and surprisingly, so that Webster could offer Britten the post of musical director at Covent Garden. The following day, Britten invited his new assistant and confidante Imogen Holst – who, fortunately, kept a lively, candid diary for her first two years in Aldeburgh – to join him on an afternoon walk across the marshes to the river wall:

As soon as he got out of the thick of High St he began to tell me about the Covent Garden crisis – David Webster wanted him to decide then & there whether he'd accept the post of musical director or not. Ben had told him that he wanted not to have to think of it while his mind was on Gloriana, but Webster insisted on having an answer. He had also said the most frightful things about Ben's 'duty' to music in England etc! Ben had said that the only thing that would make him do it would be if Covent Garden would take on all of them, ie the [English Opera] Group, with George as manager. Webster said he wouldn't do that because people would say it was turning into a clique. Ben was furious, and said that everything that ever got done in music was done by a clique – that that was the word that was used when people disapproved, and that when they approved they called it a 'group' or something else. What *amazed* Ben was that Webster had objected even before Ben had asked for the group as a whole: – he'd only asked for George when the word 'clique' was thrown at him. So he immediately felt he wanted to say No straight away. And he asked me what I thought. I said it would be wrong for him to do anything that got in the way of composing, and although he did lots of things that *appeared* to interfere, they didn't *really*: – whereas being an administrator would be fatal. He agreed. He said it would mean 6 months of the year, working in an office from Monday to Friday, which was of course impossible. At this moment he caught sight of his favourite barn owl flying over the water just beyond the ruined boat, so he stopped thinking about Covent Garden while he looked at it.[87]

Webster's proposal, which Britten anyway knew to be absurd, stood no chance against the combined forces of Imogen Holst and the barn owl. Holst's diary, which reveals her as Britten's kindred spirit in her sensitivity to nature as well as to music, provides a unique record of those afternoon thinking-and-composing walks. On one memorable occasion ('One of the best days I've *ever* had'), they drove to the hamlet of Eastbridge and walked by the dykes and flooded meadows to the ruined chapel at Minsmere: 'Well, if I thought heaven was like this I wouldn't mind dying,' said Britten.[88] On another, back on the river-wall path at Slaughden, 'He talked about the flight of birds, how they all kept perfectly together, never touched each other, and all without a conductor! "And we talk about orchestral technique & ensemble but we haven't *begun* to get near it!"'[89]

Plomer spent Christmas at Aldeburgh, before accompanying Britten to stay with the Harewoods, and by early January the libretto was complete. 'What a heavenly time that was at Harewood,' wrote Plomer on 13 January, 'and how thankful I am to have been able to contribute to your progress with *Gloriana* during these last few days – and indeed all along.'[90] Britten replied even more warmly, tactfully acknowledging that he mightn't have been the easiest person to work with: 'Writing Gloriana with you has been the greatest pleasure; more than I ever expected, & I was pretty greedy in anticipation too! I think, apart from your wonderful gifts, that you have shown the greatest possible good-temper and amenability, which can't always have been easy considering the conditions and not over-precision of your colleague on the job!' He hoped that Plomer would be able to join him in visiting John Piper for the first weekend in February, together with Basil Coleman, for 'the urgently needed preliminary discussions on the settings & production'.[91] This was followed by a play-through of the complete work at Covent Garden on 14 February; almost exactly a month later, on 13 March, the orchestration was finished.

Although Plomer had anticipated, and calmly accepted, that Britten would demand changes in his libretto, he had been unprepared for interference of another sort: he was required by the Lord Chamberlain's Office to substitute a basin for a chamber pot in Act 3, since according to 'a rule of long standing . . . the Lord Chamberlain has had *to set his face against chamber-pots*'. Tickled by this phrase, he repeated it when on 18 May he and Britten spent an evening at the Harewoods' London home, talking about *Gloriana* with the Queen and Prince Philip: 'the joke', says Alexander, 'was much enjoyed'. A few days after the gala performance – which took place, exactly as originally planned, on 8 June, six days after the Coronation – Plomer told his sister-in-law that the royal couple had 'seemed to enjoy themselves and said very nice things. He took great trouble to read the libretto & I think he now knows it better than I do.'[92] They were no less appreciative of the composer himself: in the Coronation honours list published on 1 June, Britten was made a Companion of Honour. He regarded this 'as a compliment to serious English music & what is more – opera' and told Lennox Berkeley that it made him 'feel fairly old, but not (thank God) too respectable'.[93]

Nevertheless, the first night of *Gloriana* was famously disastrous. This wasn't the fault of the work or its performers but of the audience who on the whole were as unmusical a bunch of stuffed shirts as ever sat through a new opera. At the end, to applause which was muted not only because so many hands were elegantly gloved, Britten leaned forward in his box and hissed: 'Clap, damn you.' He might have been amused and even re-assured if he could have known that a different sort of musician, John Lennon, would in 1964 urge the Royal Command Performance audience: 'Will people in the cheaper seats clap your hands? All the rest of you, if you'll just rattle your jewellery . . .'[94] Although to Plomer he put on a brave world-weary face – 'I'm a bit more used to the jungle!'[95] – Britten was devastated. 'The Queen was delighted & flattered by the occasion,' he wrote to Elizabeth Mayer. 'But – there is no way of glossing this fact over – we all feel so kicked around, so bewildered by the venom, that it is difficult to maintain one's balance.'[96] *Gloriana* was in fact well received at Covent Garden during the remainder of its run, by audiences who, as a shrewd doorkeeper told the *Daily Express*, 'are lovers of opera' and 'have paid for their seats'.[97] But it had always been destined to make enemies on both sides: on the one hand, some serious critics regarded it as clinching evidence of a once radical composer's capitulation to the establishment; on the other, some members of the establishment found a work about the ageing Elizabeth's relationship with Essex in questionable taste as a Coronation piece (and Pears as Essex a questionable piece of casting). One happier response to the royal occasion might have been an opera based on an Elizabethan comedy: *A Midsummer Night's Dream* – with its summeriness and its resolution of happy marriages, including a royal one – would have been ideal, but Britten hadn't thought of that yet.

The reviews of *Gloriana*, which mostly ranged from neutral to negative, prompted debate in the correspondence columns of *The Times*. Vaughan Williams, assuming with some dignity the role of musical elder statesman, refused to be drawn on the opera's merits 'after a single hearing' but concentrated on the fact that 'for the first time in history the Sovereign has commanded an opera by a composer from these islands for a great occasion'. Anthony Lewis asserted that 'on this historic occasion English music has been splendidly represented by Mr Britten's *Gloriana*'. On the other side of the argument, Marie Stopes, in an extraordinary letter, complained that 'the opera was unworthy of this great occasion, uninspired, missing the main glories of the times, its music inharmonious and wearisome, and with at least two scenes profoundly affronting the glorious memory of Queen Elizabeth I, hence unsuitable for public performance before Queen Elizabeth II'. And from Aldeburgh, of all places, J. Thorburn Irvine, evidently one of Lady Cranbrook's 'antibodies', lamented 'the missed opportunity of creating something to inspire other than purely musical people'. With an irony undetectable by the public, Martin Cooper in the *Spectator* attributed the negative reaction to Britten's supposedly privileged position with the establishment and 'an almost sadistic relish or glee that has little to do with the musical merit or demerit'.[98] Thanks to the *TLS*'s convention of anonymity, Cooper's readers would have been unaware that he had himself been the author of a savage attack on Britten.

Even Pears, the more metropolitan-minded of the couple, felt that the reception of *Gloriana* confirmed 'his worst fears' and that they should 'in future stick to the public that wanted them, the loyal Aldeburgh friends, and not get mixed up with something that was none of their concern'.[99] The summer of 1953 was, as it turned out, a prudent moment for Britten to withdraw for a while from the limelight for, during the autumn, Sir David Maxwell-Fyfe, the Home Secretary, was said to have instigated a witch-hunt against homosexual men, possibly triggered by the defection of the spies Guy Burgess and Donald Maclean – the latter, by a ludicrous coincidence, a contemporary of Britten at Gresham's. Neither cultural eminence nor aristocracy offered any guarantee of immunity from prosecution: among those convicted of sexual offences were John Gielgud in October 1953 and Lord Montagu of Beaulieu in March 1954. Shortly before Christmas, Britten was interviewed by officers from Scotland Yard: he was, of course, a model of decency and respectability in his private life, and no further action was taken. But the extent of anti-homosexual feeling among the public – or, at least, a section of it, for neither the people of Aldeburgh nor royalty and aristocracy seemed greatly fussed – was such that Humphrey Maud's civil servant father found it necessary to forbid his son from staying at Crabbe Street: it was, as John Maud explained to Britten during a difficult interview at his office in Curzon Street, not a matter of personal distrust but of what might be said by others. Although Britten was deeply hurt, he understood this sort of man-to-man frankness and he remained friendly with the Maud family.

Apart from Humphrey Maud, Britten's other two significant friendships with boys during the early 1950s were with Jonny Gathorne-Hardy and Paul Rogerson, when both of them were in their later teens. Jonny – who, like other members of his family, had donated his name to a character in *The Little Sweep* – remembers a steadily evolving relationship, centred on ferocious games of tennis. 'When you were beaten by him at squash or tennis, as I invariably was (though I was good at both), you did literally feel that he'd been *beating* you. If you were three down, and he could get you six down, he would.' By the time Jonny was eighteen, in 1951, he would take his post-match bath at Crabbe Street and stay to dinner; the bathroom adjoined Britten's bedroom. It was on one of these occasions, while they were wrapped in towels between bath and pre-meal Martini, that 'Ben came up with an extremely soppy, sentimental look on his face, and put his arms round me, and kissed me on the top of the head'. Jonny already had a speech prepared for this moment ('No, Ben, it is not to be!'), after which they went down to dinner in an amiable and civilised way. He was, however, sure 'that, had I relaxed, we would have been in that double bed'.[100] Today, it would be a perfectly legal place for them, but it wasn't in 1951: the gesture was, as Jonny evidently recognised, a token of Britten's trust in him. Another sort of eighteen-year-old boy would have gone off gabbling to police or press; yet another sort would have attempted blackmail.

Paul Rogerson was two years younger than Jonny Gathorne-Hardy, a cellist and a Catholic from a musical family: his father Haydn Rogerson was principal cello with the Hallé and his uncle, Thomas Matthews, leader of the LPO (he had been the soloist in the first English performance of Britten's Violin Concerto in 1941). 'Paul & I fell in love with each other, if that is how you can describe it, a whole year before we met,' Britten told Imogen Holst.[101] This was when they caught sight of each other during a Hallé concert early in 1951, where Pears was performing the *Serenade*, and it was rather less than a year before they met again at the premiere of *Billy Budd*. Britten wrote affectionate letters to 'My dear old Paul', who was away at school in Derbyshire: 'Don't forget to practice your tennis hard, & *don't* forget your cricket, because there might be a chance of playing here this summer.' Eternally schoolboyish himself, he enclosed some 'apparently mouldy bits of chocolate' which weren't 'really mouldy' but had 'arrived in a parcel from South Africa, & must have had a rough passage'.[102] During school holidays, Paul became a frequent visitor to Aldeburgh. It was a relationship founded on non-sexual devotion: Britten, Paul recalled, 'was like a godfather. He was a dear. It was an honour and a privilege, thinking back now.' As with David Spenser, there was a pattern of shared pleasures: 'We used to go out bird watching, brass rubbing, on the beach, go out with Billy Burrell, marvellous playing in front of the fire, Chenka, that sort of thing.' Or Paul would play his cello, in the sitting room at Crabbe Street, with 'one of the finest pianists in the world, certainly one of the greatest accompanists'.[103] But, during his troubled summer of 1953, Britten learned that Paul had decided to become a Jesuit: '15 years away from everyone,' noted Imogen Holst in disbelief (although in fact he would leave the order in 1959), adding that 'Ben hated the very word "Jesuit", and was appalled to think that Paul mustn't take *any* possessions away to his novitiate'.[104] Her diary entry for Tuesday 18 August, after Paul had spent a final weekend at Aldeburgh, describes his departure with Pears: 'At 10 I waited outside the front door: Paul came out to fetch me in. All three were in tears, Ben being the calmest & most matter-of-fact. He hobbled to the front door to see them off and I waved from the middle of the road till the car had turned the corner.'[105] She didn't look back, as she couldn't bear to see Britten's distress. He was prevented by a sprained ankle and a painful shoulder from driving Paul to the station at Saxmundham although, given his emotional state, this was just as well.

The ankle mended, but the shoulder became steadily more troublesome. And the summer also contained, in the weeks immediately following *Gloriana*, one more perhaps clinchingly stressful element: Britten had persuaded Auden to speak at the Aldeburgh Festival. 'Wystan came, & was provoking and brilliant,'[106] he told Elizabeth Mayer, but she wasn't taken in by this blandness: 'don't forget (I know you don't)', she replied, 'that he is a truly great person and has, of course, great faults but also great qualities (not only as a poet but as a human being)'.[107] The two men had fallen out over a decade earlier and their differences had more recently been exacerbated by Auden's collaboration with Stravinsky on *The Rake's Progress* (1951), which Britten refused to see, as he explained to Ronald Duncan: 'I've seen the score, & not withstanding the excellence of Strav. & Auden as creators I'm not awfully interested in what they think about opera . . . Opera's my life, & it's obviously not theirs.'[108] To the Harewoods he wrote that he was 'miserably disappointed . . . that easily the greatest composer alive should have such an irresponsible & perverse view of opera'; and for this he blamed Auden, 'the cleverer & more sophisticated of the two'.[109] Auden, for his part, did go to *Gloriana* during his English visit, and although he tactfully praised Britten's music to their mutual friend Elizabeth

Mayer, he added: 'Didn't care for the libretto and neither Joan Cross nor Peter should sing anymore on stage.' According to Stephen and Natasha Spender, Auden unwisely put his criticisms of *Gloriana* in writing to Britten and had his letter torn up and returned to him: 'Just an envelope, and out came the pieces of the letter.'[110] When calmer, Britten could usually manage distant civility to those who had affronted him, and that was how Auden found himself received at Aldeburgh: 'Everyone was charming, but I was never allowed to see Ben alone – I feared as much, still, I was a bit sad.'[111] Over a decade later, Christopher Isherwood, in his diary entry for 6 March 1967, recorded a remark made by Auden during a weekend visit: 'He said that Benjamin Britten was the only friend he had ever lost.'[112]

Auden had never really understood his old friend's demons: his lurches into depression and his terrifying lack of self-confidence. Walter Hussey, who preached at the festival service that year, saw both when, after the service, he went to lunch at Crabbe Street. Britten, the company was told, wouldn't be in to lunch; as the meal continued without him, there was a discussion about the parable of the talents, which Harewood, who was present, had just read as a lesson in the church. Then Britten entered, silently and 'looking like death', according to Hussey, who described what happened next:

> And we went on busily discussing the talents and almost forgot him. Then suddenly we were interrupted by a hysterical voice from the other end of the table. 'It's those who have no talents at all – they're the real problem!' And of course we were absolutely silenced . . . I said, 'Meaning yourself, Ben?' And he said in the same hysterical tone: 'There are times when I feel I have no talents – no talents at all!' And so again, a great silence. Then I leant forward and said, 'You know, Ben, when you're in this mood we love you best of all.' And he simply

gave a great shout. 'I hate you, Walter!' From that moment, he was entirely all right![113]

We can't be sure what, if anything, specifically prompted this, but Auden's presence in Aldeburgh so soon after the reception of *Gloriana* seems the likeliest cause. For Auden and Stravinsky had come to represent everything that Britten most detested and feared in the arts. Auden was clever and brilliant, but heartless and deracinated. Stravinsky wrote music of incomparable quality, yet it seemed to say nothing. Britten was a composer of music with content, rooted in a particular place and in his own troubled humanity. He was about to begin work on the song cycle which would, above all, embody these qualities.

5

'Wonderful, touching poems' was how Britten described the texts he was setting, a series of 'Thomas Hardy songs which we do at Harewood House, as part of the Leeds Festival, next month'.[114] One of them, 'Wagtail and Baby', had in fact been composed earlier in the year; the other seven were written during August and September; and the untitled group of 'Hardy Songs' – subsequently to be known, at Pears's suggestion, as *Winter Words*, Op. 52 – received its first performance at Harewood on 8 October. Isherwood had given Britten a copy of Hardy's *Collected Poems*, a nicely judged present, in 1949, and Britten characteristically made a list of twenty-one possibilities on the back flyleaf before deciding on ten to be set, two of which were excluded from the cycle. It is difficult to imagine a writer who could have spoken more powerfully to Britten at this time than Hardy, with his English rootedness, his intense humanity and his deep understanding of melancholia. We know from Imogen Holst's diary that Britten's reading went beyond the poems: she gave him her father's copy of *The Return of the Native* – presumably the one which had inspired his symphonic poem *Egdon Heath* in 1927 – while he told her that *Jude the Obscure* 'wasn't unbearable – that he minded the first bit more than the last'.[115] What moved him most powerfully in *Jude*, then, was the boy who has much in common with his own young self; who loves creatures and is beaten by the farmer for failing to scare the birds from his crops; who sets his heart on a life of learning and culture and whose 'dreams were as gigantic as his surroundings were small'.[116] It is surely no coincidence that the poems set by Britten include two solitary travelling boys, Jude Fawley's spiritual cousins.

The songs resonate with echoes from Britten's own child-hood. The first, 'At Day-Close in November', describes the month of his birth and introduces the idea of a timescale beyond human conception: 'A time when no tall trees grew here, / A time when none will be seen.' The second, 'Midnight on the Great Western', introduces the 'journeying boy', 'Bewrapt past knowing to where he was going, / Or whence he came', and his ambiguous relationship with the 'region of sin'. Next come two apparently lighter pieces, each a miniature morality: 'Wagtail and Baby', with its depiction of a humanity which is so much more terrifying than anything in nature, and 'The Little Old Table' whose 'creak' contains the 'history' of a long-forgotten love. 'The Choirmaster's Burial' is also a moral fable, directed against the mean-spirited vicar who refuses to allow his late choirmaster a funeral with music. The sixth song, 'Proud Songsters', rather surprisingly owes something to Britten's competitive streak: when Pears 'told him that Finzi had set it, "that seemed to spur him on a bit"', according to Imogen Holst.[117] The contrast between the two settings is fascinating: Finzi's is illustrative, Britten's transformative; both composers respond to the two stanzas' delicate balance, but where Finzi respectfully observes the deliberate cadence of the final line, 'And earth, and air, and rain' – and names his Hardy cycle *Earth, Air and Rain* after it – Britten finds something more intense and unsettling in it. There is no winner in this contest, but much pleasure to be had in comparing two of the finest twentieth-century setters of English verse at work on the same text.

'At the Railway Station, Upway' is the penultimate song, with its poignant trio of characters: the convict, the constable and the 'little boy with a violin'. Britten's long childhood train journeys with his viola provide, as we've already seen, one parallel to this, and we may now add a second: another journeying boy, this time with a cello, named Paul Rogerson. The final song, 'Before Life and After', returns to the first's theme of a time beyond memory:

> A time there was – as one may guess
> And as, indeed, earth's testimonies tell –
> Before the birth of consciousness,
>   When all went well.

Hardy's poem looks back in another and specifically literary sense, for its opening phrase can't help recalling the start of Wordsworth's 'Immortality Ode' (a poem Britten didn't set, although Finzi did):

> There was a time when meadow, grove, and stream,
>   The earth, and every common sight,
>   To me did seem
>   Apparell'd in celestial light,
>   The glory and the freshness of a dream.

The crucial difference between Hardy and Wordsworth – and, one might almost say, between Britten and Finzi – is that the edenic state which Wordsworth remembers persisting through childhood is pushed further into the past – even 'Before the birth of consciousness' – by Hardy. For Britten, that innocent apprehension of childhood which Wordsworth called the 'visionary gleam' seems to have become clouded and compromised early on: we are back, yet again, at South Lodge.

At first, Britten discouraged the use of the phrase 'song cycle' to describe *Winter Words*, preferring to regard it simply as a group of songs; in fact, the last poem's return to the cosmic timescale of the first is strikingly cyclical. It is among the most personal of his works for voice and piano, but in a quite different way from the *Michelangelo Sonnets*: it is grounded in his inner life and memory rather than in his relationship with Pears who, as performer, only glancingly and ironically becomes part of his own sung material when, at the end of 'The Choirmaster's Burial', we learn that this is the story 'the tenor man told / When he had grown old'. It may well have been a liberating experience for Pears to perform *Winter Words*; certainly the recording he and Britten made of it for Decca in March 1954 is one of their finest. The pointedly non-metropolitan venue of its premiere, while serving to remind doubters that Harewood was above all a musical friend, somewhat restricted the amount of press coverage; but Ernest Bradbury in the *Yorkshire Post*, after expressing mild surprise at the combination of composer and poet, noted that Britten had caught Hardy's 'sombre, ironic quality, that essential non-pitying sadness in his music'.[118] The rest of the concert at Harewood House, given by the Wind Ensemble of the LSO, consisted of music whose autumnal colours provided a perfect context for the Hardy songs, but there was also a practical reason for this: Britten's right arm had now become too painful for him to perform throughout an entire concert.

It was during this visit to Yorkshire that Britten discovered in Leeds an osteopath, Stanley Ratcliffe, who correctly diagnosed his condition as bursitis. This is a kind of inflammation 'often due' – says the *Penguin Medical Encyclopedia* – 'to wear and tear arising from a particular trade': examples include housemaid's knee, dustman's shoulder, miner's elbow and weaver's bottom, to which composer's (or conductor's or pianist's) arm seems a respectable addition. Britten was relieved to discover, after X-rays and consultations with his own doctors, that in his case it could be treated without surgery. He was, however, obliged to rest his right arm completely for several months and this, apart from 'being no end of a bore', had two consequences: the scores he wrote with his left hand could only be deciphered and transcribed by the indispensable 'Imo'; and his personal correspondence had to be typed with his left hand, a skill he triumphantly failed to master. A letter to Forster, unpromisingly dated 'sunday oct.?,,I(£/', explains: 'You see, i have had a horrid complaint boyling up for some time called BURSITIS.' Billy Burrell, he reported, had married Barbara, a hairdresser in the nearby High Street, but 'Otherwise aldebrouhg is the same'.[119] Fortunately, he had a secretary, Jeremy Cullum, to look after his professional and business correspondence and, increasingly, to act as his driver; there was now a second Rolls-Royce convertible, a 1938 Wraith. Cullum told Donald Mitchell that Britten's hatred of London caused him to devise a route 'sideways through Suffolk'[120] which would delay their arrival in the capital for as long as possible. And by this time, Britten and Pears had a new London base: after much searching, they had moved in May (or rather, Pears and Miss Hudson supervised the moving while Britten and Paul Rogerson stayed in Aldeburgh) to a 'sweet little house', 5 Chester Gate, NW1, from which they could symbolically glower across Regent's Park at Ralph and Ursula Vaughan Williams, who lived on the other side. However 'sweet' the house, it was still in London, which was where Britten would rather not be.

Before he was ordered to rest his arm, Britten travelled to Copenhagen in September, where he recorded his *Sinfonia da Requiem* and *A Ceremony of Carols*, stayed at the Hotel d'Angleterre and got 'tiddley'; back in England, he and Pears recorded *Winter Words* for the BBC Third Programme in October; and he began work, with Imogen Holst, on a Symphonic Suite from *Gloriana*. But he was unable to conduct *Peter Grimes*, when it was revived in a production by John Cranko at Covent Garden in November, and he had to cancel a planned European concert tour with Pears, the German leg of which was replaced by an extended Christmas and New Year holiday at Wolfsgarten, near Darmstadt, with Prince Ludwig of Hesse and the Rhine and his wife Princess Margaret (née Campbell Geddes). They had been introduced to 'Lu' and 'Peg' – who were to become lifelong friends, travelling companions and supporters of the Aldeburgh Festival – by Lord Harewood: 'Peg' was the founder of the Hesse Students Scheme, under which music students receive free passes to all festival concerts in exchange for organisational help, and the annual Hesse Lecture; while 'Lu', under the pseudonym Ludwig Landgraf, was the German translator of several Britten works, including the one on which he started at Wolfsgarten that winter, *The Turn of the Screw*.

The opera had been intended for production at the Venice Biennale of 1953 but, when this plan was effectively derailed by *Gloriana*, *The Turn of the Screw* was rescheduled for 1954 – a year in which there couldn't, by definition, be a biennale: instead it would form part of the 27th International Festival of Contemporary Music in Venice. More than twenty years had passed since Britten had heard a radio dramatisation of Henry James's novella, which he then read, but this passage of time had served only to emphasise its congruence with his own creative imagination. Yet, like *Peter Grimes* and *Billy Budd*, it was a perversely intractable text to transform into an opera. James's story – which concerns a governess in a remote country house, her two young charges Miles and Flora, the housekeeper Mrs Grose, and the ghosts of Peter Quint and Miss Jessel, the former valet and governess – is carefully wrapped in ambiguity: the ghosts remain invisible to the illiterate and down-to-earth (but perhaps therefore all the more reliable?) housekeeper, while the children's oddities and illnesses may be at least partly attributable to their peculiar isolation and family circumstances. Moreover, James filters and distances the tale: we have it in the governess's words, but we are to imagine these being read aloud to the remnants of a Christmas house party by a man ('Douglas') whose sister was once taught by her, at the prompting of a Jamesian first-person narrator. These framing and qualifying devices must inevitably be sacrificed when the action is presented onstage; so must the characteristic inwardness of the narrative. With a rather cumbersome writer such as Melville, this loss may be not greatly felt; with James, it is more serious. For example, James conveys the shifting, often suspicious or uncomprehending, relationship between governess and housekeeper in terms of breathtaking subtlety and aptness: 'She offered her mind to my disclosures as, had I wished to mix a witch's broth and proposed it with assurance, she would have held out a large clean saucepan.'[121] What on earth is the librettist to do about that?

The librettist was Myfanwy Piper, John Piper's second wife, who had at first suggested *The Turn of the Screw* as the basis for an operatic film, in which medium its ambiguities would have been more easily retained. She took on the task almost by accident: 'Ben said to me, "Would you try and think of a way it might be done and then we might get someone in to write it"' and, when she'd given this some thought, 'we began work on it together, and there seemed no reason to ask anyone else'.[122] The obvious candidate, William Plomer, professed himself in any case to be not much of a Jamesian. Piper's – and Britten's – solution to the challenges of James's text was a radical recasting which reduced the distancing to a modest, piano-accompanied Prologue and involved the invention of crucial scenes, such as the Latin lesson towards the end of Act 1 and the dialogue between the ghosts at the start of Act 2, into which Piper interpolated a famous line from Yeats's 'The Second Coming': 'The ceremony of innocence is drowned.' Britten's musical approach was no less daring: each of the sixteen scenes is introduced by a variation on a theme ('Scene 1: The Journey') based on a row of twelve notes, though this doesn't make it in any sense a 'twelve tone' composition. The opera is compact both in its cast – six singing roles, of which four are for women – and in its duration: two acts, each running for under an hour. Yet, as Britten himself liked to remark (on one occasion artfully ascribing this opinion to Donald Mitchell), the simpler he made his music, the more difficulty people seemed to experience in performing or understanding it.

He had intended both the children's parts to be sung by children but, after the disappointment of the first auditions, held at the Royal Court Theatre on 12 December 1953, it was clear that this mightn't be possible. The part of Flora would have to be taken by an adult soprano; however, in the absence of an available castrato, Miles could only be sung by a boy treble. Among the boys who auditioned for the role were Michael Ingram (later known as Michael Crawford) and a twelve-year-old chorister, 'one of the more bumptious boys in the choir of the Chapel Royal at Hampton Court Palace',[123] called David Hemmings. It was Hemmings who, as much on account of his engaging personality as of his rather thin voice, was recalled to a second audition with Britten and George Malcolm at Chester Gate on 27 January. He got the part and was soon invited for an extended stay in Aldeburgh, which he recalled as lasting two or three months. There, Basil Douglas of the English Opera Group was to arrange for him to have three or four hours' academic study per day while he learned the role of Miles; but there were, of course, distractions such as tennis and swimming and – when Britten gave him time off – mending nets on the beach with the fishermen, who'd take him along with them for a drink at the Mill, the pub opposite the Moot Hall. David was roguish and precocious and perfectly cast as Miles. Imogen Holst taught him to play the piano, as he would have to pretend to do onstage. His voice grew steadily stronger.

Looking at photographs of the young David Hemmings, we may feel – as perhaps Britten did – that we've seen him before: it isn't so much an exact physical likeness as an identical air of irresistible mischief that makes him so resemble another boy, Francis Barton, leaning out of a railway-carriage window with his older friend Ben in 1928. It is also, in both cases, the unmistakable assurance of being loved. Hemmings, who described himself as 'more heterosexual than Genghis Khan', had been warned about Britten in frank terms ('You know he's a homo, don't you?') by his father. The son, though similarly disinclined to mince his words, nevertheless insisted that there was no 'hanky-panky' (using the same expression as David Spenser) and described his friendship with Britten in terms which exactly echo those of his predecessors: 'He was not only a father to me, but a friend – and you couldn't have had a better father, or a better friend. He was generous and kind, and I was very lucky. I loved him dearly, I really did – I absolutely adored him.'[124] 'In all of the time I spent with him,' he said on another occasion, 'he *never* abused that trust.'[125] Maureen Garnham, Basil Douglas's secretary, recalled a moment on Crag Path, just outside the Jubilee Hall, which captured the essence of the relationship: 'David, just arrived from London, spotted Ben among the many people enjoying the sunshine, ran to him, and with a shout of greeting took a flying leap into his arms. He received in return a laughing kiss on the forehead before Ben set him down.'[126] Britten rather endearingly made his recurrent hopeless attempt to sponsor a protégé's education, even arranging a place for him at Gresham's, but by then David was beginning to set his sights on an acting career.

Held up first by *Gloriana* and then by bursitis, *The Turn of the Screw* became yet another example of Britten's compositional brinkmanship. With its Venice premiere scheduled for September, the opera was still untitled in April: Britten toyed with calling it *The Tower and the Lake*, after the two locations in which the ghosts appear, apparently failing to notice how well his musical scheme mirrored James's original title. Moreover, the seventh Aldeburgh Festival would inevitably claim much of his time in and around June; this was to be followed by four concerts in Devon at the Taw and Torridge Festival during the first week of August. And, spoilt by working with collaborators such as Forster and Plomer who were happy to spend so much time with him in Suffolk, he grumbled about Myfanwy Piper's remoteness – she was in far-off Oxfordshire – and the nuisance of her being married and a mother. Throughout the spring and early summer, composer and librettist exchanged letters, drafts and telephone calls – at least one of which was, he apologetically admitted, 'short & sharp' on Britten's part: 'I have never felt so insecure about a work – now up, now down,' he told Basil Coleman at the end of May.[127] He was also worried that Joan Cross, who was to sing the part of Mrs Grose, seemed unenthusiastic, until she explained that the problem had been finding someone to look after her elderly mother during late August and September; as with Myfanwy Piper, it simply hadn't occurred to Britten that family commitments might sometimes get in the way.

Somehow the work was finished, just in time, and the English Opera Group decamped with its child star to Venice: trusting on Italian munificence, they had wildly overspent, so it was wryly appropriate that Basil Douglas should find himself rewarded with the title 'Impresario Generale' of the EOG on La Fenice's programme. David Hemmings, who appeared from a publicity photograph to be irresistible even to the pigeons, was delighted by a headline in the *Children's Newspaper*: 'HEMMINGS THE MENACE SINGS OPERA IN VENICE'.[128] The EOG's inner circle was less cheerful: according to the stage manager, Colin Graham, 'the "family", the Pipers, Basils C. and D., Ben and Peter, and others, went about Venice as a little clique doing nothing but worry'.[129] The day of the premiere, 14 September, was accompanied – as Britten gently put it on a postcard to Lu and Peg – by 'some alarms brought on by Italian character & heat'.[130] First, the stage crew had threatened to go on strike; then, the performance itself, which was being relayed live on Radio Italia, the BBC Third Programme and other European stations, was held up by an overrunning broadcast; there was slow-hand-clapping from the impatient audience in the rose-decked Teatro La Fenice. The cast included Peter Pears (Prologue and Quint), Jennifer Vyvyan (Governess), David Hemmings (Miles), Olive Dwyer (Flora), Joan Cross (Mrs Grose) and Arda Mandikian (Miss Jessel); the production was designed by John Piper, directed by Basil Coleman and conducted by the composer. Lord Harewood, who was there, reported that the occasion was a 'genuine success', but for David Hemmings it was something more. His recollection, told half a century later to John Bridcut, of the opera's end – when, as the Governess sings a reprise of Miles's 'Malo' song from Act 1, he dies in her arms – is remarkably like Leonard Thompson's account of the *Peter Grimes* first night:

Curtain comes down. Not a sound in the audience – *not a sound*! And I'm lying in Jennifer Vyvyan's arms – who has just done this *unbelievable* aria – and then there are one or two faint claps in the audience . . . And it's absolutely *sound-throbbing*. Well, if that's not great music, I don't know what is. And I am so *proud* to be a part of it, and I'm sorry that I'm sort of weeping about it, but it was pretty magnificent stuff.[131]

There was some disappointment in the Italian press with the opera's scale and, in particular, with the modest size of the chamber orchestra; but this would have bothered Britten only superficially, if at all, since with *The Turn of the Screw* he had perfected his new 'invention', chamber opera, of which *The Rape of Lucretia* had been the prototype. A reviewer for the Paris paper *L'Express* wrote of 'the composer's customary intense preoccupation with homosexual love', which may well be, as Carpenter thought, 'the first time that homosexuality was mentioned in print in connection with Britten'.[132] That this may seem to us surprising is testimony to the power of English innuendo. In the British press, there were particularly appreciative reviews by Colin Mason in the *Manchester Guardian* – for whom, 'With the possible exception of *Billy Budd* it is in musical style the most difficult and tightly unified of Britten's operas' – and Felix Aprahamian in the *Sunday Times*: 'It is not only Britten's most gripping score: it is among his finest.'[133] Both Aprahamian and the anonymous critic in *The Times* singled out Hemmings for special praise. John Ireland, who listened to the Third Programme broadcast, thought that *The Turn of the Screw* contained 'the most remarkable and original music I have ever heard from the pen of a British composer – and it is on a firmly diatonic and tonal basis'; what Britten had 'accomplished in sound' with his thirteen instruments was 'inexplicable' and 'almost miraculous'.[134]

The Turn of the Screw was first performed in England in October that year, as part of a remarkable English Opera Group season at Sadler's Wells which also included two other Britten works – *The Rape of Lucretia* and his realisation of *The Beggar's Opera* – as well as a double bill (already presented in Aldeburgh and Devon) of *Love in a Village* by his pupil Arthur Oldham and *A Dinner Engagement* by his friend Lennox Berkeley. This prompted further reviews, including a characteristically long and thoughtful *New Statesman* piece by Desmond Shawe-Taylor, to whom Britten wrote: 'I am so glad you liked the "Screw" so much. It does work as an opera, I feel, & I think in many ways you are right about the subject being, as it were, the nearest to me of any I have yet chosen (although what that indicates about my own character I shouldn't like to say!).'[135] He also told Edward Sackville-West, Shawe-Taylor's friend and co-author with him of *The Record Guide*, that he wanted 'Decca to record it as soon as possible – before, at any rate, David's voice breaks! Isn't he a stunning little performer?'[136] Decca obliged: *The Turn of the Screw* was recorded with the original cast during the first week of January 1955, becoming the first complete Britten opera on LP. It was released too late for inclusion in the revised edition of Sackville-West and Shawe-Taylor's magisterial volume, published later that year, but it was included in their 'Supplement' of 1956: 'The libretto is extremely skilful – indeed the best yet set by the composer – and it has elicited from Britten the most completely successful expression of his constant preoccupation with the betrayal of innocence.'[137] They liked everything about the records, which they awarded their maximum two stars, though they wisely resisted the temptation to call Hemmings 'a stunning little performer'.

A leaflet published at the time of the 1954 Aldeburgh Festival had claimed, slightly disingenuously, that *The Turn of the Screw* was being premiered in Venice rather than in the Jubilee Hall because the latter was 'inadequate for the necessary lighting effects'. This leaflet was headed 'A New Theatre in Aldeburgh': the proposal was for a theatre 'of the utmost simplicity in structure and decoration, and entirely in keeping with the character of the Festival', to be built 'on an excellent site behind Aldeburgh Lodge, on high ground, with an uninterrupted view over the marshes, and near enough to the sea for interval-promenading'. The Arts Council and the English Opera Group had given their approval; so, subject to planning consents, had the Borough Council; members of the public were invited to register their interest in 'one of the books which are placed in the Festival Office and the Festival Club for this purpose'.[138] A model of the proposed building – a squat, functional 1950s affair with a barely pitched roof – was on display at the White Lion Hotel. The project came to nothing: the notional theatre was later moved to a site off Alde Lane which was eventually bought by the architect H. T. Cadbury-Brown, who built a house for himself and, in the grounds, a bungalow for Imogen Holst. Very few of those who have enjoyed the concert hall and studios at Snape Maltings would want to exchange them for the Festival Theatre that might have been. And yet 'near enough to the sea for interval-promenading' is a phrase to tug briefly at the heartstrings: the delightful thought of audiences on summer evenings wandering down the Town Steps to the pubs and the restaurants and the beach. The plans for a theatre in Aldeburgh during the mid-1950s were the last realistic chance for the festival to remain permanently based *in* Aldeburgh itself: without such a building, the festival would inescapably outgrow the town. And at that point, a distinctive part of the local and community spirit which had formed this 'modest festival' would be lost for ever.

CHAPTER 7

THE POETRY IN THE PITY
1955–64

1

While Britten was fully occupied with *Gloriana*, and when his bursitis began to restrict his piano-playing, his place as Pears's accompanist had often been taken by a young and very gifted Australian pianist, Noel Mewton-Wood. On the evening of 6 December 1953, while Britten was hosting a drinks party at 4 Crabbe Street after a 'Friends of the Festival Brains Trust', the telephone rang: Mewton-Wood, whose partner Bill Fredricks had recently died after an appendix operation, had killed himself. 'Ben came back looking distraught,' wrote Imogen Holst, but he 'didn't let everyone know, and carried on being a host'. However, the following day, he 'talked of the terrifyingly small gap between madness and non-madness, and said why was it that the people one really liked found life so difficult'.[1] A memorial concert at Wigmore Hall was scheduled for the first anniversary of Mewton-Wood's death; but as Pears – who had defied '"flu cum trachytis [tracheitis]' to sing the role of Pandarus in the Covent Garden premiere of Walton's *Troilus and Cressida* the previous evening – was unable to perform, the concert was postponed until 28 January 1955. It included works by Britten, Alan Bush, Arthur Bliss, Benjamin Frankel, Michael Tippett and

Mewton-Wood himself: the first part began with Britten's Dowland-based *Lachrymae* for viola and piano; the second with a new composition, his *Canticle III: Still Falls the Rain*, Op. 55. The text was by Edith Sitwell, from whom Britten had sought permission to set 'your very great poem from the war years', adding: 'I feel very drawn towards it, & in its courage & light seen through horror & darkness find something very right for the poor boy.'[2]

The elegiac note, so often present in Britten's writing for voice or voices, here fulfils the purpose of specific, personal memorialisation; in this sense, *Canticle III* prefigures the *War Requiem*. Musically, however, it takes the now familiar form of a pendant to Britten's most recent opera: again, a twelve-note theme is the basis of the variations, for horn, which introduce each stanza. The poem combines images of the crucifixion with an air raid during the London Blitz and interpolates a pair of lines from Marlowe's *Doctor Faustus* ('O I'll leap up to my God! Who pulls me down? / See, see where Christ's blood streams in the firmament!') which Britten treats in a Schoenbergian way as *Sprechgesang*; but it ends in redemption, with tenor and horn in unison or uneasily close harmony. Michael Kennedy describes the piece as 'Britten in a hair-shirt, flagellating his soul on behalf of suffering humanity'.[3] The first performance – by Pears, Britten and Dennis Brain – so moved Edith Sitwell that she 'had no sleep at all on the night of the performance. And I can think of nothing else. It was certainly one of the greatest experiences in all my life as an artist.'[4]

A week after the Mewton-Wood memorial concert, Britten and Pears were off to Belgium and Switzerland, followed by a skiing holiday in Zermatt with Mary Potter and Ronald and Rose-Marie Duncan. On their first day there, Mary Potter injured her leg; to provide her with some amusement, Britten promptly wrote the six brief movements of his *Alpine Suite* for recorder trio. Both he and Pears had, with Imogen Holst's guidance, become keen recorder players in the Aldeburgh Music Club, an informal group of local musicians who met regularly at 4 Crabbe Street and whose cardinal rule was that any professional musicians present must not play their first instrument. 'It is *wonderful* for the amateurs in Aldeburgh to have those two to play & sing with,'[5] Holst had enthused in 1952, shortly after the club's formation, modestly ignoring her own contribution (but she also saw how Britten's support of local music contributed to his exhaustion: 'Must try & persuade him that he already does more than enough for people in Aldeburgh,'[6] she rather hopelessly resolved). The *Alpine Suite* would be performed at Thorpeness as part of a 'Music on the Meare' event, by members of the Aldeburgh Music Club, during the 1955 festival.

Meanwhile, Britten's relationship with the somewhat eccentric Duncans had grown closer after a conversation in Devon the previous summer, in which he had returned to a recurrent theme: his wish somehow to adopt a child. As this seemed unlikely, could he not have a quasi-fatherly 'share' in the Duncans' twelve-year-old son Roger? 'I want to be as a father to him. But I don't want to put your nose out of joint,' he told Ronald Duncan. 'Will you allow me to give him presents, visit him at school, and let him spend part of his school holidays with me – in other words share him?' Acknowledging that he and his wife were not perhaps ideal parents themselves, Duncan agreed to the proposal: 'Ben was a second father to my son, giving him affection and advice as he grew up.'[7] For Britten, as he said, it filled a gap; for Roger, it meant a succession of presents (starting with a bicycle), holidays in Aldeburgh and, while he was away at school, those affectionate, perfectly modulated schoolboy-to-schoolboy letters at which Britten was so adept. As he grew older, Roger began to realise that there was a sexual element in Britten's love for him. 'I wasn't attracted to him physically,' he told John Bridcut, who asked: 'But perhaps he was to you?' 'Oh I'm sure,' Roger Duncan replied. 'That was quite plain. But he respected the fact that I was not.' Britten, he added, was 'very proper' and even 'strait-laced – he always wore a tie, and changed for dinner'. At the age of twenty, while studying law at Cambridge, Roger Duncan married; after gradu-ation, he emigrated with his wife to Canada. Until then, he was 'very honoured and privileged to spend so much time across eight years with such an interesting person'.[8]

During the spring of 1955, Britten began work on a major new commission: a score for Sadler's Wells Ballet, to be choreo-graphed by John Cranko and eventually called *The Prince of the Pagodas*, Op. 57. The challenge of writing a substantial work for stage but without words and voices – it would be his longest purely orchestral composition – proved unexpectedly daunting: for once, a deadline, instead of being just about met, was to be completely missed. But the delay would bring benefits, for at the end of October he and Pears set off on their most ambitious tour, beginning with European destinations but then venturing much further east, with momentous consequences for *The Prince of the Pagodas*. They were to be away until March 1956, a long stretch even for the travel-hardened Pears, while for Britten, now so firmly rooted in Suffolk, it must have seemed an eternity: to Roger Duncan, he confessed that he was already feeling 'a teeny bit homesick' in Zurich. He promised to keep Roger informed of their progress through a 'great series of letters'; their prep-school chumminess was no doubt both an expression of and an antidote to homesickness. Their concert engagements in Europe included Amsterdam, Düsseldorf, Stuttgart, Zurich and Salzburg. Yugoslavia, Britten told Harewood, 'nearly killed us, but with kindness, enthusiasm & genuine interest';[9] they performed four concerts and were received by President Tito.

By the beginning of December, they were in Turkey, staying at the Istanbul Hilton: 'It's really the East now – our room in this incredibly new & expensive hotel faces Asia across the Bosphorus, looking much nearer than Thorp Ness!'[10] Britten thought Turkish music – the 'Oriental stuff' – 'pretty poor & boring' but found there was a young audience hungry for Western music: 'Our concerts were a wild success, & were just like giving a thirsty person a long drink of champagne!'[11] While there, he composed, and sent to Imogen Holst, 'a silly little piece' for the timpanist, percussionist and member of the English Opera Group Orchestra James Blades, *Timpani Piece for Jimmy*, which is unquestionably the coolest title in his entire oeuvre.

On 11 December, they flew to India; though mostly based in Delhi, they spent Christmas 'at Agra, looking at the Taj Mahal'. They were 'bowled over' by the landscape, by the 'relaxed & calm' people they met – including Nehru and his daughter, Indira Gandhi, with whom they had lunch – and by Indian music: 'We had the luck to hear one of the best living performers (composer too), & he played in a small room to us alone – which is how it should be, not in concerts.'[12] The musician was Ravi Shankar and the 'small room' a studio at All-India Radio, where they afterwards attended a broadcast. Pears's appreciative account of the occasion in his travel diary is also a reminder that Shankar's work was at this time unfamiliar even to such experienced and sophisticated Western musicians as Britten, who as a student had attended a performance by Shankar's father Uday in 1933, and himself: 'Brilliant, fascinating, stimulating, wonderfully played – first on a full orchestra of about 20 musicians, then solo on a sort of zither [sitar]. Starting solo (with a plucked drone background of 2 instruments always) & then joined halfway through by a man playing two drums; unbelievable skill and invention.'[13] Their own engagements in India included recitals in Bombay, Delhi – broadcast under slightly surreal conditions involving a Bösendorfer and two rival piano tuners – and Calcutta, where Pears was so hot that he 'imagined that the great drops of sweat splashing off me were clearly audible and visible from the gallery'.[14] Despite this, there were aspects of Calcutta they were sorry to leave, such as the whispering pimp who invariably waylaid them outside the Grand Hotel: 'At first his words were quite unintelligible, (possibly Hindi or German?) then after a day or two "You like girl?" was audible, which grew into "schoolgirls?" (*con espressione*) and then "English schoolgirl?" (ah! that's got him); finally, in despair, to a quite unresponsive Ben, "FRENCH SCHOOLGIRLS?!!" We got rather fond of him.'[15] Then they were off to Singapore, which Britten said was 'like living in a Turkish bath'. For Pears, the humidity was even more troublesome: 'In one minute all one's stuffing was gone; in half an hour one was sweaty and cross.'[16] Nevertheless, they had to give two recitals, including Schumann's *Dichterliebe* and Schubert's *Die schöne Müllerin*, 'in a vast bath-like hall': 'I sang like a pig at both concerts,' wrote Pears.[17]

Among the audience at the latter concert were Prince Ludwig and Princess Margaret of Hesse and the Rhine, who had that day arrived in Singapore and were to accompany Britten and Pears on the remainder of their journey, which next took them on to Java and Bali, 'where musical sounds are as part of the atmosphere as the palm trees, the spicy smells, & the charming beautiful people'. Britten continued, in a letter to Imogen Holst: 'The music is *fantastically* rich – melodicly, rhythmicly, texture (such *orchestration*!!) & above all *formally*.'[18] His journey east had entailed a gradual surrender to unfamiliar cultures, and he was completely smitten by Bali. It had taken time and distance for him to relax from his buttoned-up or, as Roger Duncan put it, 'strait-laced' English ways; so it was symbolically apt, as well as ludicrous, that he and Pears, together with their friends Lu and Peg, should have been photographed in traditional Balinese dress on 20 January. Britten, the princess commented, 'looked like a governess at a fancy dress' and Pears 'like a Rhine maiden'. 'We laughed so much we could hardly be photographed,' she wrote. 'We four laugh and fool about so much we are a sort of travelling circus.'[19] This was a different Benjamin Britten from the one who always wore a tie. He described the music of the gamelan orchestra, not quite accurately but with wonderful enthusiasm, in one of the regular dispatches to his young friend Roger:

> It's mostly played on metal xylophones (sometimes wooden, bamboo), of all sizes, with gongs of tremendous size, long thin drums, and occasionally a curious one [in fact, two] string fiddle, & instruments like our treble recorders. They have bands of 20–30, always men, sometimes including quite tiny boys. But although it is quite unlike our music, it is worked out technically & rhythmically, so that one can scarcely follow it. It isn't 'primitive' at all, & neither are the people.[20]

To his percussive colleague James Blades, he sent a picture postcard of gongs: 'I've heard Gongs of all shapes, sizes, and metals here – producing fantastic notes – you'd be very interested. I hope to bring back some tapes of the music here.'[21] And to Ninette de Valois he sent an optimistic telegram: 'CONFIDENT BALLET READY FOR MIDSEPTEMBER LOVE BRITTEN'.[22] For he had discovered the musical language of Pagoda Land.

Britten had always been fascinated by tuned percussion; moreover, he had some previous experience of Balinese music. While in America, he met the composer Colin McPhee, who had lived for seven years on Bali and whose two-piano transcriptions of *Balinese Ceremonial Music* he performed with McPhee in 1941 (later he played them with Clifford Curzon). Britten's

copy of the published score was inscribed by McPhee 'To Ben
– hoping he will find something in this music, after all'; and,
fifteen years later, he had. Nor was this the only momentous
discovery he would make on his 'world tour'. After Bali, the
party returned to Java ('where everything went wrong, & I got
ill & had to cancel a concert');[23] then they went on to Hong
Kong, with four concerts in five days; and on 8 February they
flew to Japan. Britten, whose only previous dealing with the
Japanese had involved their commissioning and subsequent
rejection of his *Sinfonia da Requiem*, wasn't keen. It was, he
reported to Roger Duncan, 'the *strangest* country' they had yet
visited, as if it were 'inhabited by a very intelligent kind of
insect': 'They have very good manners, they bow & scrape all
the time; they have most beautiful small things, all their houses,
their flowers, the things they eat & drink out of, are wonderfully
pretty, but all their *big* things, their cities, their way of thinking,
and behaving, have all somehow got wrong.' But he 'unreservedly loved' their theatre, in particular the Noh, which was 'very
severe, classical – very traditional, without any scenery to speak
of, or lighting and there are very few characters – one main
one, who wears a mask, & two or three supporting ones &
usually a small boy too'.[24] It seems, as he describes it, already
to suggest the scale and texture of a work he might write himself;
although the 'small boy', not usual in Noh drama, was perhaps
a touch of wishful thinking.

Returning to England in mid-March was 'Lovely in many
ways, but, oh, oh, the problems . . . !'[25] Yet he added that 'one
settles into' the various crises, as if acknowledging the extent to
which problems were necessary, almost comforting parts of his
life's familiar fabric. The most pressing, apart from the matter
of a largely unwritten ballet scheduled for September, concerned
the festival and the English Opera Group. The former was going
through a period of organisational change following the

departure of its general manager, Elizabeth Sweeting: she had left the previous summer, ostensibly because the festival could no longer afford this full-time post but essentially because she and Imogen Holst simply couldn't get on; her friend Tommy Cullum – treasurer, local bank manager and father of Britten's secretary – resigned from the festival committee in protest. Although Elizabeth Sweeting was hurt by the manner of her dismissal (she found a letter waiting for her when she returned from London one day), she was given "'a marvellous send-off' – a benefit concert in which Britten and Pears took part'.[26] She was replaced as general manager by the art historian and dealer Stephen Reiss, who had lived in Aldeburgh since 1949, advising Pears on pictures and curating an exhibition at the 1953 festival; he was at first tactfully described as 'Hon. Secretary'. Imogen Holst, meanwhile, joined Britten and Pears as an artistic director of the festival from 1956, an appointment made necessary as well as desirable by their absence abroad for so many months. The crisis at the English Opera Group took a little longer to reach its conclusion. It began in December 1955, when Basil Douglas suggested that Britten might want to 'find someone stronger than myself who can manage the Group's fortunes more independently'. Britten replied from Delhi: 'I feel you've given nearly five years of your time & energy to it [the EOG], & that if you feel you want a change that is only natural. You must decide that, & we can only grin (?) & bear it!'[27] Douglas stayed, turning down a job with the BBC to do so, but during the following two years the relationship between him and Britten would become frayed until it reached its untidy breaking point.

'I have been plunged into a whirlpool of hectic work, & been made quite dizzy by it – the Ballet for Cranko has got to be ready for the Autumn and is only ½ written – and so on,' Britten told William Plomer in May.[28] He had that very day added to the 'and so on' by proposing to Edith Sitwell that he should compose a prologue and an epilogue, setting some of her lines, for the reading she was to give at the forthcoming festival, which was also to include a performance of *Canticle III: Still Falls the Rain*; the programme, entitled 'The Heart of the Matter', was given in the parish church on 21 June. The mutually adoring creative relationship between Britten and Sitwell is a little surprising, given the apparent mismatch of his sparse and her florid style, but by far its oddest consequence was his attempt to enlist her help in persuading Marilyn Monroe – whom she knew – to open a grand fund-raising garden party in aid of the Aldeburgh Festival (and its briefly revived dream of building a theatre) in September. Sitwell replied at once that 'there *isn't a hope* that we can get Miss Monroe', thus destroying any chance that Aldeburgh's most improbable guest appearance would take place. But the proposal is evidence of Britten's slightly wayward canniness: although neither taken in by Marilyn Monroe's pretended interest in high culture nor greatly impressed by her as a sex symbol, he knew good box office when he saw it.

For a while, *The Prince of the Pagodas* went 'swimmingly', but it was increasingly clear that the September deadline couldn't be met; an official announcement from Covent Garden on 9 August confirmed that the first night had been postponed because of Britten's illness and exhaustion. Another reason for the delay was the lack of a conductor: the first choice, Ernest Ansermet, was unavailable and, although there were other possibilities, Britten had gloomily remarked to David Webster in late May that it would be 'difficult to find anyone of this calibre who can fit in exactly with our dates'.[29] During the summer, Britten retreated to the Hesses' 'mountain fastness', Schloss Tarasp in Switzerland, to try and get the job finished. He made good progress, although in October, back in Suffolk, he was still 'madly busy' with a hundred pages of full score to go. It wasn't until 7 November that he could write to Prince Ludwig: 'That b. ballet is *FINISHED*, & I feel as if I've just been let out of prison after 18 months hard labour.'[30] Even then, his troubles with it were far from over. With a kind of dreadful inevitability, the only conductor 'of this calibre' available for the premiere was himself; and so, despite a recurrence of bursitis in his right arm and shoulder (the pain was too severe for him even to carry his own music case), he was soon immersed in rehearsals. 'It wasn't only that his arm was bad,' as Imogen Holst, his devoted amenuensis and music-case carrier, recalled, 'but in those days he'd *no* experience of conducting a *huge* orchestra in a *very* long work in an orchestral pit.'[31] Worst of all, she thought, was the indifference of Pears, because there was nothing for him to sing. She remembered the 'climax of that lack of interest' in the last full rehearsal, 'when Peter, having blown in for a little while, in the coffee break, halfway through, said to Ben, "Well, I'm going now; I'm going to have a haircut." And walked out of the theatre, leaving Ben bewildered and in pain and trying to fix up [a] doctor; no one to get him a taxi, no one but me to carry the bag or anything . . .'[32]

Britten conducted the first performance of *The Prince of the Pagodas* at Covent Garden on 1 January 1957; he also managed to conduct on the following two days before 'an extremely fierce doctor' forbade him (the remaining performances were conducted by Kenneth Alwyn and Robert Irving). The ballet – which starred David Blair and Svetlana Beriosova as the Prince and Princess, with wonderfullly evocative sets by John Piper – was much enjoyed by audiences, but critics tended to find Cranko's fairy-tale subject matter too conventional: Martin Cooper in the *Daily Telegraph* thought the work 'an infinitely superior pantomime' while for the anonymous critic in *The Times* it was 'a ballet for the young . . . a cake too full of plums for summary accounting; everyone must be his own Jack Horner'. Felix Aprahamian in the *Sunday Times* rather oddly complained that 'Britten's latest major work breaks no new ground' before going on to comment on the self-evidently groundbreaking 'quasi-Balinese sounds in the second act'. This aspect of the work was altogether too much for Donald Mitchell who, in a piece for the *Musical Times* which he later judged 'inept' but nobly quoted in *Letters from a Life*, thought it 'a major musical error: once the ensemble's tinkling has been savoured, its motivic stagnation becomes painfully tedious'; it was 'an indiscretion not only inappropriate but boring'. Mitchell points out that his original affronted reaction illustrates just how novel and unsettling the Balinese influence seemed at the time.[33]

The following month, *The Prince of the Pagodas*, conducted by the composer, was recorded by Decca, who evidently judged a brand-new ballet score to be more viable than the still unrecorded *Peter Grimes* and *Billy Budd*; this 'complete' version was in fact shortened by some forty cuts, amounting to twenty minutes, so that it would fit onto four LP sides. Over the next two years, the ballet was successfully staged in Milan, New York and Munich; it also had three brief revivals at Covent Garden before being dropped from the repertoire in 1960. By this time, Britten himself had come to dislike the work, which was seldom performed thereafter either as a ballet or as a concert piece. However, in 1989 it was staged at Covent Garden with new choreography by Kenneth MacMillan and in the same year recorded – for the first time in full – by the London Sinfonietta conducted by Oliver Knussen. The work has the limitation (which is also the charm) of all ballet scores: it consists of numerous short episodes and so lacks symphonic development. But Britten delights in limitation and he matches the narrative's journey from Middle Kingdom to Pagoda Land with his own musical journey from respectfully Tchaikovsky-like numbers to an eerier sound-world in which conventional Western percussion instruments exactly replicate gamelan sonorities. Although some remain to be convinced, for this listener Knussen's fine recording belatedly established *The Prince of the Pagodas* firmly among Britten's major compositions.

2

The painter Mary Potter, for whom Britten had composed his *Alpine Suite* during their skiing holiday in 1955, lived in a handsome double-gabled brick house at the end of a narrow lane off the Aldeburgh–Leiston road: it was called The Red House. Her marriage to the writer and humorist Stephen Potter had broken up: she was now on her own in a home which was too big for her. Britten, meanwhile, found that his and the festival's ever increasing fame had turned him into a tourist exhibit: his large-windowed rooms overlooking the beach were also inescapably overlooked *from* the beach and, since the other side of his house abutted directly onto Crabbe Street, there was nowhere to hide; strangers would even wander in through open doors on summer days, as if the place were open to the public. The obvious if unconventional solution to Potter's and Britten's predicaments was a house swap: this was tortuously negotiated during 1957 and the two-way move took place in November. The Red House had particular attractions for Britten, besides privacy and quiet: a tennis court on which he could practise his lethal skills away from the public courts in Park Road, and secluded gardens for Clytie, his miniature dachshund.

Yet Britten sacrificed so much in moving to The Red House: the sight and sound of the sea, his childhood companion, which had brought him back to Aldeburgh; the company of fishermen such as Billy Burrell; the sense that he was in and of the town itself. While he lived in Crabbe Street, an inevitable tendency towards remoteness and cliquishness could always be checked by the bracing reality outside the door; at The Red House, his garden backed onto the placid expanses of the Aldeburgh Golf Club (the second line of the address, which Britten never used, is Golf Lane). The lurking sense that there was now something a bit grand and courtly about him had acquired an exact physical reality: visitors arriving at the house, through the five-bar gate and over the large circular sweep of gravel with its central lawn, could be in no doubt that they were entering a private and privileged world which was very different from 4 Crabbe Street. Britten's elder brother Robert, on first seeing the place, asked: 'But Ben, do you think you really *deserve* all this?'[34] His move to The Red House separated him irrevocably from the ordinary life of Aldeburgh; in due course, the failure of the theatre plan and the conversion of Snape Maltings would do the same for the festival.

Britten accepted these changes as the price of fame and middle age, just as he accepted his transformation into a reluctant symbol of establishment respectability. When in April he was asked by Anthony Gishford at Boosey & Hawkes to list 'the various curious honours that I have received in the last few years', he found ten: an award from the Music Critics Circle of New York for Choral Music; Freedom of the Borough of Lowestoft; 'Accademico Effettivo Corrispondente' of Accademia Nazionale Cherubini; Honorary Member of the Académie Royale des Sciences, des Lettres, et des Beaux-Arts, Brussels; Mus. Doc. from Belfast University; Associate of the Royal Academy of Belgium; an award from the Catholic Stage Guild of Dublin ('A perfectly hideous statuette of a deformed St Cecilia'); 'a large certificate and a drawing of a bit of a suit I am supposed to wear as a Tonsättare' from the Royal Swedish Academy of Music; Honorary Member of the American Academy of Arts and Letters; and 'something' from the Accademia Nazionale di Santa Cecilia (Rome).[35] In July, he went to lunch with the Queen and Prince Philip at Buckingham Palace; a few days later, at the American Embassy, he received his honorary membership of the American Academy of Arts and Letters. The citation informed him that his compositions had 'been received with delight in many lands', that he had 'recaptured the great English tradition of word, song, and instrument' and that his operas were 'in the world repertory': 'They do honour to your country and to you.'[36] He couldn't fail to be touched by the generosity, nor to be embarrassed by the sententiousness. As if to illustrate the point about his operas, he travelled in August and September to Canada, where the English Opera Group performed *The Turn of the Screw* at the Stratford (Ontario) Shakespeare Festival.

In the meantime, Basil Douglas's term as manager of the EOG was drawing to its conclusion; as often happens in small organisations, especially those in the arts, a matter of policy became hopelessly entangled with a personal falling-out. In January, Britten wrote a carefully argued letter to the Group's chairman, James Lawrie, in which he suggested a scaling-down. Although the EOG had done well at festivals and in 'countries where opera is part of the daily bread', a recent season at the Scala Theatre had been financially disastrous: he therefore proposed that the EOG 'should move its office, staff and storage to Aldeburgh' where he and Stephen Reiss thought its administration could be absorbed by the Festival Office 'without much extra expense'; at this point he still assumed, incorrectly, that his projected Aldeburgh Theatre would provide new operas with rehearsal and performance space and serve as a launching pad for tours. A fortnight later, reporting to his fellow artistic directors on a meeting of the EOG's executive, he noted the 'feeling of deep regret that such a scheme would not include the services of Basil Douglas, who has worked so hard and loyally these six years, but I have felt that the extreme worry of the recurring financial crises, especially in the last few years, have been really bad for him'. It was possible, he added a bit half-heartedly, that Douglas might become operatic manager of a new venture at the Lyric, Hammersmith, or that he should act as a London booking manager for Aldeburgh 'in some form or other'.[37] He was trying hard to convince himself, and others, that dismissing Basil Douglas would be in Douglas's best interests: 'the financial aspect honestly hasn't been well handled, poor old B.D. has been laid low by worry – his health makes him a fine-weather sailor, I'm afraid', he told Basil Coleman.[38] To Douglas himself, who in March was about to take a holiday, he wrote: 'Go off, forget all about Groupy & Festivally problems, & come back strong. Remember you have many good friends (Peter & me included) who wish you so very well, & who will really do everything they can to help straighten out the future . . . so don't worry over much, will you?'[39]

When in the autumn Douglas finally learned that there would be no more work for him, even on a part-time basis, with Aldeburgh and the EOG, he did so indirectly: either from Stephen Reiss – who, according to Douglas, 'seemed surprised that I did not know' – or from Imogen Holst, who visited him at the EOG office to say, 'Basil, I want you to know that, whatever happens, I'll always love you' – which was, according to Christopher Grogan, 'the first Douglas had heard of his impending dismissal'.[40] Either way, the news evidently wasn't relayed by Britten, with whom there followed an embittered exchange of letters with a characteristic conclusion: 'Please stop "getting at" Peter and me, and try to realise we do not wish you ill; and have tried to do everything possible to help you. You have good friends in us, unless, of course, you are determined to call us enemies. The situation is in your hands.'[41] The trouble is not so much that

Britten sounds insincere (although he does a little) but that he sounds more than ever like a prep-school master: it's a tone which came too easily to him and which might be effectively directed at a twelve-year-old boy, yet it is far less helpful when the recipient is an unhappy adult. This is perhaps not his most likeable aspect. His failure to talk personally to Douglas may be easier to understand and at least partly to forgive; he simply couldn't manage such occasions, which made him physically ill.

The first work to be finished by Britten at The Red House was the little set of *Songs from the Chinese*, Op. 58, using Arthur Waley's translations, for Pears and his new recital partner, the guitarist Julian Bream: they were first performed at Great Glemham House during the following year's Aldeburgh Festival. But the first major composition to be written there might almost have been intended as an antidote to Britten's self-imposed privacy, with its enormous non-professional cast of children and audience or 'congregation': this was his setting of the Chester miracle play, *Noye's Fludde*, Op. 59. The piece had its origins in an educational commission, from the London commercial television station Associated-Rediffusion, which ended in acrimony and confusion with the dismissal of the company's Head of Schools Broadcasting, Boris Ford (although it would eventually be broadcast by Birmingham-based ATV, which held the London weekend franchise, on a Sunday morning). The medieval text – with its quirkily vivid language, talking animals, avuncular God and cantankerous Mrs Noye – was ideal for Britten's purpose, while his memories of gamelan informed the piece's adventurous and eccentric percussive effects. There were to be only three professional adult singers (for the Voice of God, Noye and Mrs Noye), nine musicians of the English Opera Group Players and half a dozen trained and experienced child singers. Colin Graham later recalled:

Some of the forces required by the opera are now legendary: the handbells from Leiston Modern School, which heralded the appearance of the rainbow; the percussion group from Woolverstone Hall, with its set of slung mugs for the raindrops which start and end the storm; the recorders from Framlingham College which vie with the wind; the bugles from the Royal Hospital School, Holbrook, which play the Animals in and out of the Ark and end the opera so poignantly. And the animals themselves, of course, who were auditioned (coincidentally in the presence of Aaron Copland) from schools right across the County of Suffolk.[42]

The slung mugs – and, we may guess, the prevalence of recorders – were the inspired suggestion of Imogen Holst, who remembered having once taught a Women's Institute percussion group how 'a row of china mugs hanging on a length of string could be hit with a large wooden spoon' to produce the sound of raindrops; it was she who took Britten on a shopping expedition to buy 'lots of mugs with "A Present from Aldeburgh" written on them'. The bells came from a chance conversation with some members of the local youth club, to whom Britten used to donate all the foreign stamps from his overseas mail, who told him they were off to practise handbell ringing: he, of course, had to hear this and invited them to perform for him at The Red House. He 'was so enchanted by the sounds they made that he gave them a part to play at the supreme moment of the drama in *Noye's Fludde*, when the rainbow appears in the sky and the Voice of God promises that all wrath and vengeance shall cease in the newly-washed world'.[43]

Noye's Fludde was first performed at St Bartholomew's Church in Orford on 18 June as part of the 1958 Aldeburgh Festival. The producer was Colin Graham and the costumes, including the animals' magnificent headdresses, were designed by Ceri

Richards; Owen Brannigan was Noye, Gladys Parr Mrs Noye and Trevor Anthony the Voice of God. The conductor was Charles Mackerras, who caused deep offence by jokily (as he imagined) remarking that the composer must be in his element with so many boys about. The comment, not made in Britten's presence, was nevertheless relayed to him; Mackerras was summoned to The Red House, 'and when I got there Ben said to me, "Because I like to be with boys, and because I appreciate young people, am I therefore a lecher?"'[44] Mackerras would repeat this story with some bemusement, apparently never quite understanding that in 1958 – when homosexual acts even between consenting adults were still illegal – Britten had every reason to be sensitive about his sexuality and especially to dislike any hint that he couldn't control it in his dealings with the young. Both men had too much invested in the festival for their working relationship to be affected (Britten was also playing the piano in Poulenc's *Tirésias*, which Mackerras was conducting) and the premiere was, as Philip Hope-Wallace wrote in the *Manchester Guardian*, 'a very happy and often strangely touching occasion'. For Felix Aprahamian in the *Sunday Times*, the 'sleepy village of Orford' proved the perfect setting for 'a curiously moving spiritual and musical experience' which 'claims a place in the national musical heritage'.[45] Some of the sleepy village's inhabitants apparently thought otherwise: they attempted to prevent the premiere from taking place in their church, to Britten's considerable distress. But for Kenneth Clark, who grew up in Sudbourne Hall, just outside Orford, the occasion was a revelatory one: 'To sit in Orford Church, where I had spent so many hours of my childhood dutifully awaiting some spark of divine fire, and then to receive it at last in the performance of *Noye's Fludde*, was an overwhelming experience.'[46] Happily, the production was revived in the same venue for the 1961 festival, with a necessarily different cast (apart from Brannigan and Anthony) and, perhaps unsurprisingly, a different conductor, Norman Del Mar; this was recorded by Decca for their Argo label, who issued it as NF1, thus giving it the equivalent of a personalised number plate.

It deserves every honour. Of all Britten's works, *Noye's Fludde* is the one to hear – or, better still, to take part in – when feeling ungrateful towards the composer or indeed towards life in general: moments such as the procession of the animals onto the ark, the storm itself (so utterly unlike the North Sea storm in *Peter Grimes*), the brilliantly adapted congregational hymn 'For those in peril on the sea' which follows it, the return of the olive-branch-bearing dove and the unfolding of the rainbow are among the most affecting in Britten's – or, for that matter, anyone else's – music. It is, as Michael Kennedy says, 'easily his most lovable work'. 'Strong men have been known to weep unashamedly at the sound of the bugles which precede the animals' march and at the appearance of the rainbow,' Kennedy adds, worrying that our response may be 'sentimental';[47] yet our emotion is, I think, not sentimentality but sheer wonder at a kind of transcendent rightness. Like two of Britten's masterpieces from earlier in the decade – *Billy Budd* and *Canticle II: Abraham and Isaac* – it ends in redemption. Despite its modest running time of less than an hour, *Noye's Fludde* is a completely satisfying dramatic and musical experience which, while it lacks the scale of the major operas or the *War Requiem*, is in every other respect their equal.

3

The troubles from which *Noye's Fludde* provided a triumphant respite were not only to do with the Aldeburgh Festival and the

English Opera Group. Britten's erratic health was treating him
to a variety of new afflictions: eye trouble, pleurisy and a form
of tinnitus which – ironically, though not at all to his amusement
– resonated on the note B. And there was disarray at his
publishers, Boosey & Hawkes. His friend and mentor Ralph
Hawkes had died in 1950 and his other longest-standing associate in the firm, Erwin Stein, died in July 1958; meanwhile,
Anthony Gishford, with whom Britten had been working
closely, was dismissed after a row involving B&H's American
operation (during which, with apparently uncharacteristic high-
handedness, Gishford sacked one of Leslie Boosey's sons and
confirmed himself as president of Boosey & Hawkes Inc.). The
relationship between Britten and his publishers had already
become strained by disagreements over matters such as permission being given for cuts in foreign performances of his operas;
now he sought urgent reassurances from them, which Boosey
and Ernst Roth did their best to provide. His commitment to
B&H, though weakened, held for the time being.

While suffering from tinnitus, Britten worked on the
Nocturne, Op. 60, for tenor, seven obbligato instruments and
strings, which had been commissioned by the Earl of Harewood
for the Leeds Centenary Festival: it was first performed there
by Pears and the BBC Symphony Orchestra, conducted by
Rudolf Schwarz, on 16 October 1958. This cycle of eight dream-
and sleep-related texts is topped and tailed by a passage from
Shelley's *Prometheus Unbound* ('On a poet's lips I slept / Dreaming
like a love-adept . . .') and Shakespeare's 43rd sonnet ('When
most I wink, then do mine eyes best see . . .'). The intervening
poems or extracts from poems – by Tennyson, Coleridge,
Middleton, Wordsworth, Owen and Keats – are introduced by
the obbligato instruments in the sequence bassoon, harp, horn,
timpani, cor anglais and flute with clarinet: these are typically
Brittenesque colours, but his avoidance of solo strings was also

due to the fact that he disliked the playing of Paul Beard, then leader of the BBC SO. Often wary about his work-in-progress, Britten expressed two unusually specific worries about the *Nocturne*: 'It won't be madly popular because it is the strangest & remotest thing – but then dreams are strange and remote,'[48] he told Marion Harewood; while to Princess Margaret of Hesse and the Rhine he wrote, 'I think it's good so far, but it is a tremendous effort to write – each note being squeezed out like that last dollop of toothpaste out of an empty tube. This tube rather wants a holiday.'[49] Both remarks are perceptive. It *is* strange and remote (and it hasn't been madly popular) because the poems are at once too similar in theme and too disparate in style; the delicious thematic juxtapositions of the *Serenade* or the *Spring Symphony* are missing. And it does at times seem effortful in that squeezed-toothpaste way, perhaps above all in the dutifully mimetic effects Britten provides for the nocturnal creatures in the Middleton setting. The *Nocturne* is a mysteriously unhappy work in which the nightmarish 'Sleep no more' of the centrepiece – this is Wordsworth in revolutionary Paris from Book X of *The Prelude* – appears to express a quite different, wholly personal anguish. Elsewhere in the cycle, panicky breathing rhythms recur in the strings, slowing to a mournful heartbeat for Owen's 'The Kind Ghosts': they create an unsettlingly vulnerable pulse (did Britten perhaps recall overhearing his dormitory neighbours' unsynchronised snores at Gresham's, a notable period of dreams and nightmares for him?).

The final setting, of the Shakespeare sonnet, is the one which has 'always mystified' Ian Bostridge, 'its lush Romanticism so at odds with the spareness of a cycle that is self-consciously constructed out of fragments and marginal texts'.[50] Bostridge ingeniously discovers the 'solution to the mystery' in Britten's borrowing of the 'repeated descending motif' from Tchaikovsky's sixth symphony, but Peter Evans finds in the tonal merging of

'two entities . . . into a higher unity' a more persistent influence
on the composer: 'one can choose to hear either key, a Lydian
D flat or a Neapolitan C minor, as predominant in the crucial
opening phrase, and the ambivalence is sustained to give impressive profundity of meaning to the simple textures, beautifully
scored to give a highly Mahlerian sound'.[51] There are clear
allusions to the Adagietto from Mahler's fifth symphony during
the sonnet's third quatrain. Yet, for all its consolatory romanticism, this concluding sonnet, which supplies the expected
reaffirmation of love between composer and singer, is qualified
by the ambiguously reversed pronouns with which it ends: 'All
days are nights to see till I see thee, / And nights bright days
when dreams do show thee me.'

The *Nocturne* was swiftly followed by the *Sechs Hölderlin-
Fragmente*, Op. 61, for tenor and piano: this short cycle, a fiftieth
birthday present for Prince Ludwig, was first performed – twice,
in a recital which juxtaposed it with songs from *Winter Words*
as well as songs by Purcell, Schubert and Schumann – by Pears
and Britten at Wolfsgarten on 20 November 1958; they also
gave the first concert performance in England as part of the
1959 Aldeburgh Festival. There are moments of extraordinarily
eloquent simplicity in Britten's settings of these six mostly brief
extracts from poems by Hölderlin: the invocation of home and
lost childhood in 'Die Heimat' and of life's changing seasons in
'Hälfte des Lebens' (both Hardyesque themes); or the epigram-
matic final song, 'Die Linien des Lebens', with its doubly
minimalist accompaniment – not only sparse but entirely
constructed of minims. Yet it's hard to avoid completely the
suspicion that this work and its predecessor were bread-and-
butter gestures for the Harewoods and the Hesses as well as
urgently needed material for Pears, who had been neglected by
both *The Prince of the Pagodas* and *Noye's Fludde*. A more obviously bread-and-butter affair was the commission in September

1958 from the University of Basel for a work to celebrate its 500th anniversary: the *Cantata Academica, Carmen Basiliense*, Op. 62. Then there was the *Missa Brevis*, Op. 63 – or, as Donald Mitchell memorably called it, 'Mass in short trousers' – for boys' voices and organ, composed for George Malcolm and the choristers of Westminster Cathedral. And, beyond all this, Britten had something larger and more enticing on his mind. Ever since his visit to Japan, he had wanted to do something based on the Noh play *Sumidagawa* (*The Sumida River*), for which William Plomer, who had lived in the country, would be the ideal collaborator; so, during the autumn of 1958, Plomer began to work on a draft libretto. At this stage, Britten was 'very keen on as many nice evocative Japanese words as possible',[52] although by the time the project eventually reached fruition, almost six years later, the setting would have shifted to East Anglia and the work's title become *Curlew River*.

On their return from Wolfsgarten, Britten and Pears immediately embarked on rehearsals for the recording by Decca of *Peter Grimes*, which took place in Walthamstow Town Hall during the first week of December. This project had been mooted over a year earlier, but it had significantly benefited from the delay: for, although Decca had been making stereo recordings for some time, *Grimes* was the first complete opera to be recorded by them in England specifically for stereo release. The executive producer was John Culshaw, who had recently worked on Solti's celebrated stereo recording of *Das Rheingold* in Vienna and who was to be closely associated with Britten's future projects with Decca and, later, the BBC; arrangements for the audio staging (by Culshaw, producer Erik Smith and sound engineer Kenneth Wilkinson) included fifteen pages of blocking diagrams. For Britten himself, who had not previously conducted the opera, the sessions 'ended in (temporary) physical disaster' when he 'managed to put a bone in my back out, which made breathing impossible';[53] further illness and his hectic schedule prevented him from hearing a complete playback until February; and, as late as November 1959, he was still 'rather anxiously awaiting news about our proposed stereophonic machine' at The Red House, having apparently inherited his father's suspicion of all such gadgets – 'We propose to have built a little cabinet to take the turntable, and are just waiting for dimensions from you,' he told a surely bemused Culshaw.[54] It would have been worth the wait; *Peter Grimes* may be described without exaggeration as a landmark in the history of the gramophone, a recording which remains artistically and technically unsurpassed over half a century later and has never been out of the catalogue. It was released in time for the 1959 Aldeburgh Festival: the stereo version, said Decca's advertisement in the programme book, had 'all the life and realism of a stage performance'. Reviewing it, Alec Robertson could 'declare with certainty that every lover of great music and great theatre will be thrilled with this magnificent achievement'.[55]

But that year's festival was overshadowed for Britten by a personal sadness so intense and so deeply rooted that he barely spoke of it: on 7 June, Piers Dunkerley killed himself at the home of his fiancée's parents in Dorset. Britten had known him since his schooldays at South Lodge; during the war, while serving in the Royal Marines, Dunkerley was wounded and captured in the 1944 Normandy Landings; after the war, he served on HMS *Vanguard* and then became ADC to the Governor of Gibraltar. His return to civilian life proved difficult: he failed to keep a job with the fuel merchants Charrington's, but he did become engaged to Jill Home, a young doctor from Bournemouth, and they planned to marry in August 1959. Dunkerley, who had kept in touch and visited Aldeburgh whenever possible, asked Britten to be his best man; to his dismay, the invitation was turned down. Although Britten pleaded pressure of work, he found his former young friends' weddings emotionally stressful and avoided all of them. Dunkerley pressed him to attend, even if not as best man: 'I only intend to get married once, and you *must* be there – I insist – and bring Peter.'[56] But he wouldn't be pressed. After an argument with Jill, Piers died of seconal poisoning, 'self-administered while his mind was befogged owing to taking seconal and spirits',[57] according to the coroner. Britten inevitably blamed himself: he would in due course find a way to memorialise his friend.

By the summer of 1959, the proposal for an Aldeburgh Theatre had been finally abandoned in favour of a scheme to renovate and extend the Jubilee Hall: the adjacent house was to be purchased and the building extended as far as Crag Path to provide a new stage with orchestra pit, acoustic panelling and dressing rooms. It would be reopened for the 1960 Aldeburgh Festival and Britten would supply a new opera for the occasion. As this typically audacious and tightly deadlined plan took shape, he made two momentous decisions. Firstly, he would dispense with the services of a librettist (although he consulted Myfanwy Piper); instead, he and Pears were to make their own adaptation of *A Midsummer Night's Dream*, Op. 64. Secondly, he would construct the opera around a particular singer's voice, but that singer would not be Pears. On 18 August, he wrote to the countertenor Alfred Deller: 'I wonder how you would react to the idea of playing Oberon . . . I see you and hear your voice very clearly in this part . . .'[58] It was a bold and risky idea; Deller himself was initially uncertain and had to be gently persuaded by Pears. Moreover, the countertenor voice was less familiar to audiences in the late 1950s than it is today and still likely to prompt strange misapprehensions: there is the story of a German woman who asked Deller, a large bearded family man, 'You are eunuch, Mr Deller?' (to which he nobly replied, 'I think you mean *unique*, madam,' as just possibly she did). It was also a risk, although

one which Britten had already taken in *The Turn of the Screw*,
to sacrifice what might otherwise have been a useful contrast of
registers between Oberon and Tytania.

At first, all went well. In September, the libretto was 'shaping
nicely', Britten told Harewood, adding: 'What a play it is!'[59]
Compositionally, he had cleared the decks (as he put it) to work
on the project, though that didn't mean he could give it an
autumn of uninterrupted concentration: there were, as ever,
recitals with Pears, as well as their appearance at a Festival Hall
concert called *Stars in Our Eyes*, in aid of the Campaign for
Nuclear Disarmament; there was next year's festival to plan and
an ambitious appeal in aid of the Jubilee Hall conversion
(including an auction at Christie's to which Henry Moore
donated a bronze which sold for 1,400 guineas – or approximately
£20,000 in contemporary terms); there was a television production of *The Turn of the Screw*, to be broadcast on the ITV network
over Christmas, for which Britten attended a rehearsal and the
press screening – it was, he told Pears, who was singing in
Switzerland, 'awfully good, scenically rather than musically, actually'.[60] He had been scheduled to accompany Pears, but had now
developed tendonitis in his left arm as well as the periodically
recurring bursitis in his right.

He was also suffering from depression, triggered by
Dunkerley's suicide and intensified by Pears's absence. Almost
at once, he was writing desolately lonely letters to his partner;
a few days later they spoke on the telephone. 'I was so saddened
by your poor old voice this morning and everything gloomy
and dismal that I have been thinking of you all the time and
wondering what I can do,' Pears wrote afterwards. 'What can I
say except that I love you very very much with all my heart.
Take courage my bee – you are so unbelievably loved by everybody.'[61] He did his best, yet he was less complicated and more
easily outgoing than his partner, and he may never have fully

comprehended Britten's plunges into depression and the paralysing lack of self-confidence which went with them. A fellow
sufferer, the gardening writer Monty Don, once explained on
the BBC Radio 3 programme *Private Passions* – presented by
Britten's godson Michael Berkeley – how a depressive crash can
be set off by an event as tiny as a leaf blowing by; how, too, some
music becomes dangerous during periods of depression. It's
equally true that something apparently trivial can quite unexpectedly lift the spirits: the friendly wave of a fisherman outside the
window on Aldeburgh beach, for example. But the beach was no
longer outside Britten's window: at such times, the isolated and
protected environment of The Red House was probably the worst
place for him to be.

'I am having rather a dreary winter,'[62] he told William Glock
in January; while at Easter he reported to Elizabeth Mayer that
it had been a 'horrid winter' during which 'everyone has been
ill, or cross or mad'.[63] He had now added gout to his other
ailments, and in February Imogen Holst was rushed to hospital
with suspected appendicitis; after an operation in March, she
was ordered to take six weeks' rest. Meanwhile, Britten had been
made at least 'cross' if not actually 'mad' by the conduct of his
old friend George Harewood, who had begun an affair with
Patricia Tuckwell (sister of the horn player Barry Tuckwell),
thus jeopardising his marriage to Britten's even older friend
Marion Stein. To the seventeen-year-old Roger Duncan, who
had been staying with the Harewoods, he wrote in strongly
moral terms:

> I wish people just occasionally would think of the result of
> their actions. I am also rather worried about you, old boy,
> worried lest you think that this kind of sexual laxity is the way
> most of the world behaves, or *should* behave. But I do know
> (I really *do* know!) quite a lot of happily married couples, with

plenty of imagination & sensitivity (*& desires*) who manage to live together happily, in spite of, I am sure, problems from time to time.[64]

This is the voice of the respectable middle-class dentist's son from Lowestoft, but it is also genuinely and straightforwardly meant; above all, it is something which Britten *could* say because his careful definition of 'happily married couples' so precisely describes himself and Pears. His simple acknowledgement that they too had their 'problems' – not least the inescapable possibility that the singer, during his frequent absences, might be enjoying himself in unreported ways – is characteristically honest.

Against this troublesome background, the deadline for *A Midsummer Night's Dream* approached. Britten now had the assistance of Rosamund Strode, while Violet Tunnard and Martin Penny stepped in to take over Imogen Holst's tasks, but 'the delays resulting from IH's indisposition meant that George Malcolm, who was training the boy fairies, did not receive the vocal score for Act III until two weeks before the performance'.[65] There were other last-minute panics, including John Cranko's inadequate direction and Deller's continuing worry that he lacked the stage experience necessary for his part: following the dress rehearsal, he told Britten to 'delete me when you think fit'. Nevertheless, the opera was successfully premiered in the refurbished Jubilee Hall on 11 June 1960 with Jennifer Vyvyan as Tytania, George Maran as Lysander, Thomas Hemsley as Demetrius, Marjorie Thomas as Hermia, April Cantelo as Helena, Owen Brannigan as Bottom and Pears as Flute; the speaking role of Puck was taken by Leonide Massine II, the fifteen-year-old son of the dancer and choreographer. As Deller had feared, critics found fault with his stage presence (though not with his singing) and he was indeed 'deleted' from the cast when the production transferred to Covent Garden – though by the opera house management rather than by Britten, who reinstated him for the work's 1966 recording.

Britten and Pears had been scrupulous about retaining, while cutting and rearranging, Shakespeare's language, to which they added only half a dozen explanatory words. The music, too, faithfully reflects the play's tripartite division: lovers, rustics and fairies have their distinctive sound-worlds. The lovers' music is the most grandly conventional as their confusion resolves into eloquence; the rustics are funny and cumbersome, breaking into barbershop harmony and aptly accompanied (Bottom by a trombone, Flute obviously by a flute); while the fairies have celesta, harpsichord, vibraphone and gamelan-influenced percussive effects. The ascending and descending string glissandi which open the opera and signal its transitions cast an oblique glance at Mendelssohn, who began his *Dream* music enigmatically with spaced chords, yet their unsettling quality also suggests a dream bordering on nightmare, like the music which opens Act 2 of *The Turn of the Screw*. The rustics' production of *Pyramus and Thisbe* is an exuberant pastiche of Donizetti, which Pears further improved by turning his Flute-as-Thisbe into a wicked imitation of Joan Sutherland, whose *Lucia di Lammermoor* at Covent Garden was still fresh in musical memories. The happy ending is intensely moving, with Shakespeare's 'And all shall be well' supplying a benign counterpart to Hardy's 'When all went well' in *Winter Words*: even the ambiguity of Puck's epilogue is softened by cutting the couplet in which he appears to question his own honesty. Nevertheless, a crucial element of the play has been lost in Britten and Pears's removal of the original Act 1, apart from an anachronistic fragment which is transplanted to Act 3. Shakespeare's play begins in the orderly 'red' world of the court, where the lovers are frustrated by their elders; it then moves to the chaotic and transformative 'green' world of the forest, from which come liberation and resolution; finally, it returns to a 'red' world made newly benevolent by love. In losing this dialectical progression, by plunging us straight into an enchanted wood, the opera diminishes the lovers' coherence and motivation as characters and, conversely, increases the likelihood of their being upstaged by the rustics and the fairies. Peter Hall, who has directed both Shakespeare's and Britten's *A Midsummer Night's Dream*, once memorably remarked that the difference between them is that in Britten's version there is no love.

4

Despite the immediate and sustained success of *A Midsummer Night's Dream*, there's a chill in Britten's music at the turn of the decade; the improbable agent of its thaw was to be Nikita Khrushchev, prime minister of the USSR from 1958 to 1964. For it was thanks to Khrushchev's encouragement of cultural exchanges with the West that on 21 September 1960 the Leningrad Symphony Orchestra, conducted by Gennadi Rozhdestvensky, appeared at the Royal Festival Hall in London; with them was the Russian cellist Mstislav Rostropovich, then in his early thirties, who was to be the soloist in the first British performance of the Cello Concerto by Dmitri Shostakovich. Since the opening item in the concert was *The Young Person's Guide to the Orchestra*, Shostakovich invited Britten to join him in his box, together with the Master of the Queen's Music, Arthur Bliss. Britten had already heard a radio broadcast by Rostropovich and been astonished by his playing; now, as he listened to the concerto, he became wildly excited, bobbing up and down and poking Shostakovich in the ribs whenever (which was often) he was especially delighted. Afterwards, backstage, the two men were introduced: Rostropovich, relieved to find

Britten 'just like his music – not spoiled by his status', immediately 'pleaded most sincerely and passionately with him to write something for the cello'.[66] Britten, who needed no persuading, at once agreed to meet the next day, with Rozhdestvensky again present to assist communication, at Rostropovich's modest hotel, the Prince of Wales in Kensington. There he proposed that he should write a sonata for cello which he would send to Rostropovich in Moscow, on the condition that it should receive from him its first public performance at the 1961 Aldeburgh Festival: it was a brilliant suggestion and, for both men, a life-changing one. Permission would have to be obtained from the authorities in the USSR but, even before Rostropovich left London, Britten had crafted for him a 'letter to the Minister . . . written in a perfect way though my personal qualities are considerably exaggerated'. It did the trick. Three weeks later, the cellist wrote again from Moscow:

> If you have no objections I intend to come ten days before our concert in Aldeburgh and to learn your sonata there putting in all my love and skill. Please don't worry that I shall not have time to learn the sonata well, for I am rather quick to learn. For instance I learned Shostakovich's concerto in four days.[67]

Britten, smiling at this, must have realised that, for sheer musical intelligence, he had at last met his equal.

Rostropovich, who was eagerly anticipating the arrival of each day's post, endured some months of agony: 'The wait was actually painful.' Meanwhile, Britten had more pressing things in his diary, including a holiday with the Hesses in Greece, a recital tour with Pears of Germany and Switzerland, and recordings of his revised two-act version of *Billy Budd* for the BBC – it was broadcast on 13 November – and of the *Spring Symphony*

for Decca. There was also a concert with Menuhin at the Festival
Hall, in aid of Christian Action, and a Wigmore Hall recital in
which Britten and Pears were joined by a boy alto, John Hahessy,
for *Canticle II: Abraham and Isaac*. It wasn't until after Christmas
that he could work on Rostropovich's sonata; by 17 January he
had 'got the cello piece in order' and played it through to Imogen
Holst, 'who was quite impressed'. Then the phone rang: 'there
was "Slava" from Paris, & I had a wild & dotty conversation in
broken German (*very* broken) with him'.[68] This common idiom,
hammered out of their different versions of German, they were
to call 'Aldeburgh Deutsch'. When the parcel of music reached
Moscow, Rostropovich 'made a dash for my cello, locked myself
in and went at that Sonata. It was a case of love at first sight.'
On 11 February he sent a telegram to Britten: 'ADMIRING
AND IN LOVE WITH YOUR GREAT SONATA SHALL
BE IN LONDON END OF FEBRUARY DETAILS BY
CABLE LOVE ROSTROPOVICH'.[69] In fact, it was 5 March
when he spent a day in London – he was changing planes on
the way to South America – and together they tried through the
piece at 59 Marlborough Place, the current Britten–Pears London
base in St John's Wood:

> Ben said, 'Well, Slava, do you think we have time for a drink
> first?' I said, 'Yes, yes', so we both drank a large whisky. Then
> Ben said: 'Maybe we have time for another one?' 'Yes, yes,' I
> said. Another large whisky. After four or five very large whiskies
> we finally sat down and played through the sonata. We played
> like pigs, but we were so happy.[70]

In a letter to Rostropovich's wife, the soprano Galina Vishnevskaya,
Britten told her how much he had enjoyed 'working with Slava',
who had 'understood the work perfectly, and of course played
it like no one else in the world could'. He hoped that she would

accompany him to Aldeburgh and 'that there will be a chance of hearing you sing'.[71]

The Aldeburgh Festival of 1961 was both significant and magical. On the one hand, the Russian visitors were treated to some wonderful events: Pears and Britten gave their first public performance of Schubert's *Winterreise*; *The Turn of the Screw*, conducted by Meredith Davies, was staged in the Jubilee Hall; and *Noye's Fludde*, conducted by Norman Del Mar, was revived in Orford Church. On the other, there was Rostropovich with the London Symphony Orchestra in the Schumann Cello Concerto and in a chamber recital with Britten which included Schubert's Arpeggione Sonata and Five Pieces in Folk Style, the Debussy Cello Sonata and the promised premiere of Britten's own Sonata in C, Op. 65, of which the last two movements were given again as an encore; after that, Rostropovich beckoned Pears onto the platform and the three of them performed a Bach aria with cello obbligato. The anonymous critic in *The Times* (William Mann) perceptively noted that Britten's new five-movement work, 'nearer to suite than sonata in character', seemed to have been intended 'to reflect his own impression of the character of the player to whom it is dedicated: gay, charming, an astonishingly brilliant executant, but behind all these qualities a searching musician with the mind of a philosopher'.[72] He might have added that this was also an accurate self-portrait of the composer. In Galina Vishnevskaya's recital, her husband was the piano accompanist: 'I can't believe such a programme was possible,' she later wrote. 'In addition to songs by Prokoviev, Tchaikovsky, Richard Strauss and Schumann, plus arias from *Norma*, *Manon Lescaut*, *La Forza del Destino*, and *Lady Macbeth of Mtensk*, for dessert I sang Mussorgsky's *Songs and Dances of Death*.'[73] But it *was* possible in Aldeburgh.

Rostropovich and his wife fell in love with the place. He had arrived first, for a rehearsal with Britten and the LSO in

London, before being driven to Suffolk in the composer's latest open-topped car, an Alvis; she joined him a few days later at the Wentworth Hotel, overlooking the sea on the northern edge of the 'wonderfully cosy and enticing town'. Then they were off to a garden party at The Red House where Vishnevskaya was introduced to Britten 'and my heart opened to him instantly': 'From the beginning I felt at ease with him; I'm sure that everyone who was lucky enough to know that charming man must have felt the same sense of simplicity and naturalness in his company.'[74] In fact, not everyone did; but the Rostropoviches – with their combination of musicality, modesty and generosity – brought out the very best in him. 'Dear, dear Ben and Peter,' they wrote, a few days after their return home, 'It is quite impossible to express in a letter our feelings of sorrow and loneliness'; they had never before met 'people so cordial and warm-hearted, so genuinely gifted, so sincere and frank . . .'[75] Aldeburgh, as Bernard Levin once put it, is a place to leave looking over your shoulder. They would be back.

Although Britten was to write another four works for cello dedicated to his friend Slava Rostropovich, it was Galina Vishnevskaya's recital which had the more immediate effect on his composing life. In October 1958, he had been approached with an invitation to write a substantial work for chorus and orchestra to mark the consecration of the new cathedral in Coventry, designed by Basil Spence, which was to take place in 1962. 'I should very much like to undertake this,' he told John Lowe, the artistic director of the Coventry Cathedral Festival, 'one of the reasons, I must confess, being the, for once, reasonable date attached.'[76] However, it wasn't until almost two years later, in the summer of 1960, that he began work in earnest on a composition which would interleave the traditional movements of the Requiem Mass with texts taken from the First World War poems of Wilfred Owen; he had already included

Owen's 'Strange Meeting' in his contribution to the BBC radio series *Personal Choice* and 'The Kind Ghosts' in his *Nocturne*. This idea of juxtaposing two very different textual sources may well have been suggested by Tippett's interleaving of his own words with songs from *The Book of American Negro Spirituals* in *A Child of Our Time*. By the following February, he had decided that the poems would be 'set for tenor and baritone, with an accompaniment of chamber orchestra, placed in the middle of the other forces' and, in a careful and respectful letter, he invited Dietrich Fischer-Dieskau to sing alongside Pears; the two had recently worked together on a recording of the *St Matthew Passion* under Otto Klemperer. Although the choice of Fischer-Dieskau was essentially a musical one, Britten also had in mind what he called 'the circumstances for this particular occasion', by which he meant that the appearance of an English and a German soloist would be an appropriate symbol of reconciliation and peace. He also vaguely thought that he would need 'a strong soprano for the Mass section'; when he heard Vishnevskaya sing at Aldeburgh, he immediately told her that 'he had begun to write his *War Requiem* and now wanted to write in a part for me'.[77] A project designed to unite performers from the opposing sides of two world wars might do the same for the Cold War as well.

It was at this point that another timely and prescient gift arrived from Christopher Isherwood. Britten had been using the Edmund Blunden edition of Wilfred Owen's poems; but now Isherwood, who was in England, sent him a copy of the first edition, edited by Siegfried Sassoon and published in 1920, which contained a photograph of Owen. Britten was 'delighted to have it – I am so involved with him at the moment, & I wanted to see what he looked like: I might have guessed, it's just what I expected really'.[78] What he expected or what he hoped? He would have guessed or known about Owen's sexuality (and, if he hadn't, Isherwood was just the friend to enlighten him); but, above all, he must have noticed the resemblance between Owen in his military uniform and a wartime photograph of Captain Piers Dunkerley, Royal Marines. His *War Requiem*, Op. 66, would carry this dedication: 'In loving memory of Roger Burney, Sub-Lieutenant, Royal Naval Volunteer Reserve; Piers Dunkerley, Captain, Royal Marines; David Gill, Ordinary Seaman, Royal Navy; Michael Halliday, Lieutenant, Royal New Zealand Naval Volunteer Force.' Burney (a friend of Pears), Gill and Halliday (Lowestoft friends of Britten) had all died in the war; Dunkerley, Britten implies, was also a casualty of the war, in the sense that it left him unable to cope with life in peacetime. Yet he knew this wasn't the whole truth, which explains his otherwise elliptical remark to the painter Sidney Nolan: 'Really what the whole thing is, it's a kind of reparation. That's what the *War Requiem* is about; it is reparation.'[79] Thus a work which had originated as a very public commission was increasingly concerned with a very private subtext.

Britten and Rostropovich next met a month later in London, where they spent two days recording three of the four items from their Aldeburgh programme for Decca; Britten noted with satisfaction that they had apparently used up six miles of tape. Two days after that, he and Pears were introduced by the Rostropoviches to the great Russian pianist Sviatoslav Richter, who was to become a regular participant in Aldeburgh Festivals, and his wife, the singer Nina Dorliak. Then they flew to Yugoslavia, to perform at the Dubrovnik Festival, where there was also a production of *The Rape of Lucretia*. At the end of August, they were off to the Edinburgh Festival – somehow contriving to fit in a concert at the Three Choirs Festival in Hereford before dashing back to Scotland – before immediately embarking on a ten-day tour of West Germany and Poland. It was, incidentally, on a fleeting back-to-base stop between Scotland and Germany that Britten scribbled his thanks to

Isherwood for the Owen book, adding: 'We are only back for 24 hours to pick up clothes & music & there are 1,000,000 things to do.' He should have been working on the *War Requiem*, but at times such as this one wonders how he managed to compose anything at all. In early October he was at the Leeds Triennial Festival, where his new arrangement of the National Anthem received its first public performance and Pears was one of the soloists in the *Cantata Academica*. A fortnight later, he and Pears gave a recital at Whitehaven in Cumbria, where *The Turn of the Screw* was also produced as part of a week-long Britten Festival sponsored by the textile entrepreneur Nicholas Sekers. Then, at last, it was back to Aldeburgh and the *War Requiem*. 'I go on working at the Coventry piece,' he told Basil Coleman. 'Sometimes it seems the best ever, more often the worst – but it is always so with me.'[80]

By Christmas, it was beginning to look as if Galina Vishnevskaya's participation in the *War Requiem* would prove a concession too far for the Soviet authorities; however, knowing that his and Rostropovich's combined charm had already worked small miracles, Britten hoped they might yet be persuaded. He finished the *War Requiem* by the end of January and then he set Goethe's poem 'Um Mitternacht' for voice and piano, a pendant to the night-worlds of the *Nocturne* and the *Dream*, before joining Pears on a three-week tour of Canada. When they returned, he learned that Moscow definitely wouldn't allow Vishnevskaya to sing at Coventry: 'the combination of "Cathedral" & Reconciliation with W. Germany . . . was too much for them',[81] he told Forster, writing on Easter Saturday from Ipswich Nursing Home, where he was being treated for haemorrhoids. Vishnevskaya herself recalled an interview with the Minister of Culture, Ekaterina Furtseva, in which she was asked: 'But how can you, a Soviet woman, stand next to a German and an Englishman and

Pears, E. M. Forster, Robin Long ('The Nipper'), Britten and Billy Burrell, 1948

Pears and Britten shopping in Aldeburgh High Street, 1948

Britten leaving the Concertgebouw after the premiere of his *Spring Symphony* at the Holland Festival, Amsterdam, 1949

E. M. Forster, Britten and Eric Crozier working on *Billy Budd* in the study at Crabbe Street, Aldeburgh, 1949

Imogen Holst conducting the Aldeburgh Music Club, including Britten and Pears, as part of 'Music on the Meare', Thorpeness, 1954

Premiere of *Noye's Fludde*, performed in the Aldeburgh Festival at St Bartholomew's Church, Orford, 1958

Pears, Prince Ludwig and Princess Margaret of Hesse and the Rhine and Britten in Balinese costume, Bali, 1956

Britten, Pears, Princess Margaret and Prince Ludwig, Venice, 1957

Britten accepting the Honorary Freedom of the Borough of Aldeburgh, 1962

Britten and Colin Graham leaving The Red House in Britten's Alvis, Aldeburgh, 1964

Britten and Meredith Davies in discussion during rehearsals for the first performance of the *War Requiem*, Coventry Cathedral, 1962

With soprano Galina Vishnevskaya after recording the *War Requiem*, London, 1963

With viola player Cecil Aronowitz during a Decca recording session of *The Burning Fiery Furnace*, Orford Church, 1967

With cellist Mstislav Rostropovich during the rehearsal for the first UK performance of Symphony for Cello and Orchestra, Blythburgh Church, 1964

Rehearsals for the television recording of *Peter Grimes* at the Snape Maltings Concert Hall, 1969

Death in Venice: the final scene, with Pears (Aschenbach) and Robert Huguenin (Tadzio), Snape Maltings, 1973

Britten and Pears at Snape, 1975

perform a political work? Perhaps on the issue in question our government isn't in complete agreement with them.'[82] Heather Harper was drafted in, despite a busy schedule (including, as it happens, *A Midsummer Night's Dream*), and she learned the part in ten days. Meanwhile, Britten, who had been assured that Coventry's new cathedral would be magnificent and blessed with perfect acoustics, visited the place, detested the building and found the acoustics 'lunatic'. (Did he perhaps make a mental note that if he were ever to have anything to do with a new concert hall for the Aldeburgh Festival, they would at least have to get *that* right?) Scarcely less lunatic was the behaviour of some Coventry clergy, who appeared determined to wage war on his requiem: there were 'really Trollopian clerical battles, but with modern weapons'.[83] Although the original plan had been for Britten to conduct the first perform-ance and Meredith Davies the second, the combination of acoustic problems and the cathedral authorities' refusal to allow a stage to be erected in front of the altar meant that each performance would require two conductors; Britten, whose arm was again troublesome, chose the secondary role of conducting the chamber orchestra (the Melos Ensemble), leaving the City of Birmingham Symphony Orchestra in Davies's hands. There were moments when Coventry seemed as obstructive as Moscow.

The *War Requiem* was first performed on 30 May 1962 and broadcast live on the BBC Third Programme. The cathedral, determined to resemble Barchester to the last, had decreed that the audience should be admitted through only one doorway and, although other doors were eventually opened, it was obvious that the performance couldn't start on time. The BBC announcer came to the end of his script and, as the producer Richard Butt later recalled, there was a long pause 'during which the radio audience heard nothing but the sound of a large, silent congregation waiting for something to happen';[84] unusually, this prompted messages of thanks from listeners who felt that the preliminary silence was suitable for the occasion and the work. Very few people who were in the cathedral that evening or who heard the broadcast were in any doubt that something extraordinary was taking place. Writing in the weekly *Time & Tide*, the playwright Peter Shaffer thought it 'the most impressive and moving piece of sacred music ever to be composed in this country, and one of the greatest musical compositions of the twentieth century', and the normally more cautious professional music critics largely agreed. 'Britten's inspiration throughout is at its highest; never before has he invented at so sustained and elevated a level,' wrote Andrew Porter in the *Musical Times*. William Mann, in *The Times*, wished that 'everyone in the world might hear, inwardly digest, and outwardly acknowledge the great and cogent call to a sane, Christian life proclaimed in this Requiem' which was 'so superbly proportioned and calculated, so humiliating and disturbing in effect, in fact so tremendous, that every performance it is given ought to be a momentous occasion'. 'It is surely a masterpiece of our time,' agreed Desmond Shawe-Taylor in the *Sunday Times*.[85] Colleagues and friends sent Britten letters of congratulation, among which was one from Harold Owen, the poet's brother, who found the *War Requiem* 'magnificent' and 'superb' as well as 'most disturbing', adding that it was 'a wonderful thought . . . that Wilfred's poetry will for ever be a part of this great work'.[86]

'My subject is War, and the pity of War,' wrote Owen in his brief preface. 'The Poetry is in the pity.'[87] That second sentence – which ought to remain surprising, despite its familiarity, since on the page the pity is more obviously in the poetry – seems here at last to make transcendent sense. Although it isn't quite fair to describe the *War Requiem* as the culmination of everything towards which Britten was striving, it is the work in which one major aspect of his musical life achieves its finest expression: he hints as much when he audaciously quotes from his own *Canticle II: Abraham and Isaac* in setting 'The Parable of the Old Man and the Young', before it reaches Owen's appallingly different conclusion. All the complex elements of this creative strand – the pacifist, the devotional and the inwardly personal – come together in the Libera me, which sets Owen's 'Strange Meeting' as a dialogue for English tenor and German baritone: the poem, which envisages two soldiers from opposing armies meeting after death, ends with the words 'Let us sleep now . . .' and leads into the *War Requiem*'s intensely moving (if harmonically compromised) invocation of eternal peace. Yet, in this context, the poem gains new resonances: this, surely, is where we will again recall Britten's remark that his visit to Belsen changed everything he wrote thereafter; while, on a differently personal level, mourning 'the undone years / The hopelessness' will remind us of the work's dedication and especially of Piers Dunkerley. The second part of the poem, which is also the baritone's last solo, proved too much for Fischer-Dieskau who, as Britten reported almost proudly to Plomer, 'was so upset at the end that Peter couldn't get him out of the choir-stalls'.[88] 'The first performance created an atmosphere of such intensity that by the end I was completely undone,' the singer himself wrote. 'I did not know where to hide my face.'[89]

When, on 1 June, the *War Requiem* was performed for the second time in Coventry, the BBC producer Richard Butt was able to experience it as a member of the audience. He sat next to the conductor Arnold Goldsbrough who, as 'the long, intense silence after the music began to dissolve', turned to him and said: 'Yes – that's what Ben had to do.'[90] He would do nothing remotely like it ever again.

5

Rostropovich, who had been unwell early in 1962 (though without enduring the 'heart attack' created by rumour and mistranslation), wrote to Britten in March: 'If you want me to recover completely I ask you to see the doctor whose address is: The Red House, Aldeburgh, Suffolk. Only he can bring me to life by composing a brilliant violoncello concerto.'[91] Britten confirmed his determination to write such a work, while refusing to set himself a deadline. This was just as well, because his progress would be delayed by commitments and ill health: in July, he warned his 'beloved Slava' to 'be patient about the Concerto' which he wanted to be 'worthy of my favourite 'Cellist'.[92] The following month, the Rostropoviches spent a short holiday in Aldeburgh, after which they were all scheduled to go on to the Edinburgh Festival; but Britten, suffering from a frozen shoulder, had to cancel his appearances there with Rostropovich and with Pears, who was instead accompanied by Julian Bream. However, this didn't deter Britten from fulfilling an important engagement closer to home, the first of a series of Bach weekends at Long Melford, held on 15–16 September: there was a programme of concertos given by George Malcolm and the English Chamber Orchestra, conducted by Britten, with the D minor Cello Suite performed by the previously unannounced Rostropovich; a late-night recital by Malcolm, Pears and Rostropovich; and a concert of cantatas with Janet Baker, Pears and John Shirley-Quirk, with the ECO conducted by Imogen Holst, to which Rostropovich added two of the suites.

Immediately after their Bach weekend, Britten and Pears set off on holiday to Venice. 'I am really very glad we came here – I am sure the complete break from Aldeburgh routine & problems . . . has done us good,' Britten told the Hesses. 'I am determined now,' he recklessly added, 'to snap out of all these stupid minor ailments, & even if they can't be cured, to ignore them.'[93] While in Venice, they dined with the avant-garde composer Luigi Nono and his wife Nuria (Schoenberg's daughter), with whom they seem to have got on splendidly, despite their musical differences. But although they had a 'lovely' fortnight in Venice, Britten 'picked up a germ there (a most rare one which has had even the Hosp. for Tropical Diseases guessing!)'[94] and on his return to England was 'absolutely laid out' for four weeks: it was a savagely ironic end to a holiday which had begun with his resolve to 'snap out of' his ailments, quite apart from the troubling echoes (and pre-echoes) of Thomas Mann's Aschenbach, Britten's own last opera and, for that matter, his own final visit to Venice in 1975. The more robust Pears found Britten's procession of illnesses immensely tiresome and wasn't invariably sympathetic, especially when the composer had to pull out of their joint tours. He was fulfilling a singing engagement in Liverpool when Britten wrote to him in late October:

My honey darling,

I am so dreadfully sorry I'm being such a broken reed at the moment – it is the bloodiest nuisance from every point of view. But I promise you that it is only a bad patch this, & I'll get it all coped with & promise to be a worthy companion for you from now on! I suppose one can't help having weak spots, and being a jumpy neurotic type – but at least I'm determined now not to be such an infernal nuisance to everyone – including myself, because it isn't fun to feel like the wrong end of a broken down bus for most of the time; I don't *like* spending most of my life sitting on a lavatory seat, because it isn't comfy, nor pretty. But from now on you'll see a new me, – I hope –, & one that's not a drag on you, a worry for you, & a bit more worthy of my beloved P.[95]

Some may dislike the childish, wheedling note in that; but more will be moved by the greatest living English composer's humility and vulnerability. Pears touches on this in his reply:

> My darling Ben –
>
> Your letter makes me go hot with shame. That *you* should be asking me to forgive you for being ill, when it is I that should be looking after you & loving you, should long ago have thrown my silly career out of the window & come & tried to protect you a bit from worry and tension, instead of adding to them with my own worries and tetchinesses. God! I think singers over the age of 14 should be wiped out . . .
>
> My honey, you *mustn't* worry about me & my affairs – & if you don't feel like coming to Switzerland on Sunday we jolly well won't go.[96]

So shy and private a man as Britten often found it difficult to cope with the consequences of his own reputation. Sometimes, his anxiety could be diffused by an appeal to his perennially youthful sense of humour, as when an unknown admirer sent him a collection of schoolboy howlers including one about himself: 'B.B. is our most famous contemporary composer. It is difficult to be contemporary because a composer isn't alive until he's dead.' But when Ronald Duncan was commissioned to write a 'profile' of him for the *Sunday Times*, he was horrified, asking Duncan not to do it and enlisting the help of Desmond Shawe-Taylor, the paper's music critic, in his effort to prevent it: 'I don't like this kind of thing – especially the (entre nous) rather chatty, gossipy things that *he* writes. I wrote and said I didn't want it done – don't want publicity (just want to write better music!).'[97] Britten did, however, enjoy one very special ceremony of public acknowledgement that autumn. On 22 October, in the council chamber of the Moot Hall – the room in which Peter

Grimes had stood before the court – he was presented with the Honorary Freedom of the Borough of Aldeburgh. 'It was done with great simplicity – only lasting half an hour, but really touching & impressive.'[98]

In his speech of thanks, Britten returns to the points about the artist and society which he had made on the similar occasion at Lowestoft over a decade earlier, but this time he adds a deeply felt personal note: 'As I understand it, this honour is not given because of a *reputation*, because of a chance acquaintance, it is – dare I say it? – because you really *do* know me, and accept me as one of yourselves, *as a useful part of the Borough* – and this is, I think, the highest possible compliment for an artist.'[99] Especially and extraordinarily, in 1962, for a homosexual artist. Towards the end of his speech – blowing, as he says, 'Aldeburgh's own small trumpet' – he reprises the theme of the artist and his community: 'It is a considerable achievement, in this small Borough in England, that we run year after year, a first-class Festival of the Arts, and we make a huge success of it. And when I say "*we*" I mean "we".' He was, he concludes, deeply grateful to be honoured 'as a symbol', 'but I can't help feeling that it is *all* of us, all of *you* who deserve it'. The only way in which he could make his achievements tolerable and manageable to himself was to feel they were shared with the community. Yet an inescapable sense of distance creeps in: twice in his speech he refers to visitors being 'charmed' (which is not a word much used by locals) by the town and in praising it he invokes the example of 'a very choosy friend from abroad who regularly re-stocks her wardrobe here, and buys most of her Christmas presents too, I believe'.[100] Were the mayor, town clerk, aldermen, councillors and people of Aldeburgh 'charmed' by the thought of Princess Margaret of Hesse and the Rhine doing her shopping among them or did they ever so slightly wince? A bit of each, surely.

The demands made by the *War Requiem* on Britten's time, and on his health, had not ceased with the first performance. There was a planned recording for Decca, for which he had to negotiate with Ekaterina Furtseva to secure the participation of Vishnevskaya and with EMI to release Fischer-Dieskau from his exclusive contract with them; tenacious and tactful, he succeeded on both counts. On 18 November, there was the work's West German premiere at the Deutsche Oper Berlin, in which he shared the conducting with Colin Davis. Three weeks later, the *War Requiem* was performed for the first time in London at Westminster Abbey, 'during one of the thickest, coldest, longest-lasting, freezing smogs the capital had known for years', according to Rosamund Strode, who was there; she added that 'Heather Harper, singing from the pulpit, couldn't even see down to the west end of the nave'.[101] Pears, who was suffering from a throat infection, missed the dress rehearsal although he sang in the performance, which was given in the presence of the Queen Mother and the Princess Royal and broadcast live on the BBC Third Programme. William Plomer, who with his German-born partner Charles Erdmann listened to it on the radio ('with tears running down our faces'), told Britten that he now grasped 'more fully the extraordinary boldness and skill with which the work is constructed, and appreciate all the more what is most Ben-like in this phrase and that'.[102] And then, between 3 and 10 January 1963, the *War Requiem* was recorded at Kingsway Hall, with Decca's senior producer John Culshaw and engineer Kenneth Wilkinson in charge; in between the sessions, the work was performed at the Albert Hall on 8 January.

Afterwards, Culshaw told Britten that he thought the recording 'a document of very great musical importance' and thanked him for his 'co-operation and understanding', while the composer responded with thanks to the producer for his

'tact, kindness, & skill & endless (necessary!) encouragement'.[103]
This was very far from mere conventional politeness on either
side, for the whole project had almost collapsed on the first
day of recording. Vishnevskaya, who had never previously
performed the work and who understood her Latin text but
not Owen's English, objected to being placed on the balcony
with the chorus, rather than with the other two soloists;
according to Culshaw, she 'lost her head, and lay down on the
floor of the vestry . . . and shrieked at the top of her voice',[104]
a performance of such intensity and duration that it was impossible to record anything at all in the building while it was going
on. The following day, however, she took her place cheerfully
and sang brilliantly – evidently, her interpreter had at last
succeeded in explaining the work's construction to her – and
the project was actually completed ahead of schedule. Culshaw
had been right about its importance, although he can hardly
have foreseen the extent of its commercial success: released in
May as a sombre black box of two premium-priced LPs, the
War Requiem nevertheless sold an unprecedented 200,000
copies within a few months. When he left Decca, five years
later, Culshaw wrote of his recordings with Britten: 'He seems
to inspire everyone around him with a different sort of single-
mindedness, which is simply that of doing justice . . . to the
music at hand.'[105]

'I gave out a great deal of myself in the War Requiem, &
my body has taken revenge!'[106] Britten told Paul Sacher – who
had wanted to commission a work to mark the composer's
forthcoming fiftieth birthday – within days of completing the
recording. Undeterred by the effects of their most recent
holiday, he and Pears were about to leave for two weeks in
Greece, followed by a fortnight with the Hesses at Schloss
Tarasp. But in Greece they were snowed in and unable to
explore; then, in Switzerland, he immediately fell while skiing

and was laid up for the rest of their stay, preventing the rest of the party from doing much. On their return to England, he had to spend some weeks hobbling around on crutches with his injured foot in plaster, when he should have been touring in Germany with Pears – which was 'quite maddening & frustrating for him, I fear, tho' not so bad for me who have been sitting, leg up, working on my new Concerto for Slava'.[107] All the same, he remained determined to travel to Moscow in early March, with or without crutches, for the British Council's 'Festival of British Musical Art': among the other musicians taking part in the fourteen concerts (seven each in Moscow and Leningrad) were the Amadeus Quartet, Norman Del Mar, George Malcolm, Barry Tuckwell and, from the host nation, Rostropovich, who was still in poor health. The visit was a huge success not only with audiences but also with the Minister of Culture, Madame Furtseva: Britten, who knew how to charm, established an immediate and valuable degree of personal rapport with her. The only dissenting note came from the English press where he was quoted as having said, in an interview for *Pravda*, 'One of the main social duties of an artist lies in the formation, education and development of the artistic tastes of the people.' There was some debate about whether or not he had appreciated the significance which a communist readership would attach to the definite article before 'people': he later told William Plomer that he had meant to give *Pravda* 'a sympathetic tactful talk, which of course the blighters got deliberately wrong'. 'However,' he added, 'that isn't unique to the USSR, is it?'[108]

The concerto which he had originally hoped to perform with Rostropovich during his Moscow visit remained unfinished: it was evolving into a four-movement symphony-shaped work which for a while he tentatively called a 'Sinfonia Concertante'. He completed the composition draft of what would in fact be the Cello Symphony – or, more properly, the Symphony for Cello and Orchestra, Op. 68 – on 11 April and the full score on 3 May. Rostropovich, recovering from his illness in a Moscow hospital, found it 'miraculous' and 'a work of genius'; recalling the terms in which he had asked Britten to write it, he added that it would be 'the best medicine for my recuperation'.[109] As he wouldn't be well enough to attend that year's Aldeburgh Festival, he magnanimously waived his right to give the work's first performance; Britten naturally declined this offer, and the premiere was postponed until the following spring. Meanwhile, he had another deadline to meet, another commission to finish: this was the *Cantata Misericordium*, Op. 69, for the centenary of the Red Cross. His original intention had been to set a medieval Latin text on the theme of the Good Samaritan, although there was some concern that a Christian text might be inappropriate for a firmly non-denominational organisation. He then enlisted the help of Patrick Wilkinson, Professor of Latin at Cambridge, and by the end of 1962 he was able to assure Frédéric Siordet of the Red Cross that they were 'going ahead with a purely humanitarian version of the Good Samaritan story'. He also – in a move clearly intended to impress Siordet as a coup and to silence any further grumbling about the text – secured the participation of Dietrich Fischer-Dieskau as the baritone soloist for the work's first performance, which was to take place at the Grand Théâtre in Geneva on 1 September; the other participants were Pears as tenor soloist, Le Motet de Genève and the Orchestre de la Suisse Romande, conducted by Ernest Ansermet.

The *Cantata Misericordium* is a more substantial work than the *Cantata Academica*; it is also another of Britten's pendants, in this case to the *War Requiem*. He was slightly disingenuous in describing it as 'purely humanitarian', for within the first few minutes the chorus issues the invitation, 'Iesu parabola iam nobis fiat fabula' ('Let us enact a parable of Jesus'). Yet the chorus's conclusion is impeccably tuned to the occasion: 'Morbus gliscit, Mars incedit, / fames late superat; / sed mortales, alter quando alterum sic sublevat, / e dolore procreata caritas consociat' ('Disease is spreading, war is stalking, / famine reigns far and wide; / but when one mortal relieves another like this, / charity springing from pain unites them'). To which the two soloists add their assent: 'Quis sit proximus tuus iam scis' ('Who your neighbour is, now you know'). Donald Mitchell, writing in the *Daily Telegraph*, thought the work 'quite exceptionally beautiful' and 'an incomparably gentle master-piece'.[110] He should perhaps have declared his interest: since the beginning of the year, he had been working for Boosey & Hawkes with special responsibility for Britten and for encour-aging younger composers. He was also compiling a definitive catalogue of Britten's work, to be published by Boosey & Hawkes to mark the composer's fiftieth birthday: he proudly reported that he had 'managed to persuade Roth to let Faber's design the typography – quite a triumph',[111] not yet guessing how closely he, Britten and the designer Berthold Wolpe would soon become associated.

That fiftieth birthday was always going to be a torment for Britten. The *Sunday Times*, having been defeated over the earlier 'Profile', wouldn't let the occasion pass: on 17 November, they published an article and interview by Desmond Shawe-Taylor, in the course of which Britten imprudently mentioned his never to be realised plan for an opera based on *King Lear*. The paper headlined the piece 'Benjamin Britten at Fifty: A *King Lear* in prospect', rather neatly confirming his point about *Pravda*'s lack of uniqueness. The same day's *Observer* carried Michael Tippett's 'Britten at Fifty' – 'Of all the musicians I have met, Britten is the most sheerly musical' – while to the *Sunday Telegraph* the composer himself contributed 'Britten Looking Back', an affectionate tribute to his friend and teacher

Frank Bridge. There were celebratory musical events, begin-
ning with an Albert Hall Prom on 12 September at which
Britten himself conducted his *Sinfonia da Requiem*, *Spring
Symphony* and, in its first London performance, *Cantata
Misericordium*. Then, on the birthday itself, 22 November, there
was a concert performance of *Gloriana* at the Festival Hall,
followed by a party at the Harewoods' London house in Orme
Square. The performance, in which Pears reprised the role of
Essex and the part of Queen Elizabeth I was sung by Sylvia
Fisher, 'went surprisingly well, & was rather interesting',[112] but
during the interval the news from Dallas, of President John F.
Kennedy's assassination, began to circulate among the audience
and cast an inescapable shadow over the remainder of the
evening.

The most ill-judged of the birthday celebrations – which
was apparently instigated by Decca's chairman, Edward Lewis,
and organised by John Culshaw, who should have known better
– was the presentation to Britten of a specially pressed LP,
bearing the number BB 50 and containing secretly taped
rehearsal material from the *War Requiem* sessions; it took him
a month to summon the courage to play it once (and to thank
Culshaw), after which it was consigned to a cupboard at The
Red House and not heard again during the composer's lifetime.
By contrast, the most perfectly judged was a Festschrift, *A
Tribute to Benjamin Britten on his Fiftieth Birthday*, edited by
Anthony Gishford and published by Faber. The contributors
to this astonishing book, of whose existence its dedicatee
managed to remain unaware until 22 November, were Julian
Bream, Kenneth Clark, Aaron Copland, the Earl of Cranbrook,
Joan Cross, Clifford Curzon, Ronald Duncan, E. M. Forster,
Robert Gathorne-Hardy, Anthony Gishford, Carlo Maria
Giulini, Lord Harewood, Prince Ludwig of Hesse and the
Rhine, Imogen Holst, Hans Keller, George Malcolm, Elizabeth

Mayer, Yehudi Menuhin, Donald Mitchell, Peter Pears, Myfanwy Piper, William Plomer, Francis Poulenc, Mstislav Rostropovich, Edith Sitwell and Eric Walter White; plates reproduced works of art or manuscript pages of compositions by Georg Ehrlich, Kenneth Green, Hans Werner Henze, Edward Hicks, Henry Moore, John Nash, John Piper, Mary Potter, Reynolds Stone and Michael Tippett. A notable absentee appears to be Eric Crozier, who did in fact offer a pungent sequel to *Albert Herring*, 'Albert in Later Life', which Gishford greatly enjoyed but regretfully declined on the grounds that 'blackmail, pederasty, pornography and arson' were not quite the subjects for the occasion. 'I am *very* proud of that book, by the way,'[113] Britten told George Malcolm.

William Walton wrote him a splendid letter on 23 November, saying that he had celebrated the previous day 'in my own way by playing my favourite works – *Spring Symphony* – *Nocturne* and *War Requiem* – each in its different way a masterwork'. 'In the last years,' he continued, 'your music has come to mean more and more to me . . .'[114] Of all the birthday cards and letters Britten received, none can have been more touching than the one from T. J. E. Sewell which concluded: 'This letter requires no answer: it is really a note of thanks to yourself and an expression of my pride that I was once your headmaster.'[115] Britten, who in May 1962 had composed a setting of Psalm 150 for the centenary of what was now Old Buckenham Hall School, obviously did reply, with his usual well-judged courtesy and friendliness. But it was to William Plomer that he had already expressed his frank opinion of this whole birthday business: 'I feel that my age at the moment is centenarian, rather than demi-c., & that these concerts are memorial rather than celebratory, & these nice things being written are really obituaries. I know what it's like to be dead, now.'[116]

6

In the course of a birthday interview with Britten published in
the *London Magazine*, Charles Osborne began to ask an unfinished question: 'I think of you as primarily an opera composer,
and –' Osborne wasn't and isn't alone: the reader of Richard
Taruskin's enormous *Oxford History of Western Music* will find
Britten unequivocally described as 'a specialist in opera'.[117] But
his interruption of Osborne's question was impatient and
revealing: 'Well, I don't know that I do. Certainly I respond
very deeply to words, but not necessarily only opera. At the
moment, I think the finest thing I've written is my work for
'cello and orchestra which hasn't yet been performed.'[118] He
would in fact only write two more operas, of which one – *Owen
Wingrave*, composed for television in 1970 – is a special and
somewhat unsatisfactory case. In the meantime, there were to
be the three vocal and dramatic, but not operatic, works he
would call his 'church parables'; and if the first of these, *Curlew
River*, Op. 71, was to be premiered as planned during the 1964
Aldeburgh Festival, it was high time it got written.

Most uncharacteristically, Britten decided to go away for six
weeks to work on it: from mid-January until late February, he
and Pears were in Venice, where they stayed in 'a rambling
flat in a crazy old Palazzo on the Grand Canal';[119] Byron had
lived in it, an unsettling companion to the city's more familiar
literary ghosts, such as Henry James and Thomas Mann. Since
returning from America in 1942, Britten had seldom composed
away from his own study, but there's a hint here that he was
finding The Red House, for all its peace and space, a less creative
environment than Crabbe Street. He also needed a break from
niggling English difficulties: chief among these was the rapidly
unravelling situation at Boosey & Hawkes. For a while, following
Donald Mitchell's appointment, he had been optimistic: 'things

are looking up at B & H quite a bit',[120] he had told Nicholas Maw in October, while a month later he was enthusiastically welcoming Peter Maxwell Davies 'into the Boosey & Hawkes fold'.[121] But in December, Mitchell was asked to resign, following a series of disagreements with Ernst Roth; while Roth himself was to be succeeded on his retirement in 1964 by David Adams, until then president of Boosey & Hawkes Inc. in New York, who seemed to have little interest in contemporary music. In a letter to Mitchell from Venice, Britten (who by now couldn't even bring himself to write the initials 'B' and 'H') concluded with an apparently throwaway line: 'Love to you all, & don't worry too much about – & –; I'm sure there'll be some future. I occasion-ally dream of Faber + Faber – music publishers!'[122] Mitchell, who already advised Faber on music books, replied: 'You say you dream of F & F Music Publishers! Perhaps we ought to try & make the dream come true!'[123] He took the suggestion to Peter du Sautoy at Faber and he in turn discussed it with his chairman, Richard de la Mare, whose response was: 'I have no idea how this can be done, but clearly we have to do it.'[124]

Curlew River was making good progress in Venice: so much so that Britten wrote to Plomer on 15 February, asking him to spend a few days in Aldeburgh at the end of the month, when he could hear it played through. This duly happened on 27 February; afterwards, back in Sussex, Plomer wrote to say that he thought it 'a work of extraordinary originality, unity, force, and vitality'.[125] A few days later, Britten was 'off Eastwards in a whirl of music, visas, warm clothes (warm enough?), & unfinished projects':[126] he was flying to Moscow to conduct the first performance of 'the finest thing I've written', the Symphony for Cello and Orchestra, with Rostropovich as soloist and the Moscow Philharmonic Orchestra, in the Great Hall of the Moscow Conservatory on 12 March. Unlike the other composers repre-sented in the previous year's Festival of British Music, Britten had already become something of a musical hero in Russia: his music was available in Soviet editions and he had a huge student following. John Warrack, who attended the rehearsal, where Britten was 'in his element among friendly musicians', as well as the concert itself, reported that at the end of the performance 'the students in the gallery were overjoyed, stamping and hand-clapping until they got the finale encored'.[127] In his review for the *Daily Telegraph*, Warrack precisely echoed the composer's own feelings about the piece: it was, he said, 'Britten's finest instrumental work to date' and it would 'nail the dying view that Britten needs words for his music'.[128] On 16 March, Rostropovich, Britten and the Orchestra of the RSFSR – which, as Yulian Vainkop remarked with justifiable pride in *Leningradskaya Pravda*, 'mastered Britten's very difficult score in an exceptionally short time' – performed the work in the Great Hall of the Philharmonia in Leningrad, where the finale was again encored; during the composer's three days in the city, admiring students at the conservatory astonished and delighted him with an impromptu performance of extracts from his *War Requiem*.

The Cello Symphony is the last and the finest of Britten's regrettably small group of major orchestral works. Its sound-world and grammar have a good deal in common with the *Sinfonia da Requiem*, with which it shares the 'tragic key' of D minor, but it is more audacious and substantial. The opening allegro maestoso is by turns thunderous and brooding: it is, David Matthews notes, among Britten's darkest movements, 'the music struggling upwards from the murky opening sounds of tuba, contrabassoon and basses, but continually being beaten down by timpani strokes'.[129] It is followed by a neurotic, panicky scherzo which ends in a plaintive catlike mewing. The linked third and fourth movements are an adagio, which contrives to be both majestic and wistful, and an overwhelmingly wonderful passacaglia. This is a characteristic quest for redemption, whose final moments of precariously achieved resolution are as intensely moving as anything in Britten. As Michael Kennedy says, 'In terms of novel instrumental colouring, absorbing interplay of motifs and the emotional eloquence of the spiritual drama being enacted, this is Britten's orchestral apogee.'[130] Steven Isserlis, who at first disliked the work but found himself invited to record it in the late 1980s, remembers the 'epiphany' in which he fell in love with it, 'because it is a masterpiece': 'I happened to be playing at around that time at Snape Maltings, and decided to take a walk across the marshes before the concert. At one point I stood still and listened to the haunting silence; suddenly the thought came to me: "This is it. This is where Britten's music comes from!"'[131]

Britten's popularity in the USSR had usefully practical consequences. He told Madame Furtseva that he would extend Rostropovich's exclusive right to perform as soloist in the Cello Symphony until the end of 1965, whereupon she granted permission for the cellist to record the work with Britten and the English Chamber Orchestra for Decca; the sessions took place at Kingsway Hall in London during July. Concert performances of *Peter Grimes* in Leningrad in late March resulted in three separate proposals for staged productions, and the Bolshoi expressed interest in *A Midsummer Night's Dream*. While in Moscow, Britten was paid four hundred roubles in royalties for an edition of his 'selected vocal music' which had been published there: this he had to leave in a Russian bank account (cheerfully enough, since he rightly anticipated further visits), although he realised that some of it belonged to Boosey & Hawkes and mentioned this to Ernst Roth. Roth's response, no doubt coloured by Britten's reluctance to assign publication rights for *Curlew River* to B&H, was discouraging: he strongly advised Britten against making his music freely available in the USSR, a country from which it was impossible to extract payment, and tetchily added

that 'Roubles in a Russian bank are no use to us'.[132] He entirely
failed to understand Britten's enthusiasm for Russia, which was
founded not only on his creative partnership with Rostropovich
but also on the rapport he had established with predominantly
young audiences. With them, he seemed to achieve the direct-
ness of communication and response for which he had always
hoped and which in England had often eluded him; perhaps,
after all, he hadn't been so badly misrepresented in that *Pravda*
interview.

Pears had not been in Russia with Britten – he had engagements in Oxford, Edinburgh, Rotterdam and Amsterdam during
March – but the following month both men were 'off East'
again, this time to Budapest and Prague, where they performed
Britten's *Michelangelo Sonnets* and *Hölderlin-Fragmente* and
Schubert's *Winterreise*. In Budapest, they met Zoltán Kodály,
another important musical friendship and (naturally) a recruit
for the Aldeburgh Festival, and a pair of twelve-year-old twin
musical prodigies, Zoltán and Gábor Jeney, for whom Britten
was to compose his *Gemini Variations*, Op. 73. Meanwhile, in
England, Faber Music – at first a division of the publishing
house, later a separate company with Britten on its board – was
swiftly becoming a reality. Richard de la Mare, having asked
himself what they would have done if Mozart had approached
them and asked them to publish his music, had only one answer:
in May, Britten signed a five-year contract which committed
him to writing 'four new major works and six new minor works
if possible'. *Curlew River* was to be the first, and it would appear
with one of Berthold Wolpe's distinctively calligraphed covers,
exactly as if it were a Faber book of poetry. Britten was delighted;
so was the firm's most distinguished poet and former editorial
director, T. S. Eliot.

Curlew River marked an ending as well as a beginning: when
her work on it was complete, Imogen Holst retired as Britten's

music assistant. She had originally intended to stay another three years, until her sixtieth birthday, before devoting herself to the promotion of her father's music in the approach to his centenary in 1974; but a resurgence of interest in Holst's music was already under way, stimulated in part by her own recording of his *Choral Fantasia* and *Psalm 86* for EMI in 1964. Moreover, she was soon to embark on the huge task of cataloguing his manuscripts and, with the help of Britten's solicitor and accountant, Isador Caplan and Leslie Periton, of reorganising the management of his estate. In any case, after a decade of working so intensely with Britten, it was time for a break: although she has often been portrayed as cranky and unworldly, in choosing that moment for herself she showed far shrewder judgement than many of her Aldeburgh colleagues. Consequently, she remained close to Britten – and involved with the Aldeburgh Festival – for the rest of his life. She was succeeded as his amanuensis by Rosamund Strode.

The 1964 festival included several momentous events, one of which was wholly unexpected. Sviatoslav Richter, unheralded by the programme, provided a 'truly unforgettable' Schubert recital in the parish church. 'Where else but in Aldeburgh,' asked the *Daily Telegraph*, 'is one likely to stumble inadvertently on the experience of a lifetime?'[133] There was the first English performance of the Cello Symphony by Rostropovich and the ECO under Britten in Blythburgh Church, 'the cathedral of the marshes', while in an actual cathedral – Ely – there was the *War Requiem*. Julian Bream gave the first performance of the *Nocturnal after John Dowland*, Op. 70, which Britten had composed the previous autumn, in the weeks before his unwanted fiftieth birthday celebrations: though it self-evidently belongs to the sequence of sleep-and-dream pieces which includes *A Midsummer Night's Dream* and the *Nocturne*, the eight disturbed and fractured variations (culminating, of course, in a passacaglia) which precede the eventual statement of Dowland's 'Come, heavy sleep' are

mostly suggestive of anxious insomnia. Britten himself said of
the *Nocturnal* that 'it has some very, to me, disturbing images
in it . . . inspired by . . . the Dowland song, which of course
has some very strange undertones in it'.[134] Although the comparison of sleep with death was much more commonplace in
Elizabethan poetry than Britten seems to acknowledge here, this
is certainly a powerfully haunting example of it:

> Come, heavy Sleep, the image of true Death,
>   And close up these my weary weeping eyes,
> Whose spring of tears doth stop my vital breath,
>   And tears my heart with Sorrow's sigh-swoll'n cries.
> Come and possess my tired thought-worn soul,
> That living dies, till thou on me be stole.
>
> Come, shadow of my end, and shape of rest,
>   Allied to Death, child to this black-faced Night;
> Come thou and charm these rebels in my breast,
>   Whose waking fancies doth my mind affright.
> O come, sweet Sleep, come or I die for ever;
> Come ere my last sleep comes, or come never.[135]

It was perhaps the duality of the second stanza, in which sleep
is perceived first as like death and then as death's only alternative, which struck Britten as 'very strange.'

The most eagerly and nervously anticipated premiere was
undoubtedly that of *Curlew River*, given – like that of *Noye's
Fludde* – in the parish church at Orford. A violent thunderstorm
on the evening of 13 June cut the power and delayed the start
for half an hour. This intensified the occasion's mystical significance for some in the audience, but it was almost too much for
the already fraught performers; Britten, however, remained
outwardly calm and in control, just as he would in a later and

far more serious crisis. There was much to be fraught about in *Curlew River*. The casting of Pears in the role of the Madwoman had already aroused reactions varying from hilarity to rage, even among those who should have known better: Imogen Holst remembered how Stephen Reiss had spent an hour one morning, when she was trying to work on the score, telling her that they 'must stop Ben writing this because of what people would think about Peter singing a woman's part'.[136] Given the work's origin in all-male Noh drama, this was of course non-negotiable. Then there was the music itself: gamelan-inspired and conductorless, for a weird concoction of instruments quite unlike the small orchestras of the chamber operas. It was meant to be loose and unsynchronised – one reason why Britten so enjoyed writing for children was their ability to get things creatively wrong – with a new notation in the score, the 'curlew mark', to indicate where the performers must listen to the others and hold a note until everything was back in place. Though *Curlew River* is a short, one-act work, it is enormously ambitious in its superimposition of different worlds: Japanese drama and medieval Suffolk in the text, an asymmetrical chiming of East and West in the music. The anonymous *Times* reviewer found it 'strange, unpretentious yet infinitely solemn' and speculated that it might be 'the start of a new, perhaps the most important stage in Britten's creative life'.[137]

In July, Britten travelled to Aspen, Colorado, to receive the first Aspen Award for Humanistic Studies. Selected 'from among more than a hundred artists, scholars, writers, poets, philosophers, and statesmen who had been nominated by leaders in intellectual and cultural fields throughout the world', he repaid the honour with the finest and fullest of his acceptance speeches – '*our* speech', as he described it to Pears, who had played a substantial part in drafting it. The theme which underpins it is the occasional nature of music and its corollary, the sense of music as an occasion. He cites the aptness and oddness of the slung mugs in *Noye's Fludde* as one instance of a composition crafted for its occasion – and for 'the pleasure the young performers will have in playing it' – and the suitability of the *War Requiem* for the vast space of Coventry Cathedral as another: 'Music does not exist in a vacuum, it does not exist until it is performed, and a performance imposes conditions.' Yet this doesn't mean that the composer should write either for 'pressure groups which demand true proletarian music' or for 'snobs who demand the latest *avant-garde* tricks'. Nor, he adds, is the composer's task made any easier by society's attitude towards him: 'semi-Socialist Britain, and Conservative Britain before it, has for years treated the musician as a curiosity to be barely tolerated'. Music should be not only an occasion but a special occasion: Britten takes a sustained swipe at broadcast and recorded music – doubtless to the puzzlement of anyone unaware of his father's formative views on the matter – and insists that a live musical performance 'demands some preparation, some effort, a journey to a special place, saving up for a ticket, some homework on the programme perhaps, some clarification of the ears and sharpening of the instincts'. It's important to note here that he is not claiming music as the preserve of the privileged or the wealthy, for whom 'saving up for a ticket' would hardly be necessary.

In the most famous part of his address – the section in which, as we've already seen, he thanks the USA for being the place in which he discovered Crabbe and *Peter Grimes* and 'realised where I belonged and what I lacked' – he returns to the subject of the 'small corner of East Anglia' where he has lived ever since then. Although, he says, he enjoys travelling, making new friends and giving concerts 'with a congenial partner', he belongs in Aldeburgh: 'I have tried to bring music *to* it in the shape of our local Festival; and all the music I write comes *from* it.'[138] The whole speech amounts to a wonderfully coherent summary of Britten's credo, yet it's significant that he no longer attempts to evoke the physical presence of Aldeburgh and the Suffolk coast, which might have been especially beguiling for his American audience. That was already beginning to seem like a place of the memory and the mind: he had stepped back from the shore.

The day after his return from America, Britten conducted, with Meredith Davies, a televised Prom performance of the *War Requiem* at the Albert Hall. By now, both he and Pears were exhausted by their extraordinary schedule of engagements, and they promised themselves a complete break from performing. 'It has been a hectic Summer – now turning into an equally hectic Autumn,' Britten told Plomer in September; 'the only way Peter & I feel we can cope is to cling like mad to our sabbatical 1965 – only 4 months to go!'[139] Inevitably, it would turn out to be more of a sabbatical for Pears than for Britten, who could no more stop thinking about music (and therefore, sooner or later, composing) than he could stop breathing. What, asked John Warrack in an interview for *Musical America*, were his plans for his year off?

> To write a lot of music! But first a holiday. We're going to India for six weeks in January and February, and in the late autumn there's a very exciting plan to drive through Russia with the Rostropoviches. Then, apart from the Aldeburgh and Long Melford festivals, composing. I'm going to do a solo cello sonata for Rostropovich – nothing down yet, though. And there is to be a song-cycle for Fischer-Dieskau, in memory of his wife, for baritone and chamber group – English poetry, but it's not chosen yet. That'll be for Aldeburgh.[140]

He added that there would also be 'another church parable kind of work' on an Old Testament subject (*The Burning Fiery Furnace*) and tantalisingly mentioned what would have surely been the most bizarre of all his unrealised projects: an opera on a modern subject which was to include 'a scene in an airport' and a tennis party.

The First Suite for Cello, Op. 72, written in December 1964, had been 'commissioned' by Rostropovich under somewhat eccentric circumstances during his summer visit to England. He and Britten, travelling north with Marion Harewood for a recital at Miki Sekers's Rosehill Theatre in Whitehaven, were to stop at Harewood House, where the Earl of Harewood's mother, Princess Mary, was in residence. In a restaurant in Lincoln, it became clear that Rostropovich had practised an elaborate curtsy which he was determined to perform in front of the elderly and easily offended Princess, whom he obstinately envisaged in fairy-tale terms. Britten, horrified by this, was obliged to sign, on the back of a menu, a 'contract' to write 'six major works for cello in recompense for which Slava Rostropovich will agree not to perform his pirouette in front of Princess Mary'.[141] In the event, he would only complete half of Bach's total. Despite the austerity of its opening Canto, the first suite is a work of charming contrasts, from its eloquently touching Lamento to its richly comic Marcia, and with a disconcerting surprise when a ghostly reminiscence of the Elgar concerto appears in the penultimate Bordone. Rostropovich was to give the first performance during the 1965 Aldeburgh Festival.

When Rostropovich reluctantly failed to curtsy to Princess Mary (whom he discovered knitting), Lord Harewood was away at the Holland Festival; his marriage to Marion had broken down completely, following the birth of his son with Patricia Tuckwell on 4 July, and Britten had consequently ended their friendship. Just before he and Pears left for India the following January, Britten wrote to Harewood suggesting that, as it would no longer be possible for him to visit the Aldeburgh Festival, he should resign as its president: this he did in due course by writing to Fidelity Cranbrook, who thought Britten had been silly and priggish. A certain priggishness was an inalienable part of his nature, yet there were nobler motives at work: his old friend George had hurt his older and deeper friend Marion; the code of loyalty, to which he steadfastly adhered in his own private life, had been affronted. No one who knew him would have expected him to behave differently. Harewood himself was saddened but not shocked and, when his mother Princess Mary died at the end of March, there was a civilised exchange of letters between the two men: in a postscript to his, Harewood congratulated Britten on having just been admitted to the Order of Merit, succeeding T. S. Eliot (who had died on 4 January) as one of the twenty-four holders of the honour and following in the footsteps of two previous composers, Elgar and Vaughan Williams. His favour with the royal family evidently remained undiminished.

CHAPTER 8

THE BUILDING OF THE HOUSE

1965–71

1

Britten and Pears set off for Wolfsgarten on 16 January 1965 to join their other royal friends, the Hesses, who were to accompany them to India: together, they flew over Yugoslavia and Greece ('with Olympus and its inhabitants over far to the right'), stopped in Beirut and Karachi, and were met by their friend Narayana Menon in Delhi, where they were to give a recital. Pears began, but failed to sustain, a detailed travel diary and wrote descriptive letters to friends; for his part, Britten sent regular dispatches to the thirteen-year-old John Newton, who had sung in the second cast of *Curlew River* and toured with the English Opera Group as Miles in *The Turn of the Screw* and Harry in *Albert Herring*. He had stayed at Aldeburgh during November, 'a sweet affectionate child – makes one rather feel what one has missed in not having a child';[1] Britten was providing some assistance with the fees at Cawston College, where he had just begun to board. 'Things will seem rather strange, but soon they will all straighten out, and you won't remember that you were ever a "new boy",' Britten reassured him in his first letter. His sympathetic understanding of the schoolboy's world was as acute as ever, although by the mid-1960s the tone may have begun to sound a bit dated, and it seemed that his magnetism for the young was international: at the Red Fort in Delhi, 'a serious young boy' had already tried to attach himself to the party, subsequently following their car through the crowded streets. When they were stopped 'by the jumble of cars, bicycles, people and cows . . . he came right up to the car window, looking appealing'; he appeared happy and well dressed, Britten noted, 'so it wasn't money he wanted'.[2] Pears thought that the boy 'seemed to regard us as some vehicles to a wider world' and added: 'Ben's heart was touched, so was the boy's.'[3]

They dined with the 'charming and intelligent' Mrs Indira Gandhi, who took them to a folk-dance rehearsal for the imminent National Day; they performed their recital ('I wasn't too hopeless on the old piano,' said Britten); they drove to Agra and revisited the Taj Mahal; then they flew to Udaipur, to stay at the Lake Palace Hotel – 'the most exquisite hotel you can imagine' or, in Pears's words, 'a white meringue in a lake'.[4] The place brought out the ornithologist in both men. Britten, in his second 'batch of diary' for John Newton, listed 'pelicans, lots of them, storks, cranes, stilts (tall white birds with red legs), cormorants (like Aldeburgh) and their bigger cousins the Indian Darters, Ibis (white and black), herons of all kinds, terns (like Aldeburgh again, but an Indian variety), kingfishers, spoonbills, green bee-eaters, flycatcher (but not the Red House kind), and on one particular island at sunset, millions of green Parakeets . . .'[5] Pears, not to be outdone, wrote to his friend Hélène Rohlfs about 'all sorts of strange birds . . . brilliant green paraqueets with long tails which fan out quickly as they land . . . storks and cranes, bright blue big kingfishers, curlews, ibis, paddy-birds, little waders, pelicans (huge yawns!), vultures, many kinds of long legged grey birds, standing up on their nests on the tops of trees'.[6] There were also crocodiles in the lake: Pears merely noted their presence, but Britten, perhaps improving on the occasion for his young reader in Norfolk, reported that the largest of the crocodiles grinned at them as 'the engine of the motor boat refused to start and we drifted helplessly on – I wondered if I'd ever see Aldeburgh, or you, or Cawston College again!'[7] He ate too much curry and endured 'the worst tummy-ache of my life'; yet, despite this and the crocodiles, both he and Pears described the place as 'paradise'.

A few days later, the slums of Bombay provided a sharp contrast, but Britten noted with admiration how clean the inhabitants were, despite their squalid surroundings. In Madras, they dined with William Paterson, the British deputy high commissioner, whose schoolboy son had been 'dotty about pop music, and suddenly developed a craze for *my* music (quite a compliment, or not, do you think??!!)'.[8] Britten's approval-seeking insecurity here is as characteristic and touching as his bemusement about pop culture: the Beatles, he would tell an interviewer in October that year, were 'charming creatures; I don't happen to like their music, but that's just me'.[9] They visited a children's home, where he met the boy whom he and Princess Margaret had sponsored on their previous visit, and the Kalakshetra School of Music and Dancing. Then they took to the hills, travelling to Ootacamund, or 'Ooty', which Britten described, with the slightest hint of disapproval, as 'a relic of the English occupation' but which was 'delightfully cool'. Cochin was different again, eight thousand feet lower and terrifically hot. Next came 'the most exciting part of our whole trip', a visit to Thekkaday in Kerala, 'a Game Reserve, round a large artificial lake, made by damming a river, the Periya'.[10] They stayed at a bungalow in the middle of the lake, and once again Britten provided an idyllic description of the place and its wildlife for John Newton. Pears also enthused, in letters to his friends Oliver Holt and Hélène Rohlfs, about 'the song of the red whiskered bul-bul, very melodious, and the sweet warble of the gold-fronted charopsis or leaf-bird', 'the hoop-hoop-hoop-hoop of the brown faced blank monkeys' and the bison, which resembled 'huge muscle-bound leather dreadnoughts';[11] although there was also an unnamed bird 'whose song is deadly monotonous and disturbs Ben, who is working on a piece for the Hungarian twin boys who are coming to the Festival with Kodály'.[12] Then it was back to Bombay – via another bird sanctuary and another magnetised twelve-year-old boy – from where they flew to London on 1 March. Jeremy Cullum met them at the airport in Pears's new Rover and drove them through snow-covered Essex home to Aldeburgh.

Colin Graham had suggested *Anna Karenina* as the basis for an opera and Britten read the novel while in India, although he rather understandably wondered how he might fit it into one evening or perhaps even two; nothing was to come of the idea. But he did finish the *Gemini Variations*, which he described to Elizabeth Mayer as 'a romp for 2 little boys': he sent it off to the Jeney twins on 13 March. Subtitled 'Quartet for Two Players' in the published score, it is a typically ingenious set of twelve variations and a fugue on a theme from the fourth of Kodály's *Epigrams*, designed for the Jeneys' multi-instrumental talents and including such instructions as 'Gábor takes Violin' and 'Zoltán first turns to page 12, then takes Flute'. Before they gave the first performance at the 1965 Aldeburgh Festival, there was to be a charming exchange of letters concerning their piano stool, which had to be specially made to their customary height of fifty centimetres: 'We hope that it will be the right size for you,' Rosamund Strode wrote to them, 'and very slippery so that you can move about quickly on it when you have to.'[13]

However, Britten's major composition that spring was the *Songs and Proverbs of William Blake*, Op. 74, written for Dietrich Fischer-Dieskau. Although he reassuringly told Pears that he found other singers 'rather non-inspiring to write for', he had already been sufficiently inspired by Fischer-Dieskau to create the baritone part in the *War Requiem* for him; now, batting aside the singer's interesting suggestion of a cycle which would have set a number of Shakespeare sonnets together with their German translation by Paul Celan, he turned to fourteen items by Blake, selected by Pears, interleaving poems from the *Songs of Experience* and *Anguries of Innocence* with *Proverbs of Hell*. He told Fischer-Dieskau that it would be 'big and serious', and he was as good as his word: in its almost unremitting pessimism, the work feels as if it is fulfilling a promise made long ago by an earlier Blake setting, 'The Sick Rose', from the *Serenade*. Even the Chimney Sweeper's transitory joy ('Because I was happy upon the heath, / And smil'd among the winter's snow . . .') barely relieves the bleakness, while 'A Poison Tree', the third song, is devastatingly powerful: as in the *Nocturne*, Britten embeds the darkest material close to the cycle's centre and, as in *Winter Words*, it takes a blameless creature of nature (here, 'The Fly') to coax him into comparatively benign mood; the final song, 'Every Night and every Morn', from *Auguries of Innocence*, is a distant cousin of the 'Lyke-Wake Dirge' in the *Serenade*. In several respects, therefore, *Songs and Proverbs of William Blake*, Britten's last cycle of songs setting English poetry, clearly connects with its predecessors; yet its interwoven construction and uncompromising starkness mark it out as something quite new. Like much of Britten's sparsely textured and (in a misleading sense) almost 'simple' late work, it is extremely difficult to get right: Fischer-Dieskau and Britten, giving the first performance in the Jubilee Hall, Aldeburgh, on 24 June 1965, evidently managed to do just that but, as *The Times*'s reviewer perceptively remarked, 'Mediocre musicians will touch these songs at their peril.' For Peter Heyworth in the *Observer*, it was 'conceivably the finest cycle that Britten has yet given us'.[14]

William Plomer had been working on the libretto for a

second 'church parable' based on the Old Testament story of the three Israelites condemned by Nebuchadnezzar to perish in the burning fiery furnace (and their miraculous survival); Britten liked to call it 'the firy boys' but Plomer, when he sent a draft version in July, gave it the novelistic working title *Strangers in Babylon*. Britten, meanwhile, had a rather tiresome commission to complete before his and Pears's next foreign adventure: this was *Voices for Today*, Op. 75, a work for unaccompanied voices to mark the twentieth anniversary of the United Nations. He chose to cram into a short piece words from fifteen suitably peaceful authors, with the result that each text has the brevity, though not usually the wit, of an epigram. Among them are 'Force is not a remedy', 'Burning stakes do not lighten the darkness' and this impenetrably gnomic sentence from Camus: 'The fruits of the spirit are slower to ripen than intercontinental missiles.' *Voices for Today* received simultaneous first performances on 24 October in London, New York and Paris.

Since their return from India, the sabbatical travellers had already spent an enjoyable if damp fortnight in the Dordogne with Stephen Reiss and his wife Beth; then, early in August, following a performance by Rostropovich of the Cello Symphony at the Festival Hall, they left to spend a month in the USSR with 'Slava' and 'Galya'. Apart from obvious indulgences – Ben's cars, Peter's paintings – they were cautious about money, carefully budgeting and itemising their travel expenses, but they were happy to accept, gratefully and politely, the hospitality of others: both the caution and the acceptance were typical legacies of their middle-class and public-school backgrounds. They may not have fully appreciated that an extended trip to Russia was very different from visiting well-off dignitaries (and travelling with royalty) in India. 'How would I feed these gentlemen for a whole month?' wondered Galina. 'Where would I find edible steak for them, and fresh fish?'[15] Britten had already sensed that

things mightn't be 'wholly happy with those two tumultuous characters'[16] and so he may not have been surprised by the eruption, on their second morning at the Rostropovich dacha, of a first-class row, 'an occasional banged door from upstairs keeping us alert, forte soprano, piano calmando legato baritone', as Pears put it.[17] Galina was protesting at the impossibility of their planned visit to the composers' colony near Dilizhan in the mountains of Armenia; however, as Pears wisely observed, 'You can't say no to Slava.' So they duly went, staying in bungalows reserved for important visitors and being handsomely entertained by members of the Armenian Composers' Union. Pears in his travel diary recorded both the magnificent landscapes and the splendid meals, although Vishnevskaya would later remark, without rancour, that neither he nor Britten 'ever knew what heroic efforts it took to arrange all those wonderful picnics, those trips high up in the mountains'.[18] But they were properly appreciative, all the same, as a postcard from Pears to Barbara Britten makes clear: 'We are in the most heavenly high green valley with glorious oak woods and v. hot sun: the wild flowers are fantastic. Galya & Slava could not be kinder & we eat & drink far too much with predictable results.'[19] Both men were astonished and impressed by the composers' colony itself. Britten, in an article called 'A Composer in Russia', published in the *Sunday Telegraph*, described how an Armenian composer could spend weeks there, with his family, at little cost: in his bungalow he would have 'a study with a piano, a living room, a bedroom and bathroom' and would 'eat in the big central building which also has a library, a room with gramophone and tape-machines'; Britten wished 'something similar could happen in England' but feared 'that composers are still not taken as seriously here as over there'.[20] Pears tried wryly to envisage a comparable institution, with comparable guests, in England: 'Can one imagine Arthur Bliss, William Walton and Ben and

lots more taking their holidays together on Windermere and entertaining Fischer-Dieskau and Henze for a month? Not quite.'[21]

As they were leaving England, Britten had bought at the airport a Penguin parallel text of Pushkin's poems; while in Armenia, he set six of them as *The Poet's Echo*, Op. 76. The cycle, dedicated 'For Galya and Slava', is precisely designed for Galina Vishnevskaya's voice: 'so much so', says John Bridcut, perhaps a little unkindly, 'that the shrill, often unforgiving tone that characterised her singing seems woven into Britten's score'.[22] Some of the piano writing too (for example, in 'The Nightingale and the Rose') has the raw, self-punishing inwardness that is the least grateful characteristic of Britten's later work, but the last song, 'Lines Written during a Sleepless Night', with its insomniac theme and ticking accompaniment, returns to an earlier, friendlier mode. When the Rostropoviches and their guests had flown back from Yerevan to Moscow, Slava insisted on driving them in his Mercedes to Pushkin's birthplace in Mikhailovskoe, a distance of some thousand kilometres, where they arrived unannounced but were warmly welcomed by the curator and his wife. After dinner, they were persuaded to give an impromptu performance of *The Poet's Echo*, part sung by Vishnevskaya and part hummed by Pears, accompanied by Britten on an upright piano. Pears noted in his diary that, when they reached the final song, 'Hardly had the little old piano begun its dry tick tock tick tock, than clear and silvery outside the window, a yard from our heads, came ding ding ding, not loud but clear, Pushkin's clock joining in his song.' He added that it 'seemed to strike far more than midnight' and that afterwards they 'sat spell-bound'.[23]

The day before Britten and Pears flew back to England, the quartet dined with Dmitri and Irina Shostakovich at their dacha outside Moscow. Delayed by extreme roadworks – at one point,

the passengers had to walk through ankle-deep mud, while Rostropovich drove gingerly on, and at another a group of soldiers cleared the surface so they could pass – they arrived three hours late to find themselves presented with an enormous meal: 'various caviars, cold meats, pâtés, yoghourts, cheese, chicken casserole, hot and cold fish, pastry, tarts, éclairs, vodka, brandy, wine, all at once'. After this, the 'welcoming and amiable' Shostakovich prevailed upon Britten and Pears to perform the Pushkin songs, to which he listened with admiration. Next morning, the company reassembled for breakfast, 'at the same table covered with much the same food': 'Ben and I both found chicken casserole perfectly possible, preceded by cognac or vodka, an important prelude, I fancy,'[24] wrote Pears blithely, although quite how Britten's delicate stomach had survived the month's culinary exertions remains a mystery. Thus fortified, they shopped and lunched in Moscow before going on to the airport and flying home just in time to rehearse for the next Long Melford Bach weekend. They sent a telegram to their Russian hosts:

DEAREST SLAVA & GALYA
WE CAN NEVER THANK YOU ENOUGH FOR OUR GLORIOUS HOLIDAY SO HAPPY SO FULL SO KIND STOP ALL ALDEBURGH IS PREPARING FOR YOUR CHRISTMAS

YOUR LOVING
PETER & BEN[25]

The Rostropoviches, after giving the first performance of *The Poet's Echo* in Moscow on 2 December, were to spend Christmas at The Red House, where they fully entered into Britten's eclectic mixture of sophisticated and childlike entertainments – proving to be virtuoso performers at Happy Families and enjoying the excellent conjuror who entertained a party of ninety in the recently constructed library on Boxing Day. The Suffolk–Russian connection, by no means the least of Britten's achievements and one which would outlive him, was now firmly established.

Meanwhile, the second church parable, *The Burning Fiery Furnace*, Op. 77, was making only slow progress: he admitted to Plomer that 'it can't be really said to have caught fire yet'.[26] The autumn had brought not only interruptions – such as a trip to Helsinki to accept a prize named after a composer he didn't much admire, Sibelius – but a distracting and distressing family crisis: the long-anticipated break-up of his sister Beth's marriage to Kit Welford. She was in the midst of divorce proceedings, drinking heavily, wandering 'helplessly from friend to friend' and proving 'very difficult to help'.[27] Then, after the jollities of a Rostropovian Christmas, Britten succumbed once again to illness. This time it was diverticulitis, which necessitated an operation and three weeks in hospital, followed by a lengthy recuperation at The Red House and a convalescent holiday in Marrakesh with Anthony Gishford. 'I do hope you don't mind too much about Morocco,' he wrote to Pears on 3 April, adding that he was 'determined to give you a lovely Easter here'.[28] Pears minded less about Morocco than about his partner's constant procession of ailments, which he found inconvenient and irritating as well as troubling. Now, once again, Britten was apologising for having been 'such a drag on you these last years' and resolving that 'you'll never have to give my health . . . another thought', a resolution whose fulfilment was completely beyond his powers. At least while Britten was away Pears could get on with yet another London move, from their flat in Anne Wood's house to 99 Offord Road, N1, next door to his niece Susan Phipps, who was now their agent: this proved to combine most of the known house-moving nightmares, including wet weather and wet paint, electricians and gas fitters getting in the way, and Pears's piano being temporarily lost. 'Thank God,' he sighed, 'that Ben was in Marrakesh!'[29]

Enforced convalescence enabled Britten to finish *The Burning Fiery Furnace* in April; it was to receive its first performance at the 1966 Aldeburgh Festival. It would, he said, use 'the same instruments' and 'the same kinds of technique' as *Curlew River*, but would be 'much less sombre, an altogether gayer affair'.[30] The instruments are in fact augmented by an alto trombone, representing the biblical sackbut, and some exotic percussion, but the form – including the monastic plainsong frame – closely paralleled that of the earlier work. Whether it is really 'altogether gayer' is debatable, although it certainly concludes more cheerfully: this is, of course, another of Britten's redemptions, and it belongs, with *Saint Nicolas* and *Canticle II: Abraham and Isaac*, to that particular sub-category in which boys are miraculously saved from apparently certain death and the element of gaiety is withheld until the very end (the same principle of delayed gratification also applies to instrumental works as different in scale as the Dowland variations and the Cello Symphony). 'If *The Burning Fiery Furnace* touches sensibilities on the raw less than *Curlew River*, its sounds are even more beautiful,' says Michael Kennedy. 'To hear the final Benedicte in the gathering darkness of a noble church or cathedral is to participate in a musical experience of rare spiritual force.'[31]

At the end of 1966, the Rostropoviches insisted on repaying the previous winter's hospitality by inviting Britten and Pears to Moscow for Christmas: as was by now to be expected on such occasions, a certain amount of organisational chaos was more than offset by their hosts' warmth and generosity. It wasn't entirely a holiday: the visitors gave two recitals, one each in Moscow and Leningrad. The first of these was at four in the afternoon on Christmas Day (which of course *wasn't* Christmas Day in the Russian Orthodox calendar) at the Moscow

Conservatoire, where there was only half an hour available for rehearsal; so they arranged to rehearse at the Rostropoviches' flat at noon. Pears takes up the story in his diary:

> After breakfast we waited. No Slava. I practised, in despair, for an hour. At last, Slava, at 1 o'clock. I had particularly asked if we could eat early, no later than 1. We sat down at 1.45. The concert got nearer and nearer. We finished with strong coffee at 2.50. Drive to Hotel, through thick snow of course, quick change, drive to Conservatoire, five minutes on stage for practice, and lights. Fuss with nice intelligent woman who will announce *Dichterliebe* as first half, instead of Dowland–Purcell–Schubert. Last-minute crowd in artists' room until I sing them all out fortissimo . . . It is a big lofty hall but beautiful, with a fine acoustic and a marvellous warm feeling. Heavenly audience, quiet as mice and immensely warm and enthusiastic.[32]

That evening they dined with the Rostropoviches – 'a splendid spread, with an excellent goose' – where Dmitri and Irina Shostakovich were the other guests (and Shostakovich the triumphant Happy Families winner); they talked 'about Stravinsky and the drivelling muck written about Dmitri by [Nicholas] Nabokov' and Britten told the assembled company of a recent dream in which Stravinsky had appeared 'as a monumental hunchback pointing with quivering finger at a passage in the Cello Symphony "How dare you write that bar?"'[33] The following day, Britten and Pears had a lengthy dinner with Sviatoslav and Nina Richter which stretched into planning Richter's programme for the following year's Aldeburgh Festival. They welcomed the new year in style at the Rostropovich dacha, with a peripatetic meal divided among three houses which ended at 3.30 in the morning.

They were hardly back in England before it was time to set off for a holiday in the Caribbean – a destination somewhat out of character, chosen because of the Venice floods, but one where 'slow-moving relaxed days seemed to go on for ever'.[34] Britten, however, returned with his traditional winter illness and in early February he was 'feeling as near death as only 'flu can make me'.[35] He had written a little folk-song-based fanfare piece for wind and percussion, 'Hankin Booby' – eventually to be incorporated into his *Suite on English Folk Tunes: 'A Time There Was'* – for the opening of the Queen Elizabeth Hall; he conducted the inaugural concert there on 1 March 1967. As he was doing so, he must have reflected with satisfaction that before long he would have a concert hall of his own.

2

When malting at Snape ended in 1965, the disused buildings across the river from the Old Mill were sold to Gooderham & Hayward, who proposed to produce and store animal feeds in some of them and to let out the rest. Stephen Reiss, in search of storage space for English Opera Group scenery, decided to have a look: some way behind the handsome frontage, with its arches and staircases and clock, he discovered a 'great barn-like place', the redundant Malt House. It was, however, only barn-like on the outside; within, it was divided by drying floors and internal walls, so it was difficult to get a sense of it as an empty space. Nevertheless, its external dimensions and its Brittenesque situation – with views across reed beds to the river and Iken Church on its promontory – irresistibly suggested a concert hall. Fidelity Cranbrook took the festival's treasurer, Charles Gifford, to see it and they were both 'aghast': 'We decided it was a madness.'[36] Britten's career had been punctuated by achieved madnesses: the wartime Atlantic crossing, the reopening of Sadler's Wells with *Peter Grimes*, the unfeasibly all-male *Billy Budd* were among the many occasions on which Britten must have said, as Richard de la Mare had said of Faber Music: 'I have no idea how this can be done, but clearly we have to do it.' And that now was Britten's attitude to the Maltings.

It had to be done. Stephen Reiss's inspired hunch was swiftly to find the right man to do it. He approached Arup Associates, who had been working on musical spaces such as the Queen Elizabeth Hall in London and 'the agony of the Sydney Opera House',[37] and was soon in touch with Derek Sugden, a regular festival-goer and, as it happened, already an admirer of the nineteenth-century industrial buildings at Snape. Sugden coped calmly with the contradictions of Britten's specification. The Maltings was to be a concert hall, not an opera house, but a hall in which opera could somehow work; and it was also to function as a recording venue for Decca and the BBC, thus further reducing the need for Britten to visit the capital, his dislike of which had by now intensified into a phobia. Consequently, its acoustics would have to be as good when the hall was empty as when it was full. Then there was the budget. Sugden knew that the Queen Elizabeth Hall, with roughly the same number of seats, was going to cost about three million pounds. Britten said they couldn't spend a penny more than £50,000; Sugden replied that it would be at least £100,000; so they amiably agreed that they would worry about that later. By the end of 1965, Stephen Reiss had produced a concise and clear brief, while Sugden had responded with a full survey and report. At that point, says Sugden, 'Stephen rang me up and just said, "Start!" I loved that.'[38]

Britten had at first imagined the project in simple terms of gutting the building and putting in the stage, seating and lighting of a concert hall, but it was far more complex than that. Years of heat had turned the original roof timbers to charcoal; and the roof would in any case have to be raised by about two feet, if only to prevent users of the bar and restaurant from continually bumping into beams. So a new roof had to be designed, brilliantly incorporating ventilators which resembled the smoke hoods of the old Malt House. Some parts of the building had heavy foundations which had to be removed and replaced; others had footings which were poor or non-existent. Excavations filled up with water and had to be pumped out, while 'Any attempt to use a mechanical digger in these conditions turned any clay present into a soup-like slurry which was nearly impossible to remove'.[39] Rather than put the project out to tender, Arup Associates wisely agreed a price with the builders William C. Reade of Aldeburgh, realising that local knowledge and loyalty might turn out to be priceless: their foreman, Bill Muttit, 'didn't have to have any project managers telling him what to do next', Sugden noted. 'It was all in his head.'[40] Meanwhile, the Arts Council, Decca, the Gulbenkian Foundation and the Pilgrim Trust had contributed to an appeal fund which was still well short of its target.

In a spirit entirely appropriate to the sparseness and bleakness of coastal Suffolk, Britten, Reiss and Sugden made a virtue of their enforced frugality. As Sugden wrote, with quiet pride, soon after the hall's completion:

There are no finishing materials, as such, at Snape; the fabric of the building forms the finish both inside and out. The roof and the pine joists in the foyer are exposed and left natural. The brick walls in the auditorium have been patched and raised with old red facing bricks saved from the demolition, and the new piers and arches in the foyer have been built in new red facing bricks. All the old walls have been grit-blasted and finished with a sealer to restore the original soft red colour of the bricks.[41]

But what to do about the seating? The BBC producer Richard Butt suggested the cane chairs at Bayreuth as a possible model: when approached, Wolfgang Wagner helpfully sent photographs, drawings and the welcome assurance that most of their chairs made in 1876 were still in use. The modest Aldeburgh budget allowed only £4 per chair, but a firm in Ipswich agreed to make them to Sugden's specification for a little over £6 each, which was still an astonishing bargain. Despite being delayed by winter storms and by practical snags with timber sourcing, the roof with its ventilators was finished in February 1967: the building was at last properly weatherproof. It would be ready ahead of schedule and in good time for that year's festival.

Britten had little faith in the 'pseudo-science' of acoustics, though both he and John Culshaw had a clear sense of how they wanted the hall to sound. He had heard it empty (on one occasion testing it with the assistance of Len Edwards, a violin-playing carpenter) but no one knew quite how it would react to an audience. So, on a Sunday afternoon in May, eight hundred local people were persuaded to come and test it, among them the London bookseller Heywood Hill (married to Anne Gathorne-Hardy and with a house at Snape), who left a splendid account of the occasion:

> There was a very good commander-in-chief (I think from Decca) who said that what he wanted first of all was utter silence for three minutes (huge exit of babies in arms). That we achieved amazingly well . . . Then he told us that the next test would be very dreadful and he gave us an example of the piercing edgy screech which he said would have to go on at various intensities for a quarter of an hour (some of the cultured

folk, who had come expecting to hear some exquisite Mozart, were seen to have tied scarves around their ears). He then said he was very sorry but now he was going to have to make three explosions and that they were going to be appallingly loud and that he advised us to block our ears as tight as possible . . . When, after that, he asked us to all stand up and to shout HELP in unison, we all responded feelingly and vociferously. He asked us to do that twice. There was then a breather, after which we were allowed some pretty music . . . We agreed that we did not think we would have behaved so well if Ben Britten and Peter Pears had not been standing near to us. I have heard they were delighted by the result and that the hall has been proved acoustically the finest in Europe.[42]

This was an opinion which in various forms – 'the best concert hall we have', 'the finest hall of its kind anywhere in the country' – was to be frequently repeated in the musical press during the following weeks, and the evidence of ears was confirmed by measurement: when full, the hall had precisely the two-second reverberation time its designers had intended.

The Snape Maltings Concert Hall was officially opened by Her Majesty the Queen on 2 June 1967, the first day of that year's festival. She and Prince Philip had flown by helicopter to the nearby RAF base at Bentwaters (which wasn't always Britten's favourite neighbour), before lunching at The Red House where, not quite coincidentally, a new entrance porch had recently been added; the other lunch guests included the Hesses, the Cranbrooks and Marion Harewood. Then the party travelled on to Snape for the opening ceremony: there the Queen used a gold-plated key to open the main door of the Maltings, inspected the auditorium and met members of the festival staff in the restaurant. A 'member of the Royal Party', presumably Prince Philip, uttered an overheard wish – 'Well, I hope the old man has written something we can understand this time'[43] – which offended Britten only because he disliked being called 'old'. Meanwhile, the hall's first audience were taking their seats for a concert which opened with Britten's arrangement of the National Anthem, with its extraordinary progression from pianissimo prayer to pealing, overlapping choral fortissimo; afterwards, the Queen was to remark that she had never been so affected by the piece, adding wryly that she had heard it once or twice before. Next came *The Building of the House*, Op. 79, a five-minute work for orchestra and massed choirs which perfectly illustrates Britten's knack for getting the 'occasional' exactly right. 'It was inspired,' he said, 'by the excitement of the planning and building – and the haste!'[44] Imogen Holst had suggested and adapted a text from Psalm 127 ('Except the Lord build the house: their labour is but lost that build it . . .') and Britten had based his composition on 'the old chorale tune which Bach loved to use': so the work is, like the building itself, both new and firmly grounded in the past. Britten conducted the English Chamber Orchestra together with 'A chorus of East Anglian choirs' – seven of them – who between them tested the hall's roof, which remained in place, as well as its acoustics. The concert also included Delius's *Summer Night on the River*, chosen for its aptness to the hall's location, and Handel's *Ode for St Cecilia's Day*, in which the soloists were Heather Harper, Pears and the trumpeter Philip Jones; between these, in a very proper acknowledgement of her role as the festival's long-serving third artistic director, Imogen Holst took the rostrum to conduct her father's *St Paul's Suite*.

The next day, the Vienna Boys' Choir – 'all sailor-suited and kissable',[45] according to Tony Palmer – gave the first performance of Britten's *The Golden Vanity*, Op. 78, a 'vaudeville for boys and pianos after the old English ballad' which tells of a sea battle and a drowned cabin boy, a sort of miniature *Billy Budd* without scenery but with costumes and mime. Although there was of course no new opera by Britten for the 1967 festival – the year's premieres were a pair of fairly unmemorable one-act operas, Lennox Berkeley's *Castaway* and William Walton's *The Bear* – Colin Graham's new production of *A Midsummer Night's Dream* was staged at the Maltings and there was a concert performance of Purcell's *The Fairy Queen* in Britten and Imogen Holst's edition. Britten had the additional pleasure of testing his new hall both with his *Spring Symphony* and with his Piano Concerto, performed by Sviatoslav Richter, with whom three years later he would record the work at Snape for Decca. Praise for the new venue from musicians, audiences and critics was unanimous: at the end of the festival, Britten with knowing understatement told Yehudi Menuhin that the Maltings was 'quite a success'.

'It's the house a composer built: it's like Bayreuth without the poison,' says Simon Rattle.[46] Not everyone would quite agree. There *was* poison at Aldeburgh in the last decade of Britten's life and some of it was connected, for all the place's incomparable virtues, with Snape Maltings. The hall would detach and alter the festival audience, and no one was more conscious of this than Britten himself. Asked that very summer by Harold Rosenthal whether there wasn't a 'danger that Aldeburgh might become too fashionable, like Glyndebourne', a question guaranteed to set his teeth on edge, Britten replied with irritated and unguarded frankness: 'There is indeed this danger; and it's not only snob audiences from London we have to worry about; there is also the "county".'[47] His hostility to snobs, whether they were Londoners or the local gentry, may mark a brisk and refreshing return to the founding principles of his 'modest festival', yet his irritation hints that he knew it was a battle he couldn't win. A visitor arriving for a concert at Snape would notice only the benefits: it was much the same journey, with a slightly different conclusion and an immensely better venue. But for the Aldeburgh resident, it wasn't the same at all: it meant travelling by car or by coach to a place with a fancy bar and a restaurant full of unfamiliar people, instead of walking to the Jubilee Hall and enjoying an interval drink in the Cross Keys. Some local people, who had originally been won over to the festival by the delicious way in which it had improvised itself in their midst, began once again to say: 'It's not for the likes of us.' Of course, there would continue to be events in the town – Britten was adamant that this should be so and it remains so to this day – but everyone who had been associated with the festival's first twenty years knew that its centre of gravity had shifted and that, from now on, most of the big operas and concerts would no longer be on their doorstep.

3

Neither Britten nor Pears was much good at dealing with the illnesses of others. Pears's characteristic response, perhaps inherited from the military side of his family, would be a simple snap-out-of-it impatience. With Britten, however, it was a matter of sensitivity and shyness, the vulnerability of having one skin too few, which made him avoid a variety of stressful occasions, from his protégés' weddings to his colleagues' sackings, where his rawness might be exposed. Those who accused him of callousness entirely failed to understand the paralysing consequences of his own deep sense of inadequacy: his appalling pre-concert nerves, when he couldn't take solid food and had to fortify himself with brandy, were another aspect of this, even though once onstage the nerves would vanish in a brilliant performance. So when in September 1967 he and Pears, visiting New York during an American tour for a concert at the Town Hall, learned that their old friend Elizabeth Mayer was in hospital after a stroke, Britten's shockingly offhand reaction – 'Well, it probably makes no sense to see Elizabeth, you know, she's in hospital'[48] – would have been prompted by nervousness rather than by heartlessness. Moreover, he had his own troubles: Pears had lost his voice, the recital was postponed and, when it had been re-arranged, his own pre-concert nausea was even worse than usual. In the end, urged by her daughter Beata, they did visit Elizabeth Mayer, while Donald Mitchell 'had a hand in arranging, at Ben's request, a modest but regular contribution to the costs of Elizabeth's hospitalisation'.[49]

Then they continued with a tour which stretched from Expo '67 in Montreal – where, besides their own recitals, the English Opera Group was presenting *Curlew River* and *The Burning Fiery Furnace* – through New York to Mexico, Peru, Chile, Argentina, Uruguay and Brazil. In Guadalajara, Schumann's *Dichterliebe* was almost drowned out by brass bands and fireworks, while in Santiago an excitable lady singer tried to join them onstage, but these were minor hazards: their reception throughout Latin America was 'absolutely wonderful everywhere'. The tour ended with the premiere on the continent of *Peter Grimes* in Rio de Janeiro, but the high point was the recital at the Teatro Colón in Buenos Aires where, according to Princess Margaret of Hesse and the Rhine, the 'magnificent' audience was 'thrilled, clapping, yelling and delighted'.[50] Britten attributed their South American audiences' enthusiasm to the fact that, while his music was well known there, his and Pears's records were difficult to obtain (although this sounds suspiciously like another reformulation of his ancient prejudice against the gramophone). They returned home, contented but exhausted, at the end of October, and on 22 November, his fifty-fourth birthday, Britten reported to William Plomer that he was 'launched on the Prodigal'.

Britten's third and final church parable, *The Prodigal Son*, Op. 81, was to receive its first performance in Orford Church like its two predecessors, as part of the 1968 Aldeburgh Festival. The idea for it had come to him during the Russian Christmas of 1966 when, the day after their Leningrad concert, Britten and Pears had wanted to revisit the Hermitage and found it closed; however, 'magic words were spoken' and they were given a private conducted tour. For Pears, the highlight was the 'big dark room with some of the greatest Rembrandts in the world in it . . . and surely the greatest of all, the *Prodigal Son* (with his broken back, shaven head, worn sole to his one foot out of his shoe, the father all loving-understanding, the three diverse characters looking on, judging, grudging, and surprised)'.[51] On returning home, Britten had written to Plomer: 'Does the idea of the prodigal Son attract you for a new Ch. Par. – inspired by a fabulous Rembrandt in the Hermitage?'[52] But at last being 'launched on the Prodigal' didn't, as Britten might by now have guessed, guarantee a smooth compositional journey. The first major interruption was in December, when he conducted Decca's recording of *Billy Budd* at Kingsway Hall, an experience which left him shattered and with a familiar exhortation from his doctor to do less. After Christmas, he retreated once again to the Palazzo Mocenigo in Venice. 'To be in a place where man can still dominate (even over the pigeons!) somehow gives one confidence again in his own capacity,' he told Plomer. He had 'worked as almost never before, with the result that I'm about 3/4 done, & have a pretty clear idea of what's to follow.'[53] What was to follow next was another illness which he first took be be a severe bout of flu; once he had been admitted to hospital in Ipswich, however, it was diagnosed as endocarditis, possibly a legacy of the heart trouble which had threatened him as a small child. He spent a month in hospital before returning to The Red House, where a nurse made daily visits to administer penicillin injections. On

29 April, he could finally reassure his librettist that 'By breaking all doctors', orders, & really thrashing my poor old self', he had 'finished Prodigal Son – score & all'.[54]

'Of all the parables in the New Testament,' wrote Plomer in his programme note, 'none has had quite such a universal and ever-renewed appeal as that of the Prodigal Son.' It is also, as he implied, yet another of Britten's redemptions: 'With its unforgettable climax of reward and rejoicing lavished not upon virtuous correctness but upon a sinner, this parable celebrates the triumph of forgiveness.'[55] Plomer's invented character of the Tempter – the role originally taken by Pears – makes it absolutely clear that in *The Prodigal Son* we are once again in a world of manipulative evil familiar from *Billy Budd* and *The Turn of the Screw*: 'See how I break it up!' he repeats, in a chilling mixture of grown-up villainy and childish tantrum, of the concord he aims to destroy. 'You have gambled and lost,' he tells the Younger Son, who thus seems to join Britten's procession of fated young men; but this is a Christian parable whose movement is inexorably towards redemption of the brother who 'was dead, and is alive again, was lost, and is found'. While *The Prodigal Son* is tamer and less groundbreaking than its two predecessors – and its first reviewers praised rather faintly, with William Mann in *The Times* finding it 'sufficiently distinctive' – it nevertheless has some claim to be regarded as the most satisfyingly coherent of the three church parables.

Another notable first performance at the 1968 festival was by Rostropovich, of the Second Cello Suite, Op. 80. This opens with a questing, introspective Largo, and indeed the whole work has an unsettled quality which makes it hugely challenging for any lesser performer; on Britten's familiar principle of delayed gratification, any hints of sweetness are reserved for the concluding Allegro. Sadler's Wells brought their revival of *Gloriana*, now fondly regarded by its composer as his 'slighted child', to the Maltings, but the opera which caused the festival's biggest stir was Harrison Birtwistle's *Punch and Judy* at the Jubilee Hall. Britten was generous in his encouragement of younger composers, from his then twenty-year-old godson Michael Berkeley and the still-teenaged Robert Saxton (who had first approached him in 1963, at the age of nine) to Birtwistle, who was in his mid-thirties. He had supported Birtwistle's successful application for a Harkness Fellowship at Princeton, where much of *Punch and Judy* was composed, and at that point had been 'exceedingly interested to hear about your projected new opera',[56] which had been commissioned by John Tooley at Covent Garden for the English Opera Group. But 'hearing about' wasn't the same as hearing, and Britten, as Tooley told Humphrey Carpenter, 'was quite appalled by what he heard' that evening in Aldeburgh: 'He hated the subject matter, he disliked the writing – I have to say in defence of Harry [Birtwistle] that it was performed in the Jubilee Hall, and the noise in there was indescribable.'[57] Accounts differ about how long Britten and Pears stayed in their directors' box – one reliable source says five minutes – before quietly slipping away for a stiff drink in the anteroom beyond. Perhaps the size of the hall *was* the problem (when *Punch and Judy* was revived at the Maltings for the 1991 festival, it seemed more manageable), yet the opera illustrated a central aesthetic dilemma for Britten, who wanted to support new music but found much of the 1960s avant-garde unendurable.

A few months later, he was asked by Donald Mitchell whether he felt 'that this is a time of acute change in music'. His reply has a touching awkwardness, as he attempts to balance tolerance with firmness:

Yes, I do. And I don't always follow the new directions, and nor do I always approve of them, but that is only purely personal to me. I mean, that there should be new directions is obvious. Any new thought, in whatever language it's couched, has got to have this new element. But I sometimes feel that seeking after a new language has become more important than saying what you mean. I mean, I always believe that language is a means and not an end.[58]

But towards the end of that interview, Britten couldn't resist mentioning 'a young composer who had a first performance of an opera not far from here' at a time when 'there were other operas being performed in the neighbourhood'. Britten thought it strange that the young composer 'didn't want to go and see how Mozart solved his problems'; for him, studying the work of other composers in order to construct his own was as natural as using a map to navigate one's way through an unfamiliar journey. The young composer was Birtwistle, the opera *Punch and Judy*.

The Maltings had to pay its way. After the 1968 festival, it began seriously to earn its keep, hosting a range of events which were listed in the introduction – optimistically headed 'The First Phase' – to the following year's programme book. These included 'a Bach week-end, an Antique-Dealers' Fair, some summer orchestral and band concerts, a highly successful series of "Jazz at the Maltings" for B.B.C. Television, a number of Decca recordings . . . and a fund-raising concert for the Aldeburgh Parish Church tower at Christmas'.[59] In December, Decca recorded Britten conducting the English Chamber Orchestra in three contrasting projects: *English Music for Strings*, including works by Bridge, Delius, Elgar and Purcell; *Salute to Percy Grainger*, with Pears, John Shirley-Quirk and the Ambrosian Singers; and the greatly admired double LP set of Bach's Brandenburg Concertos. However, the 'most ambitious and strenuous operation yet undertaken' at the Maltings was the filming for television of *Peter Grimes*.

Britten had no more enthusiasm for television than he had for records and radio, but in the autumn of 1966 Basil Coleman had directed a BBC production of *Billy Budd*, conducted by Charles Mackerras and with Pears reprising his original role of Captain Vere. This led to him 'thinking a lot about me and T.V. (!)' – the exclamation mark is his own – and to two specific proposals: one would be an opera to be composed specially for television, while the other and more urgent one was a film of *Peter Grimes*. In April 1967, he wrote to Coleman: 'I think that with Peter's performance, your understanding of the piece, & me not yet too old to conduct, we *ought* to do a really authoritative record of how we like it to go, & what it is all about.'[60] This is tactful to the point of evasiveness: Britten being too old to conduct was a more remote danger than Pears, approaching sixty, being too old to sing the part of Grimes. His intention, and Coleman's, was to pre-record the music, to which the cast would then mime during filming; but the BBC were committed to having orchestra and conductor in a separate studio, as they had for *Budd*. Britten, who wanted direct contact with the cast, then withdrew from the project and handed the baton to Meredith Davies.

It was at this point that John Culshaw moved from Decca to become head of music at BBC Television. Alert to the 'authoritative record' aspect of Britten's proposal (which a Davies-conducted version, whatever its merits, could not possess), Culshaw proposed to use his beloved Maltings as a single studio, even though this would mean cramming orchestra and conductor into the highest and hottest part of the building. Now it was Coleman's turn to withdraw: he felt, not entirely without cause, that filming in the Maltings, though it would please Britten and produce decent sound, wouldn't make the best television. Instead, Brian Large directed the production, which was filmed at Snape during the last week of February 1969. At the back of the hall, Britten sustained himself with an enormous jar of peppermints while communicating his comments and instructions via a loudhailer; at the front, after a slate-dislodging blizzard, snow fell on Auntie and her 'nieces' as they huddled round the fire in the 'Boar'. 'It was a very great experience,' he said afterwards, adding that 'the people I was working with were so musical and understood the musical side of the work so well that my task was made much easier'.[61] The resulting film achieved precisely what Britten had intended; yet it's hard not to feel a little wistful about Coleman's original plan, for *Grimes*, unlike many operas and plays, does lend itself to filmic opening-out. The Suffolk seascape and the town itself are so crucial to the work that a production shot on location might have been fascinating, despite the inevitable snags which can arise when singers mime. As it was, *Peter Grimes* was transmitted on BBC2 in November 1969.

By the time *Grimes* was filmed, Britten had already started to plan his television opera, *Owen Wingrave*, with Myfanwy Piper; but, as so often, he also had an unfulfilled commission to get out of the way. This was *The Children's Crusade*, Op. 82, a version of Brecht's *Kinderkreuzzug*, for the fiftieth anniversary of the Save the Children Fund. Michael Kennedy thought this the 'least appealing'[62] among Britten's choral works of the 1960s, and few would disagree. 'Britten was never so grim as in this piece,' says John Bridcut, before wondering rhetorically 'whether it has won many hearts'.[63] Even the composer himself described it as 'a very grisly piece'.[64] It received its first performance from the Wandsworth School Choir at St Paul's Cathedral on 19 May 1969; Adrian Thompson, who was among the boy singers, later recalled that they had at first found the work terrifying, not least in its brutally percussive opening, but that Britten's kindness and care during rehearsal had won them round. By way of contrast, and perhaps simply to cheer himself up, Britten then wrote the charming, almost eighteenth-century *Suite for Harp*, Op. 83, for

Ossian Ellis, whose nationality is deftly acknowledged by the closing variations on the Welsh hymn tune 'St Denio'.

Although the programme for the 1969 festival, now extended to three weeks, was full of confident ambition, it still retained at its core the feeling of a 'modest' event with 'a few friends'. So, alongside a new production of *Idomeneo* and a revival of *The Prodigal Son*, there were to be recitals by Pears and Britten, George Malcolm (playing the *'Goldberg' Variations*), Julian Bream, Ossian Ellis and Alfred Brendel; Britten was to conduct the hard-working ECO in the Brandenburgs, in Elgar and, remark-ably, in Mahler's Fourth, a work he had loved since his student days, with Elly Ameling as soloist in the last movement. Philip Ledger had joined Britten, Pears and Holst as the fourth artistic director, notably strengthening the baroque element of the programme. As so often in the past, the festival's musician friends reappeared in assorted combinations and wearing different hats, among them the stately ones of a mock-Victorian evening cele-brating the 150th anniversary of Queen Victoria's and Prince Albert's births in, of course, the Jubilee Hall. The opening afternoon concert, on Saturday 7 June, was given at the Maltings by the Amadeus Quartet, augmented by Cecil Aronowitz (viola), Adrian Beers (double bass) and Britten himself, playing his own Steinway concert grand, whose usual home was the library-cum-music room at The Red House, in Purcell, Mozart and Schubert. That evening, in the Jubilee Hall, there was the first performance of an operatic double bill by Gordon Crosse, *Purgatory* and *The Grace of God*, whose misfortune it is to be remembered mainly for what else happened that night. The performance began at 8.30 p.m.; by the time it ended, at around eleven o'clock, Snape Maltings was on fire.

At first, because the concert hall itself was obviously window-less, the only signs of trouble were the glowing roof ventilators; then, a customer leaving the Crown at closing time noticed a

redness in the sky above the building. When the fire brigade
from Saxmundham arrived, the roof was ablaze and about to
collapse: it didn't take the walls with it, because Derek Sugden
had providentially allowed for the roof structure to move freely
during gales. Stephen Reiss, when he heard and disbelieved the
rumour, drove straight over from Aldeburgh: the flames, he said,
were visible from Snape crossroads, a mile away, and when he
reached the Maltings, 'it was just devastation'.[65] He went back
to The Red House to break the news. Britten, about to go to
bed, was 'amazing': together with Pears and Reiss, he immediately started to sort out the practical business of how the festival
– everything, including *Idomeneo* – could go on. There were
nineteen events scheduled at the Maltings, almost all of which
would be transferred to Blythburgh Church, although the
concert by the New Philharmonia conducted by Carlo Maria
Giulini had to be transplanted more distantly to Ely Cathedral.
The only casualty was the next day's choral and orchestral
concert: this was to have opened with Britten conducting *The
Building of the House*, a work which had become quite obviously
unperformable in the circumstances. On the Sunday morning,
the Bishop of St Edmundsbury offered them the use of any
church in his diocese and the Queen telephoned personally.
Britten, who had lost not only his concert hall but his Steinway
('the nicest piano I have ever played on'), was calm, clear-headed
and impossible to argue with: when Sugden arrived from his
Hertfordshire home to assess the damage, he had already decided
that they were going to rebuild in time for the following year's
festival. The treasurer, Charles Gifford, had checked with the
building's insurers that they were fully covered: so, Britten told
the astonished but impressed Sugden, they might as well start
work straight away. Perhaps they'd even make one or two modest
improvements.

Everyone who was there remembers the rest of the 1969

festival as a series of miracles. Imogen Holst's unscheduled but superb conducting of the ECO in her father's *A Fugal Concerto* – replacing Elgar's *For the Fallen*, which required forces too large for Blythburgh – was indisputably one of them. But by some distance the most extraordinary was the performance of Mozart's *Idomeneo*, conducted by Britten, in Blythburgh Church on Tuesday 10 June, just three days after the fire. Carpenters from Reade's of Aldeburgh worked day and night to create a stage in the church and seats were borrowed from anyone who would lend them; a marquee on the lawn provided dressing rooms for the cast. Britten conducted from a cramped corner of the stage, snapping off pieces of his baton: a recurring habit which on this occasion enabled him to avoid poking orchestra members in the eye. Robert Tear, singing Arbace, recalled that 'it had the feel of an improvisation, as if it were literally a first performance. I can't begin to tell you how wonderfully Ben conducted.'[66] Joyce Grenfell, a regular festival attender, noted in her diary that it was 'an impeccable performance' and 'found the whole occasion a triumph of spirit'.[67] Because the church couldn't contain the entire audience, local people were asked to surrender their tickets so that more distant visitors needn't be disappointed, with the promise that *Idomeneo* would be restaged the following year at a rebuilt Maltings; as, of course, it was.

Just what happened in Snape on that Saturday night remains a mystery. No electrical fault was ever discovered and, because the evening's performance was at the Jubilee Hall, there was no particular reason why anyone should still have been on the premises. The fire may have started in the costume store beneath the stage, where a trapdoor may have been left open, and some of the festival's volunteer helpers, present earlier in the evening, may have been smoking. All that is perfectly possible; but so, it must be said, is arson. There were some local people – there still are – who passionately detested Britten and his festival. As he grew older, their dislike seemed to become more intense: paradoxically, he caused offence by having so completely failed to be offensive. His detractors would have found an outrageously camp or bohemian character easy to mock and to dismiss; what infuriated them beyond measure was his unimpeachable quiet respectability. I once met a man in a Suffolk pub who claimed to know who started the Maltings fire: he wouldn't say any more, but I didn't disbelieve him.

4

During the summer of 1969, Britten wrote the final song cycle in which he would accompany Pears, *Who Are These Children?*, Op. 84, setting poems and riddles by the Scots poet William Soutar (1898–1943): several are in English, but in others the dialect acts as a gauze or a veil which, while more readily penetrable than those earlier supplied by Rimbaud or Michelangelo or Hölderlin, has much the same distancing effect. At the heart of the cycle are two poems about children in wartime: one, on an air raid ('Death came out of the sky / In the bright afternoon'), leads to a reversal, which is also a corollary, of Britten's recurring corruption-of-innocence theme ('The blood of children corrupts the hearts of men'); the other, juxtaposing a 'world at war' with a fox hunt, takes us back to *Our Hunting Fathers* or even to that essay with which Britten ended his South Lodge schooldays. And perhaps South Lodge is a memory in two poems which deal with the naughtiness rather than the vulnerability of children: 'Black Day' – where the boy receives a 'skelp' (that is, a beating) from, successively, his teacher, mother, brother and father – and 'The Larky Lad', whose larks are jauntily admired by poet and composer alike. 'Nightmare', another recurrent preoccupation, has a tree which cries out and whose branches flower 'with children's eyes'; while the bleak simplicity of the last song, 'The Auld Aik', about an oak tree which is 'doun, doun', perhaps suggests a metaphor for the temporarily felled Maltings. In its pared-down reflexiveness, *Who Are These Children?* is a notable instance of 'late style'.

Britten and Myfanwy Piper had also been getting on with *Owen Wingrave*. The successful filming of *Grimes* had given Britten a rather surprising new enthusiasm for television: 'We're using the camera consciously throughout . . . I'm being very careful to think throughout of the television medium and not of the stage.' He was clear that the television audience needed 'the lyricism of the aria and the ensemble' and so, he told Donald Mitchell in February 1969, he and Piper had been 'adding arias galore'.[68] But, by the summer, the Maltings fire had reshuffled his priorities: when he and Pears visited America in October, their pre-planned recital tour had become at least partly a fund-raising exercise. Interviewed by John Tusa for BBC2's *The Money Programme* – not a show on which composers usually appeared – Britten admitted that he was 'depressed' to be raising money for the second time in five years; it did mean, however, that various improvements to the hall would be made now rather than later, since they could hardly put out the begging bowl for a third time. In the new year, he resumed work on *Owen Wingrave* while staying with Peg Hesse at Wolfsgarten, before setting off with Pears for an extended trip to Australia, where the EOG were performing the church parables at the Adelaide Festival. Despite all this travelling and hard work, he had also found time to buy another house in Suffolk.

There was, as he explained to Mitchell, a straightforward reason for this uncharacteristic extravagance: 'Silence, of course, these days, becomes a rarer and rarer presence, particularly in this house where we're sitting now, where the aeroplanes land with unfailing regularity close to the house.'[69] That was The Red House, which would remain Britten's permanent home until his death, and the planes were those from the nearby airbase at Bentwaters. So, although Aldeburgh itself seemed a retreat to their metropolitan friends, he and Pears sought a retreat from their retreat, where Britten could compose in peace and they could both escape from festival business. At first, they considered the west coast of Ireland, perhaps with a fleeting memory of Jack Moeran, who had ended his days there; but they eventually settled for Chapel Cottage at Horham, a village in inland Suffolk, not far from Chandos Lodge, Frederick Ashton's country home at Eye. This they would enlarge – it became Chapel House – and Britten would have a simple small studio in the garden. Although it may have seemed a perfectly sensible idea, it would before long cause, or at any rate contribute to, trouble.

When the rebuilt Maltings opened for the 1970 festival, audiences perceived that the superb acoustics were even better than before although, as Derek Sugden noted, they were in fact exactly the same. But there had been changes. As the introduction to the programme book, headed (with mild irony) 'The Present Phase', remarked: 'The Next Phase is indeed on us, but rather more forced on us than we wished.'[70] There was a proper chorus room, an improved lighting box, a new downstairs kitchen for the restaurant and relocated facilities for two 'principal patrons', Decca and the BBC. For the audience, the most perceptible difference was the construction of a new corridor – later known as the Marland Gallery – from the upper level of the auditorium to the bar and restaurant: the introduction's author optimistically thought that the 'interval bottle-neck should be substantially cleared' (instead of merely being moved closer to the bar). It was to be hoped that the 'expensive sprinklers' which had been installed would never be put to the test, but since the fire a new hazard had appeared: the river wall had been breached, the Alde had invaded the marshes on its south side and the grass terrace had been 'extended and fortified against it'. Once again, the Queen and Prince Philip attended the opening concert, on Friday 5 June: called 'Music for a Royal Occasion', it opened with Britten's arrangement of the National Anthem and closed with three extracts from *Gloriana*, but fate was not to be tempted by a reprise of *The Building of the House*. The following evening, Colin Graham's production of *Idomeneo* – with, thanks to the cooperation of the BBC and Covent Garden, new costumes and a slightly different set – finally reached the Maltings.

That summer, *Owen Wingrave* was finished, and in November it was filmed at Snape for transmission on BBC2 the following year. Despite some marvellous music, it's a work full of problems, many of them self-inflicted by its composer, and it hasn't been much loved. Henry James's short story had long fascinated Britten, who saw it – his first mistake – as a companion piece to *The Turn of the Screw*: 'By the way,' he wrote to Eric Walter White on 5 November 1954, 'do you know another story of James' called "Owen Wingrave" with much the same quality as the Screw?'[71] Owen, the scion of the Wingraves, is a Sandhurst cadet who rejects military life and returns home to the family mansion, suggestively called Paramore, where he eventually dies in an ancestor-haunted room. Pacifism and ghosts were, of course, both subjects which Britten had treated before, and his wish to revisit the anti-military theme had been sharpened both by the war in Vietnam and by the Soviet invasion of Czechoslovakia in 1968; he refused, when invited, to take a public stand on the latter, fearing that this might complicate matters for his Russian musical friends, but promised to make private representations, doubtless via Madame Furtseva. His second mistake was to assume that the timeliness of the opera's message would compensate for its lack of dramatic interest, and his third was to write for specific singers who would feel uncomfortable with, or simply too old for, their roles.

Some of these weaknesses might have been disguised or mitigated if only the filming itself had been a happier affair, but the pleasure Britten had taken in working on the television version of *Grimes* wasn't to be repeated. Basil Coleman, who would have been perfectly happy to direct a chamber-scale opera at the Maltings, was passed over; Colin Graham was drafted in to co-direct alongside Brian Large, a television rather than an opera man, and there was tension between the two factions. The concert hall, which had proved curiously amenable to the earlier opera's clutter, almost as if it didn't mind being put out by something so coastal and Suffolky, looked ridiculous when converted into the elaborate set of a stately home interior, which also happened to ruin its famous acoustics. Britten, exhausted by the fire and the fund-raising, and recuperating from a recent hernia operation, hated the whole business: he began to wonder whether *Owen Wingrave* wouldn't after all work better when, two years later, it was staged at Covent Garden. He donated his fee of £10,000 from the BBC to the rebuilding fund for the Maltings: his unlikely love affair with television was over. When the opera was broadcast on 16 May 1971, it was praised by William Mann in *The Times* ('the most impressive piece of ambitious TV drama I have seen') and by Martin Cooper in the *Daily Telegraph* ('one of the composer's most powerful utterances').[72] However, Britten himself was having none of it: 'But o, what a terrible medium,' he wrote to William Plomer; 'between ourselves it looked pretty awful . . .'[73] By then, he and Myfanwy Piper were already deep into 'a big new piece for Peter, which cannot be delayed';[74] Pears, he added, wasn't getting any younger.

In that long and revealing 1969 interview with Donald Mitchell, Britten explained why, in spite of being in many ways admirably suited to the role, he had never seen himself as a teacher. 'I don't exactly know why I'm so shy about teaching,' he begins, before appearing to contradict this modest assertion:

> I know that when young people come to me with their works it gives me great pleasure to go through them – these works – with the young composers. I think I'm frightened of imposing my own solutions on their problems. Although I do believe strongly that even the personality of the teacher can be absorbed without much detriment to the scholar. Because if the personality of the scholar is strong enough it can absorb it easily, and perhaps get richer from it. But I have seen so many cases in my life where the tricks, the mannerisms of the teacher have been picked up by the scholar . . . I think that the great composer, the great writer, painter, will survive almost any kind of treatment. But the great composers can look after themselves. It's the minor composers, the people who can make our lives so much richer in small ways, that I want to preserve and to help.[75]

The last point is interesting and slightly surprising, though made of the same stuff as Britten's frequently reiterated insistence on the musician's social responsibility; for the rest, however, he seems to be playing a ferocious game of tennis against himself. He then veers to a slightly different point: 'I do think that at this moment of acute change in music that I perhaps am not the right person to guide young composers. My methods, which are entirely personal to me, are founded on a time when the language was not so broken as it is now.' And from there he proceeds to the subject of the contemporary composer's relationship with musical tradition, thus perhaps preventing Mitchell from interjecting the two words which might have challenged the preceding argument: Frank Bridge. For Bridge had been both a powerful musical personality and a composer out of fashion at the time when Britten was his pupil: mightn't Britten himself have been just such an invigorating teacher? There was, of course, a further implicit reason for his reluctance: the emotional entanglement which might develop from an intense one-to-one relationship with a young student.

Coincidentally or not, a few months after that interview, Britten did accept a pupil: a fifteen-year-old Irish boy named Ronan Magill. His mother, the wife of a Dublin doctor, had written three years earlier, asking Britten to take on her son as a live-in pupil for a week now and then; this bold proposal was rejected, although Britten can't have failed to notice how it echoed the suggestion that he, when not much older than Ronan, should live and study with Harold Samuel, although on that occasion the veto had come from the opposite direction. In September 1969, Ronan, now a pupil at Ampleforth, called by appointment at the Britten–Pears London house in Offord Road, Islington, and was told that Britten could spare him fifteen minutes or, at most, half an hour. What actually happened, as Ronan Magill told John Bridcut, was rather different:

> He took a look at some pieces I had composed, and I played for him – and before I knew where we were three hours had passed. Then I joined them for lunch. I kept thinking I ought to be going, but he made no attempt at that. I played him one piece which I had written, which I am pleased to say he liked. I then played Beethoven [the 'Waldstein' Sonata] and some Brahms for him – I didn't know about his hang-ups about those composers at that time. I just played, and we talked and talked and that was that.[76]

Britten's disregard of the time is exactly like Frank Bridge's, while his tolerance of Beethoven and Brahms recalls his indulgence of David Spenser's similarly aberrant musical taste. He told Mrs Magill that they were all – he, Pears, Sue and Jack Phipps – 'enchanted' by Ronan: 'I was amazed at his general musicality and intelligence, and his is a remarkable pianistic gift.' Britten would 'see him as often as possible, help him with his composition, make arrangements here for him to have general theory tuition, and discuss his piano playing too'.[77] It can't have detracted from Britten's enchantment that Ronan was good-looking in a slightly wild, dark-haired way; but he was clearly, and significantly, a young man, not a child. When her marriage broke up, Mrs Magill and the rest of her family moved to Suffolk; Ronan became a regular visitor at The Red House and even at Horham. Britten rewarded him with the affectionately Blakeian nickname 'Tyger'.

By now, Britten was surrounded by colleagues – sometimes unkindly described, as by John Lucas in his *Observer* profile of 1970, as his 'courtiers' – who tended towards overprotectiveness. But he was experienced in self-protection: there's every reason to suspect that when he grumbled 'Oh God, Ronan again' it was mainly for their benefit and that he enormously enjoyed having a fiery young man about the place. Their lessons, which were to continue until Britten's final illness, inspired an obsessive devotion on the part of his pupil, who wrote him passionate love letters which rivalled the equally heterosexual Wulff Scherchen's. But Magill, subsequently a professional pianist, was much more than just an emotional teenager: he was learning and observing, and he has striking memories of Britten's own extraordinary pianism. 'You could see his long, spindly fingers slightly shaking as they played, as if his body was carrying a sort of live wire of feeling through it,' he says. And of Britten's performance in the Schumann Piano Quartet: 'I will never forget a colour he got in the Scherzo where he made a sort of shimmer of sound. It was just like a shudder of electricity through the body.'[78] Even Britten himself didn't know how he did it. He told Imogen Holst about an occasion when, after playing Mozart's D major Sonata for Two Pianos with Clifford Curzon, 'Clifford had been thrilled and had insisted on taking his chair & sitting by Ben's piano and asking him how he'd done certain phrases, and when he asked how he'd fingered something Ben not only didn't know but was physically incapable of playing the passage in order to find out!'[79]

Ronan Magill wasn't the only boy in his late teens to attract Britten's attention at the turn of the decade. After the Maltings fire, a full-time caretaker had been appointed and given the grander title of 'Maltings Concert Hall Warden'; his name was George Hardy, and his seventeen-year-old son Alistair helped out with practical chores – it was he who collected holly and ivy to deck the *Owen Wingrave* set – and, having recently passed his test, with driving. According to Stephen Reiss, Alistair was 'very, very beautiful' and 'more or less the prototype for the boy in *Death in Venice*': 'Ben and Peter were crazy about him.'[80] But Reiss, as we're about to discover, was a far from dispassionate witness of events at this time, while the fact that Britten and Pears were likely to be attracted by a beautiful young man seems hardly worth remarking. By early 1971, it was clear to those who worked with him at Snape that George Hardy wasn't doing an adequate job and, since a flat for the warden was nearing completion, a decision on his future had to be taken soon: it clearly wouldn't do to install a man with his family in a new home and then almost at once to dismiss him. Immediately after the end of the festival, Reiss told the warden of the general dissatisfaction and the report he must make of it, whereupon Hardy resigned. Britten and Pears had retreated to Horham for a post-festival break; when they returned to Aldeburgh, they unleashed a furious attack on Reiss for his 'sacking' of George Hardy. Reiss, finding that he had lost the confidence of the founding artistic directors, felt he had no alternative but to hand in his own resignation. Fidelity Cranbrook seriously considered resigning as chairman in protest at Reiss's treatment. And Britten drafted letters in which he proposed, while retaining his artistic role, to take no further part in the management of the festival. On 8 July, he wrote to Rosamund Strode: 'I have decided to cut out of all Management concerns now – P.P. will go on, but generally the Red House will do much less, & let 'm stew in their own juice!'[81] Had all these departures actually taken place, there might have been some difficulty in finding anyone in a position to accept anyone else's resignation. But they didn't: the Countess of Cranbrook and Britten both stayed put, while the entirely innocent party – the young Alistair Hardy – found himself invited to The Red House for dinner and offered financial help in setting up some sort of business: he had been a favourite, certainly, and Britten enjoyed helping his favourites, but that was all. Or almost all.

The fall from favour of Stephen Reiss, a man liked and admired by nearly everyone connected with Aldeburgh, was not prompted merely by an unsatisfactory caretaker and his beautiful son. It had begun on the night of the Maltings fire – on such occasions, the messenger is seldom wholly forgiven – and it gathered pace during subsequent discussions about the future at Snape. This was when the idea of a 'creative campus' really began to take shape, with the preparation by Arup Associates of a twenty-five-year plan which envisaged facilities for dance and drama as well as for music and opera, together with 'rehearsal rooms, a music library, an art gallery, artists' studios, permanent exhibition space and scenery workshops'.[82] Lurking somewhere, and perhaps not quite compatibly, in this grand scheme were Britten's fond memories of the composers' colony in Armenia, together with a notional music school of which he had once said that Imogen Holst must be the director. Although Reiss had reservations about this kind of thinking, he accompanied Britten to the Arts Council, whose expansive and expansionist chairman Lord Goodman was predictably impressed by it: Goodman's suggestion was that Britten should make over his copyrights and royalties to the nation, rather as Henry Moore had done, in return for substantial state funding. Britten, having no dependants, wanted to find a constructive use for his creative assets; he was (in Reiss's words) 'absolutely bowled over' by the proposal and correspondingly affronted by Reiss's caution. When, early in 1971, Arup Associates produced a more detailed plan for a year-round arts centre, Reiss remained unconvinced. The ground had thus been thoroughly prepared for that summer's final falling-out, of which almost the saddest aspect was the change of style and tone it signalled: Reiss had been a hands-on improviser, an enthusiastic amateur in the spirit of the earlier Aldeburgh Festivals who cheerfully manned the bar at the Festival Club when needed. If the future was necessarily to be more professional, it might also turn out to be rather less fun.

But was Alistair Hardy, as Reiss suggested, 'the prototype for the boy in *Death in Venice*'? Or was Ronan Magill? Neither and both. *Death in Venice* had certainly been in Britten's mind, as Donald Mitchell has pointed out, long before he met either of them; yet that doesn't at all rule them out as influences, for they both coincide with the period when Britten, having completed *Owen Wingrave*, was turning his full attention to his last opera. What they had in common with each other, and with Wulff Scherchen, is that they were not children but young men. And as Wulff is to Young Apollo, so Ronan and Alistair are to Tadzio.

CHAPTER 9

AS IT IS, PLENTY

1971–76

1

'I wrote this suite in the early spring of 1971 and took it as a present to Slava Rostropovich when Peter Pears and I visited Moscow and Leningrad in April of that year,'[1] said Britten of his Third Suite for Cello, Op. 87. It was their last trip together to Russia, and it wasn't without complications. They were participating in a festival of British music, which included Britten conducting the London Symphony Orchestra in his Piano Concerto (with Richter as soloist) and Cello Symphony (with Rostropovich). But although Madame Furtseva, the Soviet Minister of Culture, was happy to promote Britten's music and Rostropovich's playing of it, she wasn't at all happy with Rostropovich himself, who was in disgrace for his support of the Nobel Prize-winning author Alexander Solzhenitsyn. The official celebratory lunch at the British Embassy, at which Madame Furtseva was the principal Russian guest, while other visitors from England included William and Susana Walton and André Previn, was 'greatly delayed by the non-appearance of Slavas Rostropovich and Richter', noted Pears in his diary. He was puzzled by this: 'Will the riddle ever be solved? Did they or did they not ever receive their cards of invitation? They were

sent with the rest to the Ministry, the usual thing, to be distrib-
uted thence. They were not, or were they? Phone invitations
were also made, but. Diplomacy, umbrage, tact, obedience?'²
Displeasure had been expressed in a typically Soviet style.

Britten played through the Third Suite for Cello on the
piano at the Rostropoviches' flat to a select audience including
Dmitri and Irina Shostakovich. It is the most attractive of the
three suites, and the most Russian: its themes are three Russian
folk songs as well as 'Kontakion', the Russian Orthodox Hymn
for the Dead, on which the opening Lento is based. The work
thus carries from the start an unmistakable air of gravitas, though
not of gloom, which may signal Britten's concern for his cellist
friend in troubled times. An innocent ear might easily mistake
some of the inner movements for the work of Shostakovich, yet
the substantial last movement could only be by Britten: it is, of
course, a passacaglia, which finally resolves into a subdued statement of the 'Kontakion' theme, in a manner familiar from the
Dowland-based *Lachrymae* and *Nocturnal*. As an elegant quid pro
quo, Britten and Pears were invited to a private rehearsal performance in Shostakovich's flat of his thirteenth String Quartet; they
were so moved that they asked to hear it a second time. 'I think
Dmitri was pleased and touched by our emotion,' wrote Pears.
'He has not so many listeners whom he can so wholeheartedly
respect as Ben.'³

Because of his continuing disfavour with the Soviet authorities, Rostropovich wouldn't be permitted to perform the Third
Suite for Cello in England until 1973; instead, the somewhat
surprising Britten premiere at the 1971 Aldeburgh Festival was
Canticle IV: Journey of the Magi, Op. 86. It had been over fifteen
years since *Canticle III: Still Falls the Rain*, and many listeners
would have assumed the sequence to have petered out; moreover,
the new work was almost disarmingly straightforward. One way
of looking at it is as a sort of pre-pendant to *Death in Venice*,

since it was written for the three singers who were to feature most prominently in that opera: Pears, the baritone John Shirley-Quirk and the countertenor James Bowman. Britten harmonises the three voices in ways which range from an aptly magi-like exoticism to a rather charming approach to barbershop and, in the main, treats Eliot's poem with respect. The one uncharacteristic lapse comes with the phrase 'it was (you may say) satisfactory', where Eliot surely intends ironic understatement; Britten, however, caresses and repeats the word 'satisfactory' no fewer than nine times. The conclusion is troublingly unresolved, but then so is the poem's.

The Third Suite for Cello ends with a Song of the Dead and *Journey of the Magi* ends with the words, 'I should be glad of another death.' Both point us inexorably towards *Death in Venice*. We might suspect Britten of wilful valetudinarianism, had his sense of failing health been less well founded. Although 1971 proved to be one of his relatively illness-free years – some difficult dental extractions aside – it would have been entirely like him to suppress any worries about his worsening heart condition while he got on with the opera. At the end of January, he and Pears, together with John and Myfanwy Piper, spent a fortnight in southern France: 'Ben and Myfanwy,' Pears noted, 'are working hard & well on *Tod in V*.'[4] Frederick Ashton was to be the choreographer and the original intention was that *Death in Venice* should be staged at Snape the following autumn; but on 20 September 1971 Britten told Ashton that he couldn't 'guarantee to have the opera ready' by then and that he therefore proposed the premiere should take place at the 1973 festival. 'I am desperately keen to make it the best thing I have ever done,'[5] he added: he seems to have known intuitively that it would be his final major work. In October, he visited Venice, with Pears and the Pipers, absorbing the atmosphere and researching details such as the cries of gondoliers, and in March 1972 he put in a spell of concentrated work on the opera at Wolfsgarten. Then, during a routine check-up that summer, his doctor, Ian Tait, found signs of cardiac deterioration: Britten's obstinate and honourable response was that he must finish *Death in Venice* before there could be any thought of second opinions and possible surgery. At the end of the year, after he'd completed the composition draft, he wondered, as so often, whether it was the best or the worst music he'd ever written. Both these views have been expressed by listeners over the years since then.

As we have seen with the two stories by Henry James, *The Turn of the Screw* and *Owen Wingrave*, Britten was perfectly capable of storing material in the back of his mind for decades before making use of it. We can't be certain when he first read *Death in Venice*: his own copy of the text was an early edition of the then standard translation by H. T. Lowe-Porter, published in 1928; a dozen years later, at the Middagh Street ménage in New York, he knew Mann's sons Klaus and Golo. Given his subsequent holidays in Venice and the subject of Mann's novella, it seems inconceivable that he wouldn't have read the work many years before deciding to use it as the basis for an opera; one nudge may have come from a 1965 newspaper article whose Polish author, Wladyslaw Moes, declared himself to be the original of Mann's Tadzio. But in one sense Britten couldn't have chosen a more problematical moment: Luchino Visconti's film of *Death in Venice*, starring Dirk Bogarde as Aschenbach, was released in 1971, at first threatening difficulties over copyright and in the longer term planting a rival dramatic interpretation in audiences' minds (one, moreover, with its own specifically Mahlerian musical agenda). Visconti's film has sometimes been dismissed as soft porn, which it isn't, but it is certainly soft: Aschenbach is transformed from a writer into a composer, which makes him less verbal and intellectual, while Björn Andresen's Tadzio comes close to being a flirt. There are other wilful distortions: Aschenbach is so ill so early that he seems unlikely to survive until the film's final scene; Tadzio consciously looks and even gestures towards him too soon; Aschenbach actually warns the Polish family to leave Venice instead of finding himself unable to speak to them; and the crudely histrionic interpolated flashbacks provide Aschenbach with a different, Mahlerian rather than Mannian, past.

Gustav von Aschenbach, in Mann's novella, is a distinguished author: he seems to be in his late fifties or early sixties, roughly the same age as Britten when he was working on the opera. They are strikingly alike in other respects. In the opening pages, we are told that Aschenbach, feeling 'his life had begun its gradual decline', had an 'artist's fear of not finishing his task'; for him, writing was 'a duty he loved, and by now he had almost learned to love the enervating daily struggle between his proud, tenacious, tried and tested will and that growing weariness which no one must be allowed to suspect nor his finished work betray by any telltale sign of debility or lassitude'.[6] Later on, there's a remarkable moment as Aschenbach, intermittently reading in his beach deckchair, observes Tadzio, who is wrapped in a towel after swimming: 'It almost seemed to him that he was sitting here for the purpose of protecting the half-sleeping boy . . . And his heart was filled and moved by a paternal fondness, the tender concern by which he who sacrifices himself to beget beauty in the spirit is drawn to him who possesses beauty.'[7] For Britten too, as we've repeatedly seen, the protective and the paternal were crucial to his relationships with the young. As for Mann's Tadzio, he is 'a long-haired boy of about fourteen'; Aschenbach notices with 'astonishment' that he is 'entirely beautiful',[8] although he will in due course slightly qualify this with worries about the boy's pallor and his poor teeth. As the Polish family leave the hotel hall on their way to dinner – Aschenbach, characteristically, is the last to depart – Tadzio turns, 'and *as there was now no one else in the hall*, his strangely twilight-gray eyes met those of Aschenbach'[9] (my italics). Twenty pages, during which Aschenbach makes his thwarted attempt to leave Venice, must pass before Tadzio smiles at him and he silently utters his 'strangely indignant and tender reproaches: "You mustn't smile like that! One mustn't, do you hear, mustn't smile like that at anyone!"' After a pause, he adds 'the standing formula of the heart's desire': 'I love you.'[10] Britten and Piper will make these the closing words of their Act 1, preceded not by a chance evening encounter but by the Games of Apollo, yet in Mann they are subtly qualified by his reflections on 'the relationship between people who know each other only by sight': 'For man loves and respects his fellow man for as long as he is not yet in a position to evaluate him, and desire is born of defective knowledge.'[11]

Mann's *Death in Venice* is a work rich in echoes and symmetries. Two motifs are established before Aschenbach has even thought of leaving Munich: the images of death in the cemetery where he waits for his tram and the returned look of the stranger loitering there. Even the boat on which he travels is funereal – 'It was an ancient Italian boat, out of date and dingy and black with soot' – and this will be echoed by the sinister, unlicensed gondola on which he is rowed across a symbolic Styx. His journey is attended by a procession of sinister figures, beginning with 'the goat-bearded purser' who presciently assures him that Venice is 'A city irresistibly attractive to the man of culture, by its history no less than by its present charms'.[12] No less prescient in his way is the 'foppish old man' whose parting words – 'our compliments to your sweetheart'[13] – prefigure the hotel barber's assurance that, following his attentions, Aschenbach 'can fall in love as soon as he pleases'.[14] Other characters who emphasise Aschenbach's gathering inability to control either his destination or his destiny include the Hotel Manager and the grotesque

Leader of the Players: Britten and Piper take Mann's hints and
combine them all in a single role for baritone. Of the bystanders,
only the Englishman in the 'British travel agency', which we
(like Visconti) will recognise as Thomas Cook, is different: it is
he who, 'in his straightforward comfortable language',[15] finally
tells Aschenbach the truth about cholera in Venice.

For Britten and his librettist, who had at first dismissed
the subject as 'impossible', *Death in Venice* posed one specially
intractable problem. Since Tadzio doesn't speak, except in an
unreported way to his family and friends, how could he sing?
(And, if he had sung, would he have been an innocent treble,
an ambiguous countertenor, or a grown-up baritone like Billy
Budd?) Their solution was to turn him into a dancer, yet this
created its own difficulties: a dramatic dialogue in which one
participant remains silent makes huge demands of the other.
Moreover, a dancing Tadzio has to be physically more mature
than Mann's or Visconti's: he has, in fact, to be 'very, very
beautiful' and 'athletic to boot',[16] which are Stephen Reiss's
words about Alistair Hardy. For this part of the scheme to
work, the involvement of a great choreographer was essential;
and when Britten, no doubt feeling that their Suffolk near-
neighbourliness was a good omen, drove over to Chandos Lodge
to invite Ashton's collaboration, he was relieved and delighted
to find his proposal accepted at once. They were more alike
now than they had been at the time of *Albert Herring*: both of
them were older and sadder, of course, and they both felt that
they had been pushed aside by the fashionable young. 'You can't
believe how thrilled I am at the prospect of working with you,'[17]
Britten told Ashton. The feeling was reciprocated. Ashton also
knew and liked the Pipers, and this must have encouraged
Myfanwy Piper in her enthusiasm for the danced Games of
Apollo at the end of Act 1. She even suggested that these should
be danced naked, an idea which briefly captivated Britten before

he sensibly became 'worried lest the work might cause a certain interest that none of us really wants';[18] in the end, they had trouble enough getting permission for members of the Royal Ballet School to dance barefoot rather than in ballet shoes. The simple beach games of Tadzio and his friends were nevertheless extended into a pentathlon, which Ashton thought overlong but Britten was determined to retain; here, and in Aschenbach's dream in Act 2, Britten and Piper amplify the conflict between Apollo and Dionysus which is much more gently suggested in Mann's original version.

Was *Death in Venice*, as Britten had hoped, 'the best thing I have ever done'? On its own terms, yes. Its limitations, being self-imposed, are really choices and not limitations at all: it is a work in which the majority of the text is carried by only two voices – of the rest, a good deal is for chorus – and in which the musical palette is often restricted or eccentric. Its originality is everywhere apparent: in the sea-sickly Mahlerian motif of Aschenbach's opening words, 'My mind beats on and no words come', in which we might catch a distorted echo of Mahler's Nietzsche setting ('O Mensch! Gib acht! . . .) in his third symphony; in the foghorning brass and paddle-steamerish percussion which accompanies Aschenbach on the boat to Venice and the alternately noble and clangorous sounds of his arrival there; in the pompously insistent rhythms of the Hotel Manager's threatening welcome, dissolving into the lyricism of the view; in the continuously inventive piano accompaniments to Aschenbach's recitatives (during which he draws from his pocket a notebook, suggesting both soliloquy and a hope of turning this experience into *his* work of art); and in the gamelan-influenced tuned percussion, glockenspiel and (especially) vibraphone which always attend Tadzio, lending him, despite his extreme physicality, a ghostly air of untouchability. The opera's set pieces both dazzle and discomfort with their emotional ambiguities, as in the mysteriously grotesque laughing song which concludes the players' performance in Act 2 or the deranged pseudo-Rossini of the Hotel Barber. Like Mann (and, to give him his due, Visconti), Britten introduces an entirely new texture for the truth-telling travel agency clerk – low strings, clarinet and flute, sombre and reliably English – while in the dream sequence which follows we enter a nightmare world familiar from his earlier works. The scene of the Polish family's departure reprises and transfigures previously heard ideas, introduced by Gabrieli-like brass, briefly modulating to calm when the Hotel Manager once again invokes the famous view, reaching a menacing crescendo on 'the season comes to an end, our work is nearly done'. As Tadzio walks into the water at the end of the opera, the vibraphone diminishes to a wistful tinkle, yet the orchestral colours are, almost reassuringly, those in which Britten had habitually painted the sea.

By the time *Death in Venice* received its first performance, on 16 June 1973 at Snape Maltings, Britten was too ill to attend, let alone conduct it. The conductor was Steuart Bedford, the son of his old friend Lesley Bedford (née Duff), who worked with him closely during his last years and conducted first performances of the *Suite on English Folk Tunes* and *Phaedra*. Britten was at Horham, where he listened to the live relay of the second performance on BBC Radio 3 until he became distressed by an intermittent stray bass note, which in fact came from the equipment needed to turn the Venetian towers of John Piper's scenery. The part of Aschenbach was sung by Peter Pears, his various earthly tempters and the Voice of Dionysus by John Shirley-Quirk, and the Voice of Apollo by James Bowman; the role of Tadzio was danced by a recent graduate of the Royal Ballet School, Robert Huguenin. Critical reaction, while favourable and generous to everyone involved, tended not yet to grasp the complex resonances of Britten's achievement, although Edward

Greenfield in the *Guardian* admiringly noted that 'a compressed and intense story, an artist's inner monologue, lacking conversation, lacking plot, has against all the odds become a great opera'.[19] For Pears, who celebrated his sixty-third birthday on 22 June, it was a special triumph which he would in due course repeat at Covent Garden and at the Metropolitan Opera in New York. Before that, though, there was a private performance at the Maltings in September, so that Britten could at last see and hear his final opera. Ronan Magill, among the invited audience, was too much moved to speak to the composer; but Britten, he told Pears afterwards, 'looked so well and strong, and pleased with the performance. He looked so much better than I was led to believe – and so young.' He added: 'Please kiss Ben for me – and give him my love.'[20]

Peter Grimes, *Billy Budd* and *Death in Venice* together form a triptych. It is often enough noticed that each of these three operas pits the disturbed experience of an older man against youthful innocence – Grimes and his apprentices, Claggart and Billy, Aschenbach and Tadzio – yet they have something still more elemental in common: the presence of Britten's earliest companion and continual inspiration, the sea. It's no accident that Aschenbach's most perfect moment of calm contentment, just before his unsettling first glimpse of Tadzio, occurs in the passage beginning 'But there is the sea . . .' in Act 1 ('How I love the sound of the long low waves, rhythmic upon the sand'). For it is the consolatory sea, I suspect, which accounts for perhaps the most extraordinary aspect of Britten's *Death in Venice*: its strangely glowing subtext of thanksgiving and reconciliation. One can imagine his Aschenbach thinking to himself, like the painter Lily Briscoe at the end of Virginia Woolf's *To the Lighthouse*: 'It was done; it was finished.' Indeed, Myfanwy Piper's libretto seems momentarily to recall the same book when she has one of the hotel guests say to his son: 'If tomorrow is fine then we will go to the islands.' And surely, as he completed his incomparable late masterpiece, Britten would have fully shared Lily Briscoe's profound sense of exhaustion and relief: 'Yes, she thought, laying down her brush in extreme fatigue, I have had my vision.'[21]

2

He was certainly 'in extreme fatigue'. By the time he completed *Death in Venice*, he could no longer walk upstairs without very great difficulty. It was, he knew, his 'wonky heart', and he rightly suspected that this wonkiness went back a long way; Ian Tait, his GP in Aldeburgh, confirmed that, had he been called up for military service in the Second World War, he would have been declared medically unfit – a hypothetical sequence of events which, had it curtailed or even prevented his stay in America, might have significantly altered the history of English music. Ronan Magill, when he stayed at Horham in 1972, noticed Britten's strangely irregular heartbeat – 'It had a sort of hollow bang to it'[22] – and he felt that 'those hollow thuds embodied the origin of all the slings and arrows he had suffered in his life'.[23] Pears, who had come to believe, not wholly without reason, that most of Britten's illnesses were psychosomatic in origin, told Sidney Nolan: 'Ben is writing an evil opera, and it's killing him.'[24]

This was, of course, nonsense: for its composer, *Death in Venice* was cathartic rather than evil and its demands were likelier to prove life-threatening for Pears than for Britten. What was killing him was the cardiac deterioration which Ian Tait diagnosed in August 1972. But not until the full score of *Death in Venice* was finished – and after he and Pears had attended Peg

Hesse's sixtieth birthday celebrations at Wolfsgarten, where they performed to an audience for the last time – would Britten reluctantly allow himself, at the end of March 1973, to be driven to London for a consultation with a Harley Street heart specialist, Dr Graham Hayward. A week later, he was admitted to the London Clinic, where intensive drug treatment had little effect; accordingly, after ten days, he was transferred to the National Heart Hospital. His examination there resulted in a medical dilemma: he was likely to die soon from heart failure unless he underwent an operation to replace a valve; on the other hand, it seemed doubtful whether his heart would recover fully, even with a replacement valve, and there might be complications from the surgery itself. It was decided, reasonably, that the possibility of improvement was a better bet than the probability of death. 'Without it, he would not have been able to live very much longer,' Pears said of the operation, 'with it, there was a chance that he might regain much of his strength and stamina.'[25] Britten, when readmitted to the London Clinic on 2 May, was alarmingly jaunty, telling Ray Minshull, his producer at Decca, that he would be 'out of action all the summer, and then I should be as good as new – even conducting!'[26] However, the six-hour operation, at the National Heart Hospital on 7 May, was not a complete success: his heart was at first reluctant to restart and, more seriously, he suffered a minor stroke, perhaps caused by a particle of calcium finding its way into his bloodstream and then lodging in the brain. Although the coordination of his right hand and arm was impaired, there was at first some hope that this would be temporary.

While awaiting surgery at the National Heart Hospital, Britten had embarked on what was to be the last great friendship of his life, with the senior sister in charge of his ward, Rita Thomson. 'Don't worry about this, we'll see it through together,' she told him on his arrival; and that, at somewhat greater length than they at first anticipated, is exactly what they did. She visited him when he was returned after his surgery to the London Clinic and found him in a single room, lonely and frightened: except when working or walking, he had never been much good at being alone. While she was there one evening, he was given a huge and inappropriate meal, in unmanageable silver dishes, one of which when uncovered revealed an enormous steak: it was the sort of thing he wouldn't have wanted to eat even when fit. When the time came for him to go home to The Red House and there was no nurse available to accompany him, Rita Thomson, who had a few days' leave available, offered to stand in: Pears told Anthony Gishford that Britten was 'off to Suffolk . . . with a Sister from the Heart Hospital, with whom he has fallen in love, and she with him'.[27] Thereafter, they kept in touch and she became an occasional welcome weekend visitor. Early the following year, after she had left the National Heart Hospital to work as a freelance, Ian Tait would propose that she move permanently to Aldeburgh to look after Britten.

For a while, during the summer of 1973, there remained a vague hope that Britten's condition would improve, even though, as Ian Tait told Humphrey Carpenter, 'Ben's chances of regaining his capacity for full work and musical creation were very doubtful'.[28] There was, Tait added, 'a very strong wish to think otherwise, and also a great wish to encourage him', which natur- ally inhibited Britten's medical advisers and friends from saying what they thought: that the operation had been 'a great disap- pointment' (Tait) or 'a failure' (Pears). Britten would never again be able to conduct nor, much more distressingly, to play the piano either in public or to his own private satisfaction: when he tried, he couldn't bear to be overheard, even by a nurse outside the door, and his attempts to play duets with an Aldeburgh neighbour, Pat Nicholson, left him even more depressed. Still, he practised, in the belief or at any rate the hope that things would improve. 'When's it all going to get better?' he would ask his friends.

And then, just as that summer was turning to autumn, came the deaths of two old friends and collaborators. In the early hours of 20 September, William Plomer suffered a heart attack at his Sussex home and died in the arms of his partner Charles Erdmann. Just over a week later, on 29 September and also in the early hours, W. H. Auden died of heart failure in a Vienna hotel room. Donald Mitchell, who was with Britten when he received the news of Auden's death, says that it was the only time he ever saw the composer cry.

3

When Britten chose Auden's 'As it is, plenty' to conclude *On This Island* in 1937, he set it, with the callousness of youth, as a jauntily comical cabaret song. Yet even then the piece was bitter-sweet. The invocation 'Give thanks, give thanks' can't be merely flippant, nor can the lines which open the poem's final stanza:

> Let him not cease to praise
> Then his spacious days;
> Yes, and the success
> Let him bless, let him bless . . .[29]

This was the spirit Britten now tried more sombrely to embrace when he returned to composition in 1974. If he had looked back on his lifetime's music and declared, in a rather different tone, 'As it is, plenty', no one could have blamed him; instead, he brought his customary resourcefulness to bear on his new limitations and produced a series of important if small-scale late works.

The first of these was *Canticle V: The Death of St Narcissus*, Op. 89, for tenor and harp, written for Pears and Ossian Ellis in memory of Plomer. A little later, Britten would encourage the new performing partnership of Pears and Murray Perahia, then a young pianist whom he greatly admired and tactfully advised (once hiding behind a screen to avoid distracting him or inhibiting his playing), but he was understandably reluctant to compose material for an instrument on which he could no longer perform. The text is surprising and disconcerting: an early, posthumously published poem by T. S. Eliot, unknown to readers of the long-serving standard *Collected Poems*, yet at first startlingly familiar since it opens with lines which Eliot adapted and reused in *The Waste Land*. Less surprising is the way in which the piece seems, once again, to be a pendant to Britten's most recent opera: Narcissus, after various transmogrifications, becomes 'a dancer to God', and his music shares with *Death in Venice* a sense of resignation beneath its angst. The images of man as nature – Narcissus as a tree 'Twisting its branches among each other' and finally as 'green, dry and stained' – would also have resonated with the composer at this time, even though he said of the poem: 'I haven't got the remotest idea what it's about.'[30] Pears and Ellis gave the first performance at Schlöss Elmau, Upper Bavaria, on 15 January 1975.

Pears – whose own health problems at this time included high blood pressure and a number of throat infections – found Britten's invalid state almost impossible to cope with: his characteristic response was to throw himself into work and during the autumn of 1974 he was away from Aldeburgh for three months. He began to dread returning: writing from America to Peg Hesse on 1 November, he noted with relief that Britten hadn't 'mentioned lately my coming back for a visit', adding:

'I must say that the thought of such a visit appals me.'[31] This was shortly after his Met debut, at the age of sixty-four, in the triumphant New York premiere of *Death in Venice*, which took place on 18 October 1974; once again, John Shirley-Quirk sang the multiple baritone roles and Steuart Bedford conducted. For Pears, as he wrote to Britten on 12 October, the major disappointment was Bryan Pitts's Tadzio: although 'a much better dancer' than Robert Huguenin, 'he has *not* got *IT* at all!! Oh dear! I wouldn't dream of looking at him for more than 5 seconds.'[32] Nevertheless, the first performance was received 'with tremendous cheering and applause. I would call it a big success.'[33] There was a large 'English contingent' in support – including Donald and Kathleen Mitchell, Isador and Joan Caplan, Charles and Lettie Gifford, William and Pat Servaes – and a party afterwards given by the music publishers Schirmer's. So many of Britten's closest friends had travelled to New York that he might have felt abandoned in Aldeburgh, had he been there.

But, by way of a compensatory treat, Britten and Rita Thomson, now firmly installed as his nurse and indispensable companion, had flown by private plane to stay with Peg Hesse at Wolfsgarten. While conceding it was 'lovely here', Britten reported to his sister Beth that he'd 'had a 'fluey cold and felt lousy' and was 'very jealous of all of them in New York for D in V'.[34] Nevertheless he was trying to do 'a bit of work' on his *Suite on English Folk Tunes: 'A Time There Was'*, Op. 90, which he would finish exactly a month later. Although the ostensible logic behind this work was Britten's wish to find a home for 'Hankin Booby', the little folk-song-based piece for wind and percussion he had composed for the opening of the Queen Elizabeth Hall in 1967, as well as to memorialise Percy Grainger, another enthusiastic arranger of folk songs, the emotional impulse signalled by the subtitle was deeper and stronger. He

had, of course, set the Hardy poem from which it derives in
Winter Words:

> A time there was – as one may guess
> And as, indeed, earth's testimonies tell –
> Before the birth of consciousness,
>   When all went well.

Hardy's anguished concluding question – 'How long, how long?' –
– was precisely the one Britten continued to ask about his own
increasingly improbable recovery. Then, just as he was about to
put the finishing touches to the suite (whose last movement,
'Lord Melbourne', has a deeply moving and appropriately
English-pastoral part for cor anglais), a serendipitous piece of
broadcasting confirmed his subtitle. On 17 November, he wrote
to Pears:

> I've just listened to a re-broadcast of Winter Words (something
> like Sept. '72) and honestly you are the greatest artist that ever
> was – every nuance, subtle & never over-done – those great
> words, so sad & wise, painted for one, that heavenly sound
> you make, full but always coloured for words & music. What
> *have* I done to deserve such an artist and *man* to write for? I
> had to switch off before the folk songs because I couldn't [take]
> anything after 'how long, how long'. How long? – only till
> Dec. 20th – I think I can *just* bear it.
>
>   But I love you,
>   I love you
>   I love you – –
>   B.[35]

Pears replied from New York:

No one has ever ever had a lovelier letter than the one which came from you today – You say things which turn my heart over with love and pride, and I love you for every single word you write. But you know, Love is blind – and what your dear eyes do not see is that it is *you* who have given me everything, right from the beginning, from yourself in Grand Rapids! through Grimes & Serenade & Michelangelo and Canticles – one thing after another, right up to this great Aschenbach – I am here as your mouthpiece and I live in your music – And I can never be thankful enough to you and to Fate for all the heavenly joy we have had together for 35 years.

My darling, I love you –

P.[36]

These are both wonderful letters, but there's a crucial difference between them: Britten focuses on the present and anticipates the future, while Pears looks back gratefully to the past. Despite his ailments, Pears carried his years well: many would have thought him more handsome in his urbane sixties than in his prep-school-masterish youth. He had made younger gay friends on his travels – Donald Mitchell remembers one particular New Yorker, in leather jacket and jeans, who even turned up at an Aldeburgh Festival – and he was inevitably beginning to envisage a future without Ben.

Pears was back in Aldeburgh for Christmas and the new year. During January, Britten composed *Sacred and Profane*, Op. 91, for the unaccompanied voices of the madrigal group, named after the East Anglian madrigalist John Wilbye (1574–1638), which Pears directed: these settings of eight medieval lyrics are dedicated 'For P.P. and the Wilbye Consort' and were first performed by them at the Maltings on 14 September 1975. While Britten was working on *Sacred and Profane*, he received a handwritten letter from the Queen, whose warm personal regard for Britten and Pears stretched back through the opening (and reopening) of the Maltings to *Gloriana* and the Coronation. Would he, she wondered, consider writing something for her mother's seventy-fifth birthday in August? It was an appropriate suggestion – Queen Elizabeth the Queen Mother had accepted an invitation to become Patron of the Aldeburgh Festival a year earlier – as well as a tactful one: not an official commission nor a request for something grand, but a graceful attempt to cheer a composer in poor health. He responded at once: bearing in mind both the Queen Mother's Scottish upbringing and her titular role as the Scottish Regiment's Colonel-in-Chief, Britten proposed a cycle for tenor and harp, to be performed by Pears and Ellis, using poems by Robert Burns. Without waiting for the formality of royal approval, he set to work on *A Birthday Hansel*, Op. 92. But he could be tactful, too, and he made some textual changes: 'Health to the Maxwell's veteran Chief' became 'Health to our well-loved Hielan Chief' and 'Farewell, auld birkie' 'All hail, auld birkie', a term which gave no offence to the Queen Mother's Scottish ear. She was at the Castle of Mey for her birthday on 4 August where, among her presents, was Britten's manuscript of *A Birthday Hansel*; Ruth Fermoy, her lady-in-waiting, played the harp part for her on the piano, though it's not known if either of them sang. She was, she wrote to Britten, 'absolutely thrilled and delighted by this glorious birthday gift', and she commented in some detail on the poems he had chosen. 'I honestly do not think anything in my life has given me greater pleasure than your birthday gift,' she told him. 'It is very precious to me, and will I am sure give joy to your countless grateful admirers.'[37]

During May, Britten and Pears, together with Rita Thomson and Sue Phipps's stepdaughter Polly, had taken a holiday in Oxfordshire on a narrow boat, the *Amelia di Liverpool*, owned by John Shirley-Quirk. Britten now had padded swivelling chairs for working at The Red House and at Horham: one of these was installed at the boat's prow and there's a touching photograph of him seated in it, wearing a woolly tea-cosy hat and his characteristically resilient smile. Soon after his return to Aldeburgh, he received another personal letter from the Queen: Sir Arthur Bliss, the Master of the Queen's Music, had died on 27 March and she needed to appoint a successor. She was approaching him informally, in view of his illness, to see whether he might be persuaded to take it on; the only real compositional necessity would be something for the forthcoming Silver Jubilee. Britten declined, with real regret, on the grounds that he could no longer manage social occasions and seldom went to London: he felt the position should be held by someone lively and public-spirited who could 'write appropriate music, attend and preside over public occasions, and generally lead the musical profession'.[38] Now feeling older than his years, he seems to have decided, perhaps not quite reasonably, that the appropriate candidate should be younger than him – thus excluding Michael Tippett – and to have suggested Malcolm Williamson, whose appointment was not an unqualified success.

The Queen Mother was present at the 1975 Aldeburgh Festival to hear the first performance of the *Suite on English Folk Tunes: 'A Time There Was'*; afterwards she told Britten that she had been 'deeply moved by your glorious new piece', adding that 'Ruth & I came home all aglow!'[39] Among the other highlights at the Maltings that June was Janet Baker's incomparable performance of *Les Nuits d'été* by Berlioz, and as soon as the festival was over, Britten began to compose a piece for her to sing at the following year's festival. Almost thirty years earlier, Eric Crozier had suggested Racine's *Phèdre* as the basis for a chamber opera to follow *The Rape of Lucretia*; now Britten turned to Robert Lowell's recent version of the work, in rhyming couplets, as the text for his *Phaedra*, Op. 93, a cantata for mezzo-soprano, strings, harpsichord and percussion. There are five sections. A chime introduces the brief Prologue, in which Phaedra recalls the wedding day on which, turning aside from her new husband Theseus, she caught sight of her stepson Hippolytus. Then a short Recitative quickly brings us to the point at which 'Venus resigned her altar to my new lord'. In the third Presto section, Phaedra's description of Hippolytus as a 'monster' gives way to a confession of love accompanied by a thumpingly percussive and increasingly irregular heartbeat which surely mirrors Britten's own. Next comes a confessional Recitative addressed to Phaedra's maid Oenone: when she concludes that 'Death will give me freedom', there's a fleeting reminiscence, assisted by the accompanying strings and harpsichord, of Dido's lament in Purcell's *Dido and Aeneas*, another role Janet Baker had made her own. A characteristically energetic string passage leads to the final Adagio section, in which Phaedra confesses her love to Theseus and vows to take 'Medea's poison' before the music finally resolves into a Mahlerian chord of C major with added sixth and ninth.

Phaedra might indeed have made an excellent chamber opera, but it is overwhelmingly effective as a fifteen-minute cantata. It is, in more than one sense, a further pendant to *Death in Venice*: it concerns a mature individual's love for a beautiful young man and it ends in death; yet, as in the opera, the musical conclusion speaks once more of acceptance and redemption. Britten completed the cantata on 12 August: his amanuensis Colin Matthews played it through with him at the piano, with Britten sitting on the right of the keyboard and playing the vocal line with his left hand. Two months later, again with Matthews's invaluable help, he began his final major work, the String Quartet No. 3, Op. 94, dedicated to Hans Keller. The piece consists of five movements, of which the central one is the utterly astonishing 'Solo': here the first violin begins a rapturously unfolding song without words and modulates into a central passage of perfect birdsong – not seabirds, but inland birds from Horham – before it returns to its uncannily articulate lyricism. This is buttressed by two shorter, contrastingly boisterous movements, 'Ostinato' and 'Burlesque', and these in turn are framed by the opening 'Duets' and the concluding nine-minute 'Recitative and Passacaglia (La Serenissima)': Britten's last great composition, the finest of his string quartets, could scarcely have ended otherwise than with this movingly elegiac example of his favourite musical form. The Venetian subtitle reminds us that the quartet was completed during the holiday which he was persuaded to take in November by Bill and Pat Servaes, who had already planned a trip to Venice with their Chilean friend Esteban Cerda. Britten, now in a wheelchair, was manoeuvred with some panache by Rita Thomson: they stayed in a suite at the Hotel Danieli, with a balcony overlooking the Grand Canal, opposite the church of Santa Maria della Salute, whose bells (heard only once a year, on 21 November, a prelude to Britten's birthday) provided the basis for his passacaglia. As ever, he responded well to being 'mothered' and, as he finished the quartet, seemed like a man liberated from the pressures of a lifetime. If he had previously identified with Aschenbach, now he was exorcising him.

With Britten back in Aldeburgh before Christmas, Colin Matthews was joined by his brother David to play the quartet through to Britten as a piano duet. In his journal, David Matthews noted how well Britten looked after his holiday, despite his less firm voice and his difficulty in walking. On 17 December, the brothers at first made 'rather a botched job' of the piece but, after lunch and some more practice,

> we did produce a reasonable through-performance for him. & it was a moving occasion as the quartet is certainly a masterpiece & proves his creative powers are quite undiminished.

The long passacaglia finale is especially fine, a serene piece in
E major. After we have finished there was a silence and then
Ben said, in a small voice: *Do you think it's any good?* We assured
him that it was.[40]

Britten had been asking that question, in one form or another,
throughout his composing life: he was never quite sure. This was
among the reasons why he so needed to have trusted friends about
him, as he did once again that Christmas: Basil Coleman, their
old quarrel forgotten, was among the guests. Early in the new
year, a complete performance of *Paul Bunyan* was broadcast on
Radio 3 with Norma Burrowes as Tiny, George Hamilton IV as
the Narrator and Pears as Johnny Inkslinger; the conductor was
Steuart Bedford. Britten, when he heard it, was moved to tears:
he hadn't, he said, realised that it was such a strong piece.

It was by now clear that his condition was deteriorating
rapidly: the possibility of a further operation was mooted, but
both Ian Tait and Michael Petch, the registrar at the National
Heart Hospital, agreed that the risk was too great. In March,
Britten made a new will, in which the first priority was providing
generously for Pears: 'This is far more important to me than
anything that is going on in Aldeburgh, or anything to do with
my music.'[41] Aldeburgh and his music would be well looked
after, nevertheless, for he had never lost his ingrained habits
of frugality and he would die a wealthy man. Meanwhile, to
anyone who had managed to remain ignorant about his state
of health, the Aldeburgh Festival of 1976 might have given the
impression that Britten was composing with renewed vigour.
A Birthday Hansel, which in January had been performed
privately for the Queen Mother – with both her daughters, as
well as the composer and Rita Thomson, present – at the home
of Lady Fermoy, was performed by Pears and Ossian Ellis.
Phaedra received its first performance from Janet Baker and the

English Chamber Orchestra under Steuart Bedford. And *Paul Bunyan* was at last staged at the Maltings, directed by Colin Graham. But the second Saturday of the festival, 12 June, held a surprise in store.

By the time the guests who had been mysteriously invited to a garden party had assembled at The Red House – among them, in another reconciliation, Eric Crozier and Nancy Evans – the secret was out: Britten had been appointed a life peer in the Queen's Birthday Honours. Rita Thomson liked to take some of the credit: she said that she'd threatened never to speak to him again if he refused it (he was rumoured to have turned down a knighthood earlier). But some of his friends had reservations: Lord Harewood found it 'unnecessary' and Donald Mitchell thought 'it didn't seem sensible'. Both should have known better. Britten viewed his peerage in the same spirit as he regarded all the other honours which had come his way, as a mark of esteem not for him but for music. Also, he joked, given the trouble he now had writing, it took much less effort for him to sign letters with the single word 'Britten' than with his full name.

Although during 1976 he undertook two arranging tasks (a new set of eight folk songs for Pears and Ellis, and a version of his Dowland-based *Lachrymae* for viola and string orchestra), wrote a little cello piece as the theme for a multi-composer set of variations to mark Paul Sacher's seventieth birthday and began a long-contemplated setting of Edith Sitwell's *Praise We Great Men*, Britten was to finish only one more work: the *Welcome Ode*, Op. 95, to mark the Queen's visit to Suffolk during her Silver Jubilee year. After the festival, in an attempt to escape from what was already becoming an oppressively hot summer, he and Pears, accompanied by Rita Thomson, flew to Bergen in Norway, where they stayed at the Solstrand Fjord Hotel and Britten worked on the piece; he completed the composition sketch in August, soon after his return to

Aldeburgh, and asked Colin Matthews to orchestrate it. The *Welcome Ode*, for children's chorus and orchestra, sets three celebratory texts – 'Summer Pastimes' by Thomas Dekker and John Ford, 'The Fairies' Roundel', published anonymously in 1600, and Henry Fielding's 'Ode to the New Year' – and it would indeed be performed, by the Suffolk Schools' Choir and Orchestra conducted by Keith Shaw, at the Corn Exchange, Ipswich, in the presence of the Queen, on 11 July 1977. That the work bearing Britten's final opus number should have been for children, for Suffolk and for the Queen seems absolutely fitting.

'I don't need to fight any more,' Britten told Pears; he might almost have added, 'As it is, plenty.' There was champagne for the guests at his sixty-third birthday on 22 November, but he was too ill to drink it. Old friends trooped upstairs to his bedroom, one by one, to say – without saying – goodbye. Britten had once told Imogen Holst of his 'very strong feeling that people died at the right moment, and that the greatness of a person included the time when he was born and the time he endured'.[42] Now, when he asked Rita Thomson if he were dying, she replied: 'Well, you are very, very ill, love.'[43] Pears, who had continued throughout the autumn with his professional schedule, to the bafflement of those who failed to understand that it was the only way he could hope to stay sane, eventually cut short a Canadian tour in mid-November and returned to The Red House. The Bishop of St Edmundsbury and Ipswich came to talk, read prayers for the dying and administer Holy Communion (which Britten, according to Pears, accepted mainly to make the bishop happy). On Friday 3 December, after eating a light supper, Britten fell peacefully asleep; but later that night, Susie Walton – who was sharing nursing duties with Rita Thomson – noticed that his breathing had deteriorated. Pears, when summoned, told Rita: 'I'll stay with him, you go and sleep.'[44] At 4.15 on the morning of Saturday, 4 December 1976, Benjamin Britten died peacefully in his partner's arms.

4

I remember that Saturday morning with unusual clarity. I was a young writer and teacher, living in a small town on the Hertfordshire–Bedfordshire border. I'd decided to drive into Bedford to do the weekend shopping and thought I might treat myself to a new LP while I was there. What I wanted was the recent recording, by Anthony Rooley and the Consort of Musicke, of John Dowland's *Lachrimae* (1604): there was a basic classical department upstairs in the little HMV shop which ought to have had it. However, as I wrote in my journal for 4 December 1976:

> It wasn't there, but in order to discover this I had to leaf through the section called 'Composers A–E', since Dowland isn't popular enough to earn a section of his own. I did come across several records of Britten, including the *Serenade for Tenor, Horn and Strings* which I've been meaning to buy; I hesitated, but decided to pursue the Dowland, without success. Returning home, I heard of Britten's death on the lunchtime news, and one of my reactions was an odd sense of failure – that I hadn't got the record before I'd heard of his death, that I'd never heard him at Aldeburgh after all, that I was too late.
>
> I felt I knew Britten . . . Partly it's the absolute certainty that I could listen to and be enriched by any of Britten's work – even the enormous amount I don't know. I have confidence in it in that very rare way . . .

That last feeling – and I'd have said the same about Auden –
was, I suspect, quite commonly shared. For Britten was one of
the few exceptional creative artists whose greatness I thought I
could take on trust: if I sometimes failed to appreciate it, that
was almost certainly because I wasn't listening properly. His
death, like Auden's, seemed to shake the cultural foundations in
a way that possibly doesn't happen any more. Incidentally, that
juxtaposition with Dowland was just a marvellous coincidence:
I hadn't yet discovered Britten's *Lachrymae*.

Britten's death led the BBC news bulletins that day. The
following morning, it made the Sunday papers' front pages.
The Queen sent a personal message of condolence to Peter
Pears. On the day of the funeral, Tuesday 7 December, the
cortège looped around Aldeburgh to travel back along the entire
length of the High Street, where the shops were closed and the
festival flag flew at half mast. It was at once the town's gesture
of respect for Britten and an acknowledgement of his own respect
for the town: a burial in Westminster Abbey had been proposed,
but he hadn't wanted that. His grave in the annexe of the parish
churchyard at Aldeburgh was lined with reeds from the marshes
at Snape by Bob and Doris Ling, the caretakers at the Maltings;
inside the church, the Festival Singers performed his early *Hymn
to the Virgin* and the congregation sang the hymns from *Saint
Nicolas*. 'Ben will like the sound of the trumpets, though he will
find it difficult to believe they are sounding for him,'[45] said the
Right Reverend Dr Leslie Brown, Bishop of St Edmundsbury
and Ipswich, at the end of his address. Among the mourners
were Britten's three siblings (Barbara, Robert and Beth), Pears,
Rita Thomson, Rostropovich and Princess Margaret of Hesse
and the Rhine. In due course, Pears would be buried beside
Britten and Imogen Holst nearby: even in death, the guiding
creative spirits of the Aldeburgh Festival wouldn't forsake the
place.

Of Britten's three enduring legacies, the first and the finest is, rather obviously, his music. Perhaps because he had suffered from the whims of fashion during his lifetime, his posthumous reputation was to enjoy a long period of steady consolidation. 'Everything about Britten's style – his deliberate parochialism, his tonal orientation, his preference for classical forms – went against the grain of the postwar era,' writes Alex Ross.[46] Britten felt this unfashionability most acutely during the 1960s: his music seemed both conservative when compared with that of younger composers and hopelessly staid in a world which had begun to take pop music seriously. Yet, at the same time, part of the musical audience never quite lost its bemused sense that he was 'modern' and 'difficult', a delusion which persisted long after his death. I remember following a pair of elderly concert-goers out of the Maltings one evening in the early 1990s: on the stairs, one turned to the other and glumly remarked, 'I don't know quite what to make of Britten's so-called Cello Symphony,' exactly as if they had just been listening to a controversial piece receiving its first performance. But what looks like a pincer movement of disapproval – or, as Thersites has it, 'Fools on both sides' – may actually have worked in Britten's favour: it prevented him from being pigeonholed, thus ensuring that those who sought to denigrate his achievement would do so from laughably contradictory positions.

While his status as a great composer is now largely undisputed, there remains a good deal of lively (and healthy) debate about where that greatness is most to be found. Although the widely held notion that he was mainly an opera composer is one which he himself challenged, the central importance of the operas is undeniable. But which of the operas? John Bridcut has recently argued that *The Turn of the Screw* 'is one of the wonders of twentieth-century opera, with a strong claim to be Britten's greatest'.[47] For me, the supreme achievement lies in the group I've already defined as his sea trilogy: *Peter Grimes*, *Billy Budd* and *Death in Venice*. Choosing between them is impossible and, happily, unnecessary. While writing this book I tended to value most the one I was thinking about at the time: at this moment (partly, no doubt, because it comes last) I can readily agree with Ian Bostridge in regarding *Death in Venice* as 'perhaps his greatest opera'.[48] And mentioning Bostridge hints at a vital element in our continuously evolving perception of Britten's work: the way in which a succession of younger British tenors – among them Bostridge, Mark Padmore, James Gilchrist, Nicky Spence and Allan Clayton – have steadily liberated both the operas and the song cycles from the ghostly presence of Peter Pears. This isn't for a moment to denigrate Pears: it is simply to say that, during his lifetime, it was almost impossible for another tenor to sing Britten without sounding different and somehow wrong; whereas, after Pears's death, it was at last time for the works themselves to grow up and leave home. Nowhere is this more evident than with *Death in Venice*, which couldn't avoid being burdened by the particular circumstances of its composition and early performances and which has correspondingly benefited from the different dynamics of recent productions: for example, the DVD filmed at Teatro La Fenice in 2008 – with Aschenbach a quite spruce middle-aged intellectual and a tall, dark Tadzio – completely banishes any lurking paedophile overtones. So the operas, like the plays of Shakespeare, now make their own way in a world where they will be endlessly reinvented, with inspiring and occasionally infuriating consequences.

The song cycles, too, have been refreshed by new interpreters. When the 2009 Aldeburgh Festival included a series of concerts in which young singers, accompanied by Malcolm Martineau, performed virtually all Britten's songs for voice and piano, it felt like a deliberate gesture of handing on. Of those cycles, *Winter Words* remains for me the greatest: Britten, as we have seen, engaged with Hardy's poems at a deeper level than with anything else he set. The three major song cycles with orchestra – *Les Illuminations, Serenade, Nocturne* – are different again; here, despite the noble efforts of Bostridge and others, we must continue to give thanks for an invention Britten didn't always love, the gramophone, and particularly for Decca's loyal support of the composer and his work. To be able to hear, now and always, the *Serenade for Tenor, Horn and Strings* performed by Peter Pears and Dennis Brain, for example, is a privilege of a kind undreamed of by earlier composers and their audiences. The monumental recording of the *War Requiem* with the three soloists for whom it was written, a feat unmanaged by the first performance in Coventry, is a simply astonishing historical document of the mid-twentieth century. The disc of *Noye's Fludde*, made in the parish church at Orford, provides as great a lift to the spirit as any I know. And so on.

If we think of Britten as primarily a composer for voices or for the voice, we should remember that his career effectively began with two startling short works for orchestra: the mysteriously discarded Double Concerto and the *Sinfonietta*. Then there are the concertos for piano and for violin, the *Sinfonia da Requiem* and the amazing Cello Symphony, while many listeners are belatedly coming to admire *The Prince of the Pagodas*. For generations of children, musical education has begun with *The Young Person's Guide to the Orchestra*: mine certainly did, in the shape of the Malcolm Sargent recording on 12″ Columbia 78s, and I have them still. Away from the orchestra, Britten wrote three suites for cello and three of the century's finest string quartets, the last and most remarkable of them during his final illness. For reasons possibly connected with a day in December 1976, I've a special affection for the *Nocturnal after John Dowland* and for *Lachrymae*, especially in the late version for viola and string orchestra.

Just as everyone seems to have personal favourites among Britten's work, so most of us must own up to blind spots and regrets. My own major blind spot – as the attentive reader will already have gathered – concerns the three church parables: this is partly because, through no fault of their own, they bump into other prejudices of mine, and I may get over it. I'm also not easily persuaded by twentieth-century choral music in general: again, *mea culpa*. As for regrets, I mean those useless wishes for a composer to have written more of this or that. In Britten's case, the lack of solo piano music – and his professed dislike of an instrument he played so marvellously – remains slightly baffling; and one can't help feeling wistful about the comparatively small tally of full-length orchestral works, for no one has ever deployed instrumental colour with greater imagination or subtlety. In this, one of his few contemporary rivals was Duke Ellington, whom he might have heard in the 1930s in London, or thirty years later, when they both appeared at the Leeds Festival; yet, while Britten gratefully embraced the musical colours of the gamelan, he had a kind of shyness about learning from jazz. That, too, may be a matter for regret, as well as providing an answer to Mervyn Horder's 'salient question why Britten couldn't write, or at least never wrote, a swinging tune'.[49] But enough of regrets.

Britten's second enduring legacy is the organisation now known as Aldeburgh Music, together with the Britten–Pears Foundation and the Britten–Pears School of Advanced Musical Studies. By some sort of miracle, although not without some inescapable rows and ructions, Snape Maltings has grown into a cultural campus of performing and rehearsing spaces which surpasses Britten's most ambitious dreams. At the same time, The Red House has become an archive and exhibition centre, undergoing major extension and refurbishment for Britten's centenary year. Although there are now year-round events at the Maltings, the Aldeburgh Festival in June remains the heart of the matter: it seems entirely proper that, unlike Bayreuth or Salzburg, this hasn't become an occasion designed to honour a single composer, although the appointment of Pierre-Laurent Aimard as artistic director in 2009 raised some eyebrows when he was described in the press as 'not an unequivocal admirer of Aldeburgh's founder'.[50] The subsequent appearance of Pierre Boulez at the 2010 festival, not to mention some of Aldeburgh's electronic and multi-media adventures, would surely have had the same effect on Britten's and Pears's ghosts as the first performance of Birtwistle's *Punch and Judy*. Yet to say that is to acknowledge that any lively arts organisation will at times provoke (as Aldeburgh has always done) anger and dissent. And to lament that the festival has become tainted by modishness on the one hand and by commercial sponsorship on the other is simply to make a more general observation about the state of the arts in our time.

The last of Britten's three enduring legacies is his non-musical one. He and Pears taught gay men of my generation the astonishing lesson that it was possible for a homosexual couple to live decently and unapologetically in provincial England. As Bernard Levin put it five years after Britten's death, in his movingly eloquent portrait of the Aldeburgh Festival: 'his private life was a model of devotion and integrity – it is not at all an exaggeration to say that the example set by Britten and Pears went far to instil throughout this country a sympathetic understanding, so long and so brutally denied, of homosexual love'.[51] The fallings-out with some former friends and colleagues, which have been accorded almost delirious over-attention by some writers on Britten, are on any scale of natural justice colossally outweighed by his generosity to other friends and colleagues, to young protégés and fellow musicians and, not least, to the countless ordinary people whose musical lives he transformed, from wartime CEMA concerts to the enduring local magic of his Aldeburgh Festival. Basil Coleman said of Britten and Pears: 'I would be half the person I am if I hadn't known them; it was a privilege to be with them. They had extraordinary generosity and capacity for kindness, understanding and caring.'[52] Pears's view of Britten was even simpler: 'He was a *good* man. How could he not be having written all that beautiful music?'[53] As it is, plenty.

BIBLIOGRAPHY

There is already an enormous amount of writing about Britten, as the exhaustive bibliographies in each volume of *Letters from a Life* demonstrate. This brief list contains works I have consulted while writing this book and to which reference is made in the text, where appropriate with the abbreviations by which they are identified in the Notes.

BOOKS ABOUT BRITTEN, PEARS AND ALDEBURGH

Ariane Bankes and Jonathan Reekie (eds), *New Aldeburgh Anthology*, Boydell, 2009 [*AA2*]

Paul Banks (ed.), *The Making of Peter Grimes: Essays and Studies*, **Boydell, 1996** [*TMPG*]

Ronald Blythe (ed.), *Aldeburgh Anthology*, Snape Maltings Foundation in association with Faber, 1971 [*AA1*]

John Bridcut, *Britten's Children*, Faber, 2006 [*JBBC*]

John Bridcut, *The Faber Pocket Guide to Britten*, Faber, 2010 [*JBPG*]

Beth Britten, *My Brother Benjamin*, Kensal Press, 1986 [*MBB*]

Humphrey Carpenter, *Benjamin Britten: A Biography*, Faber, 1992 [*HCBB*]

Nick Clark, Kevin Gosling and Lucy Walker, *Young Britten: Schoolboy, Composer*, Britten–Pears Foundation, 2009

Mervyn Cooke (ed.), *The Cambridge Companion to Benjamin Britten*, Cambridge University Press, 1999

John Evans (ed.), *Journeying Boy: The Diaries of the Young Benjamin Britten, 1928–1938*, Faber, 2009 [*JB*]

Peter Evans, *The Music of Benjamin Britten*, Dent, 1979 [*PEBB*]

Boris Ford (ed.), *Benjamin Britten's Poets: The Poetry He Set to Music*, Carcanet, 1994 [*BFBP*]

Anthony Gishford (ed.), *A Tribute to Benjamin Britten on his Fiftieth Birthday*, Faber, 1963

Christopher Grogan, *Imogen Holst: A Life in Music*, revised edition, Boydell, 2010 [*IHLM*]

Christopher Headington, *Peter Pears: A Biography*, Faber, 1992 [*CHPP*]

David Herbert (ed.), *The Operas of Benjamin Britten*, Hamish Hamilton, 1979

Michael Kennedy, *Britten (The Master Musicians)*, Dent, 1981 [*MKBB*]

Paul Kildea (ed.), *Britten on Music*, Oxford University Press, 2003 [*BOM*]

David Matthews, *Britten*, Haus, 2003 [*DMB*]

Donald Mitchell, *Britten and Auden in the Thirties: The Year 1936*, Faber, 1981

Donald Mitchell and John Evans, *Benjamin Britten: Pictures from a Life, 1913–1976*, Faber, 1978 [*PFL*]

Donald Mitchell and Philip Reed (eds), *Letters from a Life: Volume One, 1923–39*, Faber, 1991 [*LL1*]

Donald Mitchell and Philip Reed (eds), *Letters from a Life: Volume Two, 1939–45*, Faber, 1991 [*LL2*]

Donald Mitchell, Philip Reed and Mervyn Cooke (eds), *Letters from a Life: Volume Three, 1946–51*, Faber, 2004 [*LL3*]

Michael Oliver, *Benjamin Britten*, Phaidon, 1996 [*MOBB*]

Philip Reed (ed.), *The Travel Diaries of Peter Pears 1936–1978*, Boydell, 1995 [*PPTD*]

Philip Reed, Mervyn Cooke and Donald Mitchell (eds), *Letters from a Life: Volume Four, 1952–1957*, Boydell, 2008 [*LL4*]

Philip Reed and Mervyn Cooke (eds), *Letters from a Life: Volume Five, 1958–1965*, Boydell, 2010 [*LL5*]

Eric Walter White, *Benjamin Britten: His Life and Operas*, second edition, Faber, 1983 [*EWBB*]

OTHER WORKS CITED IN THE TEXT

Peter F. Alexander, *William Plomer: A Biography*, Oxford University Press, 1989

John Amis, *Amiscellany*, Faber, 1985

W. H. Auden, *Collected Shorter Poems 1927–1957*, Faber, 1966

W. H. Auden, *The English Auden*, edited by Edward Mendelson, Faber, 1977

W. H. Auden, *Prose 1926–1938*, edited by Edward Mendelson, Faber, 1996

W. H. Auden & Christopher Isherwood, *Plays and other Dramatic Writings by W. H. Auden, 1928–1938*, edited by Edward Mendelson, Faber, 1989

A. L. Bacharach (ed.), *British Music in Our Time*, Pelican, 1946

Ian Bostridge, *A Singer's Notebook*, Faber, 2011

Humphrey Carpenter, *W. H. Auden: A Biography*, Allen & Unwin, 1981

Virginia Spencer Carr, *Paul Bowles: A Life*, Peter Owen, 2004

John Culshaw, *Putting the Record Straight*, Secker & Warburg, 1981

Richard Davenport-Hines, *Auden*, Heinemann, 1995

Michael Davidson, *The World, the Flesh and Myself*, Arthur Barker, 1962

Dorothy J. Farman, *Auden in Love*, Faber, 1985

E. H. Fellowes (ed.), *English Madrigal Verse 1588–1632*, third edition, revised and enlarged by Frederick W. Sternfeld and David Greer, Clarendon Press, 1967

Dietrich Fischer-Dieskau, *Echoes of a Lifetime*, Macmillan, 1989

E. M. Forster, *Aspects of the Novel*, Pelican, 1962

E. M. Forster, *Two Cheers for Democracy*, Penguin, 1965

E. M. Forster, *The Prince's Tale and other uncollected writings*, André Deutsch, 1998

P. N. Furbank, *E. M. Forster: A Life. Volume Two: Polycrates' Ring*. Secker & Warburg, 1978

Thomas Hardy, *The Complete Poems*, New Wessex edition, Macmillan, 1976

Thomas Hardy, *Jude the Obscure*, New Wessex edition, Macmillan, 1974

Matt Houlbrook, *Queer London*, University of Chicago Press, 2005

Samuel Hynes, *The Auden Generation*, Bodley Head, 1976

Christopher Isherwood, *Lions and Shadows*, Four Square Books, 1963

Christopher Isherwood, *Christopher and his Kind*, Eyre Methuen, 1977

Christopher Isherwood, *Diaries, Volume One: 1939–1960*, edited by Katharine Bucknell, Methuen, 1996

Christopher Isherwood, *Diaries, Volume Two: 1960–1969*, edited by Katharine Bucknell, Chatto & Windus, 2010

Henry James, *The Turn of the Screw* and *The Aspern Papers*, Penguin, 1984

John Jolliffe, *Glyndebourne: An Operatic Miracle*, John Murray, 1999

Julie Kavanagh, *Secret Muses: The Life of Frederick Ashton*, Faber, 1996

Constant Lambert, *Music Ho!*, second edition, Faber, 1937

James Lees-Milne, *Ancestral Voices*, Chatto & Windus, 1975

Bernard Levin, *Conducted Tour*, Jonathan Cape, 1981

Diana McVeagh, *Gerald Finzi: His Life and Music*, Boydell, 2005

Herman Melville, *Billy Budd*, New American Library, 1961

Yehudi Menuhin, *Unfinished Journey*, Macdonald, 1977

Mark Mitchell (ed.), *The Penguin Book of International Gay Writing*, Viking, 1995

Wendy Moffat, *E. M. Forster: A New Life*, Bloomsbury, 2010

Philip Norman, *Shout! The True Story of The Beatles*, Elm Tree Books, 1981

Charles Osborne, *W. H. Auden: The Life of a Poet*, Eyre Methuen, 1980

Wilfred Owen, *Collected Poems*, Chatto & Windus, 1961

Neil Powell, *George Crabbe: An English Life*, Pimlico, 2004

Alex Ross, *The Rest is Noise*, Fourth Estate, 2008

Edward Sackville-West & Desmond Shawe-Taylor (eds), *The Record Guide*, Collins, 1955

Edward Sackville-West & Desmond Shawe-Taylor (eds), *The Record Guide Supplement*, Collins, 1956

Stanley Sadie (ed.), *The Concise Grove Dictionary of Music*, Macmillan, 1988

John Saumarez Smith (ed.), *A Spy in the Bookshop: Letters between Heywood Hill and John Saumarez Smith 1966–74*, Frances Lincoln, 2006

Tony Scotland, *Lennox and Freda*, Michael Russell, 2010

Stephen Spender, *World Within World*, Faber, 1951

Stephen Spender, *The Temple*, Faber, 1988

Stephen Spender (ed.), *W. H. Auden: A Tribute*, Weidenfeld & Nicolson, 1974

Richard Taruskin, *The Oxford History of Western Music, Volume 5: The Late Twentieth Century*, Oxford University Press, 2005

Colm Tóibín, *New Ways to Kill Your Mother*, Viking, 2012

Galina Vishnevskaya, *Galina: A Russian Story*, Hodder & Stoughton, 1984

William White, *History, Gazetteer and Directory of Suffolk*, W. White, 1844

Virginia Woolf, *To the Lighthouse*, Penguin, 1992

Rob Young, *Electric Eden: Unearthing Britain's Visionary Music*, Faber, 2010

NOTES

1 *Britten Minor*

1. William White, *History, Gazetteer and Directory of Suffolk*, p. 497 • **2**. *Britten on Music*, p. 145 • **3**. Humphrey Carpenter, *Benjamin Britten: A Biography*, p. 11 • **4**. *Letters from a Life*, *1*, p. 210 • **5**. BB to Ethel Astle, 30 September 1937, *LL1*, p. 83 • **6**. Ibid., *LL1*, p. 82 • **7**. Basil Reeve, *LL1*, p. 14 • **8**. *BOM*, p. 311 • **9**. David Matthews, *Britten*, p. 1 • **10**. *BOM*, p. 177 • **11**. Beth Britten, *My Brother Benjamin*, p. 32 • **12**. *MBB*, p. 30 • **13**. *MBB*, p. 27 • **14**. *MBB*, p. 39 • **15**. *MBB*, p. 41 • **16**. *MBB*, p. 51 • **17**. Decca LW 5163, sleevenote • **18**. *Benjamin Britten: Pictures from a Life*, plate 36 • **19**. *BOM*, p. 178 • **20**. *HCBB*, p. 9 • **21**. *BOM*, p. 179 • **22**. As Oscar Wilde might have observed, to lose one school may be regarded as a misfortune, to lose two looks like carelessness (or perhaps arson). • **23**. *LL1*, p. 84 • **24**. EMI 5 56534 2, booklet note • **25**. *BOM*, p. 311 • **26**. *LL3*, pp. 48–9 • **27**. *LL1*, p. 84 • **28**. *HCBB*, p. 10 • **29**. *HCBB*, p. 21 • **30**. *Guardian*, 7 June 1971 • **31**. *HCBB*, p. 21 • **32**. Diary, 17 June 1928, *LL1*, pp. 91–2 • **33**. The phrase is Graham Greene's, from *The Power and the Glory*. • **34**. Available at www.brittenpears.org • **35**. *BOM*, pp. 61–2 • **36**. R. V. Britten to the British Broadcasting Company Ltd, ? July 1926, *LL1*, p. 86 • **37**. BB to Mrs Britten, 28 August 1926, *LL1*, p. 88 • **38**. *BOM*, p. 62 • **39**. *BOM*, p. 250 • **40**. *MBB*, p. 54 • **41**. A. L. Bacharach (ed.), *British Music in Our Time*, p. 75 • **42**. Nevertheless, *The Record Guide* of 1955 lists as still available an 'antique' recording of Bridge's *Suite for Strings* (1910) which pre-dates Bacharach's book • **43**. Argo ZK 40, sleevenote • **44**. *BOM*, p. 77 • **45**. *BOM*, p. 250 • **46**. *BOM*, p. 62 • **47**. *BOM*, pp. 250–1 • **48**. *PFL*, plate 46 • **49**. *BOM*, p. 251 • **50**. BB to Mr and Mrs Britten, 21 September 1928, *LL1*, p. 93 • **51**. BB to Mrs Britten, 23 September 1928, *LL1*, p. 96 • **52**. Michael Davidson, *The World, the Flesh and Myself*, p. 126 • **53**. W. H. Auden, *Prose 1926–1938*, p. 57 • **54**. Stephen Spender (ed.), *W. H. Auden: A Tribute*, p. 38 • **55**. *Grasshopper* (Gresham's School, 1950), *LL1*, p. 223 • **56**. *BOM*, p. 147 • **57**. *HCBB*, p. 29 • **58**. *Journeying Boy*, p. 27 • **59**. Diary, 10 November 1928, *LL1*, p. 95 • **60**. Thomas Hardy, *The Complete Poems*, p. 514 • **61**. *LL1*, p. 10 • **62**. *LL1*, p. 11 • **63**. Diary, 13 November 1928, *JB*, p. 14 • **64**. Diary, 31 July 1928, *LL1*, p. 104 • **65**. *HCBB*, p. 28 • **66**. Diary, 24 May 1936, *LL1*, p. 104 • **67**. Diary, 8 January 1937, *JB*, p. 400 • **68**. *HCBB*, p. 29 • **69**. Oliver C. Berthoud to BB, 16 March 1971, *LL1*, p. 115 • **70**. BB to Mr and Mrs Britten, 19 January 1930, *LL1*, p. 119 • **71**. Diary, 1 March 1930, *JB*, p. 35 • **72**. Diary, 22 May 1930, *LL1*, p. 97 • **73**. BB to Mrs Britten, 18 March 1929, *LL1*, p. 109 • **74**. *LL1*, p. 104 • **75**. Diary, 16 January 1930, *JB*, p. 29 • **76**. BB to Mr and Mrs Britten, 19 January 1930, *LL1*, p. 119 • **77**. Diary, 5 September 1930, *LL1*, p. 136 • **78**. J. R. Eccles to Mrs Britten, 21 June 1930, *LL1*, p. 131 • **79**. Nick Clark, Kevin Gosling and Lucy Walker, *Young Britten: Schoolboy, Composer*, p. 9

2 *Some College*

1. *BOM*, p. 232 • **2**. Charles Osborne, *W. H. Auden: The Life of a Poet*, p. 39 • **3**. *BOM*, p. 148 • **4**. Diary, 3 December 1930, *JB*, p. 57 • **5**. Frank Bridge to BB, 25 June 1930, *LL1*, p. 132 • **6**. Frank Bridge to BB, 13 August 1930, *LL1*, p. 133 • **7**. Harold Samuel to BB, 20 August 1930, *LL1*, p. 134 • **8**. Diary, 23 September 1930, *JB*, p. 53 • **9**. BB to Mr and Mrs Britten, 24 September 1930, *LL1*, p. 140 • **10**. Diana McVeagh, *Gerald Finzi: His Life and Music*, p. 34 • **11**. Diary, 28 December 1934, *JB*, p. 240 • **12**. BB to Grace Williams, 16 January 1935, *LL1*, p. 364 • **13**. Diary, 22 October 1931, *LL1*, p. 211 • **14**. Diary, 25 September 1930, *JB*, p. 54 • **15**. Diary, 22 September 1931, *JB*, p. 83 • **16**. Diary, 2 October 1930, *JB*, p. 54 • **17**. Diary, 5 December 1930, *JB*, p. 58 • **18**. Diary, 24 September 1931, *LL1*, p. 207 • **19**. Diary, 29 September 1934, *JB*, p. 226 • **20**. Diary, 9 and 16 October 1930, *JB*, pp. 54–5 • **21**. BB to Mr and Mrs Britten, 26 October 1930, *LL1*, p. 144 • **22**. Diary, 22 January 1931, *JB*, p. 61 •

23. Diary, 15 October 1931, *LL1*, p. 210 • **24**. Diary, 12 February 1932, *LL1*, p. 236 • **25**. Diary, 15 May 1931, *JB*, p. 73 • **26**. Diary, 9 May 1933, *JB*, p. 140 • **27**. *BOM*, p. 223 • **28**. Diary, 26 November 1930–8 March 1931, *JB*, pp. 57, 61, 62, 64, 66 • **29**. Diary, 4 November 1931, *JB*, p. 87 • **30**. Diary, 25 September 1930, *JB*, p. 54 • **31**. Diary, 24 October 1930, *JB*, p. 55 • **32**. BB to Mr and Mrs Britten, 26 October 1930, *LL1*, p. 143 • **33**. Diary, 12 June 1931, *JB*, p. 76 • **34**. Diary, 20 June 1931, *JB*, p. 77 • **35**. *MBB*, p. 61 • **36**. *HCBB*, pp. 39–40 • **37**. Diary, 6 January 1931, *LL1*, p. 151 • **38**. Diary, 22 September 1930, *LL1*, p. 141 • **39**. Diary, 24 October 1930, *JB*, p. 55; and 24 January 1931, *LL1*, p. 156 • **40**. Diary, 10 July 1931, *LL1*, p. 187 • **41**. Diary, 2 December 1931, *JB*, p. 91 • **42**. Diary, 22 February 1932, *JB*, p. 100 • **43**. Diary, 2 February 1932, *JB*, p. 98 • **44**. *London Magazine*, October 1963, p. 95; *LL1*, p. 234 • **45**. Diary, 1 June 1932, *JB*, p. 106 • **46**. Diary, 7 January 1933, *JB*, p. 128 • **47**. Samuel Hynes, *The Auden Generation*, p. 51 • **48**. Ibid., p. 48 • **49**. Diary, 27 January, *LL1*, p. 158, and 15 May 1931, *JB*, p. 73 • **50**. Diary, 15 April 1931, *JB*, p. 69 • **51**. Diary, 3 August 1931, *JB*, p. 80 • **52**. Diary, 17 January 1933, *JB*, p. 128 • **53**. Diary, 25 June 1932, *JB*, p. 108 • **54**. Diary, 5 August and 5 September 1931, *JB*, pp. 80, 82 • **55**. Diary, 11 April 1931, 11 May 1932, 13 August 1931, 9 September 1931, *JB*, pp. 69, 105, 80, 82 • **56**. Diary, 19 August 1932, *LL1*, p. 270 • **57**. Diary, 28 March 1933, *JB*, p. 137 • **58**. Diary, 29 November 1933, *JB*, p. 155 • **59**. Diary, 8 June 1931, *JB*, p. 76 • **60**. Diary, 2 April 1932, *JB*, p. 103 • **61**. Diary, 5 April 1932, *JB*, p. 138 • **62**. Diary, 15 August 1932, *JB*, p. 113 • **63**. Diary, 24 September 1932, *LL1*, p. 277 • **64**. Diary, 30 July 1931, *LL1*, p. 196 • **65**. Diary, 20 May 1932, *LL1*, p. 249 • **66**. Diary, 9 January 1932, *JB*, p. 95 • **67**. *LL1*, p. 148 • **68**. Diary, 26 October and 27 November 1930, *JB*, pp. 55, 57 • **69**. Diary, 11 March 1931, *JB*, p. 66 • **70**. Diary, 6 February 1931, *JB*, p. 63 • **71**. Diary, 18 February 1931, *JB*, p. 64 • **72**. Diary, 9 February 1931, *JB*, p. 63 • **73**. Diary, 28 May 1931, *JB*, p. 74 • **74**. Diary, 31 July 1934, *JB*, p. 218 • **75**. Diary, 7 February 1933, *JB*, p. 130 • **76**. Diary, 23 April 1933, *JB*, pp. 138–9 • **77**. Diary, 28 January 1931, *JB*, p. 62 • **78**. Diary, 27 January 1932, *JB*, pp. 97–8 • **79**. Diary, 20 July 1932, *LL1*, p. 265 • **80**. Diary, 30 July 1932, *LL1*, p. 267 • **81**. Diary, 9 October 1930, *JB*, p. 54 • **82**. Diary, 6 May 1931, *LL1*, p. 176 • **83**. Diary, 11 December 1932, *LL1*, p. 292 • **84**. Diary, 14 December

1933, *JB*, p. 157 • **85**. Diary, 20 January 1931, *LL1*, p. 155 • **86**. Diary, 20 September 1932, *JB*, p. 115 • **87**. Diary, 11 February 1931, *JB*, pp. 63–4 • **88**. Diary, 24 September 1931, *JB*, p. 84 • **89**. Diary, 4 February 1931, *JB*, p. 63 • **90**. Diary, 6 May 1931 and 9 May 1933, *JB*, pp. 72, 140 • **91**. *LL1*, p. 191 • **92**. Diary, 16 June 1933, *JB*, pp. 142–3 • **93**. Diary, 4 March 1932, *LL1*, p. 240 • **94**. Diary, 9 January 1931, *JB*, p. 60 • **95**. Diary, 18 November 1931, *JB*, p. 89 • **96**. Diary, 13 February and 8 March 1933, *JB*, pp. 130, 134 • **97**. *LL1*, p. 395 • **98**. *BOM*, p. 252 • **99**. Diary, 12 November 1930, *JB*, p. 56 • **100**. Diary, 9 November 1932, *LL1*, p. 284 • **101**. Decca SET 410/1, booklet note • **102**. Diary, 12 November 1932, *JB*, p. 122 • **103**. Diary, 8 February 1933, *JB*, p. 130 • **104**. Diary, 11 February 1931, *JB*, p. 63 • **105**. Diary, 24 February 1931, *JB*, p. 65 • **106**. Diary, 20 June 1931, *LL1*, p. 178 • **107**. Diary, 19 January 1932, *LL1*, p. 230 • **108**. *Aldeburgh Festival Programme Book*, 1997, p. 61 • **109**. Diary, 18 and 29 March 1932, *LL1*, pp. 244, 245 • **110**. Diary, 6 May 1932, *LL1*, p. 247 • **111**. Diary, 20 June and 11 July 1932, *LL1*, pp. 258, 262 • **112**. Diary, 16 July 1932, *LL1*, p. 263 • **113**. Diary, 22 September 1932, *LL1*, p. 276 • **114**. Diary, 29 September, 13 October, 17 November 1932, *LL1*, pp. 278, 279, 286 • **115**. Diary, 31 January 1933, *JB*, p. 129 • **116**. *The Times*, 3 February 1933, *LL1*, p. 344 • **117**. *Daily Telegraph*, 1 February 1933, *LL1*, p. 300 • **118**. Diary, 16 March 1933, *JB*, p. 135 • **119**. BB to Gerald Finzi, 15 March 1933, *LL1*, p. 299 • **120**. Diary, 3 April 1933, *JB*, p. 137 • **121**. Diary, 22 July 1932, *LL1*, p. 266 • **122**. Diary, 12 December 1932, *LL1*, p. 293 • **123**. *The Times*, 16 December 1932, *LL1*, p. 296 • **124**. BB to Mr and Mrs Britten, 22 June 1933, *LL1*, p. 304 • **125**. Diary, 10 October 1932, *LL1*, p. 279 • **126**. *Monthly Musical Record*, December 1933, *LL1*, p. 305 • **127**. Diary, 13 February 1933, *JB*, p. 131 • **128**. Diary, 11 December 1933, *JB*, p. 156 • **129**. Diary, 19 June 1933, *JB*, p. 143 • **130**. *PFL*, plate 67 • **131**. *MBB*, p. 73 • **132**. Diary, 31 December 1933, *LL1*, p. 313 • **133**. *BOM*, p. 172 • **134**. BB to Grace Williams, 3 January 1934, *LL1*, p. 319 • **135**. Diary, 10 January 1934, *JB*, pp. 195–6 • **136**. BB to Edwin Benbow, 24 January 1934, *LL1*, p. 323 • **137**. Diary, 16 February 1934, *JB*, p. 200 • **138**. Diary, 22 February 1934, *LL1*, p. 324 • **139**. Diary, 23 February 1934, *JB*, p. 201 • **140**. BB to Grace Williams, 26 February 1934, *LL1*, p. 328 • **141**. BB to Mr and Mrs Britten, 30 March 1934, *LL1*, p. 331 • **142**. *LL1*, p. 333

• **143**. *The Times*, 9 April 1934, *LL1*, p. 337 • **144**. Diary, 6 April 1934, *JB*, p. 206 • **145**. John Bridcut, *Britten's Children*, p. 57 • **146**. *JBBC*, p. 56 • **147**. *JBBC*, p. 57 • **148**. Diary, 9 April 1934, *JB*, p. 207 • **149**. *HCBB*, p. 44 • **150**. Diary, 11 April 1934, *JB*, pp. 207–8 • **151**. Diary, 20 April 1934, *JB*, p. 208 • **152**. Diary, 7 May 1934, *JB*, p. 210 • **153**. BB to Mrs Britten, 11 May 1934, *LL1*, p. 340 • **154**. Diary, 22 May 1934, *JB*, p. 212 • **155**. Diary, 18 March 1934, *JB*, p. 203 • **156**. Diary, 15 July 1934, *JB*, p. 216 • **157**. Diary, 17 September 1934, *JB*, p. 224 • **158**. Diary, 25 August 1934, *JB*, p. 221 • **159**. A. L. Bacharach (ed.), *British Music in Our Time*, p. 175 • **160**. BB to Mrs Britten, 14 October 1936, *LL1*, p. 450 • **161**. Diary, 16 December 1933, *JB*, p. 157 • **162**. Rob Young, *Electric Eden*, p. 107 • **163**. Diary, 16 March and 14 May 1934, *JB*, pp. 202, 212 • **164**. Diary, 21 October, 4 November, 6 November 1934, *JB*, pp. 228, 231, 232 • **165**. Diary, 3 November 1934, *JB*, p. 231 • **166**. BB to Grace Williams, 19 November 1934, *LL1*, pp. 357–8 • **167**. Diary, 30 November 1934, *JB*, p. 236 • **168**. BB to J. F. R. Stainer, 1 December 1934, *LL1*, pp. 358–9 • **169**. Diary, 17 December 1934, *JB*, p. 238 • **170**. Diary, 25 December 1934, *JB*, p. 239 • **171**. Diary, 28 December 1934, *JB*, p. 240

3 *Most Surprising Days*

1. Diary, 16 January 1935, *JB*, p. 243 • **2**. Diary, 27 April 1935, *JB*, pp. 258–9 • **3**. Diary, 24 May 1935, *JB*, p. 263 • **4**. Diary, 4 May 1935, *JB*, p. 260 • **5**. Diary, 5 May 1935, *LL1*, p. 372 • **6**. Diary, 1 May 1935, *JB*, p. 259 • **7**. Diary, 18 May 1935, *JB*, p. 262 • **8**. Diary, 23 May 1935, *JB*, p. 263 • **9**. 'How to Become a Composer', *The Listener*, 7 November 1946, *LL1*, p. 373 • **10**. Diary, 4 July 1935, *JB*, p. 269 • **11**. Diary, 6 July 1935, *JB*, p. 270 • **12**. Christopher Isherwood, *Lions and Shadows*, p. 112 • **13**. Diary, 11 July 1935, *JB*, p. 270 • **14**. Diary, 17 September 1935, *JB*, p. 278 • **15**. Diary, 19 June 1935, *JB*, p. 267 • **16**. Diary, 1 October 1935, *JB*, p. 279 • **17**. Diary, 19 October 1935, *JB*, p. 283 • **18**. Diary, 18 November 1935, *JB*, p. 287 • **19**. Diary, 9 December 1935, *JB*, p. 290 • **20**. Richard Davenport-Hines, *Auden*, p. 144 • **21**. Diary, 15 January 1936, *JB*, pp. 326–7 • **22**. BB to Sylvia Spencer, 17 April 1935, *LL1*, p. 369 • **23**. Diary, 16 January

1935, *JB*, p. 243 • **24**. Diary, 15 March 1935, *JB*, p. 253 • **25**. Diary, 20 January 1935, *JB*, p. 244 • **26**. Diary, 6 February 1935, *JB*, p. 247 • **27**. Diary, 11 December 1935, *JB*, p. 290 • **28**. Diary, 13 August 1935, *JB*, p. 274 • **29**. Diary, 29 June 1935, *JB*, p. 268 • **30**. Diary, 8 May 1935, *JB*, p. 261 • **31**. BB to Marjorie Fass, 24 October 1935, *LL1*, p. 379 • **32**. Diary, 10 November 1935, *JB*, p. 285 • **33**. Diary, 5 October 1935, *JB*, pp. 280–1 • **34**. BB to Henri Temianka, 15 November 1935, *LL1*, p. 386 • **35**. Diary, 13 December 1935, *JB*, p. 292 • **36**. Diary, 24 December 1935, *JB*, p. 292 • **37**. Diary, 29 December 1935, *LL1*, p. 394 • **38**. Diary, 1 January 1936, *JB*, p. 323 • **39**. Diary, 2 January 1936, *JB*, p. 323 • **40**. Diary, 30 April 1937, *JB*, p. 428 • **41**. Diary, 19 January 1936, *JB*, p. 325 • **42**. Diary, 16 January 1936, *JB*, p. 327 • **43**. Diary, 7 April 1936, *JB*, p. 344 • **44**. BB to John Pounder, 14 April 1936, *LL1*, p. 419 • **45**. Diary, 15 April 1936, *JB*, p. 346 • **46**. Diary, 24 January 1936, *JB*, p. 328 • **47**. Diary, 23 February 1936, *JB*, p. 335 • **48**. Diary, 31 January 1936, *JB*, p. 331 • **49**. Diary, 12 January 1936, *JB*, p. 326 • **50**. W. H. Auden, *The English Auden*, p. 160 • **51**. Ibid., p. 162 • **52**. Diary, 18 February 1936, *JB*, p. 333 • **53**. Diary, 19 February 1936, *JB*, p. 334 • **54**. Diary, 11 April 1936, *JB*, p. 345 • **55**. Diary, 26 February 1936, *JB*, p. 335 • **56**. Diary, 10 March 1936, *JB*, p. 340 • **57**. Diary, 8 April 1936, *JB*, p. 344 • **58**. BB to Mrs Britten, 21 April 1936, *LL1*, p. 423 • **59**. Diary, 29 April 1936, *JB*, p. 350 • **60**. Diary, 19 April 1936, *JB*, p. 348 • **61**. BB to Grace Williams, 26 April 1936, *LL1*, p. 425 • **62**. Diary, 1 May 1936, *JB*, p. 351 • **63**. Constant Lambert, *Music Ho!*, p. 10 • **64**. *The Record Guide*, p. 117 • **65**. Diary, 22 April 1936, *JB*, p. 349 • **66**. Diary, 27 April 1936, *JB*, p. 350 • **67**. Diary, 18 May 1936, *JB*, p. 354 • **68**. Diary, 11 June 1936, *JB*, p. 358 • **69**. Diary, 22 June 1936, *JB*, p. 359 • **70**. Diary, 7 July 1936, *JB*, p. 362 • **71**. Diary, 19 July 1936, *JB*, p. 363 • **72**. Diary, 20 July 1936, *JB*, p. 364 • **73**. BB to Mrs Britten, 28 July 1936, *LL1*, p. 436 • **74**. Diary, 26 July 1936, *JB*, p. 365 • **75**. Diary, 1 March 1936, *JB*, p. 337 • **76**. Diary, 30 July 1936, *JB*, p. 366 • **77**. Diary, 9 August 1936, *JB*, p. 367 • **78**. Diary, 19 September 1936, *JB*, p. 374 • **79**. Michael Kennedy, *Britten*, p. 22 • **80**. Diary, 25 September 1936, *JB*, p. 375 • **81**. Frank Bridge to BB, 30 April 1937, *LL1*, p. 433 • **82**. *LL1*, pp. 444–5 • **83**. *Observer*, 27 September 1936, *LL1*, p. 449 • **84**. Diary, 30 April 1937, *JB*, p. 428 • **85**. Diary, 10 September 1936, *JB*, p. 372 • **86**. Diary, 28 September

1936, *JB*, p. 376 • **87**. BB to Mrs Britten, 14 October 1936, *LL1*, p. 450 • **88**. Diary, 21 October 1936, *JB*, p. 381 • **89**. Diary, 30 October 1936, *JB*, p. 384 • **90**. Charles Osborne, *W. H. Auden: The Life of a Poet*, p. 129 • **91**. Diary, 2 November 1936, *JB*, p. 384 • **92**. W. H. Auden, *Prose 1926–1938*, p. 365 • **93**. Diary, 1 December 1936, *JB*, p. 391 • **94**. *MBB*, p. 98 • **95**. Diary, 7 December 1936, *JB*, p. 393 • **96**. W. H. Auden & Christopher Isherwood, *Plays and Other Dramatic Writings by W. H. Auden 1928–1938*, pp. 430–2 • **97**. Diary, 11 March 1936, *JB*, p. 340 • **98**. Diary, 10 December 1936, *JB*, p. 393 • **99**. Diary, 16 October 1936, *JB*, p. 380 • **100**. Diary, 30 November 1936, *JB*, p. 391 • **101**. Diary, 1 January 1937, *JB*, p. 398 • **102**. Diary, 1 February 1937, *JB*, p. 406 • **103**. Diary, 3 February 1937, *JB*, p. 407 • **104**. Diary, 31 January 1937, *JB*, p. 406 • **105**. BB to John Pounder, 8 February 1937, *LL1*, p. 476 • **106**. Diary, 24 February 1937, *JB*, p. 412 • **107**. Diary, 26 February 1937, *JB*, p. 413 • **108**. Diary, 3 March 1937, *JB*, p. 414 • **109**. Diary, 6 March 1937, *JB*, p. 415 • **110**. Diary, 23 March 1937, *JB*, p. 418 • **111**. Diary, 14–15 March 1937, *JB*, p. 418 • **112**. Christopher Headington, *Peter Pears: A Biography*, p. 63 • **113**. Diary, 27 April 1937, *LL1*, p. 479 • **114**. Tony Scotland, *Lennox and Freda*, p. 217 • **115**. Diary, 30 April 1937, *JB*, p. 428 • **116**. Diary, 7 May 1937, *JB*, p. 430 • **117**. Diary, 12 May 1937, *JB*, p. 431 • **118**. *LL1*, p. 502 • **119**. Diary, 15 July 1937, *JB*, p. 442 • **120**. Peter Pears to BB, 27 August 1937, *LL1*, pp. 507–8 • **121**. *CHPP*, p. 39 • **122**. *CHPP*, p. 19 • **123**. *CHPP*, p. 53 • **124**. Diary, 18 July 1937, *JB*, p. 443 • **125**. BB to Mary Behrend, 19 July 1937, *LL1*, p. 496 • **126**. Diary, 29 June 1937, *JB*, p. 440 • **127**. Diary, 11 July 1937, *JB*, p. 441 • **128**. BB to Nell Burra, 14 July 1937, *LL1*, p. 495 • **129**. Diary, 3 July 1936, *JB*, p. 361 • **130**. Diary, 26 June 1937, *JB*, p. 439 • **131**. Diary, 17 July 1937, *JB*, p. 442 • **132**. Diary, 13 August 1937, *JB*, p. 449 • **133**. Diary, 23 August 1937, *JB*, p. 450 • **134**. *JBBC*, p. 52 • **135**. Diary, 17 October 1937, *JB*, p. 458 • **136**. *JBBC*, p. 52 • **137**. Humphrey Carpenter, *W. H. Auden: A Biography*, p. 188 • **138**. Diary, 25 June 1937, *JB*, p. 439 • **139**. Diary, 3 July 1937, *JB*, p. 440 • **140**. Matt Houlbrook, *Queer London*, p. 94 • **141**. Diary, 9 July 1937, *JB*, p. 441 • **142**. *JBBC*, p. 48 • **143**. *JBBC*, p. 53 • **144**. Diary, 24 February 1938, *JB*, p. 465 • **145**. Diary, 8 September 1937, *JB*, p. 450 • **146**. BB to Mary Behrend, 17 October 1937, *LL1*, p. 517 • **147**. Diary, 20 October 1937, *JB*, p. 459 • **148**. BB to Peter

Pears, 24 October 1937, *LL1*, p. 518 • **149**. Diary, 24 September 1937, *JB*, p. 453 • **150**. Diary, 30 September 1937, *JB*, p. 455 • **151**. Diary, 7 October 1937, *JB*, p. 456 • **152**. BB to Kenneth Wright, 16 January 1938, *LL1*, p. 543 • **153**. *MBB*, p. 106 • **154**. Diary, 28 July 1937, *JB*, p. 445 • **155**. Diary, 20 September 1937, *JB*, p. 452 • **156**. Diary, 12 March 1938, *JB*, p. 466 • **157**. Diary, 14 April 1938, *JB*, p. 468 • **158**. *MBB*, p. 106 • **159**. BB to John Pounder, 4 May 1938, *LL1*, p. 554 • **160**. BB to Ralph Hawkes, 5 May 1938, *LL1*, p. 556 • **161**. Diary, 19 May 1938, *JB*, p. 471 • **162**. Peter Pears to BB, ? June 1938, *LL1*, p. 558 • **163**. BB to Wulff Scherchen, 25 June 1938, *LL1*, pp. 562–3 • **164**. *JBBC*, pp. 59–60 • **165**. *JBBC*, p. 60 • **166**. BB to Wulff Scherchen, 30 June 1938, *LL1*, p. 568 • **167**. *JBBC*, p. 63 • **168**. *JBBC*, p. 63 • **169**. BB to Wulff Scherchen, ? July 1938, *LL1*, p. 572 • **170**. BB to Kenneth Wright, 28 May 1938, *LL1*, p. 558 • **171**. BB to Ralph Hawkes, 28 June 1938, *LL1*, p. 565 • **172**. BB to Ralph Hawkes, 4 July 1938, *LL1*, pp. 569–70 • **173**. BB to Wulff Scherchen, 1 August 1938, *LL1*, p. 573 • **174**. *PFL*, plate 111 • **175**. *JBBC*, pp. 53–4 • **176**. *Musical Times*, September 1938, p. 703, *LL1*, p. 578 • **177**. Marjorie Fass to Daphne Oliver, 22 August 1938, *LL1*, p. 577 • **178**. W. H. Auden to BB, ? August 1938, *LL1*, p. 575 • **179**. BB to Wulff Scherchen, 29 August 1938, *LL1*, p. 580 • **180**. *MKBB*, p. 144 • **181**. W. H. Auden to BB, early 1939, *LL1*, p. 547 • **182**. BB to Edwina Jackson, 16 September 1938, *LL1*, p. 585 • **183**. BB to Ralph Hawkes, 29 November 1938, *LL1*, p. 597 • **184**. BB to Wulff Scherchen, 3 October 1938, *LL1*, p. 589 • **185**. Ibid., 10 October 1938, *LL1*, p. 590 • **186**. Ibid., 22 November 1938, *LL1*, p. 596 • **187**. *JBBC*, p. 71 • **188**. Tony Scotland, *Lennox and Freda*, p. 255 • **189**. Ibid., p. 257 • **190**. BB to Lennox Berkeley, 1 January 1939, *LL1*, p. 605 • **191**. Tony Scotland, *Lennox and Freda*, p. 251 • **192**. *JBBC*, p. 82 • **193**. Tony Scotland, *Lennox and Freda*, p. 258 • **194**. Lennox Berkeley to BB, n.d., *LL1*, p. 607 • **195**. BB to Wulff Scherchen, 5 January 1939, *LL1*, p. 606 • **196**. William Coldstream, *Notebooks*, *LL2*, p. 1337 • **197**. BB to Wulff Scherchen, 10 January 1939, *JBBC*, p. 78 • **198**. Wulff Scherchen to BB, 19 January 1939, *JBBC*, p. 80 • **199**. BB to Wulff Scherchen, 22 January 1939, *JBBC*, p. 81 • **200**. Tony Scotland, *Lennox and Freda*, p. 259 • **201**. BB to Peter Pears, 16 March 1939, *LL1*, p. 616 • **202**. BB to Enid Slater, 13 March 1939, *LL1*, p. 611 • **203**. Tony Scotland, *Lennox and Freda*, p. 261 • **204**. *LL1*, p. 614 •

205. Tony Scotland, *Lennox and Freda*, p. 263 • **206**. BB to Wulff Scherchen, 7 February 1939, *LL1*, p. 610 • **207**. BB to Mary Behrend, 19 April 1939, *LL1*, p. 618 • **208**. *CHPP*, p. 83 • **209**. Sophie Wyss, interview in *Composer*, Winter 1976–7, *LL1*, p. 604 • **210**. W. H. Auden, *The English Auden*, pp. 237–8 • **211**. BB to Wulff Scherchen, 19 March 1939, *LL1*, p. 617 • **212**. Ibid., 22 April 1939, *JBBC*, p. 87 • **213**. *LL2*, p. 632

4 *American Overtures*

1. BB to Wulff Scherchen, 1 May 1939, *LL2*, pp. 631–2 • **2**. BB to Lennox Berkeley, 3 May 1939, *LL2*, p. 633 • **3**. BB to Aaron Copland, 8 May 1939, *LL2*, p. 634 • **4**. *CHPP*, p. 84 • **5**. BB to Ralph Hawkes, 16 May 1939, *LL2*, p. 641 • **6**. BB to Beth Welford, 5 June 1939, *MBB*, p. 111 • **7**. BB to Wulff Scherchen, 22 May 1939, *JBBC*, p. 91 • **8**. BB to Lennox Berkeley, 19 June 1939, *LL2*, p. 668 • **9**. BB to Enid Slater, 29 July 1939, *LL2*, p. 691 • **10**. BB to Wulff Scherchen, 13 July 1939, *LL2*, p. 684 • **11**. Interview with Donald Mitchell, *LL2*, p. 674 • **12**. BB to Beth Welford, 14 July 1939, *MBB*, p. 117 • **13**. BB to Ralph Hawkes, 10 July 1939, *LL2*, p. 683 • **14**. EMI 5 58049 2, booklet note • **15**. BB to WS, 9 June 1939, *JBBC*, p. 94 • **16**. *LL1*, p. 14 • **17**. *MBB*, p. 109 • **18**. BB to Ralph Hawkes, 15 August 1939, *LL2*, p. 692 • **19**. *CHPP*, p. 91 • **20**. BB to Enid Slater, 7 November 1939, *LL2*, p. 734 • **21**. *CHPP*, p. 92 • **22**. BB to Barbara Britten, 3 September 1939, *LL2*, p. 696 • **23**. BB to Ralph Hawkes, 3 September 1939, *LL2*, p. 697 • **24**. Ibid., 22 September 1939, *LL2*, p. 701 • **25**. BB to Beth Welford, 19 October 1939, *LL2*, p. 707 • **26**. BB to Wulff Scherchen, 29 September 1939, *LL2*, p. 702 • **27**. BB to Beth Welford, 23 October 1939, *LL2*, p. 718 • **28**. BB to Hedli Anderson, ? October 1939, *LL2*, p. 720 • **29**. BB to Elizabeth Mayer, 9 January 1940, *LL2*, p. 761 • **30**. Elizabeth Mayer to BB, 3 January 1940, *LL2*, p. 754 • **31**. Peter Pears to BB, 9 January 1940, *LL2*, p. 759 • **32**. Interview with Donald Mitchell, *LL2*, p. 766 • **33**. Edward Barry, *Chicago Tribune*, 16 January 1940; Eugene Stimson, *Chicago Daily News*, 16 January 1940; *LL2*, p. 765 • **34**. BB to Beth Welford, *MBB*, p. 128 • **35**. BB to Beth Welford, *MBB*, pp. 131–2 • **36**. BB to Sophie Wyss and Arnold Gyle, 15 March 1940, *LL2*, p. 779 • **37**. *Daily Telegraph*, 31 January

1940, *LL2*, p. 782 • **38**. Lennox Berkeley to BB, 30 January 1940, *LL2*, p. 781 • **39**. BB to Antonio Brosa, 31 March 1940, *LL2*, p. 787 • **40**. BB to Leslie Boosey, 2 April 1940, *LL2*, p. 791 • **41**. BB to Beth Welford, 26 April 1940, *MBB*, pp. 140–1 • **42**. BB to Enid Slater, 7 April 1940, *LL2*, pp. 799–800 • **43**. BB to Barbara Britten, 1 August 1940, *LL2*, p. 837 • **44**. BB to Beth Welford, 26 July 1940, *MBB*, p. 149 • **45**. BB to Beth, Kit and Sebastian Welford, 30 June 1940, *MBB*, p. 147 • **46**. BB to John Pounder, 7 April 1940, *LL1*, p. 822; BB to Enid Slater, 7 April 1940, *LL1*, p. 797 • **47**. BB to Wulff Scherchen, 15 August 1940, *LL2*, p. 842 • **48**. BB to Gustel Scherchen, 22 August 1940, *LL2*, p. 853 • **49**. BB to Aaron Copland, 15 August 1940, *LL2*, p. 844 • **50**. BB to Elizabeth Mayer, 22 August 1940, *LL2*, p. 845 • **51**. BB to Ralph Hawkes, 2 September 1940, *LL2*, p. 855 • **52**. BB to Beth Welford, 25 August 1940, *MBB*, p. 154 • **53**. BB to Beth, Kit and Sebastian Welford, 25 August 1940, *MBB*, p. 160 • **54**. *CHPP*, p. 106 • **55**. *LL2*, p. 864 • **56**. Colm Toíbín, *New Ways to Kill Your Mother*, p. 202 • **57**. *LL2*, p. 865 • **58**. Virginia Spencer Carr, *Paul Bowles: A Life*, p. 171 • **59**. Ibid., p. 172 • **60**. *LL2*, p. 900 • **61**. BB to Antonio and Peggy Brosa, 20 December 1940, *LL2*, p. 899 • **62**. Dorothy J. Farman, *Auden in Love*, p. 25 • **63**. Stephen Spender (ed.), *W. H. Auden: A Tribute*, p. 101 • **64**. *CHPP*, p. 107 • **65**. BB to Beth Welford, 12 May 1941, *MBB*, p. 162 • **66**. Prince Fuminaro Konoye to the Director of the Cultural Bureau of the Japanese Foreign Office, *LL2*, p. 881 • **67**. Ralph Hawkes to BB, 20 December 1940, *LL2*, pp. 891–2 • **68**. BB to Ralph Hawkes, 27 November 1940, *LL2*, p. 888 • **69**. BB to Peggy Brosa, ? April 1941, *LL2*, p. 909 • **70**. BB to Sophie Wyss and Arnold Gyde, 15 March 1940, *LL2*, p. 780 • **71**. BB to Enid Slater, 7 April 1940, *LL2*, p. 799 • **72**. *LL2*, p. 930 • **73**. *CHPP*, p. 99 • **74**. *New York Times*, 6 May 1941; Virgil Thomson, *New York Herald Tribune*, 6 May 1941; *LL2*, pp. 915–16 • **75**. Eric Walter White, *Benjamin Britten: His Life and Operas*, p. 118 • **76**. BB to Albert Goldberg, 20 December 1940, *LL2*, p. 893 • **77**. Howard L. Koch, 'Benjamin Britten: A Reminiscence', *LL2*, p. 894 • **78**. *JBBC*, p. 118 • **79**. BB to David Rothman, 12 November 1941, *LL2*, p. 998 • **80**. *JBBC*, p. 119 • **81**. BB to Albert Goldberg, 24 May 1941, *LL2*, p. 933 • **82**. *CHPP*, p. 110 • **83**. BB to Beth Welford, 4 November 1941, *LL2*, p. 992 • **84**. E. M. Forster, *The Prince's Tale and other uncollected writings*, p. 127 • **85**. BB to Elizabeth Mayer, 29 July 1941, *LL2*, p. 961 • **86**. Peter Pears to

Elizabeth Mayer, 5 July 1941, *LL2*, p. 951 • **87**. *BOM*, p. 262 • **88**. BB to Ralph Hawkes, 8 September 1940, *LL2*, p. 858 • **89**. *BOM*, pp. 24–7 • **90**. Ibid., p. 31 • **91**. *Sunday Times*, 4 May, 8 June, 15 June 1941, *LL2*, pp. 958–9 • **92**. *Musical Times*, June 1941, *LL2*, p. 870 • **93**. Ibid., September 1941, *LL2*, p. 871 • **94**. Ibid., October 1941, *LL2*, p. 872 • **95**. BB to Beth Welford, 19 August 1941, *MBB*, p. 168 • **96**. BB to Barbara Britten, 7 September 1941, *LL2*, pp. 973–4 • **97**. BB to Wulff Scherchen, 9 September 1941, *LL2*, p. 977 • **98**. BB to Elizabeth Sprague Coolidge, 24 July 1941, *LL2*, p. 959 • **99**. BB to Peggy Brosa, 4 November 1941, *LL2*, p. 991 • **100**. Ibid., 25 November 1941, *LL2*, p. 1001 • **101**. *Chicago Tribune*, 25 November 1941; *Chicago Daily Times*, 25 November 1941; *LL2*, p. 1002 • **102**. BB to Albert Goldberg, ? December 1941, *LL2*, p. 1005 • **103**. *HCBB*, p. 163 • **104**. BB to Antonio and Peggy Brosa, 31 December 1941, *LL2*, p. 1009 • **105**. *New York World-Telegram*, 23 December 1941, *LL2*, p. 1010 • **106**. BB to Albert Goldberg, 20 January 1942, *LL2*, p. 1014 • **107**. Christopher Isherwood, *Diaries, Volume One: 1939–1960*, p. 206 • **108**. W. H. Auden to BB, 31 January 1942, Donald Mitchell, *Britten and Auden in the Thirties*, pp. 161–2 • **109**. BB to Kit Welford, 1 March 1942, *MBB*, p. 174 • **110**. Peter Pears to Antonio and Peggy Brosa, 10 March 1942, *LL2*, pp. 1023–4 • **111**. *PFL*, plate 160 • **112**. *LL2*, p. 1026

5 *Where I Belong*

1. BB to Bobby Rothman, 24 June 1942, *LL2*, p. 1067 • **2**. Peter Pears to Beata Mayer, 31 March 1942, *LL2*, p. 1027 • **3**. *CHPP*, p. 114 • **4**. BB to Bobby Rothman, 24 June 1942, *LL2*, p. 1068 • **5**. *MBB*, p. 177 • **6**. BB to Elizabeth Mayer, 4 May 1942, *LL2*, p. 1037 • **7**. Ibid., 17 May 1942, *LL2*, p. 1049 • **8**. *LL2*, p. 1059 • **9**. BB to Elizabeth Mayer, 30 September 1942, *LL2*, pp. 1087–8 • **10**. Ibid., 17 May 1942, *LL2*, p. 1050 • **11**. BB to Beata Wachstein, 6 June 1942, *LL2*, p. 1063 • **12**. BB to Peter Pears, 1 June 1942, *LL2*, p. 1055 • **13**. *JBBC*, p. 123 • **14**. BB to Peter Pears, 1 June 1942, *LL2*, p. 1056 • **15**. BB to Elizabeth Mayer, 5 June 1942, *LL2*, p. 1061 • **16**. *JBBC*, p. 124 • **17**. BB to Elizabeth Mayer, 30 September 1942, *LL2*, p. 1087 • **18**. *Observer*, 26

July 1942, *LL2*, p. 1074 • **19**. BB to Mary Behrend, 6 August 1942, *LL2*, p. 1072 • **20**. BB to Elizabeth Mayer, 30 September 1942, *LL2*, p. 1088 • **21**. BB to Ernest Newman, 18 September 1942, *LL2*, pp. 1075–6 • **22**. *The Times*, 25 September 1942; *Daily Telegraph*, 24 September 1942; *New Statesman and Nation*, 3 October 1942; *LL2*, pp. 1077–8 • **23**. *CHPP*, p. 121 • **24**. *HCBB*, p. 178 • **25**. *Observer*, 14 March 1943, *CHPP*, p. 120 • **26**. BB to Elizabeth Mayer, 30 September 1942, *LL2*, pp. 1089–90 • **27**. BB to Bobby Rothman, 29 September 1942, *LL2*, p. 1083 • **28**. *CHPP*, pp. 119–20 • **29**. BB to Elizabeth Mayer, 24 November 1942, *LL2*, p. 1073 • **30**. BB to Peter Pears, ? December 1942, *LL2*, p. 1105 • **31**. *LL2*, p. 1109 • **32**. BB to Edward Sackville-West, ? October 1942, *LL3*, p. 113 • **33**. James Lees-Milne, *Ancestral Voices*, p. 125 • **34**. Edward Sackville-West to BB, 2 December 1942, *LL3*, p. 114 • **35**. *Observer*, 6 December 1942, *LL2*, p. 1097 • **36**. Peter Pears to Elizabeth Mayer, 13 February 1943, *LL2*, p. 1113 • **37**. BB to Ralph Hawkes, 9 March 1943, *LL2*, p. 1120 • **38**. BB to Enid Slater, 8 March 1943, *LL2*, p. 1118 • **39**. BB to Ralph Hawkes, 12 March 1943, *LL2*, p. 1128 • **40**. William White, *History, Gazetteer and Directory of Suffolk*, p. 173 • **41**. BB to Elizabeth Mayer, 6 April 1943, *LL2*, p. 1144 • **42**. *MBB*, p. 181 • **43**. *HCBB*, p. 214 • **44**. *MBB*, p. 183 • **45**. BB to Enid Slater, 8 March 1943, *LL2*, p. 1118 • **46**. BB to Peter Pears, 21 March 1943, *LL2*, p. 1133 • **47**. BB to Elizabeth Mayer, 6 April 1943, *LL2*, p. 1144 • **48**. *HCBB*, p. 185 • **49**. *LL3*, p. 118 • **50**. Peter Pears to BB, late March/early April 1943, *LL2*, p. 1140 • **51**. BB to Peter Pears, 1 April 1943, *LL2*, p. 1141 • **52**. BB to Ralph Hawkes, 29 March 1943, *LL2*, p. 1138 • **53**. Walter Hussey to BB, 22 March 1943, *LL2*, p. 1139 • **54**. BB to Elizabeth Mayer, 22 May 1943, *LL2*, p. 1151 • **55**. John Amis, *Amiscellany*, pp. 173–4 • **56**. BB to Walter Hussey, 28 May 1943, *LL2*, p. 1157 • **57**. Ibid., 23 August 1943, *LL2*, p. 1160 • **58**. *HCBB*, p. 190 • **59**. BB to Walter Hussey, 26 September 1943, *LL2*, p. 1161 • **60**. BB to Elizabeth Mayer, 8 December 1943, *LL2*, p. 1173 • **61**. *Observer*, 24 October 1943, *LL2*, p. 1176 • **62**. BB to Elizabeth Mayer, 8 December 1943, *LL2*, p. 1173 • **63**. Christopher Isherwood to BB, 18 February 1942, *LL3*, p. 92 • **64**. *CHPP*, p. 115 • **65**. BB to Peter Pears, 11 March 1943, *LL2*, p. 1124 • **66**. *BOM*, p. 226 • **67**. Paul Banks (ed.), *The Making of Peter Grimes: Essays and Studies*, p. 5 • **68**. Ibid., p. 57 • **69**. Neil Powell, *George Crabbe: An English Life*, pp. 180–203 • **70**. *TMPG*, pp. 65–6 • **71**. Peter

Pears to BB, 1 March 1944, *LL2*, p. 1189 • **72**. *CHPP*, p. 135 • **73**. Peter Pears to BB, 11 May 1944, *LL2*, p. 1198 • **74**. BB to Peter Pears, 10 January 1944, ? April 1944, 12 June 1944, *LL2*, pp. 1181, 1191, 1203 • **75**. Peter Pears to BB, 15–17 June 1944, *LL2*, p. 1206 • **76**. BB to Peter Pears, 12 July 1944, *LL2*, p. 1209 • **77**. BB to Peter Pears, 20 November 1944, *LL2*, p. 1237 • **78**. BB to Mary Behrend, 10 February 1945, *LL2*, p. 1241 • **79**. *HCBB*, pp. 213–14 • **80**. *TMPG*, p. 44 • **81**. Ibid., p. 42 • **82**. *HCBB*, p. 222 • **83**. *Time & Tide*, 14 June 1945, *LL2*, p. 1260 • **84**. *News Chronicle*, 8 June 1945, *LL2*, p. 1256 • **85**. A. L. Bacharach (ed.), *British Music in Our Time*, pp. 217–18 • **86**. *Observer*, 24 June 1945, *LL2*, p. 1259 • **87**. *BOM*, p. 50 • **88**. Ibid., p. 51 • **89**. *TMPG*, pp. 46–7 • **90**. BB to Mrs Wright, 18 June 1945, *LL2*, p. 1252 • **91**. *Aldeburgh Festival Programme Book*, 1995, p. 96 • **92**. *British Music in Our Time*, p. 218 • **93**. Rutland Boughton to BB, 3 July 1945, *LL2*, p. 1945 • **94**. BB to Rutland Boughton, 29 August 1945, *LL2*, p. 1336 • **95**. Yehudi Menuhin, *Unfinished Journey*, p. 179 • **96**. *LL2*, p. 1274 • **97**. Peter Pears to BB, 1 August 1945, *LL2*, p. 1272 • **98**. *HCBB*, p. 228 • **99**. BB to Mary Behrend, 3 December 1945, *LL2*, p. 1285 • **100**. John Amis, *Amiscellany*, p. 181 • **101**. *The Times*, 24 November 1945, *LL2*, p. 1288 • **102**. *JBBC*, p. 148 • **103**. Interview with Elizabeth Sweeting, *LL3*, p. 12 • **104**. BB to Peter Pears, ? November 1944, *LL3*, p. 102 • **105**. Ibid., 24 January 1946, *LL3*, p. 139 • **106**. BB to Ralph Hawkes, 19 December 1945, *LL2*, p. 1285 • **107**. John Jolliffe, *Glyndebourne: An Operatic Miracle*, p. 47 • **108**. BB to Ralph Hawkes, 30 June 1946, *LL3*, p. 198 • **109**. BB to *The Times*, 8 July 1946, *LL3*, p. 213 • **110**. John Jolliffe, *Glyndebourne: An Operatic Miracle*, pp. 48–9 • **111**. *Sunday Times*, 21 July 1946, *LL3*, pp. 215–17 • **112**. *Observer*, 14 July 1946, *LL3*, p. 219 • **113**. *Manchester Guardian*, 15 July 1946, *LL3*, p. 220 • **114**. *New Statesman and Nation*, 20 July 1946, *LL3*, p. 222 • **115**. BB to Erwin Stein, 24 May 1946, *LL3*, p. 185 • **116**. *New York Times*, 7 August 1946, *LL3*, p. 209 • **117**. *LL3*, p. 225 • **118**. Ibid., p. 201 • **119**. Ibid., p. 265 • **120**. *PFL*, plate 212 • **121**. BB to Ernest Ansermet, 12 January 1947, *LL3*, p. 273 • **122**. Eric Crozier to Nancy Evans, 28 April 1947, *LL3*, p. 277 • **123**. Julie Kavanagh, *Secret Muses: The Life of Frederick Ashton*, p. 336 • **124**. Ibid., p. 338 • **125**. John Jolliffe, *Glyndebourne: An Operatic Miracle*, p. 49 • **126**. *LL3*, p. 277 • **127**. Eric Crozier to Hans Oppenheim, 21 June 1947, *LL3*, p. 294 • **128**. *The Times*, 21 June 1947; *Daily Telegraph*,

21 June 1947; *Observer*, 22 June 1947; *LL3*, pp. 294–5 • **129**. *JBBC*, p. 153 • **130**. Ibid., p. 156 • **131**. BB to Ralph Hawkes, 9 September 1947, *LL3*, p. 325 • **132**. *JBBC*, pp. 155–6 • **133**. BB to Peter Pears, 4 September 1947, *LL3*, p. 315 • **134**. *Aldeburgh Anthology*, p. 8

6 *A Modest Festival*

1. BB to Peter Pears, 4 September 1947, *LL3*, p. 315 • **2**. *Aldeburgh Anthology*, pp. 8–9 • **3**. *LL3*, p. 318 • **4**. BB to Lennox Berkeley, ? 15 November 1947, *LL3*, p. 335 • **5**. BB to Mary Behrend, ? 10 November 1947, *LL3*, p. 333 • **6**. *Manchester Guardian*, 12 November 1947, *LL3*, p. 335 • **7**. *BOM*, p. 75 • **8**. BB to Henry Boys, 24 November 1947, *LL3*, p. 338 • **9**. BB to Peter Pears, 18 December 1947, *LL3*, p. 344 • **10**. *LL3*, p. 300 • **11**. *HCBB*, p. 265 • **12**. *The Times*, 26 July 1948; *Observer*, 1 August 1948; *New Statesman and Nation*, 31 July 1948; *LL3*, pp. 301–2 • **13**. BB to Ralph Hawkes, 27 February 1948, *LL3*, p. 373 • **14**. BB to David Webster, 15 May 1948, *LL3*, pp. 390–1 • **15**. BB to Anthony Gishford, 20 May 1948, *LL3*, pp. 392–3 • **16**. *HCBB*, p. 262 • **17**. *East Anglian Daily Times*, 18 December 1947, *LL3*, p. 346 • **18**. BB to Elizabeth Mayer, 4 February 1948, *LL3*, p. 357 • **19**. P. N. Furbank, *E. M. Forster: A Life. Volume Two: Polycrates' Ring*, pp. 281–2 • **20**. E. M. Forster, *Two Cheers for Democracy*, p. 190 • **21**. *Aldeburgh Anthology*, p. 14 • **22**. BB to E. J. Dent, 16 June 1948, *LL3*, p. 396 • **23**. *MBB*, p. 192 • **24**. BB to Elizabeth Mayer, 4 February 1948, *LL3*, p. 358 • **25**. *CHPP*, p. 152 • **26**. *HCBB*, p. 260 • **27**. Cf. *HCBB*, between pp. 338 and 339, and *Aldeburgh Anthology*, facing p. 14 • **28**. BB to Peter Pears, 18 October 1948, *LL3*, pp. 416–17 • **29**. Peter Pears to BB, 19 October 1948, *LL3*, p. 418 • **30**. BB to Peter Pears, 22 October 1948, *LL3*, p. 420 • **31**. Ibid., 28 October 1948, *LL3*, p. 442 • **32**. Ibid., 31 October 1948, *LL3*, p. 449 • **33**. Ibid., 5 November 1948, *LL3*, p. 456 • **34**. BB to Serge Koussevitzky, 12 January 1947, *LL3*, p. 279 • **35**. BB to Peter Pears, 22 October 1948, *LL3*, p. 419 • **36**. Ibid., 5 November 1948, *LL3*, p. 456 • **37**. BB to Serge Koussevitzky, December 1948, *LL3*, p. 465 • **38**. BB to Peter Pears, before 18 March 1949, *LL3*, p. 496 • **39**. BB to Serge Koussevitzky, 15 July 1949, *LL3*, p. 521 • **40**. BB to Ralph Hawkes, 24 March 1949, *LL3*, p. 501 • **41**.

Eric Crozier to Nancy Evans, 7 April 1949, *LL3*, p. 506 • **42**. BB to Peter Pears, 8 April 1949, *LL3*, p. 506 • **43**. E. M. Forster to Eric Crozier, 24 October 1948, *LL3*, p. 429 • **44**. E. M. Forster, *Aspects of the Novel*, pp. 145–6 • **45**. E. M. Forster to BB, 11 November 1948, *LL3*, p. 411 • **46**. Eric Crozier to Nancy Evans, 11 March 1949, *LL3*, p. 498 • **47**. BB to Ralph Hawkes, 24 March 1949, *LL3*, p. 501 • **48**. Eric Crozier to Nancy Evans, 22 August 1949, *LL3*, p. 537 • **49**. Ibid., ? July 1949, *LL3*, p. 521 • **50**. BB to Ralph Hawkes, 29 May 1949, *LL3*, p. 513 • **51**. BB to Erwin Stein, 5 November 1949, *LL3*, p. 551 • **52**. BB to Nancy Evans and Eric Crozier, December 1949, *LL2*, p. 559 • **53**. BB to Peter Pears, 21 January 1950, *LL3*, p. 569 • **54**. *Times Literary Supplement*, 19 February 1949, *LL3*, p. 504 • **55**. *LL2*, p. 1011 • **56**. *BOM*, pp. 108–10 • **57**. Peter Pears to BB, 21 February 1951, *LL3*, p. 653 • **58**. BB to Barbara Britten, 30 April 1950, *LL3*, p. 587 • **59**. E. M. Forster to Bob Buckingham, 23 April 1950, *LL3*, p. 588 • **60**. Wendy Moffat, *E. M. Forster: A New Life*, p. 298 • **61**. E. M. Forster to BB, early December 1950, *LL3*, p. 618 • **62**. P. N. Furbank, *E. M. Forster: A Life. Volume Two: Polycrates' Ring*, p. 285 • **63**. BB to Erwin Stein, 9 September 1951, *LL3*, p. 677 • **64**. *JBBC*, p. 217 • **65**. Herman Melville, *Billy Budd*, p. 18 • **66**. Ibid., p. 85 • **67**. Ibid., p. 33 • **68**. Ibid., p. 59 • **69**. Ibid., p. 80 • **70**. Ibid., p. 34 • **71**. Ibid., p. 31 • **72**. *HCBB*, p. 299 • **73**. *Spectator*, 7 December 1951, *LL3*, p. 692 • **74**. John Ireland to BB, 24 December 1951, *LL3*, p. 700 • **75**. *HCBB*, p. 300 • **76**. *MKBB*, p. 200 • **77**. Ian Bostridge, *A Singer's Notebook*, p. 222 • **78**. *LL4*, p. 321 • **79**. BB to Basil Coleman, 8 January 1952, *LL4*, p. 21 • **80**. *Birmingham Post*, 23 January 1952; *The Times*, 5 February 1952; *LL4*, pp. 36–7 • **81**. BB to William Plomer, 27 April 1952, *LL4*, p. 57 • **82**. BB to William Plomer, 7 May 1952, *LL4*, p. 60 • **83**. Eric Walter White, *Benjamin Britten: His Life and Operas*, p. 79 • **84**. BB to William Plomer, 11 May 1962, *LL4*, p. 63 • **85**. Peter F. Alexander, *William Plomer: A Biography*, pp. 269–79 • **86**. *MKBB*, p. 64 • **87**. Christopher Grogan, *Imogen Holst: A Life in Music*, p. 213 • **88**. Ibid., p. 251 • **89**. Ibid., p. 201 • **90**. William Plomer to BB, 13 January 1953, *LL4*, p. 119 • **91**. BB to William Plomer, 21 January 1953, *LL4*, p. 118 • **92**. Peter F. Alexander, *William Plomer: A Biography*, pp. 278–9 • **93**. BB to Lennox Berkeley, after 28 June 1953, *LL4*, p. 162 • **94**. Philip Norman, *Shout! The True Story of The Beatles*, p. 191 • **95**. BB to

William Plomer, 20 July 1953, *LL4*, p. 165 • **96**. BB to Elizabeth Mayer, 30 August 1953, *LL4*, p. 177 • **97**. *Daily Express*, 12 June 1953, *LL4*, p. 152 • **98**. *The Times*, 18 June 1953; *The Times*, 20 June 1953; *Spectator*, 19 June 1953; *LL4*, pp. 160–1 • **99**. *HCBB*, p. 99 • **100**. *HCBB*, pp. 349–50 • **101**. *IHLM*, pp. 243–4 • **102**. *JBBC*, p. 162 • **103**. Interview with Donald Mitchell, *LL4*, pp. 68–9 • **104**. *IHLM*, p. 291 • **105**. Ibid., p. 292 • **106**. BB to Elizabeth Mayer, 30 August 1953, *LL4*, p. 177 • **107**. *LL4*, p. 164 • **108**. BB to Ronald Duncan, 11 September 1951, *LL3*, p. 675 • **109**. *HCBB*, p. 297 • **110**. Interview with Donald Mitchell, *LL2*, p. 1339 • **111**. *LL4*, p. 164 • **112**. Christopher Isherwood, *Diaries, Volume Two: 1960–1969*, p. 443 • **113**. *HCBB*, p. 328 • **114**. BB to Elizabeth Mayer, 30 August 1953, *LL4*, p. 178 • **115**. *IHLM*, p. 298 • **116**. Thomas Hardy, *Jude the Obscure*, p. 41 • **117**. *IHLM*, p. 300 • **118**. *Yorkshire Post*, 9 October 1953, *LL4*, p. 186 • **119**. BB to E. M. Forster, 25 October 1953, *LL4*, p. 187 • **120**. Interview with Donald Mitchell, *LL4*, p. 179 • **121**. Henry James, *The Turn of the Screw* and *The Aspern Papers*, p. 203 • **122**. Interview with Humphrey Carpenter, *LL4*, p. 88 • **123**. *JBBC*, p. 194 • **124**. Ibid., p. 199 • **125**. *LL3*, p. 25 • **126**. *JBBC*, p. 198 • **127**. BB to Basil Coleman, 29 May 1954, *LL4*, p. 248 • **128**. *JBBC*, p. 207 • **129**. *HCBB*, p. 359 • **130**. BB and Peter Pears to Princess Margaret of Hesse and the Rhine, after 14 September 1954, *LL4*, p. 272 • **131**. *JBBC*, pp. 207–8 • **132**. *HCBB*, p. 360 • **133**. *Manchester Guardian*, 15 September 1954; *Sunday Times*, 19 September 1954, *LL4*; pp. 275, 277 • **134**. Interview with Charles Markes, *LL4*, p. 268 • **135**. BB to Desmond Shawe-Taylor, 6 November 1954, *LL4*, p. 300 • **136**. BB to Edward Sackville-West, 16 October 1954, *LL4*, p. 296 • **137**. *The Record Guide Supplement*, p. 45 • **138**. *LL4*, p. 253

7 *The Poetry in the Pity*

1. *IHLM*, p. 318 • **2**. BB to Edith Sitwell, 27 September 1954, *LL4*, p. 289 • **3**. *MKBB*, p. 212 • **4**. Edith Sitwell to BB, 26 April 1955, *LL4*, p. 316 • **5**. *IHLM*, p. 202 • **6**. Ibid., p. 205 • **7**. *LL4*, pp. 269–70 • **8**. *JBBC*, pp. 224, 226 • **9**. BB to Lord Harewood, 9 December 1955, *LL4*, p. 356 • **10**. BB and Peter Pears to Imogen Holst, 1

December 1955, *LL4*, p. 353 • **11**. BB to Roger Duncan, 19 December 1955, *LL4*, p. 368 • **12**. BB and Peter Pears to Mary Potter, 23 December 1955, *LL4*, p. 374 • **13**. *The Travel Diaries of Peter Pears*, p. 30 • **14**. Ibid., p. 33 • **15**. Ibid., p. 35 • **16**. *CHPP*, p. 183 • **17**. *PPTD*, p. 36 • **18**. BB to Imogen Holst, 17 December 1955, *LL4*, p. 385 • **19**. *CHPP*, p. 185 • **20**. BB to Roger Duncan, 18 January 1956, *LL4*, p. 395 • **21**. BB to James Blades, 25 January 1956, *LL4*, p. 398 • **22**. BB to Ninette de Valois, 23 January 1956, *LL4*, p. 391 • **23**. BB to Imogen Holst, 8 February 1956, *LL4*, p. 400 • **24**. BB to Roger Duncan, 21 February 1956, *LL4*, pp. 408–9 • **25**. BB to Princess Margaret of Hesse and the Rhine, 20 March 1956, *LL4*, p. 429 • **26**. *HCBB*, p. 369 • **27**. BB to Basil Douglas, 22 December 1955, *LL4*, p. 371 • **28**. BB to William Plomer, 13 May 1956, *LL4*, pp. 454–5 • **29**. BB to David Webster, 28 May 1956, *LL4*, p. 456 • **30**. BB to Prince Ludwig of Hesse and the Rhine, 7 November 1956, *LL4*, p. 471 • **31**. *IHLM*, p. 349 • **32**. Ibid., p. 350 • **33**. *Daily Telegraph*, 2 January 1957; *The Times*, 2 January 1957; *Sunday Times*, 6 January 1957; *Musical Times*, February 1957; *LL4*, pp. 482–5 • **34**. *HCBB*, p. 379 • **35**. BB to Anthony Gishford, 8 April 1957, *LL4*, pp. 521–2 • **36**. Eric Walter White, *Benjamin Britten: His Life and Operas*, p. 83 • **37**. BB to the artistic directors of the English Opera Group, 31 January 1957, *LL4*, p. 503 • **38**. BB to Basil Coleman, 31 January 1957, *LL4*, p. 507 • **39**. BB to Basil Douglas, 20 March 1957, *LL4*, p. 520 • **40**. *IHLM*, p. 355 • **41**. BB to Basil Douglas, 27 October 1957, *LL4*, p. 571 • **42**. David Herbert (ed.), *The Operas of Benjamin Britten*, p. 44 • **43**. *IHLM*, p. 356 • **44**. *HCBB*, p. 385 • **45**. *Manchester Guardian*, 19 June 1958; *Sunday Times*, 22 June 1958; *LL5*, pp. 49–52 • **46**. *New Aldeburgh Anthology*, p. 96 • **47**. *MKBB*, p. 215 • **48**. BB to the Countess of Harewood, 20 August 1958, *LL5*, pp. 62–3 • **49**. BB to Princess Margaret of Hesse and the Rhine, 20 August 1958, *LL5*, p. 65 • **50**. Ian Bostridge, *A Singer's Notebook*, p. 216 • **51**. Peter Evans, *The Music of Benjamin Britten*, p. 375 • **52**. BB to William Plomer, 8 October 1958, *LL5*, p. 89 • **53**. BB to Barbara Britten, 15 December 1958, *LL5*, p. 98 • **54**. BB to John Culshaw, 25 November 1959, *LL5*, p. 68 • **55**. *The Gramophone*, October 1959, p. 189 • **56**. *JBBC*, p. 171 • **57**. *HCBB*, p. 407 • **58**. BB to Alfred Deller, 18 August 1959, *LL5*, p. 173 • **59**. BB to the Earl of Harewood, 6 September 1959, *LL5*, p. 182 • **60**. BB to Peter Pears, 14 December 1959, *LL5*,

p. 199 • **61**. Peter Pears to BB, 17 December 1959, *LL5*, p. 201 • **62**. BB to William Glock, 12 January 1960, *LL5*, p. 202 • **63**. BB to Elizabeth Mayer, 11 April 1960, *LL5*, p. 219 • **64**. BB to Roger Duncan, 13 April 1960, *LL5*, p. 223 • **65**. *IHLM*, p. 363 • **66**. *LL5*, p. 276 • **67**. Mstislav Rostropovich to BB, 12 October 1960, *LL5*, p. 278 • **68**. BB to Peter Pears, 17 January 1961, *LL5*, p. 294 • **69**. Mstislav Rostropovich to BB, 11 February 1961, *LL5*, p. 298 • **70**. 'Three Friends', *Observer*, 27 November 1977 • **71**. BB to Galina Vishnevskaya, 1 April 1961, *LL5*, pp. 324–5 • **72**. *The Times*, 10 July 1961, *LL5*, p. 301 • **73**. *HCBB*, p. 403 • **74**. Galina Vishnevskaya, *Galina*, p. 364 • **75**. *HCBB*, p. 404 • **76**. BB to John Lowe, 8 October 1958, *LL5*, p. 72 • **77**. Galina Vishnevskaya, *Galina*, p. 365 • **78**. BB to Christopher Isherwood, 11 September 1961, *LL5*, p. 349 • **79**. *HCBB*, p. 408 • **80**. BB to Basil Coleman, 29 October 1961, *LL5*, p. 356 • **81**. BB to E. M. Forster, 21 April 1962, *LL5*, p. 392 • **82**. Galina Vishnevskaya, *Galina*, p. 367 • **83**. BB to William Plomer, 5 June 1962, *LL5*, p. 401 • **84**. '*War Requiem*: The First Performances', 1986, *LL5*, p. 403 • **85**. *Time & Tide*, 7 June 1962; *Musical Times*, July 1962; *The Times*, 31 May 1962; *Sunday Times*, 3 June 1962; *LL5*, pp. 403–7 • **86**. Harold Owen to BB, 31 May 1962, *LL5*, p. 409 • **87**. Wilfred Owen, *Collected Poems*, p. 31 • **88**. BB to William Plomer, 5 June 1962, *LL5*, p. 402 • **89**. Dietrich Fischer-Dieskau, *Echoes of a Lifetime*, p. 258 • **90**. '*War Requiem*: The First Performances', 1986, *LL5*, p. 403 • **91**. Mstislav Rostropovich to BB, early March 1962, *LL5*, p. 385 • **92**. BB to Mstislav Rostropovich, July 1962, *LL5*, p. 410 • **93**. BB to Prince Ludwig and Princess Margaret of Hesse and the Rhine, 26 September 1962, *LL5*, p. 436 • **94**. BB to William Plomer, 1 November 1962, *LL5*, p. 444 • **95**. BB to Peter Pears, 29 October 1962, *LL5*, p. 445 • **96**. Peter Pears to BB, 30 October 1962, *LL5*, p. 445 • **97**. BB to Desmond Shawe-Taylor, 15 November 1962, *LL5*, p. 448 • **98**. BB to Prince Ludwig and Princess Margaret of Hesse and the Rhine, 23 October 1962, *LL5*, p. 442 • **99**. *BOM*, p. 217 • **100**. Ibid., p. 218 • **101**. *LL5*, p. 373 • **102**. William Plomer to BB, 12 December 1962, *LL5*, p. 452 • **103**. John Culshaw to BB, 11 January 1963; BB to John Culshaw, 12 January 1963; *LL5*, p. 460 • **104**. John Culshaw, *Putting the Record Straight*, p. 313 • **105**. *The Gramophone*, March 1968, p. 475 • **106**. BB to Paul Sacher, 13 January 1963, *LL5*, p. 465 • **107**. BB to Elizabeth Mayer, 1 March 1963, *LL5*,

p. 466 • **108**. BB to William Plomer, 7 April 1963, *LL5*, p. 470 • **109**. Mstislav Rostropovich to BB, 30 May 1963, *LL5*, p. 473 • **110**. *Daily Telegraph*, 2 September 1963, *LL5*, p. 496 • **111**. Donald Mitchell to BB, 3 October 1963, *LL5*, p. 506 • **112**. BB to Kenneth Clark, 28 November 1963, *LL5*, p. 525 • **113**. BB to George Malcolm, 28 November 1963, *LL5*, p. 529 • **114**. William Walton to BB, 23 November 1963, *LL5*, p. 538 • **115**. T. J. E. Sewell to BB, 21 November 1963, *LL5*, p. 532 • **116**. BB to William Plomer, 10 November 1963, *LL5*, p. 526 • **117**. Richard Taruskin, *The Oxford History of Western Music*, Volume 5, p. 224 • **118**. *BOM*, p. 245 • **119**. BB to John Piper, 25 January 1964, *LL5*, p. 549 • **120**. BB to Nicholas Maw, 27 October 1963, *LL5*, p. 510 • **121**. BB to Peter Maxwell Davies, 18 November 1963, *LL5*, p. 522 • **122**. BB to Donald Mitchell, 5 February 1964, *LL5*, p. 552 • **123**. Donald Mitchell to BB, 17 February 1964, *LL5*, p. 555 • **124**. *LL5*, p. 575 • **125**. William Plomer to BB, 2 March 1964, *LL5*, p. 563 • **126**. BB to William Plomer, 7 March 1964, *LL5*, p. 569 • **127**. *HCBB*, pp. 426–7 • **128**. *Daily Telegraph*, 12 March 1964, *LL5*, p. 572 • **129**. David Matthews, *Britten*, p. 133 • **130**. *MKBB*, p. 242 • **131**. *AA2*, p. 263 • **132**. Ernst Roth to BB, 22 April 1964, *LL5*, p. 572 • **133**. *Daily Telegraph*, 20 June 1964, *HCBB*, p. 432 • **134**. *BOM*, p. 326 • **135**. E. H. Fellowes (ed.), *English Madrigal Verse 1588–1632*, p. 466 • **136**. *IHLM*, p. 377 • **137**. *The Times*, 15 June 1964, *LL5*, p. 584 • **138**. *BOM*, pp. 255–63 • **139**. BB to William Plomer, 8 September 1964, *LL5*, p. 603 • **140**. *BOM*, p. 269 • **141**. *HCBB*, p. 417

8 *The Building of the House*

1. BB to Peter Pears, 17 November 1964, *LL5*, p. 614 • **2**. BB to John Newton, 19 January 1965, *LL5*, pp. 632–3 • **3**. *PPTD*, p. 86 • **4**. Ibid., p. 90 • **5**. BB to John Newton, 24 January 1965, *LL5*, pp. 637–8 • **6**. *PPTD*, p. 91 • **7**. BB to John Newton, 24 January 1965, *LL5*, p. 638 • **8**. Ibid., 26 January 1965, *LL5*, p. 640 • **10**. Ibid., 19 February 1965, *LL5*, p. 649 • **11**. *CHPP*, p. 215 • **12**. BB to John Newton, 1 March 1965, *LL5*, p. 651 • **13**. Rosamund Strode to Zoltán and Gábor Jeney, 12 May 1965, *LL5*, p. 656 • **14**. *The Times*, 25 June 1965; *Observer*, 27 June 1965 • **15**. *CHPP*, p. 216 • **16**. BB to Elizabeth Mayer, 29

May 1965, *LL5*, p. 677 • **17**. *PPTD*, p. 103 • **18**. *CHPP*, p. 218 • **19**. PP to Barbara Britten, n.d., *LL5*, p. 691 • **20**. *BOM*, pp. 281–2 • **21**. *PPTD*, p. 107 • **22**. John Bridcut, *The Faber Pocket Guide to Britten*, p. 436 • **23**. *PPTD*, p. 133 • **24**. Ibid., p. 134 • **25**. BB and Peter Pears to Mstislav and Galina Rostropovich, n.d., *LL5*, p. 695 • **26**. BB to William Plomer, 27 October 1965, *LL5*, p. 698 • **27**. BB to Elizabeth Mayer, 29 November 1965, *LL5*, p. 712 • **28**. *CHPP*, p. 222 • **29**. Ibid., p. 223 • **30**. *PEBB*, p. 480 • **31**. *MKBB*, p. 235 • **32**. *PPTD*, p. 137 • **33**. Ibid., p. 139 • **34**. Ibid., p. 160 • **35**. BB to Eric Walter White, 6 February 1967 • **36**. *HCBB*, p. 455 • **37**. *AA2*, p. 285 • **38**. *HCBB*, p. 457 • **39**. *AA1*, p. 27 • **40**. *HCBB*, p. 468 • **41**. *AA1*, pp. 26–7 • **42**. John Samaurez Smith (ed.), *A Spy in the Bookshop*, pp. 46–7 • **43**. *London Magazine*, November 1967, p. 68 • **44**. *PFL*, plate 342 • **45**. *London Magazine*, November 1967, p. 69 • **46**. BBC Radio 3, 12 June 2011 • **47**. *BOM*, p. 314 • **48**. *HCBB*, p. 477 • **49**. Ibid., p. 478 • **50**. *CHPP*, p. 228 • **51**. *PPTD*, p. 146 • **52**. BB to William Plomer, 6 January 1967 • **53**. *DMBB*, p. 142 • **54**. BB to William Plomer, 29 April 1967 • **55**. *AA1*, p. 263 • **56**. BB to Harrison Birtwistle, 3 November 1965, *LL5*, p. 705 • **57**. *HCBB*, p. 482 • **58**. *BOM*, p. 327 • **59**. *Aldeburgh Festival Programme Book*, 1969, p. 5 • **60**. BB to Basil Coleman, 24 April 1967 • **61**. *BOM*, p. 321 • **62**. *MKBB*, p. 230 • **63**. *JBPG*, p. 276 • **64**. *HCBB*, p. 488 • **65**. Ibid., p. 490 • **66**. Ibid., p. 493 • **67**. *AA2*, p. 259 • **68**. *BOM*, p. 322 • **69**. *BOM*, p. 325 • **70**. *Aldeburgh Festival Programme Book*, 1970, p. 5 • **71**. BB to Eric Walter White, 5 November 1954, *LL4*, p. 300 • **72**. *The Times*, 15 May 1971, *Daily Telegraph*, 17 May 1971 • **73**. BB to William Plomer, ? May 1971, *HCBB*, p. 519 • **74**. BB to Walter Hussey, 6 January 1971, *HCBB*, p. 515 • **75**. *BOM*, pp. 326–7 • **76**. *JBBC*, pp. 276–7 • **77**. BB to Joan Magill, 18 September 1969 • **78**. *JBBC*, p. 184 • **79**. *IHLM*, p. 219 • **80**. *HCBB*, p. 524 • **81**. BB to Rosamund Strode, 8 July 1971 • **82**. *HCBB*, p. 522

9 *As It Is, Plenty*

1. *Aldeburgh Festival Programme Book*, 1976, p. 50 • **2**. *PPTD*, pp. 163–4 • **3**. Ibid., p. 165 • **4**. *CHPP*, p. 242 • **5**. BB to Frederick Ashton, 20 September 1971, *HCBB*, pp. 533–4 • **6**. Thomas Mann, *Death in Venice*,

NOTES TO PAGES 439–467   *493*

in *The Penguin Book of International Gay Writing*, pp. 146–7. I have preferred David Luke's translation, which is more accurate and less mannered than H. T. Lowe-Porter's, even though this remained in print for many years as a Penguin Modern Classic. • **7**. Ibid., p. 171 • **8**. Ibid., p. 164 • **9**. Ibid., p. 165 • **10**. Ibid., p. 187 • **11**. Ibid., p. 186 • **12**. Ibid., p. 155 • **13**. Ibid., p. 159 • **14**. Ibid., p. 204 • **15**. Ibid., p. 198 • **16**. *LL3*, p. 31 • **17**. Julie Kavanagh, *Secret Muses*, pp. 535–6 • **18**. Ibid., p. 537 • **19**. *Guardian*, 18 June 1973, *HCBB*, p. 558 • **20**. *JBBC*, p. 284 • **21**. Virginia Woolf, *To the Lighthouse*, p. 226 • **22**. *HCBB*. p. 539 • **23**. *JBBC*, pp. 283–4 • **24**. *HCBB*, p. 546 • **25**. *CHPP*, p. 244 • **26**. BB to Ray Minshull, 3 April 1973, *HCBB*, p. 548 • **27**. Peter Pears to Anthony Gishford, ? May 1973, *HCBB*, p. 551 • **28**. *HCBB*, p. 561 • **29**. Boris Ford (ed.), *Benjamin Britten's Poets*, p. 52 • **30**. *JBPG*, p. 348 • **31**. *PPTD*, p. 181 • **32**. Ibid., p. 190 • **33**. Ibid., p. 198 • **34**. BB to Beth Welford, 17 October 1974, *HCBB*, p. 567 • **35**. BB to Peter Pears, 17 November 1974, *LL1*, p. 60 • **36**. Peter Pears to BB, 21 November 1974, *LL1*, pp. 60–1 • **37**. *JBPG*, pp. 168–9 • **38**. Ibid., p. 167 • **39**. Ibid., p. 164 • **40**. *DMBB*, p. 153 • **41**. *HCBB*, p. 577 • **42**. *IHLM*, p. 186 • **43**. *CHPP*, p. 273 • **44**. *HCBB*, p. 585 • **45**. *PFL*, plate 435 • **46**. Alex Ross, *The Rest is Noise*, p. 413 • **47**. *JBPG*, p. 373 • **48**. Ian Bostridge, *A Singer's Notebook*, p. 228 • **49**. *London Magazine*, February/March 1993, p. 131 • **50**. *Times Literary Supplement*, 10 July 2009 • **51**. Bernard Levin, *Conducted Tour*, p. 69 • **52**. *CHPP*, p. 268 • **53**. *HCBB*, p. 590

ILLUSTRATION CREDITS

INDEX

About the Author

NEIL POWELL is the author of biographies of George Crabbe and Kingsley and Martin Amis, as well as seven collections of poetry. He has contributed to numerous journals and newspapers, including *The Guardian* and *The Times Literary Supplement*. Powell now lives in Aldeburgh, where Britten lived for the last thirty years of his life.